The Public Administration Dictionary

THE PUBLIC ADMINISTRATION DICTIONARY

Second Edition

Ralph C. Chandler
Jack C. Plano
Western Michigan University

ABC-CLIO

Santa Barbara, California
Oxford, England

© 1988 by Ralph C. Chandler and Jack C. Plano

All rights reserved. No part of this publication may be reproduced, stored in a retrieval system, or transmitted, in any form or by any means, electronic, mechanical, photocopying, recording, or otherwise, except for the inclusion of brief quotations in a review, without prior permission in writing from the publishers.

Library of Congress Cataloging-in-Publication Data
Chandler, Ralph C., 1934–
  The public administration dictionary / Ralph C. Chandler, Jack C. Plano. — 2nd ed.
    p.   cm. — (Clio dictionaries in political science)
  Bibliography: p.
  Includes index.
  ISBN 0-87436-498-1 (alk. paper).   ISBN 0-87436-499-X (pbk. : alk. paper)
  1. Public administration—Dictionaries. I. Plano, Jack C.
II. Title. III. Series.
JA61.C47 1988
350'.0003'21—dc19   87-32045
                                                                  CIP

10 9 8 7 6 5 4 3 2 1 (cloth)
10 9 8 7 6 5 4 3 2 1 (paper)

ABC-Clio, Inc.
Riviera Campus
2040 Alameda Padre Serra, Box 4397
Santa Barbara, California 93140–4397

Clio Press Ltd.
55 St. Thomas' Street
Oxford, OX1 1JG, England

This book is printed on acid free paper ∞ .
Manufactured in the United States of America

*To Nancy Mott Chandler
and
Jay Charles Plano*

Clio Dictionaries in Political Science

The African Political Dictionary
Claude S. Phillips

The Asian Political Dictionary
Lawrence Ziring and C. I. Eugene Kim

The Constitutional Law Dictionary, Volume 1: *Individual Rights*
Ralph C. Chandler, Richard A. Enslen, and Peter G. Renstrom

The Constitutional Law Dictionary, Volume 1: *Individual Rights*
Supplement 1
Ralph C. Chandler, Richard A. Enslen, and Peter G. Renstrom

The Constitutional Law Dictionary, Volume 2, *Governmental Powers*
Ralph C. Chandler, Richard A. Enslen, and Peter G. Renstrom

The Dictionary of Political Analysis, Second Edition
Jack C. Plano, Robert E. Riggs, and Helenan S. Robin

The European Political Dictionary
Ernest E. Rossi and Barbara P. McCrea

The International Law Dictionary
Robert L. Bledsoe and Boleslaw A. Boczek

The International Relations Dictionary, Fourth Edition
Jack C. Plano and Roy Olton

The Latin American Political Dictionary
Ernest E. Rossi and Jack C. Plano

The Middle East Political Dictionary
Lawrence Ziring

The Presidential-Congressional Political Dictionary
Jeffrey M. Elliot and Sheikh R. Ali

The Public Administration Dictionary, Second Edition
Ralph C. Chandler and Jack C. Plano

The Public Policy Dictionary
Earl R. Kruschke and Byron M. Jackson

The Soviet and East European Political Dictionary
Barbara P. McCrea, Jack C. Plano, and George Klein

The State and Local Government Political Dictionary
Jeffrey M. Elliot and Sheikh R. Ali

Forthcoming

The Arms Control, Disarmament, and Military Security Dictionary
Jeffrey M. Elliot and Sheikh R. Ali

The Electoral Politics Dictionary
Peter G. Renstrom and Chester B. Rogers

The Nuclear War and Peace Dictionary
Sheikh R. Ali

SERIES STATEMENT

Language precision is the primary tool of every scientific discipline. That aphorism serves as the guideline for this series of political dictionaries. Although each book in the series relates to a specific topical or regional area in the discipline of political science, entries in the dictionaries also emphasize history, geography, economics, sociology, philosophy, and religion.

This dictionary series incorporates special features designed to help the reader overcome any language barriers that may impede a full understanding of the subject matter. For example, the concepts included in each volume were selected to complement the subject matter found in existing texts and other books. All but one volume utilize a subject matter chapter arrangement that is most useful for classroom and study purposes.

Entries in all volumes include an up-to-date definition plus a paragraph of *Significance* in which the authors discuss and analyze the term's historical and current relevance. Most entries are also cross-referenced, providing the reader an opportunity to seek additional information related to the subject of inquiry. A comprehensive index, found in both hard cover and paperback editions, allows the reader to locate major entries and other concepts, events, and institutions discussed within these entries.

The political and social sciences suffer more than most disciplines from semantic confusion. This is attributable, *inter alia*, to the popularization of the language, and to the focus on many diverse foreign political and social systems. This dictionary series is dedicated to overcoming some of this confusion through careful writing of thorough, accurate definitions for the central concepts, institutions, and events that comprise the basic knowledge of each of the subject fields. New titles in the series will be issued periodically, including some in related social science disciplines.

—Jack C. Plano
Series Editor

CONTENTS

A Note On How To Use This Book, **x**
Preface, **xi**

1. Fundamentals of Public Administration, **3**
2. Public Policy, **45**
3. Public Management, **119**
4. Bureaucracy and Administrative Organization, **161**
5. Personnel Administration, **243**
6. Financial Administration, **319**
7. Public Law and Regulation, **367**

Bibliography, **407**
Index, **415**

A NOTE ON HOW TO USE THIS BOOK

The Public Administration Dictionary uses a format that facilitates its use both as a class supplement and as a reference guide to the basic concepts of the field. Entries are arranged alphabetically within seven subject-matter chapters, which can be coordinated with many of the leading textbooks in the field. Terms relating to government organizations and structures, for example, can be found in the chapter titled "Bureaucracy and Administrative Organization," and those dealing with public employment can be located in the chapter titled "Personnel Administration." When in doubt about which chapter contains a specific term, the reader should consult the Index.

Another feature of this book is the inclusion of a special paragraph called *Significance*, following the definition paragraph. In this way, we have been able to give each defined concept some perspective by placing it in its historical and contemporary environments. To facilitate both study and reference, *See also* cross-references are included with most entries. They encourage the reader to seek additional information, either in the same chapter or in another.

Finally, the reader can use the Index to locate both major entries and the hundreds of concepts, theories and theorists, institutions, and the like, that are found within the major entries. Major entries are those that we believe are essential to understanding the field of public administration. We have highlighted them in the Index by using heavy bold type for their entry numbers, whereas concepts defined or discussed *within* major entries can be identified by entry numbers in regular type.

The special format of this book is designed to offer the reader assistance of various kinds in the quest for information about public administration. These unique features will facilitate its use as (1) a *study guide* for introductory courses in the field; (2) a *supplement* to a textbook or to a group of monographs adopted for course use; (3) a source of *review materials* for students enrolled in advanced courses in the field; (4) a *cognate-course aid* for use in related fields, such as management and general business; and (5) a *reference guide* to the specialized language of public administration.

PREFACE

Many changes have occurred in public administration since *The Public Administration Dictionary* was first published in 1982. This second edition seeks to keep the entries relevant and the significance of each one carefully delineated in both historical and contemporary terms. Twenty-five new entries have been added, and numerous existing ones revised and updated. The authors are particularly pleased that the publisher, ABC-CLIO of Santa Barbara, California, and Oxford, England, has made it possible to keep the dictionary current and useful.

Despite the advent of computer technology, the authors believe that precise language is still the most basic tool of every intellectual discipline, including public administration. We initially prepared *The Public Administration Dictionary* with this conviction in mind, and we now offer a revised edition in pursuit of the same belief.

There were additional considerations. We sought to produce a work that reflected the field in its eclectic dimensions. We were also interested in helping the student—especially the student in introductory classes—grasp some of the essential concepts of the field. We hope a knowledge of these building blocks will add meaning and interest to courses in the public administration curriculum.

One could view the *Dictionary* as a "back to basics" approach to public administration, but one caveat is in order: we did not attempt to be inclusive in selecting terms and concepts. Instead, we decided to focus our attention and that of the reader on those concepts that are fundamental to an understanding of the field. Additional but perhaps less pertinent concepts and terms are found within major entries and are listed in the Index. Complete publication information for references cited within the text may be found in the Bibliography, which also includes other important publications the authors employed in compiling this work.

In sifting and winnowing through concepts, events, strategies, theories, institutions, and leading thinkers to determine which should be included in the book as major entries, we were guided in both editions by several key questions. Does this concept improve the

Preface

ability of the student to communicate in the technical language of the field? Will it aid the reader's search for knowledge and understanding? Will it complement, as well as supplement, the materials used in most public administration classes?

Thus, the selection of major entries was determined by our best judgment of what is important in the field, not on a content analysis of the entire literature of public administration. The latter method would be most useful in producing a comprehensive reference book. This book is designed to function primarily as a teaching-learning instrument.

Although dictionary formats have remained largely unchanged since the fifteenth century, *The Public Administration Dictionary* incorporates a number of unique features. First, entries have been carefully selected based on the major foci of the field. Second, the book utilizes a subject-matter chapter format by which key concepts are grouped for study and review purposes. Because of this feature, the dictionary can be used in and out of class as a teaching-learning tool by professors, students, and practitioners. The chapters in the *Dictionary* are linked through subject matter with those found in most of the leading textbooks in the field. A third feature, also unique, is the inclusion of a paragraph we call *Significance*, following the definition of the entry. In this way, the authors lend each concept some historical perspective and bring it up to date by placing it in its contemporary environment. A fourth feature of the book is the inclusion of cross-references that function as suggestions to the reader on how to seek additional related information. Finally, the book incorporates a comprehensive Index to facilitate its use as a reference tool. Some idea of the scope and quality of coverage can be gleaned from a brief perusal of the Index. We invite potential users of the book to start their evaluation process there. Those who examine the Index will discover another feature: boldface numbers are used for the major Index entries, while entries of lesser importance appear in regular type.

Beginning students taking courses in public administration often suffer from semantic confusion. This is more true of public administration than many other fields because of its interdisciplinary nature. Many of the terms included in the *Dictionary*, for example, can be found in textbooks and scholarly articles published in such diverse fields as political science, management, economics, sociology, psychology, and history. Public administration as an academic area seeks to draw these disparate fields together into a coherent body of knowledge. This drawing together has been a major objective of the authors. We are certain some readers will find fault with our approach. We encourage everyone to communicate with us about the ways the book may be improved in its next edition.

The material for this book has been drawn from a great variety of sources. It is impossible to list them all or always to identify the original sources of ideas and phrases that have become part of the common store of information in public administration. The authors

Preface

therefore acknowledge the important contributions of the many scholars whose articles and books have enriched the language of the field. Of these, we would like to give special recognition to those authors whose books are included in the Bibliography. They often provided us with the conceptual clarity and occasionally the language used in constructing the entries of the dictionary.

Meanwhile, we wish to thank the scholars in the field who have contributed to the growing volume and richness of the language of public administration. The field has come of age and needs a working, comprehensive language to increase its effectiveness. If this dictionary in its second edition contributes toward that goal, we will feel that our efforts have been worthwhile.

The Public Administration Dictionary

1. Fundamentals of Public Administration

Administration (1)
The process by which decisions and policies are implemented. Public administration is concerned primarily with enforcing laws, making and enforcing rules and regulations, and carrying out public policy. *Public* can be contrasted with *nonprofit, private,* or *business* administration, with the latter concerned with such elements as sales, productivity, and profits. In government, administration is largely the function of the executive branch, although judicial and legislative administration are also responsibilities of those two branches. Public administration is both an art and a science which aims at managing public affairs and carrying out assigned tasks. Major components of the field include organization, personnel, and finance. Public administration as an academic discipline aims at improving problem solving in these three areas. *See also* BUDGET, 261; ORGANIZATION, 168; PUBLIC ADMINISTRATION, 21.

Significance The quality of life for millions of people within a modern state depends on the skill, efficiency, and dedication with which modern bureaucratic structures carry out their administration duties. As life becomes more complex, so do the operations of governments as they seek to cope with and manage diverse problems. As a result, new administrative organizations with large numbers of employees spending huge amounts of money have become an accepted way of life in the industrialized countries. In the United States, for example, the new Departments of Energy and Education and the Environmental Protection Agency were created to meet new challenges. Administrative units increasingly make, administer, enforce, and adjudicate law. Administrative law that relates to regulating and promoting private enterprises has become the fastest growing type of law. The view that administration is separate from policy making has been altered by actual performance wherein bureaucrats at all levels of government engage regularly in both activities. The ultimate goal of public administration, both in theory and in practice, is to develop sound techniques and procedures which make it possible to combine efficiency of operations with democratic responsibility and accountability.

Administrative Man Model (2)

A model of human behavior in organizations that stresses the nature and characteristics of leadership. The administrative man model paralleled the development of early classical theory, which emphasized formal internal structure as the key to understanding organizations. In both approaches, trait theories were tested to determine the characteristics of a leader, and theorists such as Max Weber and Amitai Etzioni developed typologies of leadership style. Weber identified three types of leadership: traditional, charismatic, and legal-rational. Etzioni typed leaders according to positional and personal power with a resulting tripartite classification system of officials, informal leaders, and formal leaders. Theorists of the human relations school, on the other hand, believed the nature of all men and women, not just of the leaders, was critical to understanding organizational functioning. Sociological and psychological views of individual behavior contributed to an emerging humanist model that identified the administrative man as a very human creature who was somewhat limited in cognitive skills but who occasionally could make rational decisions.

Herbert A. Simon wrote about these different aspects of administrative man in his book, *Administrative Behavior*. Simon identified *psychological man* and *economic man,* with *administrative man* being a combination of the two. He believed the decision-making behavior of individual persons was the key component in understanding organizations. It is from that decision-making perspective that Simon elaborated the administrative man model. The psychological man has his own set of personal goals, quirks, and motivations. He may or may not be rational in the context of organizational decision making, since each individual is different in psychological makeup. The psychological man may or may not be conscious of the organization's needs. The concept of "economic man" has long been used by economists to predict the behavior of the economy as a whole. Economic man, according to the traditional model, is totally rational and approaches a decision fully aware of all the alternatives and implications of a particular decision. Economic man is capable of "maximizing" by selecting the best alternative for achievement of organizational and individual goals. Simon's third model balanced the important aspects of economic and psychological man in an effort to understand the realities of administrative decision making. Administrative man is the cousin of economic man, perhaps even his brother, and can be compared to him in two key ways. First, administrative man "satisfices," rather than maximizes, because he can seldom see, or predict the outcome of, all possible options. Satisficing is selecting the best or most satisfactory of the immediate alternatives. Second, administrative man recognizes that his view of an administrative situation is simplified and that it is impossible to grasp the interrelatedness of all aspects of the decision-making environment. He therefore leaves out all factors he considers irrelevant, which is a large portion of an extremely complex environment. He is content in making decisions with the limited alternatives he can immediately see. This propensity to decide on the basis of partial knowledge Simon called "bounded rationality." These concepts, satisficing and bounded rationality, are central to Simon's approach to understanding decision making in organizations, and they constitute the primary characteristics of the administrative man.

Models of administrative man other than Simon's include cultural and political models as subgroups of the sociopsychological approach to administrative analysis. *Cultural* models emphasize the effect of cultural influence on organizational processes and decision making. French political scientist Michel Crozier's work, for example, compares the United States and other cultures in specific aspects of organizational process, such as specialization. *Political* models of administrative man deal with how administrators function politically in organizations. Researchers in this area have constructed typologies of administrative man in terms of the degree of his institutional commitment, specialty skills, and expertise in political gamesmanship. *See also* BOUNDED RATIONALITY, 88; ECONOMIC MAN THEORY, 38; SATISFICING, 113; SIMON, HERBERT A., 114.

Significance The administrative man model represents an important ongoing theme in the study of public administration leadership. Whether the perspective is to determine how bureaucracies affect the people within them, or how individuals affect organizational efficiency, the need to understand the nature of administrative man has provided scholars an organizing idea for research. Political behavior and administrative decision making in public organizations have particular significance for the study of administrative man. Since politics has great influence in the public sector, concepts such as political gamesmanship, bureaupathology, and "politicized experts" have become increasingly important as explanation tools for administrative behavior. Simon's model of administrative man and bounded rationality is not intended to convey a pathological symptom of modern bureaucrats, however. Instead, it is a realistic portrayal of how administrators actually do make decisions on extremely complex issues. Simon based his conclusions on empirical evidence gathered in computer simulations of decision making which paralleled actual cases of administrative choice.

Administrative Novel (3)
Fictional literature that attempts to portray the public administrator as a thinking, feeling, and searching being who directs social organizations toward particular ends. The administrative novel explores the meaning of the subjective life of the administrative man in society. It asks how reality is comprehended and *felt* within the context of administrative situations. Political scientist Rowland Egger suggests that an administrative novel's four characteristics are (1) it represents life; (2) it is interesting; (3) it makes effective use of the author's subject idea; and (4) it takes no more liberties with the subject matter than are essential to the achievement of artistic objectives. The administrative novel is aimed at enhancing the reader's understanding of administration by addressing the existential problems that are at the root of the tensions between human beings and their society. It is also directed at preserving a record of modes of response to particular social and cultural conditions. The administrative novel represents social evidence and testimony about such phenomena as role conflicts, decision-making processes, and the impact of organizational life on individuals. *See also* ADMINISTRATIVE MAN MODEL, 2; DECISION MAKING, 92–95; HUMAN MOTIVATION, 99–103.

Significance The administrative novel is one way of trying to find meaning in the art and science of administration. The novelist and the administrative theorist have in common the task of understanding the inner life of public servants. They are natural partners. In the past, novelists have portrayed administrators as parasites, heroes, faithful subordinates, and a range of other character types. The strength of the administrative novel, whatever the type of its character sketches, is that it affirms the fact that administration is to a considerable degree an artistic performance. While formal training in public administration frequently ignores fictional literature as a source of instruction, practitioners have consulted with profit such works as Dostoevsky's *The Brothers Karamazov*, particularly Book V, Chapter 5, and C. P. Snow's *Corridors of Power*.

Administrative Platonism (4)

A school of thought that believes public administrators should emphasize high ethical standards as a check on bureaucratic power and as an affirmation of democratic values and processes. Administrative platonism was first identified with Paul Appleby, who described the characteristics of the moral administrator in *Morality and Administration in Democratic Government* (1952). According to Appleby, the moral administrator has (1) a sense of responsibility; (2) skills in communication and personnel administration, including how to recruit competent assistants, advisors, and specialists; (3) the ability to cultivate and utilize institutional resources; (4) a willingness to engage in problem solving and to work with others as a team; and (5) enough personal confidence to initiate new ideas. The moral administrator seldom resorts to the use of raw bureaucratic power, preferring to be influenced by public pressures, interests, and needs. Another well-known administrative platonist is Stephen K. Bailey, like Appleby a former Dean of the Maxwell School of Citizenship and Public Affairs at Syracuse University. Bailey said the conditions surrounding policy decisions are replete with moral ambiguities and the "paradox of procedures." These procedures are designed to treat all people indiscriminately, but they result in discrimination against those who do not possess the *savoir faire* for dealing with the bureaucracy. Both Appleby and Bailey believed that optimism, courage, fairness, and charity are characteristics of ethical administrators. Both believed in the relegation of personal power to the public good. Both believed that public administrators have a responsibility to uphold the highest moral principles of the society. Disciples of administrative platonism believe that public administrators are not unlike the guardians in Plato's *Republic*. See also APPLEBY, PAUL HENSON, 8; ETHICS IN GOVERNMENT ACT OF 1978, 212.

Significance Administrative platonism competes with four other schools of thought in American public administration: scientific management, participative management, representative bureaucracy, and the new public administration. Administrative platonism has drawn a good deal of criticism from these schools because (1) Concepts such as courage and charity defy precise definition and therefore become void of meaning. As long as personal definitions of morality pertain, there can be little agreement about what constitutes the public good or even ethical behavior. When public official Daniel Ellsberg released the Pentagon Papers, he believed he was acting in accordance with high ethical principles. Others believed he was violating the public trust. (2) The guardian side of the administrative platonist, basing morality on self-conceptions rather than on commonly agreed-on democratic values, can become self-righteous enough to block political processes. (3) Administrative platonists do not clarify how ethical values are instilled in public administrators, a particular problem in the United States, where training of public administrators is not uniform and where ethics courses are not a part of most curricula. (4) Since most public administrators do not have the ethical sensibilities of Appleby and Bailey, the public cannot rely on administrative platonism to control bureaucratic power. Countervailing interest-group pressures would appear to be a more reliable means of doing so.

Administrative Theory (5)

An effort to conceptualize what public administration is, how to improve what it does, how to define what it *should* do, why people behave as they do in administrative settings, and how the administrative apparatus of government can be orchestrated and coordinated to achieve predetermined goals. Administrative theory has at least five aspects according to public administrationist William L. Morrow: descriptive theory, prescriptive theory, normative theory, assumptive theory, and instrumental theory. *Descriptive theory* describes what actually happens in administrative agencies and postulates possible causes for the behavior it observes. Administrative theorists, such as Stephen K. Bailey, suggest that we should apply the insights of the humanities and the social sciences to the study of public administration, because sociology, psychology, economics, and history can help explain why administrators act as they do. *Prescriptive theory* prescribes changes in the direction of public policy by exploiting the bureaucracy's expertise and political clout. Once descriptive theory has described the cause of an administrative disease, prescriptive theory can prescribe its cure. According to prescriptive theory, administrative theory exists to reform, to correct, and to improve the processes of government. *Normative theory* is concerned with questions of whether the public bureaucracy should be assuming the roles it is assuming in politics and policy development, and whether or not such roles should be stabilized, extended, or restricted. Should public administrators advocate the protection of the interests of the consumer and the aged? Should public administrators introduce comprehensive plans for preservation of the wilderness and natural resources? Ought bureaucrats to lobby for policies designed to solve the energy crisis? Or should the advocacy role be avoided in deference to the prerogatives of popularly elected executives and legislators? These are the primary questions of normative theory. *Assumptive theory* focuses on improving the quality of administrative practices by attempting to understand the nature of human beings as they interact with political institutions in a bureaucratic environment. *Instrumental theory* conceptualizes ways to improve techniques of administrative management to make policy goals more realizable. Instrumental theory is "pay off" theory. It is about the tools, techniques, and timing necessary to implement values prescribed elsewhere in the political system. If instrumental wisdom does not exist, and if a reliable delivery system for policy decisions is not in place, the other four elements of administrative theory are incapable of application. The "how" and the "when" of administrative theory are as important as the "why." *See also* ADMINISTRATIVE MAN MODEL, 2; ORGANIZATION THEORY, CLASSICAL, 176; ORGANIZATION THEORY, NEOCLASSICAL, 178; PUBLIC ADMINISTRATION, 21.

Significance Administrative theory is based on recognition of the fact that the enduring traditions of public administration were produced in large part by political movements directed at improving the way administrators do their jobs. Whether there is a current focus on descriptive, prescriptive, normative, assumptive, or instrumental theory depends on the political climate. All advocates of change call on descriptive theory to provide the necessary explanatory evidence on which to base reform. Policy reform eras have then stressed prescriptive, normative, and assumptive theories. An era geared to relaxing the tempo of policy innovation in deference to improved management tends to favor instrumental theory. When one type of administrative theory is emphasized at the expense of others, advantages accrue to those in control of government. President Richard M. Nixon pursued political and administrative *decentralization* to get on with what he termed "the people's business." He justified his austerity approach to welfare on the same grounds. Presidents Franklin D. Roosevelt and Lyndon B. Johnson, on the other hand, saw more political and social progress in political and administrative *centralization*. They believed the federal bureaucracy's growth and advocacy of new programs would also accomplish the people's business. Preferences for a particular type of administrative theory invariably have political underpinnings.

Agenda (6)

An action plan containing things to be considered or acted upon. Every organization or committee meeting uses a formal or informal agenda to determine what business will be considered and the order in which it will be considered. In Congress, the agenda for acting upon bills and resolutions emerges out of a complex interaction involving the use of five different calendars in the House and two in the Senate. The role of the Rules Committee is crucial in determining how and when legislation will be considered in the House, as well as the actions of the party leadership in both chambers.

Significance Often in legislative and other kinds of meetings the "battle of the agenda" is critical. Opponents often seek to kill a proposal or bill by keeping it off the agenda of the committee, chamber, or agency which would consider it. In Congress, for example, thousands of bills are scuttled each session simply by keeping them off the agenda of a subcommittee of the House or Senate. Killing bills in the Congress through committee inaction is usually referred to as *pigeonholing*. This term describes the process by which bills are filed in desk cubicles (pigeonholes) and thereafter ignored. Sometimes proposals are substantially altered as a condition of getting them on the agenda. In an unusual procedure, some states use the "sunset" system whereby laws are automatically placed on the legislative body's agenda for review after a specified period, usually six or seven years. At that time the law is either re-passed by the legislature or the sun sets on it, meaning it is permitted to expire.

American Society for Public Administration (ASPA) (7)

A national professional organization existing "to advance the science, processes, and art of public administration." The American Society for Public Administration (ASPA) was organized in 1939, and in 1987 had a membership of about 20,000. The membership is exceedingly diverse, including practitioners in local, metropolitan, state, regional, and federal government, as well as academicians, students, and community and business leaders. The organization is divided into ten regions and 106 local chapters. ASPA is governed by a national council, currently composed of 43 members, and its work is facilitated by a national staff at its headquarters in Washington, DC. ASPA's three major goals are (1) to improve the quality of human life through effective, efficient, compassionate, and trustworthy public service; (2) to develop the Society as a learning and action organization; and (3) to achieve and maintain organizational health at all constituent levels by strengthening the Society's capacity to serve its members' needs. ASPA does not focus on any one functional activity. It offers twelve special sections which members can join to become part of nationwide professional networks—for example, networks on personnel administration and labor relations, natural resources and environmental administration, or international and comparative administration. The largest ASPA section is the Section on Human Resource Administration, which seeks to advance the planning, administration, and evaluation of human resource policies and programs in the public health, social services, and human development fields. The activities of each section may include the publication of newsletters, papers, and journals; the sponsoring of panels and workshops at national, regional, and local meetings; and the creation of task forces on major issues. ASPA also publishes bimonthly the *Public Administration Review* (PAR) and, twice a month, a newspaper, the *Public Administration Times*. The *Times* carries a complete array of news items of interest to public managers, plus recruiting information, booknotes, commentary, and announcements. ASPA conducts an annual national conference and regional conferences, as well as offering membership benefits of group insurance, special publications, developmental workshops, and professional study tours. *See also* PROFESSIONALISM, 20; PUBLIC ADMINISTRATION, 21.

Significance The American Society for Public Administration (ASPA), located at 1225 Connecticut Avenue, NW, Washington, DC 20036, has played a major role in establishing public administration as a professional field. As early as 1912, public administration was recognized as a subfield of political science, with the formation that year of the Committee on Practical Training for Public Service of the American Political Science Association (APSA). This committee formed the nucleus of the Society for the Promotion of Training for the Public Service, founded in 1914, and was the forerunner of ASPA. An uneasy relationship between public administration and its mother discipline came to a crisis point in the late 1960s when public administrationist Dwight Waldo wrote that "many political scientists not identified with public administration are indifferent or even hostile; they would sooner be free of it." Since 1967, when public administration disappeared as an organizing category in the program of the annual meeting of the American Political Science Association, ASPA has grown steadily. By 1980 its numbers eclipsed APSA, whose membership stood at about 12,600. Public administration scholars were also questioning the "mother discipline" assumption, arguing that Woodrow Wilson had identified public administration as a fie of study in 1887, long before the American Political Science Assoc ation was founded in 1903.

Appleby, Paul Henson (1891–1963) (8)
American public administrator, educator, and author whose writings argued against the politics-administration dichotomy and maintained that the political involvement of public administrators acts as a check on the arbitrary exercise of bureaucratic power in a democratic state. Paul Appleby was convinced during his eleven years as an administrator in the Department of Agriculture that American public managers are very much involved in the political processes of formulating and implementing public policy. In *Big Democracy* (1945) and *Policy and Administration* (1949), Appleby showed how public administration is molded and shaped by political constraints and pressures. Politics is not separate from public administration, because bureaucrats concretize legislation by making rules, interpreting the law, and determining the rights of citizens. Bureaucrats even help members of Congress draft legislation. Appleby described public administrators as "supplementary lawmakers," who nevertheless operate under such constraints as (1) the intentions and mood shifts of Congress; (2) the judicial implications of policy implementation and the possible responses of the courts ; (3) accountability to the public and interest groups regarding decisions and policies; and (4) pressure to cooperate and coordinate with other government agencies. For these reasons and others, Appleby believed that public administration and business management are very different. One way to maintain responsibility is through *administrative pluralism*. This is a system in which administration is immersed in group competition over the shape and content of public policy. In *Morality and Administration in Democratic Government* (1952), Appleby warned that one of the unfortunate consequences of political pressure on the bureaucracy is that issues tend to be pushed to the highest levels of the organization for decision. At those levels issues are oversimplified; they become either-or options, and they lose important nuances. Top level administrators are more political than lower level ones, because they have more contact with the public and with other agencies. Appleby's ultimate goal was a reconciliation of democratic values with bureaucratic necessities. He warned that the major threat to democratic administration would come not from a politically active public service, but from the experts who would rationalize democracy out of administration under the guise of efficiency. See also PLURALISM, 66; POLITICS-ADMINISTRATION DICHOTOMY, 70.

Significance   Paul Appleby was a New Deal public administrator and former newspaperman who described the *political* rules of administration while Luther Gulick and others were advocating POSDCORB (planning, organizing, staffing, directing, coordinating, reporting, budgeting) as the basic descriptive guideposts for administration. Appleby could not bring himself to believe that administration was a science, governed by immutable laws and subject to standards of rationality. He retired to academia to refute this dogma and, as Dean of the Maxwell School of Citizenship and Public Affairs at Syracuse University, he left a legacy in support of administrative pluralism. In the old argument over the bureaucratic versus the democratic model of government, Paul Appleby introduced a workable compromise by saying that interest groups and bureaucracies can work together synergistically. The Appleby solution has remained acceptable to both rationalists and classical democrats, but has had little impact on public administration outside the United States.

Boren's Testimony (9)

"When in charge, ponder; When in trouble, delegate; When in doubt, mumble." Boren's testimony was presented to the Subcommittee on Investigations and Oversight of the Committee on Public Works of the United States House of Representatives on June 22, 1971. Its author was Dr. James H. Boren, formerly an official of the United States Agency for International Development, posing hilariously in 1971 as president of a national association of government administrators. Boren's testimony followed in the tradition of Parkinson's Law and the Peter Principle and represented for the 1970s the irreverent kind of commentary on administrative foibles that they had represented in the 1950s and 1960s, respectively. Boren spoke on the merits of "policy thwartation" and "dynamic inactivism," among other positions advocated by his organization, NATAPROBU, the acronym for National Association of Professional Bureaucrats. Boren's testimony recommended the establishment of a new cabinet level department with a number of bureaus and offices for specialized functions. Among these would be (1) the Office of Orderly Over-Runs, Permeations, and Statistics (OOOPS); (2) Governmental Linguistic Obtusity Bureau (GLOB); (3) Office of Procedural Abstraction Programs (OPAP); (4) Computerized Lethargic Output Division (CLOD); and (5) Management Unit for Maximized Budgetary and Legal Evaluations (MUMBLE). Boren's testimony poked unmerciful fun at such bureaucratic necessities as committee meetings (". . . their faces wore the frozen countenance of the professional bureaucrat, but their eyes were sparkling. They were joyously devitalizing ideas with deft thrusts of yes-buttisms and forthright twiddlisms.") and paperwork ("To deny a dedicated fingertapper an adequate supply of paper on which to record the results of his prodigious pondering is to deny him the tools of creative nonresponsiveness. To limit the number of pages on which he is to write is to limit the potential beauty of a sunset. Paper to the professional bureaucrat is as canvas to the artist.") On conclusion of his testimony, president Boren presented each member of the committee with a pencil carrying his organization's slogan, "When in doubt, mumble." The pencil had an eraser at both ends. See also BUREAUPATHOLOGY, 129; MURPHY'S LAW, 108; PARKINSON'S LAW, 109; PETER PRINCIPLE, 111.

Significance Boren's testimony was parody, but it gave sharp focus to what has been called in more serious contexts bureaupathological behavior. The fact that Congressman James C. Wright, Chairman of the House Subcommittee on Investigations and Oversight, participated fully in the questioning and was, in fact, Dr. Boren's "straight man" is some indication of congressional sympathy for the testimony's purpose.

Case Study (10)
Analysis of a variety of phenomena based on research conducted on a particular event. Case studies are not usually carried on by using the scientific method. Their effectiveness depends primarily on the use of common sense and imagination by the investigator, the thoroughness and objectivity with which the investigation is conducted, and the relationship between the case study and the understanding sought. Case studies in the field of public administration may involve observational field research. By studying a group's values, motivations, beliefs, and actions in a special environment or in dealing with a specific event or issue, the researcher's efforts can add to a general understanding of that group's behavior. See also PREDICTION, 19.

Significance Case studies are a familiar tool for gaining an understanding of diverse phenomena in the social sciences and in public administration. By a thorough investigation of an agency's actions in adopting a certain public policy, much can be learned about who makes the policy and in what manner. A study of how the Federal Communications Commission (FCC) decided upon and issued the "fairness doctrine" that governs the actions of radio and television stations, for example, explains a great deal about bureaucratic decision making. In this case it reveals what values guided the commissioners, what political pressures were exerted upon them, what role Congress played, and what the motivations were that led to the decision. When the case study approach is being considered, an investigator should first determine whether a larger sample should be used to achieve his or her research goal.

Comparative Public Administration (11)
A cross-cultural approach to the study of public administration that rejects theory rooted solely in the American experience and which assumes that cultural factors do not make any difference in administrative settings because "principles are principles." From its inception in 1960 as the Comparative Administration Group (CAG) of the American Society for Public Administration (ASPA), the school of comparative public administration has attempted to be "theory-building" in opposition to the "practitioner-oriented" bias of "parochial American public administration." The school seeks knowledge for the sake of knowledge. It addresses five motivating concerns: (1) the search for theory; (2) the urge for practical application; (3) the incidental contribution of the broader field of comparative politics; (4) the interest of the researchers trained in the tradition of administrative law; and (5) the comparative analysis of ongoing problems of public administration. Comparative public administration reached its zenith in the late 1960s, when the CAG achieved a membership of over 500. *See also* PROFESSIONALISM, 20.

Significance Comparative public administration has been more scholarly than professional in its emphasis. This proved its undoing as far as a $500,000 grant from the Ford Foundation was concerned. Prior to terminating its support in 1971, a representative of the Foundation asked the Comparative Administration Group what "all this theorizing and all this study will amount to" in terms of improving the practice of public administration. Perhaps the reason no one in comparative public administration ever really answered the question was because of its fixation on a comprehensive theory or model, which proved to be an unattainable goal. Public administrationist Robert T. Golembiewski described this fixation as a "self-imposed failure experience." The CAG was disbanded in 1973, and the field's major journal, *The Journal of Comparative Administration,* ceased to publish in 1974. Comparative public administration was "captured" in a unique way by one man, Fred W. Riggs, whose ideas dominated the CAG in the ten years he chaired the organization, 1960–1970. The classic work in comparative and development administration remains Riggs's *Administration in Developing Countries: The Theory of Prismatic Society* (1965). Reports of comparative public administration's death may be premature, however, because its adherents may yet define themselves more modestly than in terms of a comprehensive theory. Comparing the administration of public transportation systems in Japan, West Germany, and the United States, for example, or the public health systems in Sweden, China, and Israel, may prove in the future to be as practical as it is theoretically interesting.

Development Administration (12)
The enhancement or improvement of techniques, processes, and systems organized to increase the administrative capacity of a nation, usually a newly emerging nation. Development administration assumes that the rise of the modern state came hand in hand with the development of the rational bureaucratic structure. According to Lucian Pye, effective bureaucratic structures made the modern nation-state possible. Development administration evolved in the 1950s from a merger of classical economics and public administration. Its adherents tended to define development from a strictly economic perspective; it was measured solely in terms of per capita increases in the gross national product. Development was equated with the amount of tangible resources produced in relation to the size of the population, expressed in such terms as industrial output, agricultural produce, and raw materials. The determinant of the growth of productive goods, that is, output, was dependent on the inputs, or factors of production of land, labor, and capital. Technology was considered neutral. Development administration plans created in the 1950s and 1960s indicated the extent of growth expected by showing how the per capita gross national product would be increased. This emphasis gave way in the 1970s, in the developing societies themselves, to values and priorities about how effectively to mobilize in order to achieve equitable distribution of wealth and income. The developing nations were equally concerned about full utilization of manpower, better utilization of natural resources, and protection of the environment. Development administration emphasizes political commitment to specific development goals and objectives. It uses governmental power and influence to provide legitimacy to them. Development administration is at the center of the politics of developing countries. *See also* BUREAUCRACY, 126; COMPARATIVE PUBLIC ADMINISTRATION, 11; PUBLIC ADMINISTRATION, 21.

Significance Development administration has attempted to implement rational bureaucratic machinery, based on a neutral, competent civil service, in developing countries. It has worked in some cases, but it has not in many others. There are significant reasons for this: (1) A neutral civil service may be desirable later, rather than earlier, in a nation's history. It may be dysfunctional to separate policy making from administration in what needs to be an *organic* structure of government as national identities are defined. A possible effect of an early dichotomy between policy and administration in countries with still embryonic political institutions is that bureaucrats will take command of policy making as well as execution. They tend to be foreign-educated technocrats with knowledge, and, as Sir Francis Bacon said, "knowledge is power." (2) There is some reason to believe that in the history of the United States, itself adopting a civil service system over a hundred years after its founding, corruption in public and private sectors was overlooked for a long time precisely because it was a means of accelerating the pace of development. (3) In many developing countries, the universities and the government live in a state of continued tension, resulting in mutual distrust. The government tends to feel the university—with its radical element on the left and on the right—will subvert government policy. The leaders of developing countries need time to establish competing institutions, such as institutes of public administration, to assure themselves that the Weberian model will indeed be followed when put in place, that bureaucrats will follow political leadership rather than form an elite power base serving their own interests. Development administration is an instrumental means for defining, consolidating, and implementing national goals in developing countries.

Ethics (13)

The rules or standards governing the moral conduct of the members of an organization or management profession. Ethics is defined in moral philosophy as "that branch of philosophy dealing with values relating to human conduct, with respect to rightness or wrongness of certain actions, and to the goodness or badness of the motives and ends of such actions." Ethics is commonly divided into four main schools of thought, which may be understood as alternative explanations for principles of human action. Actually the schools of thought overlap. They are (1) *Empirical theory,* which states that ethics are derived through human experience and are conceived by general agreement. Some forms of warfare are commonly agreed to be unethical, for example. The use of poison gas and hydrogen bombs is unethical because there would be no way to control such weapons once they were unleashed. Empirical theory bases itself on what can be seen, quantified, and measured. "Right" and "wrong" do not have an independent existence apart from facts and deeds. (2) *Rational theory,* which states that people determine what is good or bad through reason. Ethical action is a determination of logic, not of experience. Plato, Aristotle, and Spinoza were proponents of rational theory. It maintains that each situation is unique and requires a unique application of the human power of deduction to arrive at what is right or good. (3) *Intuitive theory,* which states that ethics are not necessarily derived from experience or from logic, but that human beings naturally and automatically possess an understanding of what is right and wrong, good and bad. Intuitive theorists frequently use the phrase "natural moral law" and are well represented in the writings which inspired and explained the French and American revolutions. (4) *Revelation theory,* which states that the determination of right and wrong comes from an authority above human beings. In this view the Bible as the Word of God is the final arbiter of conduct. Furthermore, God continues to make pronouncements regarding ethical decisions which must be made. Just who God speaks through on the occasions of his pronouncements is not always clear. *See also* ETHIC OF MEANS AND ENDS, 97; PROFESSIONALISM, 20.

Significance Ethics is a relatively new concept in American public administration, although its classical antecedents are deep and varied. The reason it is new is that the closed model of organizations as represented by Max Weber, Frederick Winslow Taylor, Luther Gulick, and Lyndall Urwick, and as epitomized in the politics-administration dichotomy, had no place for moral choices. From this perspective, a public administrator needs morality no more than a hotel clerk carrying out his daily duties. Of what use was morality to a person who did no more than execute the will of the state according to certain scientific principles? As long as public administrators accomplished their given tasks efficiently and economically, they were, by definition, moral. That is, they were responsible. Morality in the sense of ethical choice was simply not a function of the functionaries. But the closed model and the dichotomy were abandoned, because they had to be. Active public administrator and educator Paul H. Appleby was one of the first participant-observers to say simply that the closed model and the dichotomy did not represent the way administration was actually done, whatever the doctrine stated. When politics and administration were recognized as being part of the same parcel, it was also admitted implicitly that morality had to be relevant to the bureaucracy. The public administrator was now forced to make decisions, not just on the comfortable bases of efficiency, economy, and administrative principles, but on the more agonizing criteria of morality as well. The question of ethics in the public service, therefore, revolves around answers to the question, "What is the public interest?" Ethics is focused on the lone bureaucrat who possesses considerable discretionary power, and who must make decisions defining the public good. The traditional schools of ethical theory may not help the administrator in this task. They do give him or her the context of the decision, however. Ethical sophistication—how to recognize it, how to develop it, how to communicate it—is at the cutting edge of modern public administration.

Fayol, Henri (1841–1925) (14)

A French industrial engineer who believed that necessary administrative functions could be written down and taught as principles of administration. Fayol did not begin to write down what he knew about administration until the age of seventy-five, after a lifetime of service, first as the manager of a group of coal mines at Commentry, France, then as head of a bureaucratic and industrial empire including not only coal fields, but blast furnaces and steel mills as well. Fayol was immensely successful because of his unique skill as a manager. He drew up plans of action, made accurate economic and technical forecasts, and evaluated the performance of the workers he supervised. He spent an enormous amount of time coordinating different units within the organization. He knew how to set up a control system to verify whether operations worked according to plan. Throughout his professional life, Fayol treated administration as a process. This was contrary to prevailing practice, which was to place administration under the control of specialists. To manage a mine, for example, one studied mine engineering. To manage an army, one specialized in military strategy. Fayol believed that good administration was a process consisting of a certain number of conditions which were common to all organizations. It did not matter whether the manager administered a mine or a regiment, or worked in an industry or a government bureau. The general principles to which Fayol referred are (1) *Unity of command,* in which each employee receives orders from one superior alone: "One person, one master." (2) *The scalar principle,* in which a chain of command reflects an organizational pyramid. In issuing orders and resolving disputes, all communications must "go through official channels." (3) *Span of control,* in which the assumption is made that there is a limit to the number of subordinates a supervisor can effectively oversee, generally set at a maximum of twelve. (4) *Centralization,* in which the organization is administered from the top down. Ultimate responsibility remains at the top rather than being lost among subordinates in the organizational mass. (5) *Responsibility,* in which executives delegate responsibility as well as authority, including the power to impose sanctions. Fayol is best known for his ideas about unity of command, the scalar principle, and span of control. Stated more accurately, these ideas are well known, although many people who are aware of them do not know that Henri Fayol stated them first. *See also* GULICK, LUTHER, 17; SPAN OF CONTROL, 115; TAYLOR, FREDERICK WINSLOW, 24; URWICK, LYNDALL F., 26.

Significance   Henri Fayol's work is significant at several levels. One is that his principles of administration were adopted by the Belgian Ministry of National Defense and the French Ministry of Posts, Telegraphs, and Telephones. Another is that his ideas inspired two important administrative novels: Emile Zola's *Germinal,* based on Fayol's handling of the great French coal mine strike of 1884, and Humphrey Cobb's *Paths of Glory,* based on a French military application, or misapplication, of Fayol's management principles after the battles at St. Mihiel in 1915. But by far the most influential application of Fayol's theory was in American public administration. Fayol's ideas were thoroughly incorporated into the classical school of American public administration—what has been called "the gospel of efficiency"—by Luther Gulick and his British colleague, Lyndall Urwick. Their *Papers on the Science of Administration,* edited in 1937, presented Fayol's "The Administrative Theory in the State" for the first time in English. This collection formed "the high noon of orthodoxy" in the science of administration. Fayol's influence was felt even more because his leading interpreters, Gulick and Urwick, were confidants of President Franklin D. Roosevelt and advised him on a variety of managerial matters.

Follett, Mary Parker (1868–1933) (15)
American administrative theorist, one of the first proponents of organizational humanism who stated in the early 1920s that *people* constitute the major challenge of modern management. Follett was trained in economics and political science and was active in many types of community service organizations, including adult education and vocational guidance. She regarded industry as the most important field of human endeavor, and management as the fundamental element in industry. Follett spent much of her life writing and lecturing on the development of management as a profession. She was fascinated with the dynamics of interpersonal psychological processes. In her first major work, *Creative Experience,* published in 1924, Follett focused on the problem of administrative conflict. Traditionally, conflict had been viewed as wasteful and harmful. She described it as a process in which important differences do occur, but the resolution of these differences might contribute in

a constructive way toward the attainment of organizational goals. Follett suggested three ways of dealing with conflict. One is by providing a victory for one side or the other and by the consequent domination of one side by the other. The second is by accommodation and compromise. The third is "integration" by finding common ground. Here each side gives up a little and both sides gain as a result of the conflict. Follett maintained that integration was difficult to achieve because it required that conflict be brought into the open, followed by careful examination of both the symbols and the realities of the conflict situation. The next stage in Follett's conflict resolution sequence was analysis and evaluation of the interests and desires revealed by the situation. This led to development of alternatives to resolve the conflict. Follett drew a careful distinction between power, which she defined as the ability to make things happen or to initiate change, and authority. She believed that leadership is determined not by traits but by situations. The legal-rational approach to organization theory had assumed that organizational objectives were met merely by giving orders, but Follett said people resent being bossed. The more bossing, the more a pattern of opposition to being bossed is likely to emerge. Authority is related more to an individual's expertise than to a grant of formal power delegated in a hierarchical framework. In short, one must develop one's own powers before one can effectively exercise power. See also ORGANIZATION THEORY, CLASSICAL, 176; ORGANIZATION THEORY, HUMANISM, 177; ORGANIZATION THEORY, NEOCLASSICAL, 178.

Significance Mary Parker Follett was a pioneer far ahead of her time in her observations about power and authority. She viewed power as something that could neither be delegated nor conferred. It is rather something to be sought by managers or workers trying to improve themselves. Much of the later work challenging hierarchy as the key to administration was seeded in the contributions of Mary Parker Follett. Herbert A. Simon's work is a lineal descendent of Follett's; the Hawthorne studies of 1927–1932 tested her ideas experimentally and gave them standing in the literature of organization theory; a company of distinguished human relations theorists including Elton Mayo, F. J. Roethlisberger, Chester I. Barnard, John Dewey, and Kurt Lewin give her credit for being the first to emphasize interpersonal communication and collective/shared decision making as essential to the analysis of organizations. Follett helped to move administration toward more human concerns by breaking with the static-principles approach, by integrating administration and psychology, and by urging studies of how people interact in organizations. She was neither an experienced administrator nor a systematic thinker who clearly organized and summarized her thoughts. She was, however, a broad thinker concerned with problems of psychology, leadership, motivation, planning, power, and authority. Few individuals have had a greater influence on the theory and practice of administration.

Gilbreth, Frank B. (1868–1925) and Lillian M. (1878–1972) (16)

Pioneers in the scientific management field whose work is remembered for the innovative technical improvements they introduced to increase productivity, and for the management concepts they developed to value workers as human beings. Frank Gilbreth launched a career as an independent management contractor in 1895. With his marriage to Lillian in 1904, his initial investigations of efficient production methods became their lifetime mutual effort to explore the fastest and best methods of accomplishing targeted tasks. The early work of the Gilbreths was coincidental with the birth of scientific management. Although they worked independently of the concept's founding father, Frederick W. Taylor, they eventually became staunch supporters of Taylorism, and many of its tenets are embodied in the Gilbreths' writings. The Gilbreths' ideal paralleled Taylor with regard to what Taylor referred to as a "mental revolution," directed at the scientific determination of the "one best way" to obtain information and accomplish a task. They believed, like Taylor, that the success of scientific management concepts rested on the cooperation of management and labor in striving to maximize profits. But, whereas Taylor believed the imposition of needed standards was solely a management prerogative, the Gilbreths maintained that cooperation from labor required its participation in planning and implementing scientific management concepts. The Gilbreths emphasized the advantages to labor of the implementation of efficiency theories. The importance of the human aspects of the workplace in the minds of the Gilbreths is demonstrated by the fact that Lillian pursued academic work in psychology to complement her husband's technical knowledge. Her orientation is apparent in their discussions of the role of worker satisfaction and pride, the need for careful selection of workers for specific tasks, and the importance of individual recognition and identity. The Gilbreths recommended giving monthly awards for employee suggestions, and they devised a rating system for workers which let them know how well they were doing. The Gilbreths also developed a list of seventeen basic motions, called "therbligs" ("Gilbreth" spelled backwards, almost), for classifying worker activities. Therbligs included such motions as "search," "select," and "hold" and were designed to eliminate all worker motions unnecessary for the task at hand. See also FAYOL, HENRI, 14; SCIENTIFIC MANAGEMENT, 22; TAYLOR, FREDERICK WINSLOW, 24.

Significance Frank and Lillian Gilbreth were instrumental in streamlining and humanizing the scientific management movement. In the early part of the twentieth century, industrialization was considered a panacea to many, often at the expense of the masses of workers. Concepts such as motivation, the importance of self-concept, and the need for careful selection of workers for each position in an organization were revolutionary at the time the Gilbreths advanced them. To some degree, the Gilbreths' ideas reflected a return to past values. They pointed out that the new methods of mass production had replaced the craftsmanship of an earlier era with mindless routine, and that worker pride and concern had subsequently suffered. More importantly, they demonstrated to management that management objectives of peak efficiency could not be achieved unless worker identity with the product was maintained. The Gilbreths were the first to say that it was in the best interest of management *and* labor to ensure worker satisfaction and to respect the value of the individual.

Gulick, Luther (1892–) (17)

An American administrative reformer who at the time of his maximum influence—in the late 1930s—was Eaton Professor of Municipal Science and Administration at Columbia University. Gulick also served as Director of the Institute of Public Administration at Columbia and as a member of the President's Committee on Administrative Management (the Brownlow Committee). Gulick's most influential piece of writing is his "Notes on the Theory of Organization," the lead article in a collection of essays edited by Gulick and his British colleague Lyndall Urwick, entitled *Papers on the Science of Administration* (1937). The *Papers* marked the high water mark of the development of American administrative science. French industrial engineer Henri Fayol had been very influential in the development of Gulick's thought. Both Gulick and Fayol believed that administration was governed by certain principles or laws, and that the job of the administrative scientist was to discover these principles. Their objective was the accomplishment of the work at hand with the least expenditure of people and materials. The principles Gulick and Fayol discovered through their gospel of efficiency favored the power of managers bent on rationalizing the operations of government and industry by institutionalizing these operations in large bureaus. In his "Notes" article, Gulick condensed the duties of an administrator into the acronym POSDCORB. Each letter stood for one of the critical functions performed by administrators: planning, organizing, staffing, directing, coordinating, reporting, and budgeting. Gulick also presented four ways of organizing work which many administrators put into practice as useful rules of thumb. Gulick suggested that each position in an organization could be characterized by (1) the *purpose* served, including component services required; (2) the *process* used; (3) the *persons or things* dealt with; and (4) the *place* in which the work was done. If people are doing the same work in the same way for the same people at the same place, there would be little difficulty in designing an organizational unit for supervision and control purposes. If there is not a perfect correlation of these elements, however, the hierarchy and authority structures would look quite different. Gulick said that hierarchy and control constituted only one-third of the basic principles of management. Every executive also must be concerned with the division of work. "Work division is the foundation of organization; indeed, it is the reason for organization." Without specialization, there would be little need for coordination and, hence, little need for administrators. *See also* FAYOL, HENRI, 14; POSDCORB, 180; SCIENTIFIC MANAGEMENT, 22.

Significance Luther Gulick has been one of the most influential figures in American public administration. Although POSDCORB became symbolic of all the early errors critics believed were produced by those who first ventured into the science of administration, it represented pioneering insights as well. Gulick's ideas are still widely used in government, primarily because his critics did not have better ones to suggest. Far from being outmoded, as late as 1971 a distinguished academic ended his guest editorial in the *Public Administration Review* with the plea: "Let's give evaluation its due— let's put an E in POSDECORB." Gulick's ideas are long-lived because he was a pragmatic classical theorist. He tried to explain administrative structures by filling in some of the specifics which were implied in the Weberian ideal type of bureaucracy. Yet he was not as particularistic as Frederick W. Taylor and the scientific managers. He argued in fact that good administration is a process distinct from the *particular* management task at hand. All managers have to establish some system of hierarchy and authority, and some system of specialization. They have to institutionalize the power to control and coordinate operations, usually in a staff. A system of rules, personnel administration, and some system of budgeting and financial management must be established. Managers have to set forth objectives and improve employee motivation through human relations techniques. These are the elements of administration as presented by Gulick, and they are still widely taught and practiced.

They are called classical because they are fundamental to any administrative enterprise.

New Public Administration (18)

An effort by a school of professional administrators and academicians in the 1970s and 1980s to refocus public administration away from its traditional concerns for efficiency, effectiveness, budgeting, and good administrative techniques to a concern for social equity. The new public administration is characterized by an interest in normative theory, philosophy, and activism. It deals with values, ethics, and the personal development of individual members of the organization. Its tone is moral. Social needs, particularly the problems of urbanism and violence, are its primary focuses of attention. The new public administration was inaugurated in September 1968, when Dwight Waldo, as Albert Schweitzer Professor in Humanities at Syracuse University and as editor of the *Public Administration Review,* sponsored a conference of young public administrationists to consider the new approach. The meeting was held at the Minnowbrook conference site at Syracuse, hence occasional references in the literature to "the Minnowbrook perspective." Its proceedings were published in 1971 as *Toward a New Public Administration: The Minnowbrook Perspective,* which remains the key work in understanding this school of thought. *See also* ADMINISTRATIVE THEORY, 5; PROFESSIONALISM, 20; SOCIAL EQUITY, 23.

Significance   The new public administration movement paralleled a "new political science movement" and occurred simultaneously with the movement to rid political science of its emphasis on behavioralism. Both movements were led by "young turks" who had broader normative concerns than currently predominant technical emphases in the two fields would recognize. Many of the young turks soon became older turks who attained positions of high responsibility in public administration. H. George Frederickson, for example, one of the Minnowbrook participants who remarked during the conference that the new movement was "in alignment with good, or possibly God," became president of the American Society for Public Administration (ASPA) in 1977. The new public administration was a declaration of independence from both political science and administrative science. Advocates of the new public administration noted that political science, its mother discipline, had practically disowned it. In 1962, public administration was not included as a subfield of political science in the report of the Committee on Political Science as a Discipline of the American Political Science Association (APSA). By 1967, public administration had disappeared as an organizing category in the program of the annual meeting of the American Political Science Association. In the year he called the Minnowbrook Conference, 1968, Dwight Waldo wrote that "many political scientists not identified with Public Administration are indifferent or even hostile; they would sooner be free of it." He stated that the public administrationist had "second-class citizenship" in political science. Between 1960 and 1970, only 4 percent of all articles published in the five major political science journals dealt with public administration. New public administration adherents noted also that public administrationists had not fared much better in administrative science departments. The technical approach of statisticians, systems analysts, and economists which dominated administrative science in the 1960s left little doubt in many public administration minds that the *public* in public administration was being lost in the business-administration-school location of most administrative science departments. The business school was typically profit-conscious. The public administrationist had a sense of the public interest, without which many believed administrative science could be used for *any* purpose, no matter how immoral. The new public administration was therefore a reconsideration of public administration's traditional intellectual ties with both political science and administrative science. It was a contemplation of the prospects of academic autonomy.

Prediction (19)
A stated expectation of what will happen under specified conditions. Prediction can be contrasted with forecasting in that the former anticipates outcomes if certain conditions are met while the latter is a description of future outcomes without specifying essential conditions. In public administration, prediction often takes the form of anticipating future outcomes in the form of tendency statements. *If* certain conditions exist, *then* there is a likely tendency that specified results will follow. This is called *if-then* analysis. In the natural sciences, the ability to predict with certainty that specified results will occur is an essential element in the scientific method. Prediction typically begins with a hypothesis, a statement of expected relationships between variables that can be tested and proved empirically. If there is enough certainty about outcomes that different people utilizing the same procedures can achieve the same results, prediction then becomes deterministic rather than probabilistic. *See also* ADMINISTRATIVE THEORY, 5.

Significance   The field of public administration has placed increasing emphasis on predicting outcomes. Some predictions relate to events that have already occurred, the objective being to better understand decision making and individual and group activities by analyzing (and predicting) the relationships between dependent and independent variables. Other predictions, as in the field of planning, for example, seek to anticipate the future by studying observed regularities in the operations of government agencies and other public bodies. Because prediction is the essence of science, the value placed on enhancing the ability to predict outcomes in the field of public administration is linked to the discipline's efforts to become more scientific.

Professionalism (20)

The development of a specialized body of knowledge and expertise by one group that excludes from membership in that group any who do not possess those specialized skills. Professionalism in public administration dates back to the reform era of the 1880s. Political science Professor Woodrow Wilson was the first to point out the importance of public administration as a profession in 1887. Wilson's arguments led eventually to the founding of professional organizations of public administrators. The largest of these professional organizations is the American Society for Public Administration (ASPA), which had a 1987 membership of about 20,000, both practitioners and academics. ASPA exists "to advance the Science, Processes, and Art of Public Administration." Since specialized knowledge is part of professionalism, college or university degrees have become a symbol of merit and a way of earning admission into the profession. The professional organization that attempts to control degree requirements in the field is the National Association of Schools of Public Affairs and Administration (NASPAA). According to NASPAA's recommended core curriculum, a Master's Degree in public administration should include at least the following components: (1) the political, social, and economic contexts of administration; (2) quantitative and nonquantitative analytical tools; (3) individual, group, and organizational dynamics; (4) policy analysis; and (5) administrative/management processes. If schools of public administration want to earn the approval of NASPAA as an accrediting body, they must adopt these guidelines. Professionalism incorporates the idea that knowledge is power. Public administrationist James D. Carroll predicts that "noetic authority"—power that derives from knowledge—will eventually be more important for professionalism than authority derived from position and wealth. *See also* AMERICAN SOCIETY FOR PUBLIC ADMINISTRATION (ASPA), 7; PUBLIC ADMINISTRATION, 21; PUBLIC PERSONNEL ADMINISTRATION, 238; WILSON, WOODROW, 29.

Significance Professionalism has expanded dramatically in the public sector in recent years. In 1976, for example, professional, technical, and kindred workers comprised 21 percent of the federal civilian work force, 37 percent of the state work force, and 42 percent of the local work force. These high percentages have resulted in many problems and conflicts. Traditionally, other professionals such as doctors, lawyers, and educators have looked down on bureaucracies and bureaucrats. Professionals who have chosen public service sometimes feel they must overcome this dislike of bureaucracy if they are to perform their duties effectively. Many others ignore the pejorative remarks they receive that dub them "pseudoprofessionals." Public administration professionals are also frequently involved in rivalries within the civil service. Whereas the focus of public administration professionalism is on the person and his or her expertise, the focus of the civil service is on the position. The conflict is one of job versus how one does the job, and it has yet to be resolved. Some agencies are almost entirely controlled by certain professions, which become an elite within that agency. The profession's primary means of control is the construction of a personnel system which discourages entry of new professionals or independent experts. New employees enter the agency at the lowest level and gradually move up a pyramid-shaped organization to the top. As one moves up, competition increases, and some professionals or potential professionals are "selected out." They do not get promoted, so they leave the agency. There is little lateral entry into an elite profession. Thus the profession in control perpetuates itself by offering little chance for new opinions or methods to gain recognition. The result may be an agency that cannot respond to new and different demands. It develops and constantly reinforces its own values and norms. The conflict area of the professional versus the politician is basically that of specialized knowledge and presumed rationality opposed to the art and necessity of negotiation and compromise. Professionals usually deal with problems in a manner dictated by their professional standards. What happens if the path chosen by the professional does not coincide with the wishes of the people? In democratic theory, politicians represent the wishes of the people and therefore must contest with professional heads of agencies. The conflict may be even more intense when professional organizations act as interest groups attempting to influence policy decisions. Professionalism has increased the expertise and efficiency of agency administration while simultaneously creating its own set of problems and conflicts.

Public Administration (21)
The process by which public resources and personnel are organized and coordinated to formulate, implement, and manage public policy decisions. Public administration is characterized by bureaucracies, large-scale activities, and distinctively public administrative responsibilities. James W. Fesler, in *Public Administration, Theory and Practice,* published in 1980, notes distinctions between *public* and *private* administration. For Fesler, public administration is the administration of *governmental* affairs. Whereas the objective of most business corporations is to make a profit, an objective that is single and clear, few government departments and bureaus have profit as an objective, and their objective is usually plural. Similarly, a corporation's performance is easily measurable in terms of profit or loss, and internally a corporation can judge its individual products, divisions, and employees by cost-effectiveness standards. The typical government agency, however, provides services that are not sold on the market, since they are financed by general governmental revenues. There is generally no direct comparison between an agency's costs and the value of its services to the public. In terms of decision making, the private corporation has a limited public, which is perceived almost entirely in economic terms. The corporation does not need to concern itself with anyone's welfare but its own. The federal government, on the other hand, has a large public—240 million customers in the United States and more beyond. Most of these customers are suppliers of tax revenue as well as beneficiaries of governmental services. Public agencies pursue the interests of the society. The obligation of an individual agency to relate its actions to values and clienteles extending far beyond its specific assignment has become commonplace in the public sector. The final difference between public and private administration is the degree of publicity associated with administrative performance. Public administrators tend to live in a goldfish bowl. They must appear before congressional committees and subcommittees, grant interviews, hold press conferences, receive interest-group representatives, and endure attacks in newspaper columns, editorials, and magazine articles. Many of their decisions can be made only after public hearings. A public administrator's life is lived in the bright light of publicity and in response to the public's right to know.

Beyond public administration's distinction from private administration is the definitional factor of size. Public administration is large-scale administration. In 1976, the two largest industrial corporations in the United States, Exxon and General Motors, had sales much smaller than the outlays of either the Department of Health, Education, and Welfare (HEW) or the Department of Defense (DOD). In June 1976, General Motors, the largest industrial employer, had fewer employees than the *civilian* employees of the Department of Defense. Of the fifteen largest organizations in the nation in 1976, by number of employees, seven were government organizations. Public administration is not only *public* and large, it is also defined in terms of *policy* formulation and execution. Administrative agencies are among the most important sources for proposals for statutes and amendments to statutes. An agency has a great deal of factual information about needs and trends in its program field. It has discovered the defects which existing statutes inevitably have. It has specialized competence from which it advises the chief executive in his role as policy leader of the government. After statutes are on the books, administrators frequently must *interpret* complex or deliberately vague legislative mandates. For example, Congress broadly forbids "unfair methods of competition . . . and unfair or deceptive acts in commerce." Administrators and judges must give content to the terms *unfair* and *deceptive*. Policy execution, whether of an ambiguous law which requires the administrator to make policy, or of a very specifically worded law which draws taxes, sets interest rates, or grants permission to license radio stations, translates paper declarations of intent into reality. In the final analysis, public administration is the process of converting words into actions and form into substance. *See also* ADMINISTRATION, 1; BUREAUCRACY, 126; BUREAUCRATIC EXPERTISE, 128; PROFESSIONALISM, 20.

Significance Public administration is an ancient human activity. Written records of some of the earliest societies show that people were organized formally to attain certain public objectives, such as building monuments, aqueducts, and cities, or to conduct commerce or war. In the Bible the patriarch Joseph was a public administrator. He was given the responsibility for planning and distributing the food supply in ancient Egypt. Moses was instructed by his father-in-law, in the eighteenth chapter of Exodus, about the principles of delegation of authority and span of control. Solomon was presented as a master administrator throughout the early chapters of I Kings as he directed the establishment of elaborate trade agreements and supervised the building of Solomon's temple, which was planned so carefully "there was neither hammer nor ax nor any tool of iron heard in the house while it was in the building." In modern times, the weakness of public administration has often tended to enfeeble the political system itself.

In developing countries, for example, the critical problem seems not so much political instability or the government's inability to devise rational programs for development, but administrative incapacity to carry out the government's decisions and programs. Public administration is as varied in policy execution as delivering the mail, collecting the trash, and putting a man on the moon. It is as complex as it is important, and because it has expanded as societal needs have expanded, its boundaries have never been precisely defined.

Scientific Management (22)

An American organization theory popular in the early 1900s that emphasized rationalism, efficiency, and productivity through established rules, laws, and scientific principles. Scientific management, also known as "Taylorism," was founded by Frederick Winslow Taylor, who summarized the basic concepts in his book, *Principles of Scientific Management,* published in 1911. A mechanical engineer with a background in steel production, Taylor reacted against the inefficiency, resource waste, and corruption of the post-industrial revolution era by proposing that management could be a true science and that productivity could be increased by systematic application of scientific principles. The concepts behind Taylor's science of management formed the framework for the organization theory that dominated private and public administration for the first four decades of the twentieth century. Although other works, such as the time and motion study design of Frank and Lillian Gilbreth, contributed to the scientific management era, Taylor's work is equated with the theory. Central to the practice of scientific management was the idea that there is "one best way" to perform any task. To determine and implement that one best way required a series of steps to be performed by the management scientist. First, the job was analyzed, breaking it down into its smallest possible segments, determining what the outputs were, and identifying unnecessary movements or procedures. This analysis provided the basis for the scientific redesign of the "best" way rather than relying on what Taylor called the "rule-of-thumb" traditional knowledge kept in a worker's head. Time and motion studies were used extensively to determine exactly how long each segment of a task did, or should, take. Once the most efficient way was determined, tools and procedures were standardized to allow for maximum productivity, and a rate of pay was determined. A fair day's pay was something to be determined by scientific management rather than by negotiation between management and labor. Efficiency was greatest when workers "fit" the machines, so the right workers were selected according to their capabilities to meet the required tasks. Selected workers were then trained in the standardized procedures—what Taylor called "bringing scientific management and the worker together." Scientific management considered the worker a necessary instrument for production. The worker was a tool that had to be adapted to the system to achieve efficiency. A key to the success of scientific management was considered to be cooperative management-worker relations, but in the end the fastest way to efficiency often required forced standardization. Scientific management believed that workers were rational, self-serving, somewhat simpleminded, and motivated only by economic incentives. Since scientific management based payment to workers on productivity, it did not foresee any problems since the objectives of workers and those of management would be the same: high productivity.

Scientific management, as part of formal, classical organization theory, operated in an organizational structure with a narrow span of supervision, centralized authority, and a pattern of authority flowing *one* way: from the top of the hierarchy down. Management was entirely responsible for implementing a system where outputs are maximized by the fastest, most efficient, and least fatiguing methods of work. Supervisory work responsibilities were expanded and work was dovetailed between worker and supervisory operations to allow close control. Functional management was introduced as the most efficient use of supervisory expertise. Under functional management, a worker may answer to several different supervisors, depending on what aspect of the operation is involved. For example, machine set-up and material packing would be handled by two different supervisors. Having more than one boss proved ineffective, however, and the functional supervision arrangement was later abandoned. The practice of scientific management expanded quickly and widely in the years following the publication of Taylor's book in 1911. A Taylor Society was established in 1915 to promote the principles of scientific management, and it prospered for many years. *See also* ORGANIZATION THEORY, CLASSICAL, 176; TAYLOR, FREDERICK WINSLOW, 24; TAYLORISM, 25.

Significance Scientific management was one of the first efforts to analyze work methods systematically and to estimate management influence on productivity. Although it was abandoned as a comprehensive theory, scientific management provided measurable impact on the subsequent development of management and organizational theories. Scientific management has been criticized as incomplete because it failed to consider the human element in production, the importance of informal organizations, and the effect of organizational environment. With its obsession with efficiency and maximum productivity, it also failed to consider organizational goals and occasions when maximum productivity may not be desirable. Nevertheless, some organizations still operate on scientific management principles, and even those that do not often contain remnants of the Taylor system. For example, time and motion studies are still used by industrial engineers and by job analysts for training and appraisal purposes. Industrial psychologists sometimes use scientific management standards as part of employee selection criteria. Finally, scientific management had a direct impact on the establishment of public administration as an academic field. Early public administration theorists welcomed the idea of private sector scientific management because that meant *public* management might also be elevated to the status of a legitimate science. Among the public administrationists who were greatly influenced by Taylor's work, and who used it as a springboard to launch new theories of their own, were Leonard White, Luther Gulick, and Lyndall Urwick. The "principles of administration" movement which became popular in the 1930s was directly related to the scientific management movement of the previous generation.

Social Equity (23)

A normative standard that makes equity in the delivery of public services the criterion for judging the value of administrative policy. Social equity is the principle on which the new public administration movement of the early 1970s was based. Classical public administration asked two questions of public policy: (1) Can better services be offered with available resources? (2) Can the level of services be maintained while spending less? In addition to these questions of efficiency and economy, the new public administration asked a third question: Do the services enhance social equity? The standard of social equity requires the fair and equitable distribution of services to eliminate any injury done to people by previous programs or lack of programs. It attempts to make certain that if inequities exist, they benefit previously disadvantaged groups. The normative emphasis of social equity developed out of discontent with the status quo of traditional administration and the perceived neglect of the social responsibilities of government. From the social equity perspective, administrators should understand the ethical framework on which government is based, and they should be advocates of disadvantaged people. Proponents of the new public administration see the pursuit of social equity as a healthy desire for change which will ultimately enhance the traditional public administration values of economy, efficiency, and administrative effectiveness. They predict initial tensions as administrative changes bring about resource redistribution, and they foresee the probability of administrators having to trade support from traditional public administration sources for support from disadvantaged groups, but they believe social equity is worth the risks. Part of the approach includes the belief that bureaucracy cannot be neutral. It is, and must be, involved with clients as human beings, and it must bend the rules for them or take risks for them if necessary. Proponents of social equity say the role the average public servant can play in promoting it is to impress on higher level policy makers, sometimes forcefully, the basic values of democracy and actively to advance the cause of social justice. An attendant goal of the new public administration is increased citizen participation as a way of gaining more direct involvement of disadvantaged and minority groups in the decision-making processes of government. *See also* CITIZEN PARTICIPATION, 131; NEW PUBLIC ADMINISTRATION, 18; PARTICIPATORY DEMOCRACY, 64.

Significance Social equity has been a major moving force in the last decade of American public administration. Although all the principles of the new public administration have not taken hold, the idea of a more humane bureaucracy has gained influential proponents. Affirmative action and equal employment opportunity programs have aided the cause of social equity, as have the activities of feminist groups. Critics of the social equity standard say the pursuit of economic well-being as an end in itself creates as many problems as it solves. They see new public administrationists as being elitists themselves to the extent that they oppose legislative intent and public opinion, even if the policies they advocate are more humane. Finally, there is the problem of how social equity can be defined and measured, and whether American taxpayers can tolerate a de-emphasis on efficiency and economy in a time of retrenchment management.

Taylor, Frederick Winslow (1856–1915) (24)
An American mechanical engineer considered the father of scientific management, i.e., the science of discovering the most efficient method of performing any job. Taylor developed his philosophy of work while employed at the Midvale Steel Works in Philadelphia during the 1880s. The key to Taylor's system was his ability to discover scientifically the shortest possible time for performing any specific job. His tool was the stopwatch. Taylor would stand behind every worker in the machine shop at Midvale and record the time it took him or her to perform the most elementary motions: finding a steel rod, settling

it on a lathe, picking up a tool. By studying a large number of workers, Taylor could identify the shortest possible time for performing each individual motion. By combining the best times, discarding useless motions, and adding in gaps for unavoidable delays and rest breaks, Taylor established a pattern of work that was invariably shorter than the workers' informal pace. By the time Taylor left Midvale in 1890, his time and motion studies had led to a complete reorganization of the firm: the centralization of planning and engineering, the centralization of purchasing and inventory control, the centralization of maintenance, the introduction of centralized cost accounting, and the development of assembly-line techniques on the job. Taylor attempted to introduce scientific management into public administration beginning in 1906, first in government arsenals and then in navy yards. When the workers at the Watertown, Massachusetts Arsenal heard that Taylor was coming, they went out on strike, the army placed a guard at the arsenal gates with fixed bayonets, and a special congressional investigation committee was formed. Louis Brandeis, Walter Lippmann, Georges Clemenceau, and V. I. Lenin all took Taylor's side. But Congress banned stopwatches in government-run factories, a law that remained on the books for forty years. Taylor had other failures, notably as general manager of a pulp-and-paper mill and as a consultant to the Bethlehem Steel Company, all for the same reason. Workers resisted Taylor's system because it dehumanized them. They resisted despite the promise that their greater productivity would earn them more money. Despite his failures, however, Taylor's principles of specialization were popularized by scholars such as Henri Fayol and Luther Gulick and became a part of their classical synthesis. Taylor's main contributions were (1) the *division of work*, or the principle that work ought to be divided up so as to take maximum advantage of the specialized skills of the employees; and (2) the *principle of homogeneity*, also called unity of direction, which asserts that similar activities ought to be grouped together in the same unit under a single supervisor and a single plan. See also FAYOL, HENRI, 14; GULICK, LUTHER, 17; SCIENTIFIC MANAGEMENT, 22; TAYLORISM, 25.

Significance Frederick Winslow Taylor created a world of work which was scientific rather than spontaneous. He ventured into a philosophy of human control that contains the potential for tyranny. Taylor's view of the effective administrative state was one in which experts determined the one best way of working and standardized that method. The experts then controlled the worker through incentives and threats so as to maintain the central work standard. This made the study of work a science. The selection and training of workers was also a science. Scientific management took away from workers their ability to control the flow of work by elevating it to a science of administration run out of a central office. The worker became just another machine in the technology of progress. The extent to which Taylor's principles were applicable over time was called into question by the Hawthorne Studies commissioned by the National Academy of Science in 1924. But, for a generation, scientific management was as American as baseball.

The efficiency standard which Taylor helped establish has been roundly criticized by humanists who abhor the man-as-machine concept. It is easy, however, to forget two things about Taylor's principles. One is that the standard industrial system of Taylor's day paid workers by piecework, which meant workers who were more productive earned more for themselves as well as their employers. The other is the possibility that efficiency can serve humanism as well as any other value. Taylorism, however, continued to antagonize many workers and contributed to the growth of the labor union movement. The man-as-machine model is still very much a part of federal government personnel administration practice. One example is the use of psychotechnology by the National Aeronautics and Space Administration (NASA) in its training of astronauts. The objective of NASA's use of psychotechnology is to integrate the astronaut with the technological environment of his or her space capsule or station, both mentally and physically, in order to reduce response time. Psychotechnology is essentially Taylor's work updated, but with the added element of psychoemotional as well as physical conditioning being practiced.

Taylorism (25)

The set of beliefs ascribed to Frederick Winslow Taylor (1856–1915), a mechanical engineer who pioneered the scientific management movement in large U.S. organizations from 1885 to 1911. Taylorism is focused on the mechanistic characteristics of administration. With stopwatch and measuring tape, Taylor conducted precision studies of the physical movements of individual workers, demonstrating empirically that organizations could and should convert the management process to a system of scientific laws in which efficiency, standardization, and savings were the ultimate organizational goals. There was "one best way" to manage workers and "one best way" for workers to carry out their tasks. Otherwise, they would waste both time and motion. Taylorism thus stressed high productivity and disciplined labor. *See also* POLITICS-ADMINISTRATION DICHOTOMY, 70; SCIENTIFIC MANAGEMENT, 22.

Significance The development of Taylorism paralleled the rise of large public and private organizations in the United States and Europe. It transferred to human beings the established industrial criterion of proper mechanical functioning. Thus each worker was trained to perform those tasks for which he or she was best suited. This mechanistic view of human labor generated a deep reaction among humanists. Yet, its doctrine of efficiency and amorality simultaneously supported other current ideas about the splitting away of public administration from its political setting, of separating policy implementation from policy making. By looking at the activities of public administration as the "machinery of government," which should be "oiled properly" and "kept running smoothly," Taylorism downplayed notions of the public interest and the complex psychological drives of human beings. It encouraged a generation of scholars to consider bureaucratic organization and management efficiency as two of the main concerns of the field of public administration.

Urwick, Lyndall F. (1891–1983) (26)

A British military officer (seven years), bureaucrat (seven years, five as Director of the International Management Institute at Geneva), business executive (eight years in glove manufacturing and confectionary), and consulting industrial engineer (twenty-nine years as founder and chairman of Urwick, Orr and Partners, Ltd.). Urwick, whose distinctions include membership in the Order of the British Empire (O.B.E.), lived in retirement in Australia. He is best known in public administration circles as Luther Gulick's collaborator in editing the *Papers on the Science of Administration* in 1937. Urwick himself contributed two highly influential essays to the collection: "Organization as a Technical Problem" and "The Function of Administration." In those articles, Urwick elaborated what Dwight Waldo believed to be "probably the most pervasive and important model in American administrative study in the twentieth century—the *machine model*." Achieving efficiency in administration was conceived by Urwick as being analogous to achieving efficiency in machine performance. There must be good design-organization charts and blueprints; parts must be adjusted properly to one another; friction must be reduced; and power loss must be prevented. Organizing, according to Urwick, is determining plans and assigning people to implement them. Individuals should be assigned on an objective basis, without regard to incumbency. Efforts must be made to admit people into the organizational structure and to force them to fit the organization, not to alter the organization to fit them. Urwick criticized the slow, cumbersome character of boards and commissions, noting that well-run government agencies were administered by a single individual. He believed that because the human span of attention is limited, no supervisor could adequately direct the activities of more than five or six subordinates. Urwick's colleague, Luther Gulick, believed that the optimal number of subordinates was difficult to fix with precision, but was limited in any case by factors relating to knowledge and energy. Urwick's writing is held together by the central theme of efficiency, which he felt is to be achieved by task specialization and by the structuring of formal relations among functional, line, and staff managers. Line management, including the general manager, department manager, and foreman, is responsible for production. Functional managers deal not with the product or service but with tasks such as budgeting and planning. Staff managers have neither direct-line nor functional responsibilities but are in charge of overall planning, coordination, and policy making. Each component of the organization is to be organized and staffed in the most *efficient* manner, that is, in a fashion that will maximize a unit of output for a unit of input. *See also* FAYOL, HENRI, 14; GULICK, LUTHER, 17; SCIENTIFIC MANAGEMENT, 22; TAYLOR, FREDERICK WINSLOW, 24.

Significance Lyndall Urwick was a popularizer in the best sense. His works were more a synthesis than an original contribution. His article, "The Function of Administration," for example, is largely an exposition of the work of Henri Fayol. He also drew heavily from the work of Frederick W. Taylor and from Mooney and Reiley's *Onward Industry*, which had been published in 1931. Urwick's contribution should not be minimized, however, because scientific management writing was, up to 1937, highly fragmented and begging for integration and interpretation. Urwick helped familiarize thousands of public and private managers with such principles as the importance of fitting people to the organization structure; the need for unity of command and the use of specialized and general staffs; departmentalization by purpose, process, persons, and place; the delegating and balancing of authority and responsibility; and the definition of span of control. Urwick's writing was strongly influenced by his military experience. While the military is especially amenable to his kind of organization and routinization, there are obstacles to putting Urwick's ideas into practice in public bureaucracies and complex private organizations. The formalist-rationalist approach of not only Urwick, but Max Weber, Frederick W. Taylor, Henri Fayol, and Luther Gulick as well, has the following deficiencies as summarized by James March and Herbert Simon: (1) The motivational assumptions underlying the formal theories are incomplete. (2) There is insufficient appreciation of the role of intraorganizational conflict of interest in defining the limits of organizational behavior. (3) The constraints placed on the human being by his limitations as a complex information-process system are given little consideration. (4) Little attention is given to the role of cognition in task identification and decision. (5) The phenomenon of program elaboration is not considered. To these limitations may be added the observation that formalists such as Urwick omitted any consideration of the presence, role, status, or performance of women. In the words of Rosabeth Moss Kantor, "A 'masculine ethic' can be identified as part of the early image of managers. This masculine ethic elevates the traits assumed to belong to some men as those desirable for effective management: a tough-minded approach to problems; analytic abilities to abstract and plan; a capacity to set aside personal, emotional considerations in the interest of task accomplishment; and a cognitive superiority in problem solving and decision making. These characteristics supposedly belong to men, but then practically all managers were men from the beginning. However, when women tried to enter management jobs, the 'masculine ethic' was invoked as an exclusionary principle." Despite the incompleteness of Urwick's ideas, they have persisted through the years as successive government reorganization committees and commissions have incorporated them in the structures of federal, state, and local governments. One of the reasons for this, and perhaps the most important contribution of Urwick, is that he established a "language of management." Lyndall Urwick and his peers did not invent the relationships now referred to as line and staff, but they did provide the concepts which allowed managers and theorists to discuss them for years to come.

Waldo, C. Dwight (1913–) (27)

American professor of public administration who helped discredit Luther Gulick's "gospel of efficiency" with publication of the classic *The Administrative State* in 1948, and who has done much to shape the development of public administration in the United States. Waldo has attempted to explain the "identity crisis" created by the proliferation of approaches in public administration; and in 1968, as Albert Schweitzer Professor in Humanities at Syracuse University, Waldo organized a conference of young public administrationists for the purpose of considering possible future directions in the field. The conference resulted in the "new public administration" movement. From 1966 through 1977, Waldo was editor-in-chief of the leading journal in the field, the *Public Administration Review*. In *The Administrative State* Waldo attacked the criterion which had guided American administrative science through World War II. This was the idea of efficiency. Waldo said the 1930s' exponents of administrative principles and laws, although they frequently used the name of science, did not come close to using established scientific methods. Their principles were derived from experience, common-sense conclusions, and collections of information. Their assumption was that, if enough data were collected, a science of administration would somehow emerge. F. S. C. Northrop's distinction between "observed fact" and "described fact" was not understood. The former is a fact apprehended without relation to theory. The latter is an observed fact interpreted in relation to a theoretical framework. Waldo believed that in the apocryphal example of Newton and the apple, it was not because Newton saw many apples—or anything else—fall that he was able to formulate in his mechanics the laws of gravitation. As Newton himself stated, the basic concepts of his system, such as mass and momentum, are not common-sense notions but theoretical concepts. The facts Waldo objected to were the empirical data from time and motion studies, which regarded people and organization parts as more or less interchangeable pieces of modern machinery. Waldo asked simply if the "laws of mechanical science" have an existence apart from the "idiosyncracies" of the metals, fuels, and lubricants which constitute an engine. Although the human relations school was already in being when Waldo came on to the scene, the Hawthorne studies and the writings of Barnard and Follett had had little visible impact. Waldo did a great deal to establish intellectual respectability for organizational humanism. *See also* GULICK, LUTHER, 17; NEW PUBLIC ADMINISTRATION, 18; ORGANIZATION THEORY: HUMANISM, 177; URWICK, LYNDALL F., 26.

Significance   Dwight Waldo's effective work in helping to destroy a science of administration based on a single theory of management sent scholars off in many different directions. Some went to sociology and psychology in an attempt to create a science of organization based on an understanding of human behavior. Others went to political science to gauge the effect that politics had on the administrative process. Both groups sought a "realistic" public administration. The result was a fragmentation of public administration which Waldo attempted to address as responsibly as he had the subtle elitism of scientific management. The realism requirement was largely the result of the experiences that many academics had in government service during World War II. In Fritz Morstein-Marx's edited volume *Elements of Public Administration* (1946), each of the fifteen contributing authors, all but two of whom were academics, had just finished with wartime government service. They painted a picture of a highly political public administration, with the public administrator as political operative. The politics-administration dichotomy did not apply to the real world in which they had lived. Waldo recognized that by the 1970s public administration was in a full-blown "time of turbulence" that was brought on by controversies over such doctrines as the dichotomy, as well as over problems of approach and method. Waldo advised public administration to celebrate its diversity. It should think of itself as roughly analogous to the medical profession, he said. Medicine is guided by no single theory; instead, it draws on a number of different medical sciences to treat the multiple ills of the human patient. Schools of medicine are in business to train practitioners to use different academic disciplines. Public administration should see itself in an equivalent posture: assembling knowledge from different disciplines to prepare practitioners for careers in public service. Waldo told his colleagues to quit worrying about their place among the disciplines and "seek what we need wherever it may be located." It is a measure of Dwight Waldo's stature in the field that many administrationists took his advice.

White, Leonard D. (1891–1958) (28)

American administrative theorist, historian, author, reformer, and sometime Chairman of the United States Civil Service Commission. Leonard D. White was a political scientist and historian at the University of Chicago who published the first text in public administration, *Introduction to the Study of Public Administration,* in 1926. Some believe this work spawned public administration as a separate field of study. Like Henri Fayol, White believed that public administration had universal applicability and principles that pertained to a variety of organizations. The assumption underlying White's pioneering text was that public administration was not based in the law or the court system but in management. Unlike other management texts, however, White's work emphasized personnel administration. White's corollary belief that political science was also foundational for public administration was illustrated in his famous administrative histories, *The Federalists* (1948), *The Jeffersonians* (1951), *The Jacksonians* (1954), and *The Republican Era* (1958). White was deeply affected by the reform movement in public administration and was himself an ardent advocate of it. He devoted himself to the personnel issues which had emerged as part of the reform agenda: recruitment, dismissal, standardization of salaries, personnel evaluation, promotion, morale, and retirement. In the late 1920s White conducted the first study of public opinion about public employees. He sent out questionnaires to people of different occupations and social status, discovering a widespread negative opinion of public administrators. Federal employment had greater prestige than state and municipal employment, but two-thirds of the respondents regarded private employment more favorably than public employment. Private sector employees were judged to be more trustworthy, polite, and competent than their counterparts in public service, findings which were verified by Brookings Institution studies in 1964. White influenced the creation of the Junior Civil Service Examination in 1934 as a vehicle for establishing a formal system of recruitment for public administration generalists who could develop expertise in specific areas of public service. The examination paved the way for later improvements in the overall system of securing adequate manpower for the federal service. *See also* FAYOL, HENRI, 14; PUBLIC PERSONNEL ADMINISTRATION, 238; WILSON, WOODROW, 29.

Significance Leonard D. White was one of the architects of American public administration. His *Introduction to the Study of Public Administration* competes only with Woodrow Wilson's 1887 essay, "The Study of Administration," and the writings of Frank J. Goodnow as the work most responsible for the beginning of public administration as a distinctive field of study. White made personnel administration central to the field, although later texts gave budgetary matters equal emphasis. As White published his histories, public administrationists came to respect and value historical study in a new way. Previously, historians had focused only on specific institutions rather than on public administration *per se*. White's interest in reform also led him to do pioneering work in the areas of public opinion, prestige, and morale. White was greatly influenced by Max Weber's use of the term *prestige* and was one of the first theorists to apply the word to public administration. He believed the morale of public administrators is directly related to their prestige. Favorable public opinion enables administrators to have increased public support and compliance, which in turn increases job efficacy and morale.

Wilson, Woodrow (1856–1924) (29)

American educator, historian, public administrator, and twenty-eighth president of the United States. Wilson is widely credited with being the first American scholar to advocate the systematic study of the operations of government. As a political science professor, he wrote a famous essay in 1887 entitled "The Study of Administration," which marked the beginning of American academic interest in professional public administration. Wilson's essay reflected the values of the progressive movement which four years earlier had gained passage of the Civil Service Act and which was pressing to reform the

Fundamentals of Public Administration

management of American government at every level. Typical of these powerful citizen associations were the Civil Service Reform League, of which Wilson later became president, and the New York Bureau of Municipal Research, which was founded in 1906. The reformers were motivated by a sense of outrage against the corruption of the spoils system and by the belief that they could never bring "efficiency and economy" to government so long as the vagaries of party politics interfered with governmental management. Public administration could be made scientific only if administrators were free to concentrate on the execution of policy after the legislature and chief executive defined it. Both politics and policy making were therefore to be taken out of public administration. According to James W. Fesler in *Public Administration, Theory and Practice* (1980) Wilson stepped boldly into this movement with advice for both reformers and scholars. He asked them to forget their "paper pictures" of good government and study how administration really worked. The French and the Prussians, Wilson pointed out, had developed the most advanced administrative systems in the world, and Americans should study them to learn how to manage public programs. Wilson took exception to his colleagues in jurisprudence and politics who were concerned with the great constitutional issues, such as the separation of powers. Such debate was largely irrelevant to the reforms needed in public administration. Wilson established four guiding assumptions to chart a course for the immediate future in the study and practice of public administration: (1) the science of administration should be based on a single organizational prototype universally applicable to all political regimes; (2) any good science of administration must divorce itself from the field of politics; (3) the guiding value of the science of administration is efficiency; and (4) efficient public administration requires a single dominant center of governmental power. Despite public administration's later discomfort with Wilson's paradigm, and Herbert Simon's blistering attack on it, the paradigm remained for many years in the mainstream of academic public administration. Simon tried to demonstrate that the basic principles of administration, being imprecise, would produce *inefficiency*. But he was unsuccessful in his attack because he failed to erect any alternative model in the place of Wilsonian orthodoxy. Simon suggested that scholars study administrative decisions, but the idea never caught on. See also CIVIL SERVICE REFORM LEAGUE, 200; POLITICS-ADMINISTRATION DICHOTOMY, 70; SIMON, HERBERT A., 114.

Significance Woodrow Wilson's influence on the development of American public administration—its theory, study, and practice—can hardly be overestimated. Yet his analysis of the universal elements of public administration—those independent of time, place, and political system—contained a central and profound contradiction. Basic to much of Wilson's thought was his perception of administration as a neutral instrument, distinct from policy, politics, and particular regimes. Such a perception seemed essential to define a distinct field of study, separate from the study of policy and politics. It was a critical assumption for Wilson's thesis that nowhere in the whole field of politics can the historical, comparative method be used more safely than in administration. Wilson firmly believed that Americans, therefore, could learn administration from the Prussian and French (Napoleonic) autocracies without being infected by their political principles. Wilson advanced two themes contradictory to this line of argument. One was that administration must be fitted to a particular nation's political ideas and constitutional system. The science of administration, Wilson opined, has been adapted to the needs of a compact state, and to centralized forms of government. We must Americanize it. The second contradictory theme blurs the distinction Wilson made elsewhere between policy and administration. Wilson therefore pleaded for the vesting of large powers and unhampered discretion as the indispensable conditions of administrative responsibility. This is hardly the limited role for public administrators Wilson insisted on earlier. These contradictions in the thought of Wilson do not detract substantially from his achievement, however. They illustrate the varied positions that together form the whole truth about public administration. Modern scholars still debate the extent to which Woodrow Wilson was ambivalent about what public administration really is, but none dispute the impact of his one unambiguous thesis—that public administration is worth studying.

2. Public Policy

Circular A-95 (30)

An instruction issued by the Bureau of the Budget, now the Office of Management and Budget (OMB), in July 1969, ordering better communication and consultation among governments at state and local levels as a condition of their applications for federal grant monies. Circular A-95 was designed specifically to implement the evaluation-and-review provisions of the Model Cities Act of 1966 and the Intergovernmental Cooperation Act of 1968. The Model Cities Act stipulated that grant applications from local governments in metropolitan areas must first have been screened by an areawide comprehensive planning agency. The Intergovernmental Cooperation Act made it national policy to seek maximum congruence between national program objectives and the objectives of state, regional, and local planning. This mandated coordination was necessary in the face of widespread state and local unwillingness to consider effects of their own programs and planning on those of neighboring jurisdictions. Circular A-95 went further than the two acts in the following respects: (1) it required all local aid applicants to forward their proposals to an areawide screening agency; (2) the screening agency was required to inform other governments in the area of a proposal's contents and to solicit reactions from those governments; (3) the local government was required to consider the responses received and to modify its own proposal if it chose to do so; (4) the screening agency was required to evaluate the proposal for consistency with existing state, regional, and local planning; and (5) the screening agency was then required to forward the package of documents to the federal agency from which the grant would come. The aim of Circular A-95 was to weed out requests that could be met some other, better way; those which, if approved, would conflict with another approved grant proposal; and those which duplicated other allocations for similar or even identical purposes. *See also* FEDERALISM, 47; FEDERALISM, FISCAL, 49; INTERGOVERNMENTAL RELATIONS, 153.

Significance Circular A-95 provided a more systematic process than any which had operated previously to require an aid applicant to coordinate a grant proposal with other governmental jurisdictions that might be affected in some way by the applicant's receiving the grant. In his 1978 book *Public Administration in America* (now in its third edition), public administrationist George J. Gordon pointed out two typical instances of the effect of Circular A-95. (1) After one city had applied for a sewage treatment construction grant, officials discovered that a neighboring jurisdiction was about to apply for the identical grant. Instead of both cities applying, the decision was made to collaborate on the project and apply for a single, somewhat larger grant—a better use of public funds. (2) Local officials discovered after they had applied for a recreation development grant for a nearby lake that a city on the other side of the lake had already received a grant for expanding its water supply—drawing its water from the same lake! The benefits of prior "review and comment" would have saved the former city a good deal of grant proposal work. Circular A-95 applied at its inception to some fifty governmental programs, most of them having to do with planning and direct physical development managed by federal agencies. In April 1971, a major expansion of program coverage was instituted, bringing the total to almost one hundred, including many social and human resource programs, such as facilities for the mentally retarded, law enforcement action grants, neighborhood development, education facilities, and manpower planning. In November 1973, the Office of Management and Budget (OMB) added thirty-five more programs, including health, adult and vocational education, job opportunity, and rural development programs. Gradual additions in subsequent years mean that currently Circular A-95 requirements apply to some two hundred programs. In the words of political scientist James Sundquist, OMB as a central coordinator "expedited, facilitated, and even coerced" better lateral coordination among equals. While there have been undeniable positive effects of Circular A-95, and while the review process is now very well established within the grant system, some problems remain in this aspect of fiscal federalism. First, it is not clear that the "vertical functional autocrats" who are still largely responsible for administering grants-in-aid have cooperated more willingly than before at any level of government in the effort to secure a more rational, consistent grant system. Second, the state and local clearinghouses which refer proposals for review and comment vary considerably in how carefully they evaluate grant proposals, resulting in very uneven patterns of coordination. Third, local governments appear to be much more concerned with getting their aid applications approved than with more abstract matters of coordination, except when improving coordination will also work to their programmatic or fiscal advantage. Fourth, it is difficult to evaluate grant proposals for consistency with existing state or local plans when, as is sometimes the case, no such plans exist. Fifth, there is concern that the states and localities have been co-opted into the decision-making process of the national government via Circular A-95, thus damaging the essential nature of the federal system. Although Circular A-95 was a mixed blessing, it helped to reduce wasteful and duplicative spending and to foster better overall cooperation among thousands of local governments.

Clientele (31)

The recipients of an agency's services, frequently organized into *groups* for the purpose of influencing an agency's policies. A clientele may be potential or actual. For example, the formation of the American Legion in 1919 represented a *potential* veterans clientele group. The Legion's successful lobbying efforts produced an *actual* agency clientele in 1921 with the formation of the Veteran's Bureau, which continues today as the Veteran's Administration (VA). The relationship of a clientele group to its agency varies with the agency's purpose. In the case of welfare recipients and the food stamp program, for example, the relationship is one of dependency. The clientele group could not survive without the benefits the program provides. In the case of the Food and Drug Administration (FDA), however, clientele relationships tend to be adversarial. The FDA exists in part to regulate the pharmaceutical industry. In its effort to protect one clientele group, drug consumers, the FDA sometimes comes into conflict with another clientele group, drug manufacturers, who not infrequently believe the FDA is being either overcautious or overzealous. The influence of clientele groups in defining bureaucratic environments was dramatically illustrated in the Equal Opportunity Act of 1964, which urged the "maximum feasible participation" of an agency's clientele in agency decision making. Beginning in the late 1960s, model cities and community action programs were based largely on clientele participation. In the case of a local Community Action Agency (CAA), the law requires that one-third of the board of directors be representatives of the poor. Clientele groups are strong believers in the lobby, especially clientele groups that were either instrumental in an agency's formation or those that exist in a regulatory relationship with it. The American Legion and the Veterans of Foreign Wars continue to lobby both the Veteran's Administration and Congress to increase the number of benefits provided to veterans. The transportation industry, regulated by the Interstate Commerce Commission (ICC), lobbies its regulators for good rates and as much deregulation as the system will allow. *See also* CITIZEN PARTICIPATION, 131; CLIENTELE AGENCY, 32; COOPTATION, 34.

Significance   A clientele group can effectively shape the direction of a service agency's policies if it is well financed, has general respectability or status, and if the members have knowledge of governmental processes. A strong combination of these factors can transform a clientele group into a subgovernment. Without these factors, clientele groups such as those dependent on public assistance programs can be ignored. If people do not have the money to feed themselves, they cannot hire an advocate. Perhaps the outstanding example of a powerful clientele group is the tobacco industry and its success against the Federal Trade Commission (FTC). In the early 1960s, researchers determined there was a direct link between smoking and lung cancer. In response, the FTC issued a directive that all cigarette advertising and packages must include the statement: "Cigarette smoking is dangerous to health and may cause death from cancer and other diseases." The tobacco industry, realizing such a warning would reduce sales, lobbied Congress, which subsequently overruled the FTC. Today the warning reads: "Quitting smoking now greatly reduces serious risks to your health." Clientele groups can also enhance the position of an agency in its battles with legislative bodies and elected executives. The promise of electoral involvement, for or against an elected official, is sometimes enough to protect an agency's budget, preserve a threatened program, or decide a controversial issue. Clientele groups are an important part of a public agency's political environment.

Clientele Agency (32)

An administrative unit that carries on operations that directly affect an economic or social group. A clientele agency may be concerned primarily with regulating the group's activities, as in the case of the Antitrust Division of the Department of Justice in its role in breaking up trusts and monopolies. Or it may be concerned primarily with serving or promoting the group's interests, as with the Bureau of Indian Affairs in the Department of the Interior. Many agencies, such as the Department of Agriculture, engage in both regulatory and

Public Policy

promotional functions in their relationships with their clientele group. *See also* INTEREST-GROUP LIBERALISM, 56.

Significance Although all governmental agencies tend to have some of their operations directed toward a group or several groups, the main functions of a clientele agency relate to a single group. Many clientele agencies were established as a result of the pressures generated by an economic or social group for support or protection of its interests. Client groups typically influence the agency's operations on a continuing basis. If its activities are mainly promotional, strong support links are sought with Congress and congressional committees, with state governmental decision makers, and with other administrative units and their decision makers. If the agency's main role is considered to be harmful to the interests of the client group, the latter will seek to have it abolished or weakened, or will try to moderate its operations through changes in personnel or in its authorized operational powers.

Computer (33)

A multifunctional electronic device with the ability to process large amounts of data at high speed, to recover stored information instantaneously, to integrate a number of data sources, and to remember and apply decision rules. The computer allows government agencies to process and store much of the enormous volume of information generated by modern society. Computer principles were first described in detail by production engineer Charles Babbage in 1840. He called the computer a "difference engine." It was seventy more years, however, before a difference engine was successfully constructed. Computer principles are summarized in the computer programmer's basic philosophy: "Even the most complicated subjects and operations can be reduced to a series of yes-no questions." Computer communication involves the refining of procedures for exact, detailed, and penetrating yes-no questions and answers. The computer is neutral regarding the focus of authority in organizations. However, scholars are divided in their opinions about the computer's effect on decision making. Some are sure that computers aid centralizing tendencies in government; others are equally convinced computers aid decentralization. Most are agreed that one of the computer's major roles is in simulation, a technique used to experiment with solutions to problems. In the simulation process, the computer's ability to make complicated mathematical calculations with great speed allows the testing of a number of variables. *See also* ELECTRONIC DATA PROCESSING, 40; SYSTEMS ANALYSIS, 83.

Significance   The computer allows a new focus on detail. It allows the decision maker to ask questions that he or she may have formerly overlooked, and it helps the decision maker answer questions which previously may never have been asked. The use of computers allows people at all levels of the organization to participate in the decision-making process. The increasing use of minicomputers allows sophisticated decisions to be made at lower levels of the organization. Minicomputers also serve as a high-quality data source in support of the central organizational system. Computer usage is changing the nature of virtually every job in modern organizations. The computer's greatest effect is in the middle management area, where increasingly the traditional role of middle manager is being overtaken by computer capabilities. The result may be a drastic change from the pyramid organization structure to one with an hourglass shape, as middle managers are squeezed into the hourglass's "bottom half role" as tenders of the machines. In public administration a properly utilized computer can make more time available for the administrator to deal with people problems and with public policy issues. The tendency in public agencies, however, is to look on the computer as an electronic file cabinet. Managers at times overlook the computer's capability of applying logic to its stored materials. More often the computer has been underutilized in public agencies. The primary philosophical problem with computer technology is that it makes the world more impersonal and less private. The computer tends to suffocate the rights of the individual. There is also a growing fear of the invasion of privacy which results from the ready access to computer printouts by many individuals and organizations. The computer is basically a neutral device, however, which can be put in the service of the public by responsible managers. Computers can only be as accurate and as useful as the data which are programmed into them. In the language of computer operators, this is described as "'Gigo'—Garbage in, garbage out!"

Cooptation (34)
Strategies employed by administrative agencies to avoid hostile opposition to their own and to their clients' programs by broadening participation to encompass elements that otherwise would threaten the agency and its program. Cooptation is defined by political scientist Philip Selznick as "the process of absorbing new elements into the leadership or policy-determining structure of an organization as a means of averting threats to its stability or existence." Political scientist William L. Morrow contrasts cooptation to pacification as an informal purpose of participatory democracy. Whereas pacification seeks to

mitigate opposition to programs by tolerating the formal involvement of citizens, cooptation involves the actual conversion of would-be opponents to the cause of the establishment. Instead of passively accepting a participation revolution, as is the case with pacification strategy, the strategy of cooptation deliberately seeks participation as a means to gain public acquiescence to agency programs. Selznick elaborated the cooptation concept in his 1949 book, *TVA and the Grass Roots*, in which he divided cooptation into formal and informal relationships. *Formal cooptation* is the public absorption by an agency of new elements of potential opposition in openly avowed and formally ordered relationships. In the case of the Tennessee Valley Authority, this meant bringing into the decision-making family local farm bureau organizations, land grant colleges, fertilizer associations, and rural electrification cooperatives. *Informal cooptation* is a response to the pressure of specific centers of power within the community. This cooptation response is not to the people as a whole or to an institutional environment which may have been absorbed by formal cooptation, but to specific individuals or interest groups that are in a position to enforce demands. The latter, as Selznick says, are interested in the substance of power and not necessarily in its forms. The program or agency agrees to share power under informal cooptation but does not publicly acknowledge it, because the program or agency does not want the public to feel it has given up sovereign power. *See also* CITIZEN PARTICIPATION, 131; INTEREST-GROUP LIBERALISM, 56; ORGANIZATION THEORY: PLURALISM, 179.

Significance   Cooptation reduces potential policy challenges and is a relatively inexpensive organizational strategy. It reduces tension between an agency and its social environment. Cooptation's primary disadvantage is that it narrows the available alternatives an agency has in administering its programs. In the case of the TVA, the record clearly shows that citizen participation in the form of cooptation resulted in a negation of attempts at comprehensive planning. Cooptation also frequently degenerated into simple involvement as opposed to meaningful participation. As far as the TVA was concerned, the lack of citizen participation signified the success of the cooptation strategy because, in Selznick's words, the opposition had "the illusion of a voice without the voice itself." Opposition was stifled without the TVA having to alter policy. More recent examples of cooptation can be found in the representation of the poor on local Community Action Agency boards. Representatives tend to be warned away from the economics and sociology of the poor by the middle-class status acquired by virtue of board membership. Cooptation fulfills several important administrative functions: (1) it establishes communication channels for information and coordination; (2) it permits the use of untapped administrative resources; (3) the broad policies of an agency may be adapted to local conditions because of the decentralization involved in cooptation; and (4) sharing of responsibility increases the public's identification with and commitment to an agency's programs. The success of the TVA's "grass roots ideology," which basically involved the administration of the TVA through existing institutions within the community, is on the public record. In this instance, cooptation worked as a mechanism of social control. It has worked in other contexts too, but with less clear results.

Cost-benefit Analysis (35)

A means of budgetary analysis that measures relative gains and losses resulting from alternative policy or programmatic options. Cost-benefit analysis is usually referred to in quantitative terms, with an assumption of implicit objectivity. On the *cost* side of cost-benefit analysis, an effort is made to allocate research and development costs, investment and operating costs, and opportunity costs through a discounting procedure, and to do so with projections over a five-year period. *Discounting* in this context refers to a calculation of the extent to which tax revenues invested in a public works project would approximate what the same resources could have earned in the private sector. An *opportunity cost* is charged against the public investment for foregoing private utilization. The discounting procedure is based on the following formula:

$$\frac{\text{Annual revenues or costs}}{(1 + r)^n} = \text{today's discounted value of a sum in } n \text{ years hence}$$

r = the discount rate
n = number of years until that cost or revenue is realized

For example, cost-benefit analysis can answer the question: Is the construction of a toll bridge, estimated at $20 million, a worthwhile venture if annual operating costs are $12 million for twenty-five years and annual revenues will be $14 million for the same period? The above formula with a discount rate of 10 percent would produce an unfavorable cost-benefit ratio. A discount of 5 percent, however, would make the proposal look attractive. *The percentages applied to discount rates is a subject of great controversy in cost-benefit analysis.* One school of thought suggests that the discount rate should be the net interest rate the government must pay to borrow money for its projects. Another argues for the private rate of interest the funds could earn in the private sector with comparable risk. On the *benefit* side of cost-benefit analysis, some kinds of government activities are natural subjects for the quantification necessary to build cost-benefit tables. It is a straightforward task, for example, to calculate indices of benefit on the dollar value per acre feet of water for irrigation versus power generation for the Grand Coulee Dam. In other cases, however, quantification is almost impossible, such as numerical values for benefits from federal aid for school construction versus federal welfare payments. Cost-benefit analysis is the only component of the planning, programming, budgeting systems (PPBS) concept to remain in general use as a managerial support activity. Cost-benefit tables enable administrators to see interrelationships more clearly, to ask tougher questions, and perhaps to make better decisions. *See also* PLANNING, PROGRAMMING, BUDGETING SYSTEMS (PPBS), 283; POLICY ANALYSIS, 68; SYSTEMS ANALYSIS, 83.

Significance   Cost-benefit analysis suffers from both the advantages and disadvantages of the highly rational, mathematical decision-making model brought to government in the early 1960s as part of the planning, programming, budgeting systems (PPBS) revolution. Given adequate information, cost-benefit analysis can be very useful in narrowing a range of choices to those most likely to yield desired gains for an affordable cost. Knowledge is power in administrative politics, and cost-benefit analysis greatly enhances a manager's ability to obtain, organize, and apply relevant information in the course of choosing desirable program options. The major disadvantage of cost-benefit analysis is the difficulty of quantifying benefits in a soft-goods agency. How can a park superintendent figure the benefit of band concerts? What arithmetic can be applied to the benefit of a life saved in a seat-belt program, or of a new procedure for treating schizophrenia? Even hard-goods departments must use nonquantifiable estimates, as when an analysis of rival weapons systems shows graded "benefits" for a "show of force" of long endurance aircraft versus Minuteman ICBMs versus the Polaris missile system. Close observers of the PPBS experiment such as political scientists Aaron Wildavsky, Frederick Mosher, and Allen Schick have described the benefit calculations of cost-benefit analysis as "gamesmanship at its worst."

Decision Tree (36)

A management technique for organizing and displaying facts pertinent to an anticipated decision. A decision tree may be visualized as a picture of a tree without leaves, turned on its side. The initial issue requiring a decision is the trunk, and alternative choices are the branches. As each choice is considered, further decisions may be required, and these decisions are shown as branches off the branches. Theoretically, there is no limit to the number of steps which may retreat from the trunk decision. *Mental* decision trees are common in human decision making. By putting the process on paper, in a picture, the decision maker is helped to focus on alternative choices. One management decision frequently leads sequentially to a series of other decisions, causing the decision maker to become overwhelmed if he or she cannot visualize the whole sequence. A decision tree provides a graphic representation of decision options for further analysis and permits the decision maker to look ahead to the implications of an initial decision by portraying all the potential outcomes in their order of occurrence. The process forces the decision maker to attempt to determine the outcome of each alternative course of action. Once the decision tree is drawn out, each option, or branch, is assigned a value, usually through decision tables and simulation techniques. Each of these values is assigned a probability index, a cost factor, a "certainty equivalent," which is the minimum decision result acceptable at each decision point, and an expected monetary value; these values can then be used for purposes of analysis. *See also* COST-BENEFIT ANALYSIS, 35; DECISION MAKING, RATIONAL-COMPREHENSIVE, 95; SIMULATION, 79.

Significance The decision tree technique of decision making theoretically reduces conflict because emotion and personal interest are minimized in the decision-making process, and teamwork is encouraged. The technique pins down the logical order of outcomes, making it easier to compare the advantages and disadvantages of each. It tends to improve decision making because alternatives are easily weighed and the decision maker can look ahead to implications of initial decisions. The primary advantage of the decision tree is that it provides an organized way of subdividing a complex problem and allowing the decision maker to judge the odds. The decision maker is forced to consider factors over which he or she has no control and to determine the risk he or she is willing to take. There are also difficulties with the technique. The process can become extremely complex and unwieldy unless the number of alternatives is limited. Some managers are hesitant to make assumptions and estimate probabilities, and not all decisions are appropriate for the decision tree model. It is uneconomical, for example, if the decision to be reached is a relatively simple one. There is also the danger that managers will try to use the decision tree as an answer machine rather than carefully checking their own assumptions. The numbers portrayed on the decision tree are not magic. They simply help the administrator zero in on the alternatives open in the decision situation, so that he or she can choose something, rather than puzzle over everything.

Delphi Technique (37)
A method of long-range planning that systematically pools the opinions of experts by using a process called "cybernetic arbitration." The Delphi technique was developed in the late 1950s by the Rand Corporation. Its name refers to a priestess at the center of ancient Greek worship who sent out runners to all parts of the country to bring back opinions about important topics from the wise men of the land. Delphi is a method of searching for and predicting new breakthroughs and opportunities. Business uses Delphi to predict new advances in technology. Public administration uses it to predict trends in the social climate and changes in the economy. The cybernetic arbitration process begins when an operator presents all the necessary data on the problem to be studied, along with a questionnaire, to a chosen group of experts. This can be done by mail or via computer. The results are gathered and then sent back to the participants with a mean prediction, interquartile range, and supporting comments. The participants are given the opportunity to study the responses and to change or adjust their own responses. The new set of responses is again collected, processed, and sent back to the participants for a third and fourth iteration. One of two results most often occurs in using Delphi: (1) *unimodal convergence* in which a single opinion emerges; or (2) *bimodal convergence* in which two opinions emerge. Each iteration typically results in more critical thinking and, in most cases, a convergence of opinion. Decision makers use the results for planning. *See also* PLANNING, 65.

Significance The Delphi technique arose from dissatisfaction with unstructured group decision making. It eliminates committee activity in order to reduce the influence of psychological factors, such as an unwillingness to abandon publicly expressed opinions. It equalizes the persuasive power of an articulate, powerful, or loud advocate. And it limits the bandwagon effect of majority opinion. Delphi can do these things because its participants are physically dispersed and are anonymous to each other. No one is embarrassed about changing an answer. A particular strength of the Delphi technique is that it can elicit objective answers about subjective questions. As one proponent says, Delphi is a way of developing rational decisions about unquantifiable problems. Delphi can be expensive, especially if done by computer, and time-consuming if done by mail. Records show that the time-lag between rounds averages two hours when all respondents are linked by a computer or at a single site, and two months when administered by mail. To be certain that a desire to conform with the majority did not exist, tests have been conducted in which respondents were asked to reflect on their answers and to rethink the decisions, without receiving a report on group response. Even in these cases, estimates in the second round are closer together than they were in the first. Delphi demonstrates that the opportunity to reflect on a previous answer, and information about what other people think, serve to bring estimates together. When consensus has not evolved, and two schools of thought emerge, it appears that opinions are based on different sets of data or different interpretations of the same data. In the latter case Delphi still serves its purpose: crystallizing the reasoning process while identifying and clarifying major alternatives.

Economic Man Theory (38)

The idea that human beings will always behave rationally, making choices which will maximize their efforts to obtain desired values. Economic man theory is based on the belief that individuals can know all the alternatives available in any situation and can understand the consequences each alternative will bring. Karl Marx (1818–1883) identified this value as material well-being. Since the material conditions of life are what really count, people can be changed or motivated only by the radical transformation of the economic system they work within. For Marx, economic man theory expanded logically into a general theory of economic determinism. Looking through his historical window, economic man theory also meant a necessary shift from capitalism, in which people work for someone else, to socialism, in which people work for themselves. Before Marx, Jeremy Bentham (1748–1832) and John Stuart Mill (1806–1873) had advanced the notion that the primary value of human beings, and the chief goal of their behavior, was to seek pleasure and avoid pain. This philosophy led to the assumption that economic man constantly seeks to maximize. Any action or object can be evaluated according to the ratio of its pleasure-giving utility to its pain-giving utility. The utilitarian position is that all human behavior is guided by a calculation of the course of action which will result in maximum pleasure and minimum pain. The assumption of rationality which economic man theory makes is based on the belief that individuals are able to order their preferences according to their personal hierarchy of values, but that they always seek to maximize some desired value. *See also* DECISION MAKING, RATIONAL-COMPREHENSIVE, 95; PLANNING, PROGRAMMING, BUDGETING SYSTEMS (PPBS), 283; SATISFICING, 113; SYSTEMS ANALYSIS, 83; TAYLORISM, 25.

Significance   Economic man theory was the basis of Frederick W. Taylor's assumption about productivity: pay workers more and they will produce more despite the drudgery of their work. It was also the basis of the classical view of decision making: decisions are directed toward a single, unchanging goal, and rational decisions can be made to reach that goal. Microeconomic theories are based on the economic man theory as well: there is always an attempt to maximize profits. Despite the wide application of economic man theory, however, it is obviously irrational to assume that individuals always behave in a rational manner. Economic man theory also erroneously assumes that once an imbalance has been resolved by an appropriate decision, the matter is permanently settled. Perhaps the sharpest critic of economic man theory was Nobel Prize–winning economist Herbert A. Simon, who wrote in 1947 that the theory is invalid because individuals are never completely informed and are seldom able to maximize anything. He argued that the assumptions of economic man theory are not applicable in real situations where decisions must be made by a manager and not by a theoretician. In practice, only a *few* alternatives and consequences can be known. Future values can only be anticipated as projections of the imagination. Simon called for more modest assumptions about "administrative man," that is, he is a "satisficer" rather than an "optimizer," and frequently settles merely for the best he can get. Despite Simon's trenchant criticism of economic man theory, it survives in many forms today, particularly in the *reward-seeking* philosophy of psychologist B. F. Skinner. Behavior is a function of its consequences, says Skinner, who developed an approach to behavior modification which relied on positive rewards to reinforce desired behavior. When Skinner endorsed managerial use of incentives to stimulate workers' productivity, he was not far from Taylorism and the scientific management school of a half century earlier. Economic man theory maintains its vitality because the materialism and pleasure-seeking tendencies of human beings are too obvious to deny.

Economic Planning (39)

Identification of economic goals and objectives and the means for achieving them. Some measure of economic planning is carried on, implicitly if not explicitly, by all private businesses, but the concept more appropriately refers to government planning concerning the economy of the nation, a state, or a local unit. In the United States, economic planning is aimed at leveling out the more drastic swings of the business cycle by trying to plan for steady economic growth. On the state and local levels, attention is given mainly to planning ways and means of attracting industry, expanding jobs, and increasing the tax base. The other extreme from this type of modest governmental planning is found in the Soviet Union and other Socialist countries where government planning is linked with direct government control and direction of investment, production, and consumption. *See also* COUNCIL OF ECONOMIC ADVISERS (CEA), 267; KEYNESIANISM, 57.

Significance Economic planning, as it relates to maintaining stability and growth in the national economy, dates back to the Great Depression of the 1930s. In 1934, the National Resources Planning Board began a program of long-range resources planning aimed at controlling the more violent swings of the business cycle. The Roosevelt administration was particularly concerned with avoiding a return to the kind of economic malaise that still plagued the nation's economy in the year the board began its activities. In the Employment Act of 1946, economic planning was turned over to the Council of Economic Advisers (CEA), which became the President's chief advisory body for economic planning. The passage of the Employment Act in effect constituted the nation's acceptance of Keynesianism, an approach that substitutes an orderly, predictable pattern of governmental control and direction over the economy for the free, unrestricted workings of the marketplace. Its main objectives involve recommending policies that will promote full employment and economic growth and avoid inflation and boom-and-bust business cycles, all in a short-run period. Although the Keynesian approach was used successfully to overcome a number of serious economic recessions since 1946, by the late 1970s the simultaneous existence of serious inflation and heavy unemployment—a condition known as "stagflation"—provided a new challenge for economic planners. Other industrialized countries of the West suffered from similar malaise. In the 1980s, most of the world— including the Communist countries of Eastern Europe and China— moved away from heavy dependence on economic planning toward increasing privatization and a growing emphasis on laissez-faire policies as the best approach to economic growth.

Electronic Data Processing (EDP) (40)

The systematic use of computers to perform operations such as sorting, storing, calculating, and presenting information in a usable form for government agencies, businesses, scientific laboratories, and other organizations. Data processing is associated with digital type computer systems that consist of units for three distinct functions: input, processing, and output. The input function converts data coming from a variety of sources—such as reports, statistical compilations, sales manuals, drawings, charts, and graphs—to electronic impulses which are later automatically interpreted. The data are fed in as coded and key-punched cards or magnetic tapes. The input unit is called the card reader. Once the data are converted into electronic signals and read into the data processing system as directed by a program, it becomes possible to store, retrieve, and control the data. The data can be manipulated logically or mathematically to serve any desired end. The processing unit is the prime apparatus of the system, since it is here that the plan of the user is imposed on the data. The output unit of a data processing computer is the printer, which relays answers in a variety of forms and images on cards, teleprocessing systems, magnetic tapes, or display screens. There are at least five kinds of data bank systems emerging in U.S. public administration: (1) statistical systems for policy studies; (2) executive systems for general administration; (3) systems designed to centralize data gathered by other agencies; (4) individual agency data bank systems; and (5) mixed public/private systems. *See also* COMPUTER, 33; SYSTEMS ANALYSIS, 83.

Significance Electronic data processing equipment has become the *sine qua non* for large-scale government and business operations. As the memory capacity of data processing systems increases, they acquire a greater capability for a broad range of applications and operations. Some of these are sorting and rearranging, judging its own performance, recognizing errors, and protecting information from unauthorized users. The major advantages of data processing systems are their speed of processing and their unlimited capacity to store information, thus saving organizations time and manpower. Federal government agencies use about 10 percent of all the automatic data processing systems operating in the United States. The Census Bureau, the Internal Revenue Service (IRS), and the Social Security Administration (SSA) rely almost totally on data processing systems in performing their missions. The federal government maintains major data banks on the status of the nation's natural resources, the economy, the military, and industrial capability. At the state and local level, data processing is used in such activities as vote counting, court scheduling, and keeping police records. The optimal use of computer-based information storage and retrieval systems is inhibited by (1) the unfamiliarity of top-level government executives with EDP and management science; (2) a lack of qualified personnel to perform the necessary kinds of systems analysis; (3) the need to rewrite laws in order to permit the integration of files and information-sharing arrangements; (4) a general lack of coordination among government agencies; (5) the parochialism of many agencies; and (6) popular and official fears of privacy invasions and of a *1984* technocratic state. The question of who controls the technological capacity of electronic data processing remains a key political and power issue.

Elite (41)
Those men and women who occupy positions of influence in the body politic. The elite have been termed the *power elite* by U.S. sociologist C. Wright Mills, who described them as those persons who command the major hierarchies and organizations of modern society. According to Mills, they run the major corporations, operate the important agencies of government, and direct the military. They are in effect the "establishment," the wielders of influence that follows wealth and social standing. U.S. political scientist Harold Lasswell also defines elites in terms of power, describing political elites simply as "power holders." In Lasswell's analysis, political elites sit astride positions of authority, the bounds of which are determined by the reactions of the public toward those who hold power. Political elites exist as long as the source of their dominance—the authority of hierarchical bureaucratic structures which they control—maintains legitimacy in the eyes of the people. Both Mills and Lasswell use power and control of hierarchies as common elements in identifying elites. Theories of elites usually include the following ideas: (1) Small groups of people control most of the decision making that determines national policies. (2) Members of the elite are the heads of multinational corporations, top officials in the government, and key military personnel. (3) The elite have subtypes—for example, corporate, government, and military—that are closely associated because of the "revolving door" phenomenon. This is the process by which corporate executives move in and out of government service, or military officers become corporate executives on retirement, so there is general interchange between and among the elite subtypes. (4) Although there are occasional conspiracies among members of the elite, conspiracies are usually unnecessary because of the community of interest among the subtypes. (5) The elite hold their influence by virtue of their offices in critical bureaucracies. (6) Directly under the elite there is a group of people with "middle range power," such as congressmen, state government officials, and lower ranking military officers who carry out the wishes of the elite. (7) The U.S. government is essentially undemocratic. The

Public Policy

elite governs by orchestrating interest-group demands and systematically discriminating against the masses of the people. *See also* IRON LAW OF OLIGARCHY, 104; SUBSYSTEM, 80; WEBER, MAX, 187.

Significance The elite exist in all times and places because of the unequal distribution of talent, wealth, and political influence in society. Supporters of elitist theories argue that this is a natural phenomenon. Elitists transfer the advantages they hold into formal bureaucratic structures and use those structures to exercise, aggrandize, and protect their power. In democratic countries the elite are recruited from a broader base than in nondemocratic countries, where the elite spring from a narrow base, often from only a few families. There are established elites, and there are emerging elites in every society. In many Third World countries, for example, the old landed gentry are today challenged by the rising power of the industrial and commercial elite. There is even a hierarchy among elites. The political elite have been referred to as the *strategic* elite whose actions and judgments so affect the political, economic, military, moral, cultural, and scientific environment that they are indeed the superior class. As is true with all superior classes, the political elite frequently make decisions in the form of nondecisions. Power is wielded not only in initiating, approving, or vetoing public policies, but in preventing issues which might threaten elitist interests from being publicly considered at all.

Eminent Domain (42)
The power of government to purchase, confiscate, or expropriate private properties, and selectively to utilize and control them in the pursuit of specific public purposes. Eminent domain is usually associated with a government takeover of land holdings, as when a state highway commission acquires private lands to build highways, but the power of eminent domain has other applications as well. The public regulation of private enterprise is construed legally as an application of this authority, for example. While eminent domain normally includes the responsibility of government to provide fair compensation to property owners, the compensation is not necessarily uniform or consistent when applied. Eminent domain is also linked to the power of government to confiscate personal property when private ownership is viewed as representing a threat to the established order, or when private ownership itself is a direct violation of local, state, or federal law. Under such conditions governments are empowered to seize property in order to execute a public policy or to avert a potential crisis in the governmental system. Confiscation may involve

compensation but does not require it. Nationalization, or expropriation, is another aspect of the power of eminent domain. It is the process whereby a government may transfer ownership of privately held units to itself. Government then assumes either partial or total responsibility for managing and controlling the expropriated enterprise. Nationalization applies equally to locally owned, as well as to foreign-owned, businesses and may or may not involve compensation. While governments vary widely in terms of how the power of eminent domain is applied, and the type and amount of compensation provided, it is universally recognized and practiced. Typically, the invoking of eminent domain is carried out by administrative officials, with the courts rendering the final decision concerning its validity and the appropriateness of the compensation.

Significance Eminent domain is highly controversial in Western societies. The high value placed on the ownership of private property has sparked a long-standing debate over the utilization of this authority. Its application is heavily monitored in the United States and controlled through the judicial process. Related questions concerning the definition of the public interest and fair compensation are raised, debated, and resolved on a case-by-case basis. While opponents of the power of eminent domain argue that it violates the constitutional rights of persons and/or groups to own private property, its proponents contend that governments lacking such authority would be powerless to effect important changes aimed at improving the human condition. Programs designed to stimulate urban renewal and slum clearance, for example, and the development of public highways, utility systems, and housing authorities would be impossible without such power. The capacity to apply checks on business practices through regulatory agencies such as the Federal Trade Commission (FTC) would be impossible as well. While eminent domain is usually associated with government *purchases* of business and land holdings, its application is not confined to this kind of activity. It is widely used during periods of war. At the conclusion of World War II, for example, the United States confiscated large holdings in both Germany and Japan to exert control over these countries. Eminent domain is exercised when law enforcement agents confiscate illegally owned items, such as weapons, gambling equipment, narcotics, and other controlled substances. Eminent domain is illustrated in the nationalization practices of many Socialist and Communist-bloc countries, where the expropriation of major wealth-producing institutions is a regular practice and is prerequisite to the achievement of a socialized system. The Chilean government, for example, expropriated U.S. copper industry holdings in the 1970s as part of a nationwide move to socialize all wealth-producing segments of the economy. Such practices usually include little, if any, compensation. The power of eminent domain thus has universal applications. The systematic study of them is important for an understanding of the manner in which governments exert administrative control within their jurisdictions.

Enterprise Zone (43)
An approach to economic well-being that offers inducements designed to attract business and industry to a designated area or region of economic and social distress. In 1984, President Ronald Reagan proposed that Congress enact legislation to implement the enterprise zone scheme nationally. Although Congress rejected the proposal, nearly one-half of the states subsequently adopted enterprise zone legislation modeled largely on the Reagan administration proposal. The state systems typically establish eligibility criteria that include pervasive poverty with a high unemployment rate, slumping property values, a high crime rate, population losses, chronic building abandonment, and high levels of tax delinquency. Each state system typically starts with the creation of an Enterprise Zone Authority composed of high state government officials plus private sector members appointed by the governor. The Authority's major function is to receive, review, and make decisions about local enterprise zone applications. Each state law also establishes general criteria to determine which local units of government qualify as enterprise zones. The state systems frequently include a citizens' council charged with advising local governmental units and recruiting business and industry to participate in enterprise zone initiatives. The limitations on incentives that an enterprise zone can offer, particularly in reduced taxes, are spelled out in each state law. *See also* PRIVATIZATION, 71.

Significance Enterprise zones are basically an effort by government to cope with the many pockets of poverty that exist in the United States because of changing markets and foreign competition. The idea of reviving areas of economic and social malaise by finding ways to attract new business and industry is an approach employed by many countries, not the least of which is the People's Republic of China. Critics charge that the approach only gives official sanction to the already active and highly competitive search for jobs through the acquisition of new capital by a variety of questionable means. As long as unemployment remains high and pockets of extreme poverty exist, enterprise zone competition is likely to continue and expand. President Reagan's efforts to establish a national program were in keeping with his supply side economic philosophy which maintains that tax cuts are the best incentive to economic growth. Congress, however, rejected the Reagan proposal on the ground that federal tax reductions are not in keeping with the effort to reduce the huge budget deficits now threatening the economic stability of the nation.

Environmental Impact Statement (44)
A provision in the National Environmental Policy Act of 1969 that requires all federal agencies to consider the effect that any federally financed project or any federal policy may have on the environment. For example, if any federal, state, or local agency using federal funds undertakes a project that may threaten to produce substantial environmental damage, an environmental impact statement can be demanded under the law. By this means, private citizens, members of Congress, or governmental officials can undertake legal action to stop the project until its impact on the environment can be determined. Many state and local units of government have established similar requirements, so that an environmental impact statement is required in almost all cases before private parties begin a major development project.

Significance The requirement of an environmental impact statement was the product of a concern for the preservation of ecological stability arising in the 1960s. The enactment of the National Environmental Policy Act of 1969, the establishment of a Council on Environmental Quality in the Executive Office to advise the president, and the Environmental Protection Agency (EPA), which administers federal programs to control pollution, were also products of that concern. Because of concern over energy shortages, Congress set requirements aside in order to construct the Alaskan Pipeline project. Many in the energy field have continued to attack the environmentalists and requirements to avoid environmental damage while bringing new sources of energy into production. The environmental impact approach has helped to protect environmental stability in some areas by preventing some projects, altering others, and by encouraging the inclusion of ecosystem considerations in long-range planning. In some cases, major projects, such as the building of new dams, have been delayed or prohibited because of the impact they might have on fish species or wildlife. The building of many nuclear power plants has been delayed or canceled because of escalating costs and delays occasioned by public hearings and prolonged debates on the environmental issues involved. In 1976, the Supreme Court upheld the constitutionality of requiring an environmental impact statement. The Court determined that the National Environmental Policy Act can require an impact statement for each mining operation in a region, but not a regional impact statement (*Kleppe v. Sierra Club,* 427 U.S. 390). Requirements on the national, state, and local levels for environmental impact statements have brought administrators directly into public controversies involving environmentalists and conservationist groups, and with those groups that place primary emphasis on shaping nature to provide energy and other needs for human beings.

Environmental Turbulence (45)
A characteristic of organizational environmental activity in a time of rapid technological change and sociopolitical uncertainty that involves input elements interacting *with each other* as well as with the organization. Environmental turbulence is an open-system concept first used by psychologist F. E. Emery to describe an evolutionary model of system functioning. The turbulent field is the fourth environmental type in an evolutionary progression which also includes the placid-randomized type, the placid-clustered type, and the disturbed-reactive type. The first three types are used in the analysis of systems functioning in the fields of economics and biology. The turbulent environment type is used primarily to analyze complex organizations. The degree of turbulence in an organization's environment changes over time and varies among organizations at any given time. An organization interacts with many elements of the environment including technological, cultural, political, legal, and economic components. According to systems theory, an organization processes inputs and adapts to outputs through a feedback loop. Increasingly more complex interactions among the input components make the boundaries between organizations less defined and make organizations less autonomous and more permeable. If an organization does not adapt to these increasingly complex interrelations, a system overload occurs and the organization may collapse. The increased uncertainty in a turbulent environment changes the status of a previously autonomous organization to that of a subsystem in a larger system. For example, a small agency in a placid, stable environment can predict the reactions of a stable constituency or an unorganized labor force. An agency in a rapidly changing environment cannot rely on predictable ways of responding when it is dealing with several other rapidly changing subsystems, such as an organizing labor force or politically powerful interest groups. Operating at this level of complexity, the environment exerts a great deal of force on an organization. Theorists have suggested several adaptive mechanisms for organizations to use as

survival strategies in such a turbulent environment. These require an emphasis on flexibility, a responsiveness to change, and the expansion of communication channels to as many other organizations as possible, including private, public, and academic systems. See also SYSTEMS ANALYSIS, 83; SYSTEMS THEORY, 84.

Significance Environmental turbulence and the ability of the environment itself to be a principal generator of change in organizations are important considerations in the analysis of the effectiveness of public agencies. Turbulence is often used as a descriptive concept in the analysis of public policy making, intergovernmental relations, and administrative politics. Theorists differ in their opinions about the degree and extent of turbulence in contemporary organizational environments, but most agree that environmental turbulence can inhibit long-range planning efforts and policy reform under traditional incrementalism. Incrementalism is unable to assimilate large quantities of technological information when considering, coordinating, and administering large programs. In a time of rapid change and uncertainty, the incremental approach to decision making does not satisfy the systems requirement for occasionally dramatic adaptations. Bureaucracies by definition seek established procedures and predictable interactions. Their hierarchical structure impedes drastic change. The concept of environmental turbulence suggests that in times of demand for change an organization must restructure and redesign its patterns of assimilation and interaction to be able to survive.

Fair Labor Standards Act (FLSA) (46)
A federal law enacted in 1938 that established minimum wages and maximum working hours for employees of companies involved in interstate commerce, and regulated the use of child labor in businesses and industries engaged in interstate commerce. The Fair Labor Standards Act provided for an eight-hour work day and a forty-hour work week, with time-and-a-half pay for work exceeding forty hours. A minimum wage per hour was also established ($.25 per hour in 1938, and $3.35 per hour in 1987). Workers not engaged in interstate commerce are not covered by the act, although many states have legislated similar provisions to provide for this category of employee. In 1985, the Supreme Court ruled in *Garcia v. San Antonio Metropolitan Transit Authority* that state and local government workers are henceforth to be covered by the act, a decision that prompted Congress to enact extensive amendments to the FLSA later that year. Under the amended law, overtime would have to be paid to all state

Public Policy

and local government employees who work beyond what the Department of Labor defines as a normal work day. Legislated exceptions to *Garcia* include elected officials and their staffs; executive, administrative, and professional employees; and teachers. According to a 1982 Census Bureau report, there are approximately 3,000 counties, 19,000 municipalities, 17,000 towns and townships, and 15,000 school districts in the United States, with a total number of full-time employees approaching 7 million. There are also several million people employed by state governments. Thus the *Garcia* decision and the amendments to the FLSA have substantially affected large numbers of U.S. workers. The hours of work and general work schedules for such employees as fire fighters, members of the police force, and hospital workers, for example, have been significantly altered.

Significance Congress has progressively increased coverage of the Fair Labor Standards Act since 1938. Although certain categories of workers are still excluded from its provisions, almost all state and local public employees are now covered by it. In 1941, the Supreme Court upheld the constitutionality of the act by rejecting long-held notions that Congress could not regulate production or working conditions. The decision ended a lengthy process of legal challenges to the power of Congress to control business practices that directly or indirectly affect interstate commerce. The act has also successfully dealt with some of the more flagrant abuses of child labor. By establishing federal guidelines, the Fair Labor Standards Act tended to reduce, although it did not eliminate, the substandard working conditions and low wages that are part of the competitive environment among states and local units of government trying to attract industry. The Equal Pay Act of 1963, passed by Congress as an amendment to the Fair Labor Standards Act, requires employers to pay equal wages to men and women doing the same work.

Federalism **(47)**
A structure of government that divides power between a central government and regional governments, with each having some independent authority. Federalism is considered to be the cornerstone of the U.S. governmental system. Although interpretations of the optimum balance of power have changed significantly over the last two hundred years, the original purpose of maintaining the benefits of a centrally coordinated government, with a balance of state and local power, has remained intact. Legally, local government has no independent standing within the framework of federalism. Politically, however, local governments frequently possess autonomy from the

states that created them. Characteristics of a federal system include a separation of powers, in which neither partner owes its legal existence to the other, and a system of checks and balances, in which neither partner can dictate the policy decisions of the other. This type of balance results in a division of decision-making power between a semiautonomous central system and semiautonomous state systems. Originally outlined in the Constitution of the United States, federalism's essential legal boundaries were defined by the Supreme Court in the early nineteenth century. Throughout the 1800s, traditional "old style" federalism was concerned with defining the separate spheres of authority and jurisdiction between national and state governments. Questions of federalism focused only on which level of government should take which actions on specific policy matters. This traditional concept of governmental relations, sometimes called dual federalism, has also been characterized as "layer-cake federalism." The layers of the cake are the separate functions performed by the federal government, the state governments, and the local governments. The layers are pictured as totally distinct and layered one on top of the other.

A transition began in the early twentieth century from the old style to a new style of federalism. Characteristics of "new style" federalism as described by political scientist Michael Reagan are (1) an interest in the political and practical nature of governmental interactions, stressing *interdependence,* and (2) the sharing of functions between the national government and state and local agencies. The years following the New Deal saw an increase in federal policy making and yet an increase in decentralization of authority as well. State systems were given greater opportunity to implement policy decisions. *Cooperative federalism* thus became the new term for intergovernmental relations where both central and regional governments shared the administration of domestic programs. National involvement was seen as a necessary unifying force. Decentralization and the need for local cooperation were attributed to the immense growth of local units of government following World War II. A *marble-cake* concept of federalism became popular as an alternative to *layer-cake* federalism. It represented the fluidity of governmental processes and the involvement of all levels of government in administering programs. Marble-cake federalism acknowledged the importance of ongoing and intertwined intergovernmental relations. It contributed to the establishment of cooperative mechanisms for implementing intergovernmental agreements. Since the late 1950s, there has been a concerted effort to eliminate unnecessary jurisdictional disputes in federalism and strengthen relations among national, state, and local agencies. In 1959, for example, the Advisory Commission on Intergovernmental Relations (ACIR) was established. The commission has

Public Policy

been active in framing intergovernmental agreements. In 1969, ten federal regions were established to work closely with local governments to identify and resolve conflicting policies. As a result of some disillusionment with the marble-cake approach to federalism, a *new federalism* movement began in the early 1970s and continued in the 1980s with the purpose of involving local governments to a greater degree in the administration of domestic programs. Critics of new federalism believe it is overly decentralized and that it is not in the nation's best interest to allow state and local agencies the kind of freedom they have under new federalism principles. Historically, critics argue, principles of social equity have been better served by the enforcement of national standards. *See also* DECENTRALIZATION, 135; FEDERALISM, FISCAL, 49; INTERGOVERNMENTAL RELATIONS (IGR), 153.

Significance Federalism has immense importance for the study and practice of public administration. The issues and controversies of federalism are particularly relevant to issues such as the level of funding for social programs, cutback management, and public housing. Each of these policy areas involves problems of jurisdiction and separation of powers—the question of which level of government should be doing what. The contemporary problems of federalism concern parallel activities going on at different levels of government simultaneously. The future of U.S. government is tied closely to the coordination of these activities and to developments in intergovernmental relations. The Advisory Commission on Intergovernmental Relations has suggested four criteria that should be considered in defining future intergovernmental relationships under federalism: (1) economic efficiency, (2) equity, (3) political accountability, and (4) administrative effectiveness. Because the "new federalism" depends on increased state and local tax income, and because the states and local units of government compete with each other in trying to attract industry and jobs by keeping taxes low, standards of performance in many social categories have been seriously weakened.

Federalism, Cooperative (48)

The system that has evolved within the American federal union that views the national, state, and local governments as partners working together to solve common problems. Cooperative federalism has largely replaced the older idea of competitive federalism by which the states and the national government were expected to function as antagonistic competitors within the constitutional check and balance system. Through cooperation, the three levels operate as independent units but share their interest, involvement, and funds in common programs. Cooperative federalism was first developed through early grant-in-aid programs wherein the national government funneled large amounts of money into the states. In exchange, the states agreed to match the federal funds, accept some measure of federal standards and oversight, and assume responsibility for administering the programs. Diverse cooperative programs in fields such as health, welfare, education, conservation, and transportation were developed through this sharing of dollars and responsibility. New developments or emphases in cooperative federalism have been assigned descriptive titles that reflect these changes. *Permissive federalism* is a general term used to describe efforts during the 1960s and 1970s to carry out policy reforms aimed at streamlining the system of intergovernmental cooperation so as to achieve better results. First used by Michael D. Reagan and John G. Sanzone in their book, *The New Federalism* (1972), the emphasis in permissive federalism is on giving the state and local units greater freedom and support in terms of their political as well as their policy needs. In 1965, President Lyndon B. Johnson gave cooperative federalism a new twist by stressing intergovernmental and private group collaboration. Referring to it as *creative federalism,* President Johnson and the Congress began to implement the new approach by pouring huge amounts of money into the states, especially into the big cities, in an attempt to avoid urban crises by coping with problems before they became hopeless. In 1969, President Richard M. Nixon unveiled a *new federalism* as his administration's approach to making cooperative federalism work. Nixon's mentor, President Dwight D. Eisenhower, had not succeeded in his efforts to reverse the flow of power to Washington by revitalizing state and local governments. President Nixon reasoned that the failure had been the result of weak financial resources in the states and a fear of levying new taxes. Thus, the key to Nixon's new federalism became a revenue-sharing program which funneled huge amounts of federal funds into the state and local units without the usual federal requirements and controls found in the grant-in-aid programs. Although some of the revenue-sharing funds were designated for general program categories, most were simply handed over to be expended as the states and local units determined. *See also* FEDERALISM, 47.

Significance Cooperative federalism has given the U.S. system of government the flexibility needed to cope with many of the contemporary problems of society. Most voters, political leaders, interest groups, private organizations, and administrators involved in such programs support the intergovernmental cooperation approach to problem solving. Many differences arise, however, over how programs should be financed, which governments should make the key decisions, and should centralization or decentralization of program administration prevail. The new adaptations found in the ideas of creative federalism and the new federalism reflected acceptance of the basic idea of intergovernmental cooperation but were tempered by the liberal philosophy of President Johnson in the first case, and the conservative philosophy of President Nixon in the second. From a public administrationist's point of view, the increasing tendency toward organizational and managerial decentralization poses a difficult administrative challenge. Some, however, support the trend on the ground that, since the problems involved are so intractable and persistent, experimentation encouraged by decentralized decision making is the best approach. The search has continued in the 1980s to find some middle ground between the extremes of centralization and decentralization that will give cooperative federalism a new opportunity to prove that it is the key to effective government in the United States.

Federalism, Fiscal (49)

The transactions involved in the transfer of funds from one government entity to another in a federal system. Fiscal federalism is a major feature of contemporary intergovernmental relations. The transfer of funds downward through levels of government has been common in the United States since the 1930s, but it has been only in the last twenty years that fiscal federalism has exploded in terms of the number of grants made and actual amounts of money dispersed. The most common form of fiscal transfer is from the national government to state and local governments in the form of grants-in-aid. However, state to local transfers also play an important part in intergovernmental fiscal relations. The year 1960 marked the beginning of the grants explosion. The need for fiscal sharing was a result of the rapid growth of state and local governments and the expansion of domestic programs administered at the local level. Because local governments had a weaker, more restricted economic base than did the national government, a system of revenue sharing was devised to support locally administered domestic programs. The national government took this opportunity to use financial assistance as a way to expand and upgrade public services to meet national priorities. Thus a series of grants-in-aid transactions transferred money to lower levels of government for specific purposes with varying degrees of administrative control. From 1960 to 1970, grant authorizations increased from 45 to 530, and by 1970 grants-in-aid provided approximately a quarter of all state and local revenues. Grants have been used primarily in the areas of public assistance, education, and highways.

Some grants require matching funds, some provide 100 percent support, and some fall in between, depending on the priority Congress has placed on the purpose of the grant.

Grants-in-aid requirements vary according to how much discretion the federal government wants to allow in a particular policy area. Categorical grants, for example, are narrowly defined and leave little room for discretion. Block grants are given in specific policy areas and allow some flexibility and discretion in expenditures. Categorical grants may be made by individual application or by formula. Formula grants are available across the board to all who are eligible in a category, such as the category of "the blind." Application, or project, grants are made available only for specific purposes, however, and require a complex application procedure. The paperwork required for project grants has given rise to the art of professional grant writing. About two-thirds of categorical grants made are project grants, and the remainder are formula grants. Revenue sharing was established in 1972 by the State and Local Fiscal Assistance Act, in part because of criticism of the grants-in-aid system. Revenue sharing was intended to supplement grants by making a portion of federal tax revenues available quickly to state and local governments, with a maximum amount of local discretion built into the transfers. One result of revenue sharing has been a tendency to favor richer units of state and local governments as defined by their tax base, with most of the expenditures going for projects of the middle class. Critics describe revenue-sharing expenditures as having a minimum emphasis on social services for the needy. State to local grants, although not as common as national to state and local grants, comprise nearly a third of the activity of fiscal federalism. State to local fiscal assistance is accomplished through straight grants for specific purposes or through the sharing of taxes. Also included in the local benefits of fiscal federalism is "direct federalism," which involves the transfer of some funds directly to localities from the federal government, bypassing the state entirely. Examples of direct grants are in local housing projects and pollution control. *See also* BLOCK GRANT, 259; FEDERALISM, 47; REVENUE SHARING, 287.

Significance Fiscal federalism and national involvement in grant administration have had important effects on public management through all levels of government. The early 1960s marked a turning point in public policy making when the grants-in-aid system, instead of continuing to support policy determinations by state and local governments, shifted to what Congress determined to be in the national interest. Local projects and program objectives had to reflect national priorities to be eligible for federal revenues. Expansion of fiscal federalism in the 1960s opened grants to private corporations, universities, and nonprofit organizations. Not only were eligibility categories broadened, but more emphasis was placed on urban problems. The process of sharing revenues through all levels of government promoted interactions among those levels that would not otherwise have occurred. Fiscal federalism has contributed to the development of intergovernmental relations and is the backbone of cooperative mechanisms in the policy areas of public assistance, public housing, education, and transportation.

Freedom of Information Act (FOIA) (50)
A law enacted by Congress in 1966 that requires federal agencies to provide for citizen access to public records on request. The Freedom of Information Act provides for exceptions to this general rule of openness, including files connected with confidential personnel matters, national defense, law enforcement, and financial records. When information is withheld under these exemptions, however, the law provides that interested parties denied access can sue to seek disclosure. Under a 1974 amendment to the act, agencies are required to expedite information disclosures to private parties, access to the courts is facilitated, and judges are empowered to determine whether information is properly or improperly withheld under provisions of the act. *See also* GOVERNMENT IN THE SUNSHINE ACT, 52.

Significance The Freedom of Information Act was regarded at the time of its passage as a major step toward a purer form of democracy by opening government to public scrutiny. Subsequent disclosures of violations of individuals' constitutional rights by federal investigatory agencies proved that such concerns were well founded. Individuals who made inquiry under the act, for example, found their names included on special surveillance lists drawn up by the Federal Bureau of Investigation (FBI) and the Central Intelligence Agency (CIA), with individual dossiers filled with malicious hearsay and rumors. By opening government agencies to public scrutiny, the law serves to hold public officials more effectively accountable for their actions. It also has tended to counteract the natural bureaucratic tendency toward classifying much of the regular actions of agencies as "confidential," i.e., not open to the public. Legitimate areas of secrecy have been recognized by the courts, such as the development of new weapons systems and government financial information, which if disclosed could help private individuals reap huge profits in the stock market or other speculative arenas. Several states have followed the federal lead by adopting freedom of information laws that apply to all state and local public bodies.

Game Theory (51)

A mathematically based analysis system that utilizes modeling procedures to determine optimal human strategies in conflict situations. Game theory is based on two branches of mathematics: combinatorics and set theory. It employs techniques such as matrices and tree graphs to explore conflict situations, which it calls *games*, involving two or more participants engaged in trying to maximize their gains and minimize their losses. A participant may be any decision-making unit (e.g., a country, a politician, or an administrative agency), and the games considered are games of strategy rather than games of chance. The game plan, or strategy, of a participant includes all possible options for contingencies arising from the strategy of other participants, or the interplay of natural events. Strategies are evaluated in terms of payoff. Numerical values are assigned to the outcomes of particular plays or moves. *See also* DECISION MAKING, RATIONAL-COMPREHENSIVE, 95; SYSTEMS ANALYSIS, 83; SYSTEMS THEORY, 84.

Significance Game theory has both normative and empirical applications in the study of human behavior. The prime motivation underlying its development was to provide information on strategies that should be adopted. Employment of an optimal strategy is referred to by game theorists as "rational behavior." The descriptive value of game theory, though not the original intent of its creators, provides opportunities for behavioral scientists to observe the responses of participants in carefully structured models of real-world situations. The prisoners' dilemma, a game in which both participants must take a risk and sustain a minor loss to avoid disastrous consequences to both, is an example of a game in which behavioral scientists study participants' responses in conflict situations. They use the data to formulate generalizations about human behavior. As is generally the case with mathematical proofs, several underlying assumptions must be accepted for the proofs to be valid. In the case of game theory these assumptions directly contradict the real-world situations which the models purportedly represent. For instance, game theory assumes complete prior knowledge of all possible plays and adherence to unambiguous rules. However, in certain negotiations the "rules" or legally and socially accepted actions of one opponent may be misunderstood by the other. Possible compromises or bargains, called *plays*, may not be discovered until the last moments of the game. Game theory also assumes known payoffs with a constant value. The real-world payoff may be full of surprises, however, and the value of various payoffs may differ for real participants. Neither are the emotional stability, intelligence, and other intangible human traits of participants considered in game theory. In many ways the system is predicated on a pessimistic view of humankind; that is, one's opponent will try to inflict the maximum damage possible. In some life situations this approach may be valid, but it is not the case in all conflict situations. The techniques used by a game theorist to examine possible options encourage participants to diagram and graph possible plans and to anticipate responses of other parties. A system such as game theory which encourages thoughtful examination of options prior to action is obviously useful to policy makers. Its danger lies in a rigid and simplistic overdependence on the theory.

Government in the Sunshine Act (52)

A law enacted by Congress in 1977 that requires all multiheaded federal agencies to conduct their business in sessions open to the public. The Government in the Sunshine Act of 1977 applies to all regulatory commissions, independent agencies, commissions, and advisory committees, but the major cabinet departments are exempted. The Sunshine law also forbids the holding of unofficial meetings between agency officials and individuals involved in matters under consideration by the agency. The law specifies some exceptions to the open meeting rule, such as those in which discussions are held on national defense, personnel matters, or those that may involve court proceedings. *See also* FREEDOM OF INFORMATION ACT (FOIA), 50.

Significance   The Government in the Sunshine Act of 1977 is part of the general movement in the United States to remove secrecy from government proceedings wherever possible. Other actions include the right of individuals to examine the files kept on them by surveillance agencies, and the right of the news media and others to extract information from previously secret files. Many states have moved in the same direction, adopting "open meeting" laws that prevent state or local governmental bodies from excluding the public from their meetings. The movement toward openness gained great momentum as a result of the Watergate disclosures of illegal, immoral, and unethical conduct carried on by public officials under the guise of the need for secrecy. More and more, the principle of the public's "right to know" has been expanded to include not only the results of official deliberations but of the processes that led to those decisions as well. The Sunshine Act encourages legal action by private individuals whenever an official meeting is closed to the public.

Group Theory (53)

An approach that is aimed at explaining human behavior primarily through study of the nature and interaction of social groups. Group theory is based on explanatory statements about the characteristics of sets of human beings with regular interaction who recognize a degree of association and/or interdependence. Group theory attempts to understand the character of group life and its impact on people. There appear to be at least four types of groups, according to public administrationist J. D. Williams: (1) *formal groups,* defined by institutional structures and including titles, distinctions, rules, prerogatives, and sanctions; (2) *informal groups,* defined by unwritten codes, and including cliques which confer benefits and impose penalties on their members despite the absence of authorized powers; (3) *highly institutionalized allied groups,* including employee unions and department councils which are almost as formally bureaucratized as the department itself; and (4) *informal allied groups,* including the bowling league and the backpackers club. Group theory speculates about the internal structure of each of these groups, such as how significant others, leaders, and followers are determined, and what their belief systems, behavior norms, and sanctions for noncompliance are. Group theorists are convinced that each of these facets of group life affect the way employees perform. The group influence begins with one of the new employee's first calculations: What kind of conduct on my part will get these people to like me? Group theorists call this *role taking* and define "these people" as the *significant others* who loom large in anyone's immediate circle. Role taking leads to *role playing,* as people act in a way they hope will gain the approval of others in the group. The cues one receives on how to behave and who counts are the office *norms,* the setting of which group theorist Tamotsu Shibutani calls one of the most important functions of the group. Shibutani says that group-determined norms are universal in all groups, from the Girl Scouts to the Mafia. However, norms do not only include loyalty, decency, and sincerity. They also include when to come to work, how long a coffee break is, what is prudent to feed back to the boss, and if it is safe to excel. *See also* FOLLETT, MARY PARKER, 15; HAWTHORNE STUDIES, 54; PLURALISM, 66.

Significance   Group theory serves the public administrator by suggesting that there should be some congruence between agency norms and group norms. What constitutes a day's work? How are leave regulations complied with? How is confidential information about clients handled? For example, a reorganization of the copy-pulling section of the United States Patent Office ran into difficulty in trying to increase the number of patents pulled to 800 per day in the face of a work group standard that 300 constituted a full day's work. Another example is from the Watergate transcripts. They reveal a group norm in the White House that changed the constitutional norm for the President to "preserve, protect, and defend the Constitution of the United States." At one point presidential adviser H. R. Haldeman said to President Richard M. Nixon: "The way to contain any meaningful investigation of the Watergate break-in is to have the CIA tell the FBI, 'Stay the hell out of this. . . . '" Nixon replied: "Right. Fine. . . . Play it tough. That's the way they play it and that's the way we're going to play it." Groups possess highly effective sanctions to bring and keep their members in line: warm acceptance and praise; ridicule; the silent treatment; ostracism; and, on occasion, physical abuse as when strikers and strikebreakers clash during a protracted labor dispute. Group theory's fundamental message to administrators is that there is security in numbers. Employees use group identity as their first refuge against the winds of chance in an agency. A positive aspect of group life on the job is that if a natural work group forms, and people who like each other are able to work on tasks together, agency productivity is significantly enhanced. Such psychic payoffs on the job demonstrate the error of the early scientific management school of thought, which saw work as something *external* to life.

Hawthorne Studies (54)

A series of experiments that provided the foundation for the development of the human relations school of organization theory. The Hawthorne studies were conducted from 1927 through 1932 by Professors Elton Mayo and Fritz Roethlisberger and their associates of the Harvard Business School. The site of the studies was the Western Electric Company's Hawthorne plant in Chicago. The purpose of the experiments was to determine the basis of productivity among workers. The experiments began by placing a group of five female workers in a test room, where observers carefully recorded changes in rates of production as working conditions were altered. The women's job was to assemble telephone relays. Twelve physically based variables were introduced into the workers' environment, such as work-room illumination, number and duration of rest periods, and length of the work day and work week. Contrary to the assumptions of scientific management, the productivity of the five workers continued to rise regardless of the favorableness or unfavorableness of the changes imposed. The control group on the main assembly line did fluctuate in rate of productivity as working conditions were altered. It became clear that physical surroundings and work hours were not the central influences underlying the behavior of the five women in the relay assembly test room. The researchers concluded that the operative influences were the workers' opportunity to function as a small primary group and the psychological payoffs that came from their being the steady objects of attention in the experiment. It was theorized that the workers on the main assembly line produced less than they were physically capable of because of social norms and controls imposed by co-workers. This effect was termed "artificial restriction of output." The major findings of the Hawthorne studies were summarized by sociologist Amitai Etzioni: (1) The level of production is set by social norms, not by physiological capabilities. (2) Noneconomic rewards and sanctions affect the behavior of workers and limit economic incentive plans. (3) Often workers act or react as members of groups. *See also* GROUP THEORY, 53; HUMAN MOTIVATION, 99–103.

Significance   The Hawthorne studies introduced a social-psychological perspective to industrial management and opened the way to investigation of management factors other than formal organizational structure and process. These further investigations provided additional evidence for the human relations school of organizational theory, although the school did not have its full impact in terms of practical applications until after World War II. When the practical applications were made, subsequent reorganizations of businesses resulted in as much as a 30 percent increase in worker productivity. Further research also showed the Hawthorne experiments to be somewhat restricted in scope and interpretation and rather artificially controlled. New organizational theories would more comprehensively address the complex interaction of the human personality with the environment. The lasting impact of the Hawthorne studies was in the emphasis placed on the increased status of workers and the shared sense of participation felt by workers as members of a primary work group. Marxists and neo-Marxists explained the workers' increased productivity by referring to the increased power the worker had over the work situation. A revisionist view of the Hawthorne experiments was presented by R. H. Franke and J. D. Kaul in an article in the *American Sociological Review* (1978). An application of modern statistical techniques to the Hawthorne data convinced Franke and Kaul that most of the gain in productivity of the five relay assembly workers could be explained by (1) the assertion of managerial discipline in replacing two of the original five workers; (2) the onset of the Great Depression and consequent fear of job loss; and (3) the introduction of rest periods. They downplayed the social and psychological payoffs the workers received as part of the experiment. The description of these payoffs has been described in subsequent literature as the "Hawthorne effect."

Health Maintenance Organization (HMO) (55)

A group of physicians, surgeons, dentists, psychologists, and other professionals who provide medical, dental, pharmaceutical, general health, and mental health treatment for its members through a health care center. The purpose of the Health Maintenance Organization is to provide a new, alternative system for the financing and delivery of medical services. Unlike conventional health care that is provided by individual physicians and is usually covered by a medical insurance policy, the HMO offers a wide range of services to members who pay a stipulated fee. It also makes arrangements for members who need particular kinds of health care not directly offered by the HMO staff. The health maintenance organization is a management organization that assumes legal, financial, public, and professional accountability for its services. In 1973, Congress encouraged the formation of HMOs by enacting legislation that required employers of twenty-five or more people to offer the health maintenance organization as an alternative to their insured health benefit plans. The 1973 act also set forth the standards HMOs need to meet to gain federal recognition. It spelled out the basic services that each HMO must offer, and it provided that consumers of health services must make up one-third of the HMO's policy-making board.

Significance   The health maintenance organization approach to health care tends to reduce medical costs and improve general medical services, especially preventive care. Despite its support by Congress and its apparent effectiveness, however, the HMO movement did not initially achieve the support and growth anticipated by its sponsors. Among the early problems of HMOs were the requirements imposed on them by Congress, including liberal benefits for all group members and open enrollment to applicants regardless of their physical condition. Early opposition to HMOs by the American Medical Association (AMA) also contributed to a slow start for the concept. Amendments to the 1973 act in 1976 helped to stimulate new growth in health maintenance organizations, and today they constitute a viable alternative to traditional medical care.

Interest-group Liberalism (56)

A perspective on the policy-making processes in which government distributes policy-making privileges to interest groups, thereby limiting government's choices and its ability to do long-range planning. Interest-group liberalism was advanced as a concept by political scientist Theodore Lowi in the late 1960s. Lowi observed that policy alternatives advanced by interest groups are typically seen as legitimate and equivalent to the public good. The public in fact relies on interest groups to propose what is good for all the people. Interest-group liberalism can be viewed as an extension of the capitalist competition which flourished in the early part of the twentieth century. The acceptance of competition as a viable means of distributing policy rewards is transplanted into the policy-making arena. This perspective is similar to a marketplace, or a grand bazaar. The image of a policy marketplace included independent, relatively autonomous agencies dispensing money, advice, and services to those interest groups that advance the most lucrative offer in the hectic atmosphere of the market. Lucrative offers are proposals that match agency policy commitments and other mutual advantages determined by negotiation and barter. The more overlapped the agency's jurisdiction (duplication of wares between merchants), the more successful the system, since interest groups have bartering leverage and multiple access to the bureaucracy under those conditions. The result of this pressure system, according to Lowi, is the corruption and impotence of the democratic form of government. The idea of group policy formation parallels the theory of pluralism and the doctrine that group compromise is synonymous with the common good. The contrast between pluralistic theory, which stresses competition among groups resulting in compromise, and interest-group liberalism is that interest-group liberalism condones specific groups *capturing* and *controlling* parts of agencies without having to compete for policy rewards. Since these specific, powerful groups neither overlap nor encourage new group formation, there is no system of checks and balances that could force a compromise between interests. To counter the corruption and impotence of such a vulgarization of pluralism, Lowi encourages a return to judicial democracy in which the law rules and under which there is limited administrative delegation of authority. With limited administrative discretion, agencies would be less easily coopted by interest groups. *See also* ADMINISTRATIVE DISCRETION, 86; CITIZEN PARTICIPATION, 131; PLURALIZATION, 67; SUBSYSTEM, 80.

Significance Interest-group liberalism has important implications for the concepts of new public administration, citizen participation, and administrative discretion. The new public administration emphasizes goals of comprehensive planning, decentralization, and maximum citizen participation. Lowi's argument is that this combination of objectives really does not work. Decentralization leads to a fragmentation of authority and an increase in administrative discretion. The increase of available power through administrative discretion encourages strongly led elite groups to gain access to agency decision making, thus promoting interest-group liberalism. Since interest-group liberalism narrows the scope of interests that are taken seriously, comprehensive planning becomes impossible.

Keynesianism (57)

An economic approach fostered by the British economist John Maynard Keynes that emphasizes the role of government in strengthening and providing stability for a free enterprise economy. Keynesianism is both a general philosophy and a set of assumptions and theories that guide decision makers in democratic states. Keynes believed that the Great Depression of the 1930s was unnecessarily prolonged because of a failure to use governmental fiscal policies with skill and effectiveness. The main problem in a free economy, according to Keynes, is oversavings, which, if uncorrected by fiscal policy, tends to lead to stagnation and an equilibrium far below maximum utilization of manpower and resources. Government programs must be directed toward encouraging the channeling of savings into investment and mass consumption. Such actions, however, must be undertaken with restraint to avoid catastrophic inflation. Government fiscal policies, if used with sophistication and skill, can thus be used to correct the imbalance typical of a free enterprise system between *potential* output (determined by supply factors) and *actual* output (controlled by the aggregate demand of investors, consumers, and government). To make his system work, Keynes held that the rational decisions of political leaders must supplement and complement the free interplay of market forces. These decisions should be based on a great variety of information provided by economic indicators that enable policy makers to strengthen capitalism by developing an orderly, predictable pattern of economic activity. *See also* FISCAL POLICY, 272; MONETARISM, 61.

Significance Keynesian and neo-Keynesian policies have dominated economic decision making in most of the industrialized states of the West since the end of World War II. In recent years, however, the Monetarist school, led by Nobel-Prize-winner Milton Friedman and supported strongly by many of his colleagues in the economics department at the University of Chicago, has tended increasingly to influence the thinking of many government leaders. Whereas Keynes placed most of his emphasis on governmental manipulation and support of the economy through fiscal policies such as budgeting, spending, and tax policy, the Monetarist school tends to limit or reject government's role while placing primary emphasis on monetary policy and the self-regulatory nature of the free market. The key decisions to be made by government officials are those made through the Federal Reserve System, which determines the volume of money and credit available in the nation. The growing interest in the ideas of the Monetarist school stems partly from the failures of Keynesian fiscal policies to cope with unemployment and economic stagnation without producing heavy inflation simultaneously, a condition referred to as "stagflation." By using Keynesian policies, government leaders have tried to avoid serious cyclical movements, heavy unemployment, and economic stagnation, while at the same time encouraging growth and stability in the nation's economy. High levels of inflation, however, have made the use of fiscal policy to stimulate the economy a dangerous maneuver because of the likelihood that much of the stimulus will be eaten away in a new burst of inflation. Public administrators are intimately involved in controversies over which economic policy is best for the nation, since not only their budgets and programs are involved but, in many cases, their agency's continued existence. Often, major Keynesian policies to stimulate the economy back to health from a severe recession have taken the form of increased defense expenditures, which make federal deficits politically acceptable but may feed the fires of inflation, because the goods produced do not go into the general consumer market.

Management Information System (MIS) (58)

A special type of information system, usually computer based, designed for higher decision making at the level of strategic planning. A management information system (MIS) formally organizes the information managers need to plan the future course of an organization and to make decisions on the optimal allocation of resources. A management information system is frequently constructed following these steps: (1) *Analysis of the decision system.* The objectives of the organization are determined, and the types of decisions that must be made to achieve organizational objectives are identified. Flowcharts and decision tables are useful methods of representing these elements of the decision system. What are the important decisions that are not being made or that are being made by default? An accurate model of the decision process provides the basis for analyzing information requirements. (2) *Analysis of information requirements.* Information requirements vary according to the type of decision being made. Proper sources of information for routine managerial decisions are well established in most organizations. For more complex decisions, managers may know what information they need but not how to optimize it. In this case a computer simulation of the decision can clarify the situation. For highly complex decisions, no one may be able to agree on what information is needed. The MIS may lead

Public Policy

the organization in a search for new, untapped sources of data. (3) *Aggregation of decisions.* This is a grouping together of decisions with similar information requirements. Aggregation results in information efficiency, and it helps the manager become more of an expert on a given subject. (4) *Design of an information processing system.* This is the mechanics of a management information system: collecting, storing, retrieving, and reporting the data. Key to this part of the MIS is the selection of programs for processing the data and the type of computers which will do it. The choice of where and how to gather the raw data is strategic in itself. If garbage is fed into the system, garbage will come out of it. The system must also have the capability to answer questions that have not been asked, by reporting any deviations from expectations. Thus an exception reporting system is required. A manager who only knows how to *listen* to an information system, but has no idea how it works, will not be able to use the system effectively. (5) *Design of a control system.* The management information system will probably prove to be deficient in some way. A standardized procedure must be established for reviewing deviations from expectations and for determining if the deviations are the result of faults in the information system itself. How can the system be corrected? The correction process requires close cooperation between computer specialists, information specialists, and managers. A management information system can add a high degree of rationality to decision making if properly programmed and used. *See also* COMPUTER, 33; DECISION MAKING, RATIONAL-COMPREHENSIVE, 95; SYSTEMS ANALYSIS, 83.

Significance   Management information systems have been widely adopted by business executives who use them to analyze the performance of the firm, forecast future economic conditions, and signal variations from desired plans. Public administration has moved more slowly in adopting management information systems except in metropolitan government and in defense planning. Public managers can make good use of MIS because, paradoxically, they frequently suffer from an overabundance of information. Since they often have more information than they can use, administrators can utilize a system that filters and condenses data so that only those bits of information they need arrive on their desks. The primary function of management information systems is not information gathering, but information discrimination. Information may, of course, be used as a weapon in the struggle for power within public agencies or any organization. Factions may try to manipulate the data being fed into the information system in order to protect their own positions and discredit their enemies. A management information system is essentially a neutral instrument, however, that may provide public servants an opportunity to make better decisions.

Micro-macro Analysis (59)

An analysis continuum used as a point of reference in the study of interrelated economic, political, and social units. Microeconomic analysis examines units that are not further reducible by economic theory. Consumers or individual firms, for example, are treated as single units. Macroanalysis examines units that in practice are reducible but, for theoretical reasons, are treated as whole units. Examples of units treated under macroeconomics are employment, the gross national product, and national income. Macroeconomics, also known as Keynesian economics, studies overall averages and aggregates of a system, whereas mircoeconomics looks at individual outputs. The micro and macro distinction in economic analysis is clear-cut and stays relatively constant. Analysis of political and social units, however, is not as clear-cut, since the primary analytic concern is the linkage between different types of units and the impact of one unit on the other. In analyzing the impact of one unit on another, the theoretical perspective may change, which in turn may change the level of analysis. When studying voting behavior, for example, the unit identified as a particular state may be analyzed at the macro level if the *state* is the unit of study, or at the micro level if the *country* is the unit of study. The location on the continuum of any particular unit is determined by the perspective at which the study begins. Moving toward the micro end of the continuum requires the addition of more valid and reliable empirical data, but sacrifices some of the overall significance of macroanalysis. Conversely, as the level of analysis moves toward the macro end of the continuum, it gains in significance but loses the validity and reliability that can be demonstrated by empirical data. In micro-macro analysis the goals and "health" of a unit at one level may not be compatible with the goals and "health" of the other level. What may be of maximum value at a micro level can be detrimental to the goals of an overall macro unit. A company which dumps pollutants in a river, for example, may be optimizing resources, and it may have a sound market and full employment; yet the pollution from the plant may adversely affect the entire community at the macro level of analysis. *See also* SYSTEMS ANALYSIS, 83; SYSTEMS THEORY, 84.

Significance   Micro-macro analysis issues arise most often when attempts are made to analyze the policies and actions of large groups, institutions, and states. The dilemma is how to make meaningful statements about large systems from inquiries into the behavior of individual actors in the system. The ancient dictum of inductive reasoners and classifiers such as Aristotle that "the perfectly described particular is a universal" is limited by the degree of perfection in the description. Two distinct problems arise for the micro-macro analyst. First is the problem of extrapolation from a micro to a macro description. The sum of the individual parts does not necessarily represent what the whole system looks like or how it reacts. Second is the problem of personifying large-scale descriptions at the individual level in an effort to characterize such phenomena as the "national character." Related to this analysis problem is the issue of using both discrete and aggregate data in the analysis of a unit's behavior. Moving from statements about the behavior of aggregates, such as electoral districts, to the behavior of any one individual within that aggregate involves risky inferences. Macroanalysis in public administration activities, such as program evaluation, forecasting, and planning, is likely to conceal a good deal of variance in the behavior of individuals.

Modeling (60)

The process of identifying the significant components of a system, outlining a structure through which these components are related, and proposing measures of effectiveness for the comparison of alternate policies suggested by the relationships. Modeling can be as simple as a paper airplane or as complex as a mathematical programming model for exploring policy impacts of social service systems. Models can be highly abstract or virtual replications of an existing system. The common element of all models is that they represent reality and allow the study of some aspect of reality in a laboratory setting before taking it into the real world. Modeling provides an explicit identification of a problem and the assumptions the model makes about it. The model provides for empirical evaluation and encourages the application of highly developed forms of analysis, as well as providing a vehicle for the discussion of issues. If successful, a model can prove the existence of certain relationships among components of a system and provide the basis for optimizing decisions. Operations research projects require the use of a model as a representation of the system studied. Modeling is a major step in linear programming, computer simulations, and mathematical gaming. One of the first operations research projects designed during World War II used reproduction models of fighter planes to determine why so many damaged planes did not return to base. It was determined through the plotting of actual hits on the models that the placement of fuel lines caused an inordinate number of planes to go down. In complex mathematical models, components of a system are assigned numbers or economic values and are related to each other through logic and probability formulas. The values are manipulated to determine the optimal solution of an operational problem. Included in the modeling of an operations research project is a process called *iteration*. Iteration involves the feedback of later stage findings to question the design and underlying assumptions of the original model. Models have been used in a wide range of public policy and political activities, including how to achieve optimal distribution of resources in a political campaign, how to redistrict school and Congressional districts, and how to optimize economic planning. The boundaries of modeling are usually defined by time and money. Since most organizations have a limit on both resources, modeling can usually provide only a partial picture of reality, but one which can improve the perception of it by decision makers. *See also* OPERATIONS RESEARCH, 62.

Significance Modeling in administrative processes is very different from modeling physical phenomena. The fact that a model can capture only a fraction of reality is even more true in the public sector, since measures of administrative effectiveness are difficult to define. A useful model requires a precisely formulated problem, an ability to assign numerical or economic values to it, and reliable sources of measurable data. None of these are easy to negotiate in public administration contexts. Modeling has been used successfully in military problem solving for over thirty years. Its utilization in public agencies started in the early 1970s, and courses in its techniques are steadily being added to public administration curricula. Modeling approaches are being introduced at state and local levels of government as well, with urban planning, for example, making good use of simulation and linear programming exercises. Modeling helps enhance the appreciation of decision makers for the scope of their decisions.

Monetarism (61)

An economic system based primarily on the operations of a free market and on the use of monetary policy by government to determine the money supply. Monetarists believe that the classical economists' ideas concerning the self-regulating and self-adjusting nature of the economy remain applicable to the complex economies of today's world. The key role for government is to determine the correct supply of money to be injected into the system. Too large a supply will create a runaway boom and great inflation, and too little will produce recessions or a depression. The correct amount will, according to the Monetarists, stimulate the private sector into healthy growth and continuing stability. Leading theorist and advocate of the Monetarist school is the Nobel-Prize-winning economist Milton Friedman of the University of Chicago. Monetarists are sometimes referred to as "Friedmanites" or members of the "Chicago school" of economic thought. *See also* FEDERAL RESERVE SYSTEM (FRS), 271; KEYNESIANISM, 57.

Significance Monetarism is a new conservatism that seeks to apply classical economic ideas to the contemporary world. Monetarist thought rejects the state interventionism and central planning advocated by Keynesian and neo-Keynesian schools of economic thought. If necessary, Monetarists are willing to sacrifice the goal of full employment in the interest of bringing inflation under control and keeping government's role limited. Price and wage controls are also considered unworkable, unable to bring inflation under control, and likely to have a deadly impact on the economy. In the late 1970s, Great Britain became one of the first nations to try to implement the ideas of Monetarism under the leadership of Prime Minister Margaret Thatcher. By 1981, some of the results of that experiment were disastrous, with double-digit inflation and the heaviest unemployment since the Great Depression plaguing the British economy. On the other hand, Monetarists point out that many of the economic troubles besetting Great Britain were the result of external factors not likely to be affected by the supply of money in the system. Moreover, they emphasized that it takes several years to wring inflation out of the system, and that for the first time in years the pound sterling had risen sharply in value against other major currencies. A final verdict on the effectiveness of Monetarism as a practical economic system remains to be handed down. Meanwhile, it has become a major political issue in Britain and in those other countries where leading electoral candidates advocate Monetarism as the only meaningful answer to the major inflation that has swept over much of the world.

Operations Research (62)

A technique of systems analysis used to identify efficient courses of action in a management system and to determine the impact of those and alternative courses of action as an aid to decision making. Operations research borrows methodologies from linear programming, program evaluation and review technique (PERT), game theory, queueing theory, and probability theory. Operations research got its start in Great Britain during the late 1930s. The British military establishment, like other large organizations, had experienced a great deal of technological advancement in the first thirty years of the twentieth century without much managerial experience to go along with it. The term *operations research* was first applied to the British effort to learn how to manage their newly developed radar system. The effort was successful enough that the concept of an operations research component was expanded to other projects and staffs in the military system. Operations research was used extensively throughout the British and U.S. military establishments during the 1940s for analysis of bombing strategies, submarine deployment, and other weapons systems analyses. After World War II, the United States Department of Defense continued to be the chief government promoter of operations research, although by the middle 1950s it was being taken seriously in U.S. private industry. The aspects of operations research that distinguish it from other management techniques are a strong systems orientation, the use of interdisciplinary teams, and the adaptation of scientific method to organizational constraints. As a systems analysis technique, operations research attempts to look at all the possible impacts of a problem on other operating components of the organization. Mathematical modeling is frequently used. This involves quantifying the variables of the problem, exploring its structure, and developing optimal solutions. Simulations are often used so that the real-life organizational system is not affected by problem-solving experiments. Examples of simulation in operations research are found in game theory and computer-based decision making. All operations research adaptations require mathematical applications of some sophistication, including the calculation of sequence, function, and probability. Operations research has been used since World War II in such public policy areas as school bus scheduling, land use, and urban planning. It has also been used in a number of client service, personnel, and finance areas. Queueing studies, for example, have been conducted to determine the best ways to move clients through a human services agency with the greatest amount of efficiency. In public personnel administration, operations research has analyzed absenteeism, turnover, and optimal staff mixes in an office. In finance and accounting operations, research has been used to design auditing procedures and to develop sampling procedures for finance control. *See also* GAME THEORY, 51; SIMULATION, 79; SYSTEMS ANALYSIS, 83.

Significance Operations research was one of the earliest forms of systems analysis. It is a form of "applied science" that makes it one of the social engineering fields. It has not been used extensively in the public sector because public goals are usually more difficult to measure and are less clear than in a private corporation. The outlook, however, is that as operations research techniques become more sophisticated there will be an increased utilization of them in public policy analysis. The primary criticism of operations research is that its methodology can become an end in itself and can mask faulty reasoning.

Organization Chart (63)
A tool used to illustrate formal organizational structure, including chain of command and communications flow. The organization chart is traditionally associated with classical organization theory because of its emphasis on structure, formal organization, and hierarchy. Use of organization charts by early classical theorists, such as Luther Gulick and Lyndall Urwick, was an attempt to establish and encourage strictly patterned interactions and accountability relationships among organizational components. Organization charts are still used by management as skeletal plans for implementing organizational objectives. They also provide a reference point from which reorganization can be planned. Charting is used not only to analyze the formal and informal structure of organizations, but to illustrate sociological interactions in groups, such as in the study of family or gang relationships. The drawing of an organization chart requires a two-dimensional representation using boxes to identify positions, connected by vertical lines to depict superior-subordinate relationships, and horizontal lines representing the interaction of equal positions. Most charts, however, are severely limited in their ability to depict *all* authority and transactional relationships. Chart representations usually distinguish between line authority positions and staff positions and are usually accompanied by position descriptions for the functions identified on the chart. When used to analyze organizational structures, the overall shape of the chart is significant. A *pyramid,* for example, represents an organization in which a level on the chart has fewer people than the level immediately below it, but more than the level immediately above it. The shape of the pyramid is an indicator of the span of control practiced and the degree of centralized authority present. A tall, narrow pyramid represents a narrow span of control and a centralized authority structure. A short, flat pyramid represents a broad span of control and more decentralized authority. Most modern organization charts resemble a *diamond* rather than a pyramid, with most positions in the central section of the diamond. Relative status and authority in an organization can be determined by the distance of a position from the top of the chart and the number of positions below that level. Relative status, however, as

indicated by the location on a chart, represents the *position* rather than the individual filling the position. The status of the individual is more a function of the *informal* organization, which cannot be portrayed on an organization chart. In addition to showing relative status, there is a sometimes invisible division on a chart that identifies two separate status groups. Examples of this kind of status schism are the line between management and labor or between officers and enlisted men. Organization structure research analyzes organization charts for indicators of organizational complexity and intraorganizational relationships, such as vertical differentiation, horizontal differentiation, and spatial dispersion. *See also* GROUP THEORY, 53; ORGANIZATION DEVELOPMENT (OD), 169; ORGANIZATION THEORY, CLASSICAL, 176.

Significance Organization charts, although familiar as modern management tools, are not a modern invention. A two-dimensional representation of formal organizational structure is an old concept that can be traced to records of ancient Chinese empires. Early references to organizational charts can also be found in the Bible. The Roman republic used elaborate organization charts and explicit qualifications for office, practices which had great impact on public administration throughout the Western world. Organization charts were also discussed in early industrial management writings. Entrepreneur Charles Babbage's nineteenth-century work on factory organization, for example, involved complex formal organization plans and contributed to the later development of scientific management principles. Since the two-dimensional organization chart is a static representation of dynamic relationships, each time a major reorganization, or sometimes even a relatively minor change, occurs, a new organization chart must be drawn. Formal structure is an important aspect of management planning, and it is necessary to understand organizational functions. But organization charts cannot identify *informal* leadership, *informal* group links, and the *informal* communication patterns that are frequently more important than formal relationships in understanding organizational transactions.

Participatory Democracy (64)
A general model for political, social, and economic decision making based on the assumption that decision-making processes are most effective under conditions of direct participation by those persons most affected by decision outcomes. Participatory democracy involves the deliberate, systematic mobilization of constituent groups around issues and problems of common concern, the organization of forums for the expression of alternate views on the issues, and the

Public Policy

implementation of decision-making procedures based on majority rule. Each member of the collectivity is allotted one vote, and, according to democratic voting procedure, the accumulation of votes on a given issue determines the policy outcomes with respect to that issue. Participatory democracy is often used in conjunction with the term "direct democracy." Direct democracy refers to a system of governance in which persons gather periodically and function as a legislative body in discussing and debating important issues by voting on these issues and, in so doing, establishing governmental policy. As a theoretical decision-making model, participatory democracy is distinct from two other more commonly recognized models—the power elite model and the pluralist model. In contrast to these models, both of which systematically remove persons from the means of political, economic, and social control, participatory democracy enables people to establish and maintain control through direct involvement. Under a pluralist system, citizen input into decision making is welcomed. Under participatory democracy it is expected and made possible. *See also* CITIZEN PARTICIPATION, 131; INTEREST-GROUP LIBERALISM, 56; PARTICIPATIVE MANAGEMENT, 110.

Significance Participatory democracy was first developed in the Greek city-states. The same idea was applied later in the Swiss cantons and in New England villages. In each of these contexts, public gatherings were held at regular intervals to make major policy decisions. More recently the term has been associated with a variety of grass-roots movements in the United States. During the late 1960s, radical groups pushed for participatory democracy as a cure to what they believed to be the unresponsiveness and repressiveness of traditional decision-making mechanisms. During this same period participatory democracy came to be associated with a number of federally sponsored social programs under the Office of Economic Opportunity Act of 1964. Under this act, a number of programs were instituted with the objectives of eliminating poverty and enabling the poor to gain control over decisions affecting their lives through direct participation in agency operations. Local agencies were required to recruit, train, and incorporate service recipients as program decision makers. They were thought to possess a unique perspective that should be recognized in program planning and administrative decision making. During this period the term "maximum feasible participation" evolved into a cornerstone principle of all programs associated with the War on Poverty. While the term participatory democracy is generally associated with various efforts to promote humanitarian values, it has been criticized as being impractical. Critics say that historically it has been used with small homogeneous collectivities, and that it has never proven successful with large and scattered heterogeneous groups. Critics also point to the lack of political interest and knowledge exhibited by the masses of people as evidence for the superiority of other decision-making models.

Planning (65)

Conceiving meaningful goals and developing alternative choices for future action to achieve these goals. Planning involves a systematic procedure for the reduction of many alternatives to an approved course of action. It determines not only goals but the sequential order in which they are pursued, the need for coordination, and the standards for maintaining control. Control is the instrument employed to assure that activities or events conform to plan. French administrator Henri Fayol (1841–1925) summarized the attributes of a good plan. (1) It is based on clearly defined objectives stated in a concise manner. (2) It covers all actions that are required for the plan to be fulfilled. (3) It is flexible so that it can be adjusted to meet unexpected conditions. (4) It contains contingency plans to cover areas that are most uncertain. (5) It allows for frequent feasibility checks. (6) It has been properly disseminated to all who are committed by the plan. (7) Resources made available match the tasks assigned. (8) It is reduced to writing. Planning is usually divided into *long-range planning* and *short-range planning*. Long-range planning is focused on such questions as: *What must we do?* This is the preparation of stated goals. *Where are we now?* This is an internal assessment of present operations and trends. *What are the alternatives open to us?* This is a review of the range of feasible operations for the agency. *How are others similarly situated?* This involves comparisons with alternative approaches to meet the problem. *Which course should we follow?* This is a decision to make a commitment of resources. *Who will do what, when?* This is a schedule of key events. *How will we know how well we are doing?* This is the arrangement for feedback and evaluation. Short-range planning is concerned predominantly with events occurring within a one-year time span or less and fits into the scope of long-range planning as a phase of its execution. The results of short-range planning tend to be translated into numerical goals. The most common short-range planning takes place in preparation of an annual budget. *See also* FAYOL, HENRI, 14; MANAGEMENT BY OBJECTIVES (MBO), 279; PLANNING, PROGRAMMING, BUDGETING SYSTEMS (PPBS), 283; PROGRAM EVALUATION AND REVIEW TECHNIQUE (PERT), 73.

Significance Planning is represented in public administration by a wide range of instrumentalities. Among these are planning, programming, budgeting systems (PPBS); management by objectives (MBO); program evaluation and review technique (PERT); and many others. These systems all indicate that there is a highly rational dimension to planning which begins once the goals for planning are articulated. Goals inevitably encompass value judgments. They are formed in the political process through compromise involving a multitude of interests. Planning can never be better than these compromised goals. Because goals are frequently ambiguous, incompletely formulated, or unclear, planning can only proceed within the constraints of complexity that characterize the goals themselves. Planning has therefore been described as "improvisation on a general theme." Another limitation of planning is that it looks into the future. Because no one can see the future with a crystal ball, the accuracy of planners' forecasts and the premises derived from them are sometimes lacking. Despite the limitations of planning, however, the planning process produces people better trained to imagine the unforeseen, to analyze the unpredicted, and to winnow out for decision makers the choices that would be too costly to postpone.

Pluralism (66)

A model of political decision making in which multiple and competing elites determine public policy through a process of bargaining and compromise. Pluralism posits that the best policy decisions emerge from clashes of interest groups in the political arena, where issues are freely and openly discussed, and where an overall balance of power is maintained. The roots of pluralism are in Aristotle's theory of balance, whereby justice and political stability require a representation of all the major groups of society sufficient to give each the confidence that its interests are protected against the possibility of abuse from the others. Pluralism as a political doctrine in the United States was first advanced by James Madison at the Constitutional Convention of 1787, and later elaborated in *The Federalist*, Number 10. In answering the charge of the aristocratic faction at the convention that a democratic government could open the door for oppression by the majority, Madison replied: "The only remedy is to . . . divide the community into so great a number of interests and parties, that in the first place a majority will not be likely at the same moment to have a common interest separate from that of the whole or of the minority; and in the second place, that in case they should have such an interest, they may not be apt to be united in the pursuit of it." Madison's *countervailing theory* assumes that interest groups counteract one another in such a way that no single interest or group of interests can become permanently dominant. Thus public policy in a pluralist democracy is not necessarily majority preference, but an equilibrium of interest interaction. Advocates of pluralism point out that three features of the American political system encourage the maintenance of equilibrium: (1) the separation of powers among the legislative, executive, and judicial branches; (2) federalism, or the separation of the national government from state and local governments; and (3) the widespread participation of individual citizens in voluntary associations. See also ELITE, 41; PLURALIZATION, 67.

Significance Pluralism is a pivotal concept in explaining decision making in heterogeneous societies such as the United States. Arthur F. Bentley wrote about it as early as 1902 in *The Process of Government,* and Mary Parker Follett followed suit in *The New State* (1921). More recent discussions of pluralism have been less sanguine about its serviceability for democracy, however. Sociologist C. Wright Mills wrote in *The Power Elite* (1956) that Madison's countervailing theory is no longer operative, that an *imbalance of power* has overtaken the U.S. system, and that in fact decision making is a highly centralized process in the hands of a few. Many critics of pluralism maintain that voluntary organizations that early theorists of pluralism relied upon to sustain the individual against a unified, omnipotent government have now become oligarchically governed hierarchies. The criticism of pluralism tends to converge around three themes. (1) The present system of government excludes some segments of society while favoring others. (2) Many issues are not brought to public attention because interest groups do not give them a high priority. (3) Concerns which might apply to large groups are not sharply defined in the bargaining process of seeking interest-group agreement.

Pluralization (67)
The process of creating new, distinct, but interdependent organizational units as a government response to social needs. Pluralization is a Small Business Administration (SBA) emerging to protect the small businessperson against giant corporations, or an Environmental Protection Agency (EPA) created to control sources of air and water pollution. If the need for these social services changes, however, the agencies continue to exist. With the help of interest groups and congressional leaders, they become social systems themselves, giving bureaucrats life economically, professionally, culturally, socially, and psychologically. According to William L. Morrow in *Public Administration: Politics, Policy, and the Political System* (1980), agency members acquire a sense of identity with their agency's mission, and in the case of high-prestige agencies, such as the Forest Service, the Bureau of

Standards, and the Foreign Service, members are deliberately conditioned to serve the agency's traditional goals. There is a social marriage between the career administrator and the agency. The pluralization process creates new agencies in the public interest, but the autonomy the agencies attain, and the jealousy with which they guard their jurisdictions, makes pluralization also responsible for a fragmented, atomized system of governance. The pluralization of administrative agencies is reflective of the pluralism in U.S. society as a whole. Pluralism refers to the existence of a mutual balance of power among religious, ethnic, economic, and geographical groups, with overlapping membership, all of which participate in policy making through mutual adjustment of conflicting goals within political arenas. Pluralism and pluralization are viewed by many public administration theorists not only as social and political facts, but as desirable goals. Multiple agencies, multiple groups, and multiple access mean that major social ills and grievances will work their way to decision-making arenas for action.

The virtues of pluralism were extolled by both James Madison and Alexis de Tocqueville as contributing to the stability of the social and political system. Historically, however, pluralization has produced elites. Wealthy, historically dominant, and leadership-rich groups traditionally have had more access to decision-making arenas and therefore more influence on public policy. In the public agencies that pluralism has established, advantaged corporate and military interests frequently render obsolete pluralism's assumed group equality. Whereas classical pluralism views administrators as objective arbiters of conflicting group demands, elitism encourages them to become spokespersons for, and clients of, the privileged few. However, the structured biases of older agencies are themselves continually under attack by the process of pluralization. New policy issues are frequently handled by creating new task forces, coordinating committees, boards, councils, departments, and offices—new organizations superimposed over existing ones—which increase the number of separated but functionally interdependent centers of decision. *See also* ADMINISTRATIVE THEORY, 5; SUBSYSTEM, 80.

Significance Pluralization has important consequences other than organizational sprawl. Two major implications for administrative behavior are (1) *Massive jurisdictional redundancy.* Agencies frequently duplicate work performed by others. (2) *Self-direction bureaucracies.* The organizational patchwork which pluralization has produced encourages agencies to go their separate ways, independent even of organizationally superior executives. The merit system and careerism accentuate this tendency because they reward specialization and increase the tenure and professionalization of the career bureaucracy. Aware that they will outserve their transient political superior, career civil servants see little advantage to pursuing, against their will, policy courses of temporary political superiors. Political scientist James David Barber has enumerated seventeen possible consequences of pluralization for government. Among the more salient of these for the theory and practice of public administration are (1) *Pluralization is self-reinforcing.* As each new organization is established in response to a policy problem, a new example is set for future institutional responses to policy problems. The need for more coordination among units increases with the number of units in need of coordination. New units seek to amplify their power through specialization, which, in turn, creates a need for more coordination. (2) *Pluralization increases the incidence of conflicts within the system, but decreases the intensity of these conflicts.* The number of conflicts is increased because the need to coordinate brings individuals and agencies with different goals into contact with each other, because communications between disparate units are often misinterpreted, and because of jurisdictional redundancy. Intensity of conflict is reduced because the number of disputations means agencies must cover themselves in all arenas of conflict. Agencies must economize their energies. (3) *Pluralization encourages governing units to stress interunit relations and coordination at the expense of substantive policy making and evaluation.* The proliferation of agencies concerned with a given program means that as many biases have to be placated as there are concerned agencies. Coordination and bargaining force compromises in the basic character of the legislation itself. Reaching an agreement becomes more important than the character of the agreement itself. Pluralization militates against the development of rational, comprehensive policies; against normative theory; and against the objectives of the new public administration. Pluralization celebrates the fragmentation of government.

Policy Analysis (68)

An attempt to measure organizational effectiveness through an examination and evaluation of the qualitative impact of an agency's program. Policy analysis is a systematic and data-based alternative to intuitive judgments about the effects of policy or policy options. It is used (1) for problem assessment and monitoring, (2) as a "before the fact" decision tool, and (3) for evaluation. As an assessment and monitoring device, policy analysis is usually a means of establishing benchmarks and critical indicators. Public health agencies, for example, monitor the incidence of particular diseases in a geographical region and set certain critical levels beyond which it is assumed that a disease has reached epidemic proportions, demanding a government policy response, such as warning the public to obtain flu shots. Statistics on the incidence of crime, numbers of mental patients, percentage of the population in poverty, literacy rates, and other social indicators inform policy makers about the vital signs of social well-being. As a "before the fact" decision tool, policy analysis includes such techniques as cost-benefit analysis, public choice modeling, operations research, simulation, gaming, and other techniques generally rooted in mathematics. As a means of evaluation, policy analysis frequently uses economic categories, which are particularly useful in determining the indirect or spillover impacts of policies. Direct economic effects are evaluated by measuring change for a group of people over time on a critical variable, such as employment, criminal behavior, or educational attainment. A job training program, for example, can be analyzed according to how many clients received employment after exposure to the program, if they received employment *because* of the program, and what the net improvement of their economic condition is. *See also* COST-BENEFIT ANALYSIS, 35; OPERATIONS RESEARCH, 62; PROGRAM EVALUATION, 72.

Significance The spread of policy analysis has served to encourage public officials to be more systematic in their efforts to ascertain the quality of public policy. Case studies have shown, however, that policy analysis has often been oversold. It has rarely if ever been responsible for radical change in the quality of policy making. The principal reason is lack of agreement about what constitutes "good" policy analysis. In the physical and social sciences, scientists share certain values and norms for good research, that is, that it should be generalizable, that it should be based on high-quality data measured precisely, that as much control should be exercised as possible, and that research should be integrated into well-developed theoretical explanations and scientific laws which have been advanced over the years. The parascience of policy analysis, on the other hand, has no paradigm. Standards and norms are not agreed on, findings are not as generalizable, data are often poor and unreliably measured, research is hard to control, and no well-developed body of policy theory serves as a source of insight and inspiration. In addition, policy analysis is frequently performed by a consultant or consulting organization from outside the agency being evaluated. The consultant is sometimes captive to the agency, has been chosen for the wrong reasons, or the public administrator is not able to understand the results of the policy analyst's work. Finally, there is the problem of limitations placed on satisfactory data collection by lack of resources. If an administrator has good reason to believe the benefits of an educational program for underprivileged preschool children will be realized gradually over twenty years, for example, the expense of long-range data gathering may constitute an insurmountable obstacle to proper analysis of the administrator's belief.

Political Economy (69)
A descriptive term emphasizing the role of government in all economic activities. The concept of political economy for several centuries linked production, trade, and finance on the one hand with governmental policies about fiscal, monetary, and commercial matters on the other. In the nineteenth century, however, scholars began to study and analyze economic factors and events apart from the role of government. Although the field of economics remains a separate discipline today, the factors that link economics and political science are more obvious and important than ever before. This linkage is the result of the increasingly complex involvement of government in the economic life of the nation.

Significance One of the main functions of every government is to create and sustain a viable national economy. Many nations, however, have vacillated between a governmentally dominated economic system and one that leans in the direction of laissez faire or limited governmental intervention. Critical in any system of political economy are the foreign trade and investment factors. A serious disequilibrium in a nation's balance of trade or overall balance of payments, for example, can result in severe political problems and governmental instability. Contemporary ideologies such as capitalism, socialism, and communism differ fundamentally about issues of political economy, focused in such areas as ownership of land and capital and the nature of the proper relationship between government and the economic system of a nation.

Politics-administration Dichotomy (70)
The view that public administration should be premised on a science of management and kept separate from traditional partisan politics and general policy making. The politics-administration dichotomy suggested to American readers by Woodrow Wilson in his 1887 essay "The Study of Administration" posits a major distinction

between politics and administration. Politics is the proper activity of legislative bodies and other policy-making groups. Administration is the proper activity of administrators, who carry out the policies stated in the laws of the jurisdiction or political unit. The context of the dichotomy was the reform movement of the 1880s, which had resulted in enactment of the Civil Service Act of 1883. Reformers, such as U.S. Senator George H. Pendleton, argued that public appointments should be based on fitness and merit rather than partisanship. Hence, "politics" was out of place in public service. The classic justification for the separation of policy and administration was made by Max Weber at the University of Munich in 1918. The essence of administration is to execute conscientiously the order of the political authority, he opined, even if it appears wrong to him. In the Weberian version of the politics-administration dichotomy, the administrator is impartial, passionless, and assumes no personal responsibility for policies executed. In modern life, the complexities of governmental operations have increasingly permitted and even required administrators to become involved in making "political" decisions, especially in the regulation of the private sector. *See also* APPLEBY, PAUL HENSON, 8; WEBER, MAX, 187; WILSON, WOODROW, 29.

Significance The politics-administration dichotomy was accepted somewhat uncritically in public administration until shortly before World War II. Wilson's theme fell on the fertile intellectual ground of the Progressive movement in the United States, and Weber's related ideas captured the authoritarian predisposition of the cameralist tradition in Europe, which was primarily concerned with developing administrative techniques for managing highly centralized states. The dichotomy broke down in the United States under the practical demands of loosely phrased laws which urged public administrators to carry out the public interest. Because much discretion was available to administrators, they, along with judges, became supplementary lawmakers. Paul H. Appleby observed in *Policy and Administration* (1949) that legislatures merely hold reserve powers to be invoked only if administrators violate the implied limits of their discretion. Administrators also blur the politics-administration distinction by formulating recommendations for legislation, by entering alliances with interest groups, and by withholding or giving only selected information to legislators. As early as 1930, Harold Lasswell, in *Psychopathology and Politics,* argued that the real significance of the dichotomy was that "the internal bureaucrat" who viewed his agency's goals through "psychological spectacles" was able on the basis of his "hidden agenda" to exercise power which was informal, unseen, and greatly underestimated by doctrinaire proponents of the dichotomy.

Privatization (71)
A policy whereby certain public service functions usually carried on by national, state, or local units of government are administered by the private sector. Privatization may involve either continued ownership of public facilities by the government, but with private sector management, or a transfer of ownership, as well as operation, from the public to the private sector. The theory underlying privatization holds that publicly owned enterprises are less efficient and less flexible than privately owned companies. Some cities have contracted with private companies to provide services such as street repair, park maintenance, janitorial work, security, and waste collection and disposal. The city of Phoenix has a unique policy of permitting private contractors to bid against city departments to provide municipal services at the lowest competitive cost. *See also* ENTERPRISE ZONE, 43; PUBLIC CHOICE ECONOMICS, 75; PUBLIC POLICY, 76.

Significance According to its supporters, privatization restrains the need for tax increases to provide subsidies for government enterprises. Privatization has become the buzz word used by those who support a reduction in government services and an expansion of private sector business opportunity. The movement was ushered in by President Ronald Reagan, whose policy it was to carry out a revolution in the size and scope of the operations of government. During his administration, numerous federal programs were sold to private owners, and many more—such as the Federal Housing Authority (FHA), the Bonneville Dam, Dulles National Airport, and weather satellites—were proposed for sale but rejected by Congress. The philosophy of privatization won many supporters on the state and local levels of government as well as on the federal level and internationally. In Great Britain, for example, the Conservative government sold several major government enterprises in an effort to balance the budget and stabilize the economy. Although privatization has many supporters, its critics argue that (1) private operations are not necessarily more flexible and efficient than governmental operations; (2) while tax burdens may be somewhat decreased, consumers of the services eventually pay more to support the profit structure; (3) sale of government enterprises provides only a temporary fix for budget problems; and (4) privatization gives private interests unprecedented political and institutional power in areas where only democratic government should legitimately exercise responsibility.

Program Evaluation (72)

An assessment of the effectiveness of a program through the application of a research design aimed at obtaining valid and verifiable information on the structure, processes, outputs, and impacts of the program. Program evaluation is an effort to help decision makers determine whether to maintain, modify, or discontinue a specified program. Program evaluation is concerned with whether program activities have been successful in resolving the public problem identified, and the extent to which other factors may have contributed to the problem's resolution. If the problem would have gone away on its own, the program's worth may be questionable. There are three phases in program evaluation. (1) *Selection and identification of the goals and objectives of the program.* This is not always easy, since legislation and agency goals are often either vague or general. Without precise goals there can be no standard against which to measure a program's success. (2) *Execution of the evaluation according to scientific guidelines.* Involved in phase two are the study design, sample selection, measuring devices, and validated statistical methodology. The task of analyzing statistical data is value laden in itself and can greatly affect the outcome of the evaluation. (3) *Feedback of results and recommendations.* Phase three provides management with the findings of the evaluation for the purpose of modifying operations and planning for future programs. Among the most common ways to approach the evaluation of an ongoing program are to estimate (1) the performance effort, or the quality and quantity of the work being done; (2) the effectiveness, or the results of the work, including relative effectiveness of different strategies within the program; (3) the efficiency, including cost effectiveness and whether the same result could have been achieved at a lower cost by using alternate methods; (4) the impact, or the degree to which the program meets stated objectives; and (5) the process, to determine if current strategies are adequate to achieve the stated objectives. Program evaluation projects have been used for reasons other than a pure interest in the effectiveness of a program. They can be used to endorse a program, to lay blame for failures, or to bring about a reorganization or change in leadership. The initiation of program evaluation can come from within the evaluated organization to attract favorable attention in order to obtain a bigger budget or to secure a

The Public Administration Dictionary

promotion for a successful administrator. *See also* ACCOUNTABILITY, 85; COST-BENEFIT ANALYSIS, 35.

Significance Program evaluation developed in the 1970s as part of an increasing congressional and executive branch commitment to the comprehensive analysis of public programs at all levels of government. Evaluation activities at the federal level can be found in congressional budgetary deliberations, General Accounting Office (GAO) audits, and Office of Management and Budget (OMB) reviews. Requirements for self-evaluation or provisions for scheduled evaluations were included in many laws of the 1970s, such as the enabling statute of the Office of Economic Opportunity. In 1974 the Office of Management and Budget created the Evaluation and Program Implementation Division, which was specifically designed to evaluate federal domestic programs. State and local evaluation programs also began in the 1970s, and several states now have program evaluation departments. The use of evaluation mechanisms is an important tool in determining the health of public programs. Government has no profit line to report, by which it can justify continued support by taxpayers. Instead, it must demonstrate efficiency and effectiveness in the use of increasingly limited resources.

Program Evaluation and Review Technique (73) (PERT)

A systems analysis and scheduling plan that specifies for the administrator how various parts of a project interrelate, especially what parts of the project must be completed before the remaining parts can be started. PERT was developed in the late 1950s by Booz, Allen, and Hamilton, a consulting firm employed by the United States Navy to assist in the complex task of constructing the Polaris missile system. PERT made it possible for the system to be completed two years ahead of schedule. The program evaluation and review technique is represented by a PERT *chart,* which depicts in network-analysis form the points and paths that must exist to get all the parts of a project to occur. The steps involved in constructing a PERT chart are (1) identification of all activities necessary to complete the project; (2) arrangement of these activities in the most opportune order with respect to the time each requires and the sequence in which the activities occur; (3) charting itself to determine and show in months, weeks, days, and hours the time each task will require; and (4) rearrangement or reorganization of any activities that may streamline the tasks. For each time period, three estimates are given along with the associated cost: the optimistic completion time, the most likely completion time, and the pessimistic completion time. The formula for determining activity time is as follows:

O = optimistic completion time
M = most likely likely completion time
P = pessimistic completion time

$$\frac{O + 4M + P}{6} = \text{activity time}$$

PERT is thus an attempt to quantify program planning and control. It differs from other planning systems in that it seeks to systematize and mechanize the planning and control process by using computers and network flow plans. The flow plan is the fundamental tool used in the PERT approach, because once the schedule is created, continuing review by managers assures that actual progress conforms to planned accomplishment. Managers can intervene at appropriate times to correct deviation from planned objectives. In those cases where corrective action cannot put the project back on course, the whole time schedule must be recomputed. *See also* COMPUTER, 33; MANAGEMENT BY OBJECTIVES (MBO), 279; PLANNING, 65.

Significance Program evaluation and review technique (PERT) has been implemented by almost all federal government research and development agencies. It is used by all United States military services, the National Aeronautics and Space Administration (NASA), the Federal Aviation Agency (FAA), the Nuclear Regulatory Commission (NRC), and the Office of Management and Budget (OMB). The Soviet government uses a variant of PERT for developing its five-year economic plans. As a management tool, PERT forces managers to focus attention on planning control and coordination. It facilitates conversation and cooperation between lower and upper level administrators because it emphasizes a bottom-up approach. The people who will eventually have to implement the plan are the ones responsible for putting the time estimates and schedules together. PERT is a catalyst for creating an atmosphere of teamwork and communication, commitment, and intelligent planning. PERT is not an advisable approach for mass production systems except in their design and development stages. Once an assembly line is set up and functioning, it would be expensive and wasteful to monitor repetitious production by network analysis. But for single-use plans or one-time events, PERT has not been equaled as a planning and monitoring system since its widespread application in the early 1960s.

Proposition 13 (74)

A 1978 California initiative constitutionally limiting taxation on real estate, which passed by a two to one vote. Proposition 13 placed a taxation ceiling of 1 percent of a property's 1975–1976 assessed value, held assessment increases to 2 percent a year, and restricted the state legislature's ability to increase other taxes by requiring a two-thirds vote on any new taxes. Proposition 13, also known as the Jarvis-Gann amendment to the state constitution, effectively reduced property tax revenues in the state of California by $7 billion. The reasons for Proposition 13's overwhelming voter approval can be traced to the nature of California's real estate market. Real estate speculation, along with a severe housing shortage in the state, inflated home prices far beyond the national average. If a house were sold, every other house in the neighborhood had to be reassessed according to new, higher market values. The initiative campaign was bolstered by the optimistic predictions of Nobel Prize–winning economist Milton Friedman and University of Southern California economics professor Arthur Laffer, a leading exponent of the tax-cut theory of economy stimulation. Legal challenges to Proposition 13 were rejected by the California Supreme Court in September 1978. While the state constitution stipulates that an initiative may contain only one subject, and Proposition 13 clearly violated that by calling for a tax limitation and requiring a two-thirds vote to pass new taxes, the court declined to oppose a constitutional provision that had received a two to one voter mandate. *See also* CUTBACK MANAGEMENT, 91; ZERO-BASE BUDGETING (ZBB), 291.

Significance Proposition 13 and its broad-based support raised a fundamental question about the function of taxation in a democratic society. Since the Progressive and New Deal eras of U.S. history, the economic system used taxation as a means to fulfill the promise of equal opportunity for all citizens. Everyone, through government programs, assumed some responsibility for the welfare of everyone else. If the California "taxpayer revolt" becomes a way of life in the United States, all levels of government face the predicament of how to deliver a variety of services. If traditional revenue sources are limited and fixed, either new revenue sources must be found, or services must be cut back. Municipalities in this situation have frequently resorted to "user fees," that is, the charging of fees sizable enough to provide the basic financial support to keep needed services in operation.

However, in its first two years of application, Proposition 13 did not cause the major cutbacks in government services that were predicted. One UCLA study had said that 450,000 jobs would be lost if the initiative passed. Surplus funds from the state treasury were able to provide $4.2 billion in aid to local governments, and 500,000 new jobs were created, enough to absorb the 102,000 which were eliminated from the public payrolls. The new jobs were the result of a healthy economy spurred by the $7 billion Proposition 13 cuts, and a $1 billion cut in the state income tax pushed through in its wake. Professor Laffer may have been right for California, but not all state economies have California's characteristics. Proposition 13 has been called zero-base budgeting in extremis.

Public Choice Economics (75)

The view that public agencies should compete to provide citizens with goods and services instead of acting as monopolies under the influence of organized pressure groups. Public choice economics argues that under the current administrative system public agencies are institutionally incapable of representing the demands of individual citizens. Since the citizen is a *consumer* of government goods and services, administrative responsiveness to individual citizen demands would be increased by creating a market system for governmental activities based on microeconomic theory. In this market system the citizen-consumer would be given a *choice*, as in free-enterprise economics, between competing services. Public choice economics is illustrated by two typical proposals discussed by Howard E. McCurdy in *Public Administration: A Synthesis* (1977): the voucher system and the Lakewood plan. The *voucher system* is based on the contention that public primary and secondary education in the United States is characteristically monopolistic. The consumer receives education through a plant that serves its own monopoly clientele. All schools within a district are virtually identical. They are administered by a central bureaucracy which is controlled by professional educators who have a stake in maintaining a large, uniform system that promotes their interests. Most school systems, therefore, grow inflexible and are not responsive to new or diverse demands. The solution to such a situation for public choice economists is to give parents vouchers worth a certain amount of education. The student, in conjunction with his or her parents, would select the school he or she wishes to attend. The school would exchange the vouchers it collected from parents for the public funds it needed to finance its operations. The consumers of education would select those schools that most effectively responded to the public's needs, and the others would wither away. The *Lakewood plan* is based on the experience of a small residential community adjoining Long Beach, California. Rather than allow themselves to be annexed by the city of Long Beach and swallowed up by the Long Beach bureaucracy, the residents of Lakewood incorporated and hired ten employees. Instead of creating municipal departments, they purchased all of their services from other governments and contractors in the greater Los Angeles area. Lakewood became the first complete "contract city" in the United States. Public choice economists point out that the success of the experiment was based on the fact that the city officials who represented the residents were completely separated from the officials who produced the services to satisfy local demands. Lakewood officials were in a position to bargain over the provision of municipal services. They encouraged neighboring cities, the county of Los Angeles, special districts, and private vendors to compete with each other by submitting competitive bids to provide alternative services. Public choice economics seeks to provide bureaucrats with a new set of incentives to produce better public goods and services. *See also* CUTBACK MANAGEMENT, 91; PLURALIZATION, 67; PROPOSITION 13, 74.

Significance   Public choice economics challenges the validity of the assumptions on which government is based. Modern government is run under the assumption that groups are good. In this view individuals join groups to further their common interests. This was also John Locke's assumption as he formulated the concept of the social contract, an unspoken agreement which brings civilized people together to draft constitutions and form governments. The assumption is crucial to the theory of democratic pluralism, outlined by public administrationist Paul Appleby, who viewed the public interest as a product of the activity of organized groups. Management scientist Chester Barnard used the assumption of group cooperation to help formulate the foundations of modern organization theory. In the face of these doctrines of pluralist faith, public choice economics refuses to view government as a gargantuan voluntary association. Despite the logic of its position, the programs of public choice economics never caught on. The voucher system was tested, for example, but was discarded under bureaucratic and political pressure. The central question of public choice economics remains unanswered. How can the preferences of individual citizens be maximized in a government where bureaucratic forms are dominant?

Public Policy (76)
Strategic use of resources to alleviate national problems or governmental concerns. Public policy takes four forms. *Regulatory policy* relies on deterrents such as fines and incarceration to enforce compliance with prevailing standards of conduct. It maintains equitable access to public necessities, such as air and water, and protects the health and safety of individual citizens. The primary tools of regulatory public policy are rulemaking, in which laws are clarified, law enforcement, and adjudication. Examples of public agencies charged with implementing regulatory policies are the Food and Drug Administration (FDA), the Federal Bureau of Investigation (FBI), and the Federal Communications Commission (FCC). Because of its watchdog function, regulatory policy suffers from low clientele support.

Redistributive policy reflects the Robin Hood motif: take from the rich and give to the poor. In practice, however, redistributive public policy may tax lower and middle income earners more heavily than it does the wealthy, as in the case of social security. Through redistributive policy, government tackles the problem of meeting the minimal physical needs of its citizens. The primary means used to achieve this end are *taxes* channeled into various public assistance programs. Redistributive policy generally enjoys strong clientele support, but is frequently jeopardized by partisan political considerations.

Distributive policy focuses on governmental concern for equal access to resources. This classification covers such diverse public programs as national parks, which ensure that all citizens have an opportunity to appreciate national physical resources; government subsidized research, which makes available to small businesses and the general public intellectual resources which otherwise would be accessible only to large corporations with capital outlays for research; and distribution of financial assets through direct subsidies and insurance. Since distributive public policy benefits individual citizens, it receives strong clientele support. It allows individuals to decide whether to take advantage of particular benefits.

Constituent policy serves the nation as a whole by protecting national security and by meeting the operating needs of governmental agencies, such as minting money and hiring personnel. The tools of constituent policy are knowledge and technical expertise. It does not focus on specific individuals or organizations, but uses its power and resources to alter the total environment. The impersonal aspect of constituent policy does not encourage clientele support, which would not be an asset to constituent policy anyway. Constituent policy avoids ties with special interests, and ideally is detached, neutral, and technical, arising from knowledge rather than in response to clientele interests. *See also* DECISION MAKING, 92–95; POLICY ANALYSIS, 68.

Significance Public policy allows government to assume a parent's role in citizens' lives. It provides opportunities; it guards one's physical well-being and safety; it provides financial security; and it maintains the security of one's homeland. Citizens take sanctuary in this security while chafing at the constraints it places on personal freedom. But unlike the child come of age in the child-parent analogy, the individual citizen or the small business cannot go forth into the world—a world of corporate power—and compete on an equal footing. Public policy also means, therefore, continuing intervention by government on behalf of the powerless to allow them to hold their own and to assure balanced participation in government.

Responsible Party System (77)

A system in which political parties enunciate clear policy goals among which the electorate may choose, with confidence the majority party will attempt to implement these policies while in office. A responsible party system theoretically bridges the gap between the people and the complex policy requirements of modern government. Since U.S. politics is decentralized and complex issues are difficult for individual citizens to understand, they often feel no sense of power in relation to government. People tend to vote without comprehension of policy, and politicians, in turn, feel no obligation to implement policies mandated by the public. In the responsible party system model, based on the British system, voters choose between candidates representing policies that are made clear to the public during the campaign. The party receiving the majority of votes becomes the government, which the bureaucracy functions to serve, while the minority party serves as critic. The party continues to be directly responsible to the people. The responsible party system must (1) evolve and enunciate a reasonably explicit statement of party programs and principles; (2) nominate candidates loyal to the party program; (3) conduct its electoral campaigns in such a way that voters will grasp the programmatic differences between the parties and make voting decisions on that basis; and (4) guarantee that public office holders elected under the party label will carry the party program into programmatic activity, thus enabling the party to take responsibility for its actions.

Significance The responsible party system has been the subject of continuing debate in American political science since the 1950s when the *Report of the Committee on Political Parties of the American Political Science Association (CPP)* advanced the views of those who were critical of the present diffused party system. The reform goals of the CPP stressed the "strengthening of political control over Congress and the bureaucracy by the President, acting through the medium of the party." The president would be the representative of the majority and would work with the congressmen of his party to convert his electoral mandate into legislation. This system would, of course, require a strengthening of, and cooperation between, the state and national party networks. Among the problems of the responsible party system idea are the relationships between *party* leadership and *government* leadership. Those relationships need to be carefully delineated. There is also a fear that identification with parties on the basis of issues alone could lead to extremism. And amidst the diversity of American society, who is going to formulate the policy on which the parties base their platforms? Similarly, a party system must fit into the structure of the society in which it exists. Either basic structural changes would have to be made in American society, because it is so stratified, or the responsible party system model itself would have to undergo some alteration. It is clear that the U.S. government needs a better way of translating policy concerns into legislation. It is also clear the nation needs a greater sense of cohesion than the present political system affords. The system does not pull people together, but rather increases their feelings of distrust and alienation. The responsible party system is one way of addressing this increasingly serious problem.

Robotics (78)

The study and development of applications for robots. According to the Robot Institute of America, a robot is "a programmable multifunctional manipulator designed to move material, parts, tools, or other specialized devices through variable programmed motions for the performance of a variety of tasks." The key words in the definition are *programmable* and *multi-functional.* Unlike conventional automated equipment that performs the same activity over and over again, robots can repetitively perform the same task on identical workpieces, perform different tasks on the same workpieces, or be reprogrammed to perform entirely different tasks. The term *robot* became popular after the success of Karl Capek's play *R.U.R. (Rossum's Universal Robot)* in 1923. *Robot* comes from the Czechoslovakian word, *robota,* meaning servitude or forced labor. In the play, a robot was "a zombie-like device, a mute but capable servant." The term robotics was coined by Isaac Asimov in 1942.

Significance Robotics has the potential to revolutionize the world. It remains to be seen, however, whether the revolution will actually take place. What industrial robots are able to do is determined by both their hardware and their software, and the purpose to be served decides which available hardware and software will be employed. In theory, robots can be designed as general purpose machines, but in reality they are built to perform restricted classes of tasks. Personal robots were first introduced to the market in 1983. The first commercial home robot was the HERO-1, produced by the Heath Company of Benton Harbor, Michigan. Despite the extensive use of robots in automobile production, especially in welding and spray painting, the world's leading maker of robots, Unimation, had fallen on hard times by late 1986. Financial analysts have estimated that sales will increase by only 5 percent in the robotics industry as a whole for the foreseeable future. The main reason for the slowdown is the expense of developing the complex software needed to allow robots to communicate with other machines in the factories in which they are employed. If and when the software becomes available, particularly in electronic applications, the incipient revolution will resume. Meanwhile, job displacement has been forestalled. In 1987, a General Motors plant in Lake Orion, Michigan, replaced twelve robot painters with hourly workers using spray guns.

Simulation (79)

The imitative representation of the functioning of an actual system or process gained by observing the functioning of another, or the process of obtaining the essential qualities of reality by studying a hypothetical situation. Simulation is an attempt to construct a situation that illustrates a procedure or practice in a realistic manner and teaches or emphasizes a lesson at the same time. Simulation is similar to scientific experimentation in its methodology. In the physical sciences, experiments are performed in the laboratory using small models of a process or an operation. Complex variations are possible in these tests, and the results obtained indicate what happened under certain controlled conditions. In the social sciences, the underlying concepts of a social situation are drawn from reality or fact. From these concepts, theories are developed to focus on some part of the complex whole. Models are then conceived or built in order to test or represent the theories. The practical use of the models in attempting to identify and/or reflect the behavior of a real process or system is simulation. In public administration, managers are able to evaluate proposed projects or strategies by constructing theoretical models. They can determine what happens to these models when certain

Public Policy

assumptions are tested. Simulation is thus trial-and-error problem solving. It is also a planning aid of considerable value. The use of simulation ranges from simple "in-basket" exercises, used in personnel testing and training, to complex simulations of space vehicles for the preparation of space travel. Highly sophisticated computer simulations are used by policy analysts and planners to determine defense strategies and cost-benefit ratios for social programs. *See also* GAME THEORY, 51; SYSTEMS ANALYSIS, 83.

Significance Simulation models are a major tool for the modern public manager. They are applied in environmental planning, for example, to analyze existing river and lake conditions and to determine the cause-and-effect relationships of water pollution practices. Computer simulated models are used to help planners find answers to sewage disposal problems and the effects of waste on aquatic life. In military planning, computer-based simulation makes "war games" possible, to give military officers experience in decision making. In the area of social welfare, simulation models have been developed to estimate the effects of housing developments on juvenile delinquency. Such models give statistical evidence about what happens to juvenile delinquency when more public housing is built, or when certain units of social programs are implemented. In urban planning, simulation models are applied to help solve traffic congestion problems and to study traffic flow patterns. They take such factors as travel modes and routes traveled and estimate the variables of travel time, cost, and convenience. Simulation is also used to plan new roads and the efficient use of existing roads, while simultaneously taking into consideration competing community needs for recreation, housing, and other land-use projects.

Subsystem (80)

Any political alliance uniting some members of an administrative agency, a congressional committee or subcommittee, and an interest group with shared values and preferences in the same substantive area of public policy making. Subsystems are informal alliances or coalitions that link individuals in different parts of the formal policy structure. Their members have influence in the policy-making process because of their formal or official positions—bureau chief, committee or subcommittee chairman, or member. The essential strength of a subsystem is its ability to combine the benefits of bureaucratic expertise, Congressional leverage, and interest-group capabilities in organizing and communicating to the government the opinions of those most concerned with a particular public issue. Subsystem activity tends to be behind the scenes. Bureaucrats derive considerable benefit from subsystem arrangements, because they can count on political support from within government (i.e., Congress) and from without (i.e., interest groups). The three-sided relationship allows any one component of the subsystem to activate a joint effort toward common objectives, with the willing cooperation of the others. Unless challenged from outside—by other subsystems or adverse publicity, for example—a subsystem can dominate a policy-making area. Policy is made in a spirit of friendly, quiet cooperation among various influencial people. A subsystem depends on a larger political entity, but in actuality it functions with a high degree of autonomy. *See also* BUREAUCRATIC EXPERTISE, 128; INTEREST-GROUP LIBERALISM, 56.

Significance A subsystem is illustrated by the so-called military-industrial complex, composed of a minimum of civilian and military personnel in the Pentagon bureaucracy, key members of the House and Senate Armed Services Committees and each chamber's Appropriations Subcommittee on armed services, and major government contractors for military hardware. The presence in this subsystem of large industries supplying military equipment expands the number of affiliated legislators. By being located in New York state, for example, Grumman Aircraft can influence the votes of New York's congressional delegation. Boeing Aircraft can do the same in Washington state, where one of Washington's two United States Senators is jokingly called "the Senator from Boeing." McDonnell-Douglas Aircraft can influence congressional votes from Missouri, and Lockheed Aircraft can frequently deliver key congressmen from Georgia. There is also a highway subsystem composed of members of the House Public Works and Transportation Committee, officials of the Bureau of Public Roads, and powerful interest groups such as automobile manufacturers, automobile workers' unions, tire companies and their unions, road contractors and their unions, and oil companies and their unions. This subsystem has a common interest in maintaining and expanding automobile and highway usage. Congress has thus given ground very reluctantly on expansion of mass transit funding. A powerful subsystem can generally be successfully challenged only by another powerful subsystem. An example of this is the tobacco subsystem, which for years resisted all efforts to limit or regulate the sale of cigarettes and other tobacco products. Since tobacco is largely a southern crop, and congressional committee chairmen, including the chairman of the House Agriculture Committee, were disproportionately from the South because of the seniority system, it took a system with principal strength elsewhere finally to regulate tobacco. That subsystem was the United States Public Health Service, the Federal Trade Commission (FTC), and their allies. Thus, a subsystem is a pooling of political resources to achieve a purpose common to each ally.

Sunset Legislation (81)
A termination mechanism by which legislatures periodically reexamine designated programs and agencies of government to determine whether they should be continued or permitted to die. Sunset legislation requires the reauthorization of funded programs and agencies, or they go out of existence. The sun sets on them. A common form of sunset law establishes a timetable for review of a group of programs, agencies, or laws. These automatically terminate on established dates unless recreated by statute. The threat of termination forces evaluation. Sunset legislation is seen as an effective means of eliminating unnecessary spending and of imposing discipline on the legislature to exercise real, rather than perfunctory, oversight of administrative agencies. The purpose of sunset legislation is the same as that of zero-base budgeting: to have agencies justify their existence and defend each of their programs—old, new, and proposed. *See also* LEGISLATIVE OVERSIGHT, 105; PROGRAM EVALUATION, 72; ZERO-BASE BUDGETING (ZBB), 291.

Significance Sunset legislation attempts to arrest the tendency of agencies to proliferate and perpetuate themselves. Although legislatures already have the power to dismantle agencies and terminate their programs, they have tended to neglect the legislative oversight function in the past. Evaluation is a difficult, time-consuming task which is easy to put aside. Legislatures are typically looking to the future. Sunset legislation takes each of these tendencies into account by automatically changing the status quo instead of continuing it. Sunset is viewed by its proponents as a partnership between the legislative and executive branches to make government work. Evaluation is considered by them to be the key to increased accountability. In an era of scarcity, accountability is a priority responsibility of government. Sunset is seen by its opponents, however, as a tool for those who would destroy government and its services. Such legislation, they charge, can be used to manipulate as well as placate the public. The first sunset law was passed in Colorado in 1976. Florida has also adopted the sunset mechanism.

Supply Side Economics (82)

A body of economic theory that calls for a macroeconomic approach to the allocation of the nation's resources and emphasizes the role played by business and industry in making allocation decisions. Supply siders believe that policies insuring favorable treatment for business and industry will likely benefit the entire economy by reducing unemployment, controlling inflation, and stimulating economic growth. Supply side ideas originated with Jean Baptiste Say, a French economist, who argued that the goal of government should not be to encourage consumption but to stimulate production. Supply side economic theory holds that the primary role of government should be to remove impediments to the effective use of the implements of production—land, labor, and capital. The applications of the theory include removing disincentives to work and investment, reducing taxes, and encouraging competition in labor and product markets. *See also* KEYNESIANISM, 57; MONETARISM, 61.

Significance During the 1980s, supply side economics was often referred to as "Reaganomics." Conservatives generally applaud supply side policies whereas liberals question both their utility and their fairness. In practice, the supply side approach represents a return to classical economics with roots that go back to Adam Smith and his celebrated treatise, *Wealth of Nations* (1776). Contemporary economists often call supply side economics the new classical macroeconomics. Opponents, however, refer to it as the "trickle-down theory" by which government policies enrich business and industry and are justified on the assumption that some of the financial largess produced will in time trickle down to the masses of consumers.

Systems Analysis (83)

A quantitative approach to problem solving using analytical methods to identify alternative solutions. Systems analysis methods yield a specified degree of effectiveness for the least cost or the greatest effectiveness for a given cost. Systems analysis, sometimes called systems theory, is a way of dealing with the basic economic problem of how best to use limited resources. It develops information that will help the policy maker select the preferred way of achieving a stated objective. It defines alternative ways of achieving the objective, and it estimates in quantitative terms the benefits to be derived from and the cost of each alternative. Aspects of the problem which cannot easily be quantified are explicitly stated. Systems analysis is frequently aided by large-scale computer simulations. The computer enables the systems analyst to examine a much larger number of alternatives in a shorter period of time than would otherwise be possible. But systems analysts view the computer as a mechanical aid in their work and not as the substance of their work. Systems analysis is accomplished by the following steps: (1) defining the problem and the goal, including correct diagnosis of what the problem is by asking the right questions; (2) designating the criteria and constraints within which an acceptable solution lies, including the vectors of ethics, legality, the attitude of others, resources, and time; (3) searching for and measuring alternative solutions, including processes of intuitive brainstorming, use of the computer, the decision tree, and cost-benefit analysis; (4) deciding, including a review of priorities, and the policy maker's estimate of the consequences of the decision; (5) putting the decision into effect in the form of task assignments, the specification of resources, and a time frame; and (6) providing feedback, which measures compliance with the decision. *See also* COST-BENEFIT ANALYSIS, 35; DECISION TREE, 36; SIMULATION, 79.

Significance Systems analysis is a unique combination of selected principles of economics, engineering, mathematics, physics, psychology, and political science. It is an attempt to apply the scientific method to public problem solving. Its chief proponents, among them economist Alain C. Enthoven, describe systems analysis not as a science, however, but as an art. Like the art of medicine, it uses a method that is open, explicit, verifiable, and self-correcting. It combines logic and empirical evidence; yet the governmental applications of systems analysis in the Defense Department of the 1960s leave its usefulness in some question. The first step in the systems analysis process, for example, is to define the problem to be solved. If the wrong questions are asked, and if the problem is ill-defined or misperceived, the analysis that follows will merely compound the error of perception. The original wrong question in Vietnam, for example, was "How do we help the French retain their empire?" The right question was: "Is the French position in Southeast Asia proper and defensible?" In goal setting, systems analysis is most helpful when goals can be defined with quantitative precision as: "We desire to reduce traffic fatalities per million passenger miles by 3 percent in the next two years." The goal then lends itself to a cost-benefit table, in which programs for reducing automobile fatalities might be weighed. The following programs could be appraised: (1) compulsory drivers' education; (2) better highway design; (3) more traffic officers; (4) mandatory seat belts; and (5) stiffer penalties for violaters. Because the cost-benefit ratio for the seat belt option is probably more attractive than the others, the systems analyst would be likely to make that decision. The statistics gathered for a cost-benefit table do not replace the policy maker's sense of nuance and feel, however. "Feel" may tell him or her that everything cannot be quantified and that, despite the cost, some "dead man's curves" need to be straightened out in the highway system, or the budget priorities must be adjusted to pay salaries for additional traffic officers. Such a decision might also reflect the public's apathy and dislike for compulsory seat belt laws.

Systems Theory (84)

An effort to generalize about *all* organizations, public and private, large and small, drawing on analogies to physical and biological phenomena. Systems theory posits either a *closed* or an *open* system. A closed-system theorist says an organization is analogous to a physical system, such as a machine, whose operation is substantially unaffected by its environment. An open-system theorist says an organization is like a biological organism. It exchanges with its environment as an animal or a plant does. Systems theory is fascinated with nature's processes, particularly with the way nature mechanically and homeostatically restores equilibrium to elements out of synchronization. Systems theory models tend to have a conservative bias, making them static, rather than dynamic, models. Organizational theorists who use the systems approach usually treat an organization as an open system, one that interacts with its environment. The essential parts of an organization or administrative system in this view are *inputs, throughputs, outputs,* and *feedback.* Inputs are interactions in the system emanating from the environment, such as the energies of employees. Throughputs are the transformation of environmental factors such as supplies into outputs. Outputs are interactions initiated by the system, such as products or services. Feedback can flag the system's output mistakes so they can be corrected at the input stage. The input-output distinction is the key to understanding systems theory as it is applied to classical administrative and bureaucratic theories. Both systems and organizations must have boundaries so that one can tell what is within the system or organization and what is outside it. The systems theorist needs to identify inputs to the system from the environment and the system's outputs to the environment, and these transactions occur at the system's boundaries. A public agency must know its boundaries too—in the form of its jurisdiction and purpose. Many public agencies do not have precise boundaries. The Department of Agriculture, for example, is allowed far less autonomy than a corporation might have because of its complex legal, political, and organizational environment. Yet the Department of Agriculture does have a distinctive identity within the executive branch, resting on its core of concerns, if not on the sharpness of its boundaries. Systems theory provides a "cognitive map" for researchers, reminding them of classes of variables which are significant and analytical postures which might be useful. *See also* ORGANIZATIONAL THEORY, CLASSICAL, 176; POLICY ANALYSIS, 68; SYSTEMS ANALYSIS, 83.

Significance Systems theory has a good deal in common with classical organization theory. The latter proposed that the executive branch *should* be organized at the top by major function. Systems theory goes further by asserting that every organizational system *has* a purpose, goal, or objective. Systems theory, therefore, carries the public administrationist beyond the pluralist view that a system's objective is simply to survive. Long life is not necessarily the measure of a system's success. Unlike most biological organisms, but like humans as moral beings, an organizational system seeks to serve a purpose beyond itself, even if the pursuit or achievement of that purpose may lead to the organization's death. The public agency's purpose may be elusive, or it may have several purposes. The *purposes* of the Department of Agriculture, for example, are to advocate the American farmer's interests *and* to assure that the agricultural sector contributes to the stability and growth of the national economy and serves consumer needs. The Department of Agriculture serves the interests of large-scale, commercial farm corporations *and* reduces the poverty of small-scale farmers and migratory farm workers. Congress has assigned the department a multiplicity of purposes, which are often at odds with one another. The Department of Agriculture operates in a *field of activity*, therefore, which has imprecise boundaries, just as national defense, transportation, and public health have imprecise boundaries. The requirement of systems theory that every organization have exactly described boundaries and purposes must be relaxed for governmental agencies.

3. Public Management

Accountability (85)

A condition in which individuals who exercise power are constrained by external means and by internal norms. When defined in traditional, legal, or formal terms, accountability refers to the institution of checks and balances in an administrative system. In its external sense, accountability means being held to account for stewardship of resources or authority. Administrators have various kinds of accountability, including (1) *fiscal accountability*—responsibility for public funds; (2) *legal accountability*—responsibility for obeying laws; (3) *program accountability*—responsibility for carrying out a program; (4) *process accountability*—responsibility for executing procedures; (5) *outcome accountability*—responsibility for results. The internal norms associated with accountability refer to professional, ethical, and pragmatic guides to the exercise of responsibility which govern the individual administrator's conduct according to the standards and ideals of a profession. An accountable public servant will, for example, resist the pursuit of personal gain in the performance of his or her duties. Accountability of the executive to the legislative branch is an established characteristic of both presidential and parliamentary democracies. Congressional investigations and postappropriation budget controls are two widely used tools of accountability in the United States. Accountability is assured by agency accounts, earmarked or obligated funds, monthly cash balances, the preaudit, and the postaudit. The budget, which is generally a compromise between the executive and legislative branches, is made an instrument of accountability by the specificity of its provisions. Payments by authorized officers for approved projects, for example, must be made to appropriate suppliers at the proper rates. *See also* BUDGET, 261; BUREAUCRACY, 126; GENERAL ACCOUNTING OFFICE (GAO), 274.

Significance Accountability has grown in importance because every advance in government control and regulation tends to increase the power and influence of the bureaucracy. To control this power and keep officials accountable, codes of ethics have been established for both elected and merit system officials. Frequently, however, they are merely guides to action and do not provide for criminal prosecution in cases of the abuse of power. Accountability emphasis in recent years has been placed on trying to identify more clearly what the major abuses of power are in the bureaucracy. Examples include (1) the failure of government to deliver the programs and services that have been authorized and funded; and (2) the displacement of publicly determined program goals with organizational aggrandizement and personal objectives, such as job security and promotion. If public administrators are "accountable" in the emerging sense of the term, they are improving the capacity of government to achieve publicly articulated goals and objectives. Administrators must recognize that they translate publicly determined intentions into outcomes, and that they must assume the responsibility for developing a public interest philosophy which demonstrates the congruence of self-interest and public interest.

Administrative Discretion (86)

The freedom administrators have to make choices which determine how a policy will be implemented. Administrative discretion is the result of the interaction between politics and administration. Contrary to Woodrow Wilson's insistence that these two aspects of government be held separate, the modern legislative process has led to jurisdictional overlaps of politics and administrative applications of politically determined policy goals. The growth of administrative discretion has resulted. Legislators in the process of framing legislation are subject to pressures from various interest groups, as well as their constituents at large. Often they are unwilling to make decisions that might alienate one group or another. Resulting legislation is sometimes left purposely broad or vague to allow room for discretionary decision making by administrators. Public administrationist James W. Fesler in his 1980 book, *Public Administration: Theory and Practice,* points out several reasons for a delegation of authority to public managers: (1) The legislation may be in a new policy field where there is no accumulated experience. (2) The technology in the legislated policy field is expected to change rapidly, so the agency needs flexibility to adapt to new developments. (3) Sometimes there are contradictory guidelines in the same piece of legislation. The agency must therefore choose between and among interpretations of legislative intent. Similarly, there may be a need to reconcile statutes on the same subject passed at different times. (4) Funds may be insufficient to meet all the stated purposes of the legislation. Thus administrators must prioritize decisions. Lack of time in the legislative process, lack of interest on the part of legislators, and lack of information and/or expertise on the part of legislators may also contribute to their delegation of authority to the bureaucracies. An agency administrator not infrequently must take vague legislation and make it specific enough to be implemented. The legislation establishing the Interstate Commerce Commission (ICC), for example, requires the railroads to fix "just and reasonable" railroad rates. What is "just and reasonable"? An administrator must make that decision. The Federal Communications Commission (FCC) is required to license television broadcasters for "public convenience and necessity." Again, an administrator must decide what is "public convenience and necessity."Administrative discretion means the administrative process has become part of the legislative process, and that political considerations are important elements in the execution of policy. *See also* ETHIC OF MEANS AND ENDS, 97; PROFESSIONALISM, 20.

Significance Administrative discretion affects everyone directly or indirectly. The fact that a person may be stopped for a speeding ticket, and then released with merely a warning, is a result of administrative discretion by the individual police officer. The fact that automobile manufacturers must comply with antipollution emission standards set by the Environmental Protection Agency (EPA) is the result of discretionary decisions by that agency. The EPA has spelled out a specific policy that pursues the *intent* of a law passed by Congress. Because they are constantly having to make policy decisions of this sort, agencies and their administrators are subject to pressure from a variety of sources. The laws, rules, and regulations passed by Congress must first be heeded. These give the administrator the limits within which he or she must work. The president, various congressional committees, and their staffs often have strong ideas about how certain laws should be implemented. Although they may have avoided having these ideas included in the legislation itself, they can, and often do, pressure agencies to include desired stipulations in the implementation stage of policy making. The courts are continually making discretionary decisions of their own that shape policy. Strong pressure for certain kinds of discretionary decisions sometimes comes from other administrative agencies, as well as interest groups, political parties, and the media. Administrative discretion can get out of control and become dangerous. Public management areas incorporating a high degree of discretion, such as law enforcement, have problems with overzealous use of it. Research shows that as discretion increases, the scope and frequency of choice increases. As greater choice is exercised, adherence to policy goals decreases. Thus discretion must be controlled or goal displacement occurs. Organizational expectations must be made clear to all members of the agency, and care must be taken to ensure that those persons making discretionary decisions are well informed and qualified to make them.

Authority (87)
The right to invoke compliance by subordinates on the basis of formal position and control over rewards and sanctions. Authority is institutionalized power. A power relationship is based on the ability to coerce compliant behavior if necessary. Without authority, power relationships develop according to status, knowledge, and informal characteristics. Authority, however, is based on legitimate foundations that formally establish structure and position within an organization. As social groups are formed, superior-subordinate relationships form. These power structures are perpetuated by tradition and eventually legitimized by law, statute, or formal rules. German sociologist Max Weber identified three types of authority. *Charismatic authority* depends on the personal characteristics of the authority figure. *Traditional authority* is the stabilization of informal roles over time. *Rational-legal authority* is formally legitimized as when a state grants institutional rights to a corporation. This type of authority, like others, is delegated through hierarchical patterns and depends on effective flow of direction from top to bottom if it is to succeed. *See also* HIERARCHY, 147.

Significance Authority has a "zone of acceptance" according to organization theorist Herbert A. Simon. Unless a directive falls within this zone, it will not be effective, since it will be rejected by subordinates. Thus formal authority is limited. More and more in modern organizations, workers are questioning formal authority. If a synthesis of Weber's three types of authority were used, the "zone of acceptance" would widen and the authority should become more effective. In the typical hierarchical organization, formal authority is located at the top. Often, however, this top position is dependent on people in lower positions possessing special knowledge or skills, in order to develop plans and give proper direction. Often these persons are advisors not in line positions of authority. Thus various staff positions might acquire "functional authority." Persons in these staff positions have little formal authority, but the top decision makers depend on them for advice or information. Authority is necessary to get the job done. The extremes of authority—anarchy and authoritarianism—can, however, become dangerous. The ideal would be an organization with enough authority at the top and among the managers to ensure cooperation and achievement of goals, while allowing enough freedom for creativity. Anarchy leads to chaos, but it is often individuals struggling against authority who bring about change and progress.

Bounded Rationality (88)
The behavioral principle that the rationality demanded of human beings by classical theories of rational choice is not observable in human behavior. Those who support the principle of bounded rationality argue that rationality is inconsistent with what is known about human capabilities for processing information. The position was developed by Herbert A. Simon in his 1947 book *Administrative Behavior,* in which he stated: "The capacity of the human mind in formulating and solving complex problems is very small compared to the size of the problem. It is very difficult to achieve objectively rational behavior in the real world . . . or even a reasonable approximation to such objective rationality." Rational theories of choice assume that choice is constrained only by such external factors as availability, cost, technology, and time. Bounded rationality adds the idea that the list of constraints should include such human limitations as faulty memory, inadequate computing power, and the tendency to "satisfice," or settle for a decision which is merely "good enough." *See also* DECISION MAKING, 92; SATISFICING, 113; SIMON, HERBERT A., 114.

Significance Bounded rationality pointed out important behavioral complications for conventional theories of rational decision making. The number of such complications has grown measurably since 1947. Simon is a management scientist and economist who won the Nobel Prize in Economics in 1978. Like most economists, he began his related work in public administration with the assumption that human choice behavior is intentionally rational. He assumed that decision makers have a set of criteria known to them in advance of their actions, and that they make choices by measuring estimates of the consequences of alternative actions against the criteria. Simon found this "economic man" model to be unreflective of actual administrative behavior. "Administrative man" typically stops short of finding "the one best way" to solve a problem. While this may be a good diagnosis, the solution remains problematical.

Bribery (89)

The act of corrupting or influencing the actions of a public officer, or anyone in a position of trust, by promising, giving, receiving, agreeing to receive, or soliciting any sum of money, favors, or gifts. Bribery is a misdemeanor in common law, but in Volume 18, Chapter 11 of the *United States Code* (1948, 1962), it is a felony. Offending officials are subject to criminal prosecution and dismissal. Under old English law, only officials who had authority of discretion, such as judges and magistrates, were held accountable for bribery. Minor public officials were exempt. However, the modern definition of bribery as a penalty offense encompasses all public officials. Under special provisions of law, voters, jurors, witnesses, and other lay participants in official and political proceedings can also be punished for bribery. A wide range of bribery legislation is enforced nationwide. *See also* ETHICS IN GOVERNMENT ACT OF 1978, 212; MALFEASANCE, 318.

Significance Bribery of public administrators, inspectors, officers, and agents is all too common a practice, according to political scientist Peter Blau, who has researched the subject. Yet, comparatively few cases are reported and prosecuted. Blau believes there is a taboo on reporting offers of bribes. Often those who do report them are ostracized by their colleagues. Other factors are compassion for victims of bribes and fear of entering into collusion with bribers, even to expose them. If a public official meets with a briber and takes his or her offer, the official may assume guilt, whatever the official's ultimate intent may be. Bribery is the subject of increasingly strict codes and crackdowns. Media investigative reports and FBI secret operations, such as ABSCAM (wherein FBI agents posed as rich Arab oilmen and offered bribes to congressmen who in many cases accepted them), have led to the indictment and prosecution of public officials on bribery charges in recent years.

Coproduction (90)

Direct citizen involvement in the design and delivery of urban services. Coproduction involves a critical mix of regular producers (professional service agents) and consumers (the citizenry) in an effort to compensate for the dramatic decrease in government funds available to municipalities. The most common form of coproduction is citizens providing assistance to public agents, as when citizens of the city of Detroit, for example, formed a police reserve of over 1,300 people to alleviate the effects of a 20 percent reduction in the city's police force. A fire department auxiliary was developed for the same purpose, and an adopt-a-park program was instituted to help beleaguered city officials take care of the many parks and vacant lots in the city. Neighborhood associations are also a form of coproduction in their efforts to restore property values and provide security against theft and vandalism. More subtle forms of coproduction are participative-management service on governmental boards and commissions and doing such mundane chores as placing garbage at the curbside to be picked up rather than leaving it behind the house. Thus sanitation crews can serve more households, costs can be cut, and tax money can be saved.

Significance   The idea of coproduction goes back a long way in U.S. history: to colonial times when citizens formed groups of militia to maintain peace and order, extinguish fires, and provide for the common defense. Self-help activity was deemed essential for the community's survival for decades. Today collective coproduction makes possible a redistribution of urban resources so that benefits accrue to the city as a whole rather than to individuals or small groups economically well placed to receive them.

Cutback Management (91)

Directing organizational change toward lower levels of resource consumption and organizational activity. Cutback management, sometimes called retrenchment management, involves making hard decisions about staff reductions, which programs will be scaled down or terminated, and what clients will be asked to make sacrifices. Pressures for retrenchment are increasingly generated in modern society by popular demands, by inflation, and by other economic and political events. Public managers have at least three strategic choices to make in response to the pressures for retrenchment. These are (1) whether to resist the pressures or accept them and smooth the decline; (2) whether to cut back immediately so as to avoid a tax or service fee increase, for example, or to meet retrenchment demands voluntarily by reducing the agency's use of resources by spreading reductions over a period of time; and (3) whether to allocate cuts across-the-board to all units in an agency to help maintain morale and good team spirit in the organization, or to cut selectively those activities where there is political visibility and where there is a possibility of ending public pressures more quickly. Managers who embark on the cutback process typically follow four major steps:

confronting, planning, targeting, and distributing the cuts. In distributing cuts, there may be an opportunity for a trade-off between efficiency and equity. The manager may identify the organization's most important functions, procedures, and long-term capacity, and protect them against demands for equity. Using technical tools available to the manager—for example, hiring freezes, seniority, productivity criteria, and the applications of zero-base budgeting—the manager can distribute the cuts as equitably as maintenance of the organization's central purpose allows. *See also* PROPOSITION 13, 74; ZERO-BASE BUDGETING (ZBB), 291.

Significance Cutback management is a major new direction in public administration brought about by deteriorating revenue bases, changing demographic patterns, and rising expectations of public services. The tools and techniques thus far applied by cutback managers have indicated that organizations cannot be cut back by merely reversing the sequence of activity and resource allocation by which their problems were originally assembled. Not only are organizations organic social wholes whose parts recombine on injury, but they exist with a set of managerial and societal assumptions which sometimes limit the capacity of managers to adjust to new circumstances. Public managers tend to operate, for example, on the assumption that growth is good. Not only is growth assumed to be good, it is often also assumed to be ever present, with unlimited prospects. Despite the fact that an increasing proportion of most public budgets is considered uncontrollable because of fixed costs for established programs, many public managers seek additional ways to expand their agency budgets. Growth assumptions and practices went largely unchallenged in U.S. public administration until the early 1970s, when an era of comparative scarcity forced itself on the consciousness of the American people. Then, in the later 1970s, a popular tide against government taxes and spending was unleashed across the country starting with the adoption of Proposition 13 by a direct vote of the people of California. The basic objective of this state constitutional amendment was to force local government to undertake a major program of cutback management. The requirements of cutback management call into question the critical assumptions which have guided U.S. public administration for at least five decades. Prominent among these assumptions is the desirability of growth, expansion, permanence, and the sanctity of precedent. Cutback management also requires a fundamental alteration of the managerial "mindset" in a period labeled by Kenneth Boulding "The Era of Slowdown." The manager must confront trade-offs between new demands and old programs rather than simply expand when a new public problem arises. If cutback management is to succeed, efforts should be directed at sustaining the morale and productivity of public employees in the face of increasing control from above and shrinking opportunities for creativity and promotion. Also, in the new retrenchment milieu, clients must find alternative sources for services governments may no longer be able to provide.

Decision Making (92)
A process in which events, circumstances, and information precipitate a choice designed to achieve some desired result. Decision making is a major managerial function. Specifics of the decision-making process vary with the context, but general steps that are frequently followed include (1) a careful analysis of objectives; (2) a search for possible alternative solutions; (3) an estimate of total costs for each alternative; (4) an estimate of the effectiveness of each alternative; and (5) a comparison and analysis of each alternative. The last step leads to the selection of a preferred alternative. These steps are often modified, rearranged, changed, or deleted, but the basic outline remains the same. Decision making is a process of narrowing down a body of information, identifying primary problems, and choosing among alternative solutions. The sequential format of decision making in no way implies that it is a linear process, however. Frequently it is a process in which adjustments, reevaluation, backtracking, and revision occur. It is also rare for decisions to be made in isolation. Particularly in organizational contexts, not only are groups of people involved, but the circumstances and information relative to the decision are in a state of flux. Three models of decision making are commonly cited. The *rational-comprehensive* approach advocates logical decision making, including the consideration of all possible alternatives, cost-benefit analysis, and the choice of the best alternative. The *incremental* approach accepts the existing situation, considers only a limited number of variables at one time, and adds small improvements or changes which are politically acceptable. The *mixed scanning* approach is a combination of the rational-comprehensive and incremental models. *See also* DECISION MAKING, 93–95.

Significance Decision making involves risks and the possibility of failure. But progress cannot be made without it, and the successful manager accepts the consequences of his or her decisions. The importance of the decision-making process has enticed a wide variety of disciplines to contribute to its study. Although psychological, cultural, social, economic, and political aspects of decision making have been extensively explored, relatively few universal principles have been validated. Much of the early research in the field relied very heavily on normative views and utilized mathematical models that failed to account for important human elements in decision making. An eclectic approach to the subject is currently popular, with one fruitful line of interdisciplinary inquiry combining statistical and psychological expertise in an exploration of human beings as decision makers. Bayes's theorem is a statistical rule that revises probabilities to accommodate additional evidence. Psychologists use the rule as a yardstick against which to compare human abilities to reevaluate a decision in terms of additional information. Using a probabilistic information-processing (PIP) system, which combines the calculations of Bayes's theorem with human judgment, accuracy in predicting results has exceeded both Bayes's theorem and human judgment alone. Additional interdisciplinary studies of decision making are needed if its intricacies are to be fathomed, and if an understanding of its processes is to lead to more effective management.

Decision Making, Incremental (93)

A major approach to problem solving that suggests a conservative and practical view to administrators in order for them to meet new challenges slowly and progressively. Incrementalism recognizes that in their decision making administrators typically start with an existing body of policies, the most recent funding levels of programs, the store of knowledge each participant has of other participants' views, and the resources they can mobilize to influence the outcome of the process. Incrementalism prefers only minimal departures from the status quo, and decision makers are viewed primarily as problem solvers who may lack the intellectual capacity or the time to make a wide search for alternative solutions. Incrementalist policies are almost always more politically expedient than alternative approaches. The rational-comprehensive and mixed-scanning policies, for example, typically do not take into account the process of conflict, negotiation, persuasion, and cooperation among the private and public groups, institutions, and individuals with stakes in particular policies and decisions. The incrementalist decision-making sequence calls upon the decision maker to (1) identify the problem; (2) investigate how similar problems have been handled in the past; (3) analyze and evaluate a few solutions that appear to be plausible; and (4) choose one that makes some contribution to solving the problem without drastically altering existing processes and institutions. Incrementalism's main defender, Charles E. Lindblom, called this the science of muddling through. Administrators, according to Lindblom, muddle through in response to current events and circumstances rather than by the will of those in policy-making positions. *See also* DECISION MAKING, 92, 94, 95.

Significance Incremental decision making describes the most common form utilized in U.S. public administration. Its strength is that it reflects the society's commitment to gradual change and accepts the pluralism that exists among clientele groups and within public agencies. Incrementalism takes into account the triangular alliances that sometimes exist among an agency, its related congressional committees, and its clientele interest groups. It is short-term decision making in that decisions are a reply to immediate needs without much consideration for the long-term results. Yet, Lindblom may have claimed too much for incremental decision making when he argued that small changes help avoid monumental errors. That would be true only if the status quo itself were sound and conditions affecting it remained static. U.S. history is replete with examples of the necessity of bold and innovative changes in public policy, such as the freeing of slaves, regulating public utilities, and protecting consumers from false advertising. Still the prevalence of the incrementalist model illustrates its utility. The most powerful participants in the decision-making process often compromise using incrementalist techniques, each accepting a suboptimal service of an individual goal in order to get something out of the process. Each participant knows that the decisional process of incrementalism is episodic and diffuse. What is lost in the maximization of one's goals this year may be regained next year in another decisional arena. Since the values affecting incrementalist decisions are not distinct, the means of attaining such values, or ends, are also indistinct. Thus means-ends analysis is inappropriate and limited because means and ends are intertwined throughout the process.

Decision Making, Mixed Scanning (94)

A "third approach" to decision making, which attempts to integrate the incremental and the rational-comprehensive models. Mixed scanning involves the collection and evaluation of general data on a broad range of topics and detailed analysis of particular issues. It was suggested by Amitai Etzioni in the *Public Administration Review,* December 1967, because the incremental and rational-comprehensive models are not pure types. A particular decision, according to Etzioni, will probably have elements of both approaches. Mixed scanning therefore recognizes the limited human capability to secure purely rational decisions, while continuing to value the systems analysis techniques applied in the rational-comprehensive process. Mixed scanning adherents applaud the motto: "It is better to be roughly right than exactly wrong." The decision-making process followed by mixed scanners begins with a systematic review at set intervals of their entire areas of responsibility. However, since detailed comprehensive coverage may be impossible, mixed scanners intentionally truncate the scope of their review. They invest selected resources of the agency in detailed analyses of only "important decisions," defined as those with the broadest impact. They focus only on alternative solutions their scan has identified as plausible and promising. The systematic overview provides a context for application of the incremental model in reaching less important decisions. Mixed scanning improves on incrementalism by being less concerned with how a similar problem was solved previously, leading to a more creative search for alternatives. It improves on systems analysis in its more realistic assessment of the time available for policy analysis. *See also* DECISION MAKING, 92, 93, 95.

Significance Mixed scanning corrects what Israeli political theorist Yehezkel Dror identifies as a serious shortcoming of incrementalism; that is, the marginal changes acceptable to incrementalists may not suffice to meet growing policy demands. As policy needs change, decision makers may have to develop innovations bolder than those contemplated by the incremental approach. Incrementalism justifies the "conserver" bureaucrat who is chiefly interested in maintaining power, prestige, and income, and who takes a cautious, low-risk approach to decision making. Etzioni agrees with Dror but is more constructive with the procedural suggestions of mixed scanning. The primary significance of mixed scanning is that it distinguishes between fundamental and nonfundamental decisions. For nonfundamental decisions, the incremental approach is entirely valid and appropriate. In making fundamental decisions, however, the decision maker needs to have wider perceptual horizons than incrementalism affords. Incrementalists tend to decide only nonfundamental matters, stemming from their emphasis on the "troubleshooter" approach to solving problems. The importance of the mixed scanning model is illustrated by Etzioni's analogy of the high-altitude weather satellite in orbit around the earth. On board the satellite are two cameras, one equipped with a wide-angle lens which can scan a large area and record major weather patterns, the other equipped with a narrow-angle lens capable of zeroing in on turbulence and examining it in much finer detail. Either camera without the other would supply some useful information, but much more can be obtained when they are used in combination. The analysis provided by the narrow-lens camera (the incremental model) is more intelligible when meteorologists have some idea of the size, exact location, and boundaries of the total weather system (the rational-comprehensive model).

Decision Making, Rational-comprehensive (95)

A systems analysis approach based on principles of scientific investigation and scientific problem solving. The rational-comprehensive model of decision making is described by American political scientist Charles E. Lindblom as involving five features: (1) clarification of values; (2) means-ends analysis; (3) choice of most appropriate means to achieve desired ends; (4) comprehensive analysis; and (5) analysis that is theory-based. Rational-comprehensive analysis defines the problem, develops alternative solutions, places values on the consequences of various alternatives, assesses the probability that they will occur, and makes a decision based on logical rules. It seeks to sort out and achieve the goals decision makers believe are most valued. The model attempts to serve the ideal embodied in Max Weber's view of bureaucracy in which decisions are based on impersonal rules and techniques. Rational-comprehensive decision making draws heavily on the economists' vision of how a rational "economic man" should make decisions. It also relies on rational decision-making models developed by mathematicians and psychologists. The economics/mathematics/psychology analyses describe a single person—rather than a group or an institution—faced with the need to make a decision. These analyses also tend to idealize the decisional situation. The decision maker, for example, knows the objective clearly and is perfectly informed on all possible means to that end, including how much it will cost in money, time, and resources, and the degree of certainty with which each alternative will achieve the goal. Rational-comprehensive analysis assumes a static situation in which relevant conditions do not change, and no new information becomes available during the time period of analysis and decision. *See also* DECISION MAKING, 92–94; PLANNING, PROGRAMMING, BUDGETING SYSTEMS (PPBS), 283; SYSTEMS ANALYSIS, 83.

Significance Rational-comprehensive decision making is at one pole of a continuum that includes incremental decision making at the opposite pole, and mixed scanning in the middle. Whereas incrementalism emphasizes political rationality, the rational-comprehensive approach emphasizes economic rationality. The systems analysis techniques that are at the core of the rational-comprehensive model were in fact widely utilized in the administrations of Presidents John F. Kennedy and Lyndon B. Johnson, particularly in the Department of Defense under Secretary Robert S. McNamara. Author David

Halberstam and other close observers of the systems analysis approach in the Kennedy-Johnson years charge that public administrators rarely have the brains and never the time to complete the laborious steps of analysis involved in the systems analysis process. They also charge that cost-benefit analysis has no applicability to nonquantifiable areas of public policy, and that high-level decision making is far more a matter of political insight and widsom than it is an act of comprehensive rationality. Three Canadian researchers have concluded that the rational-comprehensive approach is rarely used in government despite widespread discussion of it. Of 83 discrete policy choices, the researchers found serious analytic techniques employed in only 18 of the cases. Despite a management literature replete with examples of systems analysis, this empirical study shows that in case after case only one policy alternative is fully explored. What the Canadians documented was not rational-comprehensive decision making but what Herbert Simon has called "bounded rationality" and what Amitai Etzioni has called "mixed scanning." Critics generally emphasize that the most important issues in government cannot be resolved by numbers, computers, or cost-benefit tables. On complex issues, there is more likely to be conflict than agreement on values, and conflict over values is essentially a political question which cannot be subordinated to economic-modeled analytical techniques.

Delegation of Authority (96)

The transfer of authority and responsibility from a higher to a lower administrative official for purposes of decision making. Delegations of authority usually involve transferring powers assigned to an elected or appointed executive official to a subordinate administrator. Such transfers are typically done under clearly defined standards with subsequent implementations subject to continuing review. The basic legal power to carry on such functions remains with the delegator and can be withdrawn at any time from the delegatee. *See also* HIERARCHY, 147.

Significance Delegations of authority are commonplace in all major administrative structures. In the national government, for example, Congress assigns full responsibility to the heads of all agencies for carrying out their basic operational missions, but direction and supervision of the diverse activities of such units cannot logically remain in one person's hands. The result is that each agency head delegates some authority to subordinates. Generally, such delegations tend to improve the operations of the agency for several reasons. For one, the agency head is not overburdened and can concentrate his or her time and attention on the most important matters of decision making. For another, greater specialization can grow naturally out of the division of authority. In many cases, however, the agency head only grudgingly delegates authority, or does not delegate power and authority equal to delegated responsibility. The latter problem is particularly acute in that the most fundamental rule of good administration is that all officials exercise authority equal to their responsibility. Some high officials, both elected and appointed, delegate very little authority out of fear of losing control over the agency's operations, because of personality problems that make it difficult for an individual to give up power and authority, or because of fear that lower officials will make the wrong decisions.

Ethic of Means and Ends (97)

The question of whether public officials and administrators, in making decisions and taking actions on behalf of government, can legitimate them on the basis that the end justifies the means. The ethic of means and ends involves the question of *raison d'état*, or reason of state. Public administrationist J. D. Williams asks, for example, if there are circumstances in which the glory or the safety of the state justifies violations of commonly agreed-on ethical standards and the law itself. In 1513, Niccolo Machiavelli in his famous book, *The Prince*, answered the means-ends question with the following reasoning in his advice to the ruler of Florence, Lorenzo de Medici: "Everybody sees what you appear to be, few feel what you are, and those few will not dare to oppose themselves to the many, who have the majesty of the state to defend them; and in the actions of men, and especially of princes, from which there is no appeal, the end justifies the means." The public administration corollary of reason of state is *reason of agency*, which is defined as whatever strengthens or protects the agency in the service of its mission is justified by the ends assigned to it as part of the national interest. *See also* MALFEASANCE, 318; MISFEASANCE, 319; NONFEASANCE, 320.

Significance The ethic of means and ends provides the context for some of the most controversial decisions in U.S. administrative history. Williams points out that in 1942, for example, President Franklin D. Roosevelt ordered that 75,000 Japanese-American citizens be isolated in relocation camps following the Japanese attack on Pearl Harbor. Roosevelt concluded that the "end" (national security) was so critical it justified the "means" (incarcerating Japanese-Americans without a trial). The great civil libertarian justice of the

Supreme Court, Hugo Black, sanctioned Roosevelt's action in *Korematsu v. United States* (323 U.S. 214: 1944), holding for the Court's majority that ". . . when under conditions of modern warfare our shores are threatened by hostile forces, the power to protect must be commensurate with the threatened danger. . . ." The ethic of means and ends recognizes that good ends frequently become unattainable or undesirable through the use of unethical means to achieve them.

Groupthink (98)
A mode of thinking and problem solving in which loyalty to the group and the seeking of agreement replaces innovation, objectivity, and careful analysis. Groupthink was coined by social psychologist Irving L. Janis in his 1972 book *Victims of Groupthink,* a study of the faults of group decision making. Janis listed seven characteristics of groupthink: (1) a shared illusion of invulnerability, which generates false optimism and lack of caution; (2) direct pressure on deviants; (3) a fear of disapproval, which keeps new alternatives from emerging; (4) an illusion of unanimity, so that when someone representing the majority view speaks, his or her pronouncement is seen as accepted by everyone else in the group; (5) a failure to explore the moral or ethical consequences of group decisions; (6) "mindguards" who protect the leader from criticism; and (7) group efforts to rationalize or deny all ill omens. If there is opposition to the group, two other characteristics come into play: (1) a shared and mistaken belief that the leaders of the opposition are evil and stupid; and (2) an air of detachment which minimizes the emotional stress of decision making. Groupthink attempts to explain a psychological process of group dynamics that prevents members of the group from realistically evaluating alternative courses of action. It occurs in highly cohesive groups in which the participants place a high value on belonging and have a strong motivation to continue as a member. Janis equates groupthink with deterioration of mental efficiency, escape from reality, and faulty moral judgment resulting from in-group pressures. The group completely ignores considerations of how a chosen plan could be hindered by political opponents, bureaucratic inertia, or derailment by accidents. Groupthinkers therefore typically fail to work out contingency plans to cope with foreseeable setbacks which could endanger the success of the chosen course of action. *See also* DECISION MAKING, 92–95.

Significance Groupthink may have played a decisive role in many of the miscalculations of modern times. Janis describes in detail the otherwise inexplicable failure of the U.S. government to react to clear warnings of a Japanese attack on Pearl Harbor; the decision to authorize the United Nations attack on North Korea, despite impressive evidence of the probability of Chinese intervention; the "perfect failure" of the Bay of Pigs invasion of Cuba; the irrational decisions to escalate the war in Vietnam; and the collective rationalization of the Watergate defendants, which included an unquestioning belief in the moral rectitude of the group. The removal of Secretary of Defense Robert McNamara from the cabinet of President Lyndon B. Johnson in 1968 because of his dissenting view on Vietnam war policy illustrates the application of direct pressure to any member of the group who argues strongly against the group's illusions, stereotypes, or plans. Janis suggests that policy-making groups can reduce the chances of falling victim to the groupthink syndrome by facilitating critical inquiry and assigning the role of critic to members. The exposure of a wide range of alternate courses of action, while group members are restrained from the early expression of opinion, will also help to provide an atmosphere of open inquiry. The tendency toward isolation can be countered by bringing outside experts into the discussions to challenge group perceptions. Knowledge of the phenomenon of groupthink is valuable to administrators if it alerts them to take precautions to assure critical and open consideration of decision options.

Human Motivation: Motivation-hygiene Theory (99)

A description of two factors believed to be present in every job: the maintenance factor and the motivation factor. Motivation-hygiene theory, also called two-factor theory, was developed by Frederick Herzberg in 1959. Herzberg was then a psychologist at Case Western Reserve University in Cleveland. He conducted experiments in motivation with two hundred engineers and accountants, finding that certain maintenance needs had to be met before the worker could begin to be motivated. The maintenance factors were identified as (1) company policy and administration; (2) technical supervision; (3) interpersonal relations with supervisor; (4) interpersonal relations with peers; (5) interpersonal relations with subordinates; (6) salary; (7) job security; (8) personal life; (9) work conditions; and (10) status. Herzberg called the maintenance factors *dissatisfiers*. They could not motivate, but they were prime negative factors if they were lacking. The motivational factors were identified as (1) achievement; (2) recognition; (3) advancement; (4) the work itself; (5) the possibility of growth; and (6) responsibility. These factors Herzberg called *satisfiers*. They are the things that could really bring about worker dedication to a job. *See also* HUMAN MOTIVATION: NEED

THEORY, 100; HUMAN MOTIVATION: THEORY X, 101; HUMAN MOTIVATION: THEORY Y, 102.

Significance Motivation-hygiene theory is an organization development concept that can be used in attempts to motivate an employee by increasing his or her satisfaction with work. The satisfiers are in agreement with Douglas McGregor's "Theory Y" view of organizations and with the top levels of Abraham Maslow's "ladder of needs." The principal contribution which motivation-hygiene theory makes to motivation theory is its focus on *the job itself.* The factors a worker can really sink his teeth into are not peripheral and extrinsic, such as another water fountain or carpets on the floor, but the job itself. Improving surroundings and developing harmonious relations among co-workers and supervisors may generate some euphoria, but what really produces high-level morale and productivity, according to motivation-hygiene theory, is doing a job worth doing. Herzberg saw that most organizational efforts to "motivate" employees are really aimed at affecting the hygiene factors. People cannot be motivated by cutting the work week. Motivated people do not seek less time on the job; they want more. Such devices as human relations and sensitivity training merely deal with improved supervision and interpersonal relationships. These cannot motivate employees. They can only make them not dissatisfied. Motivation-hygiene theory leads directly to a strategy of job enrichment for organizations convinced of the theory's utility. Job enrichment can be achieved if jobs can be restructured to involve the theory's motivator factors.

Human Motivation: Need Theory (100)

The belief that human needs are primary job motivators. Need theory was first advanced by clinical psychologist Abraham H. Maslow in "A Theory of Human Motivation" published in the *Psychological Review* in 1943. Maslow said there are five basic human needs that are sequential in nature, that is, they are arranged in a stepladder chart, with the most basic needs at the bottom of the ladder. The needs are prepotent. Until each one is relatively satisfied, a person will not strive very hard to meet the next level of need. The needs are (1) physiological; (2) safety and security; (3) love and belonging; (4) self-esteem; and (5) self-actualization. The most basic need is for air, food, shelter, sex, and elimination. Then comes physical safety, job security, and provision for old age. Because safety and security needs are *second* on the list, a person can reconcile a daily trip to work in dangerous mines or on lofty scaffolding to satisfy his or her need for food and shelter. Love and belonging are the individual's group needs, the need to be loved and accepted by significant others. Maslow's clinical data indicated that the failure to love and be loved is at the heart of many individual and group social problems. Self-esteem is the yearning to see oneself as a worthy and admirable person. How can we really like ourselves? Can we be right with ourselves by using the right deodorant and driving the right car? Maslow's data brought into serious question the accuracy of advertisers' promises of self-respect through possessions. Finally, self-actualization is an innate striving among human beings to create and to maximize one's talents. Self-actualized persons are fulfilled persons who demonstrate the following characteristics of mental health: (1) they can accept the way things are; (2) they are not afraid to get close to others; (3) they are efficient judges of situations; (4) they are creative and appreciative; (5) they march to a different drummer; and (6) they are willing to learn from anyone. Need theory maintains that when a person is reasonably well fed, secure, loved, and confident, he or she then has the physical and psychic power to begin to create, self-direct, and accomplish. But the most basic needs must be met first. When there is no bread, humans live by bread alone. *See also* HAWTHORNE STUDIES, 54; HUMAN MOTIVATION: MOTIVATION-HYGIENE THEORY, 99; TAYLORISM, 25.

Significance Need theory was developed from clinical experiences with brain-damaged and mentally disturbed persons. The tone of Maslow's philosophy is extremely positive. He saw human needs and drives as good rather than evil. He felt that each person has a natural drive toward health, happiness, and accomplishment, rather than a negative desire for failure and self-destruction. Need theory's emphasis on people instead of formal organization was the second major attack on Taylorism to come in a decade. Combined with the implications of the first attack, the Hawthorne studies, need theory provided the underpinning for a new approach to management in the United States. Yet, as discussed by J. D. Williams in *Public Administration: The People's Business* (1980), Maslow's work has been roundly criticized. The principal elements of criticism are (1) There is little empirical support for the hierarchy of needs theory in field studies. M. A. Wahba and L. G. Bridwell reviewed eight field studies, for example, and found no confirmation of the five-level needs ladder. (2) Culture makes a crucial difference in both the determination of needs and of how they are to be satisfied. The needs are not instinctive at birth. (3) Job satisfaction is heavily influenced by such factors as worker IQs, personalities, the technology employed, and many other factors unrelated to Maslow's restrictive list. (4) Self-actualized workers, each marching to the beat of their own drummers, would approximate organizational chaos. (5) The manager's real world includes many workers who are not, and probably will never be, self-actualized. Managers have to accept less than full worker motivation as a fact of life and adopt a more authoritarian leadership style than would be appropriate for a fully self-actualized work force. F. K. Gibson and C. E. Teasley suggested in the *Public Administration Review* in 1973 that need theory is based more on metaphysical attraction than empirical evidence.

Human Motivation: Theory X (101)

A task-oriented theory of management that maintains an organizational climate of close control, centralized authority, autocratic leadership, and minimum participation in the decision-making process. Theory X was advanced as a typology by Douglas M. McGregor in his 1960 book, *The Human Side of Enterprise*. The assumptions of Theory X are (1) the average person dislikes work and will avoid it as much as possible; (2) most people have to be forced or threatened by punishment to get them to make the effort necessary to accomplish organizational goals; and (3) the average person is basically passive and therefore prefers to be directed, rather than assume any risk or responsibility. Above all else, he or she prefers security. Under Theory X, management's task is to harness human energy to meet organizational requirements. There is a well-defined organizational hierarchy with a narrow span of control. Workers are considered to be extensions of machines. The organizations that use Theory X successfully are highly mechanistic. They have a pronounced division of labor, direct supervisory controls, and formal rules to assure that the workers' contribution to the enterprise is simple labor. A Theory X organization has jobs of high task simplification and low task difficulty. The jobs are routine, repetitive, and simple, as in an assembly line. Conventional programs of performance appraisal apply, such as rewards geared to numbers of pieces produced. Organizations that apply Theory X seldom create opportunities for workers or encourage their growth. They provide strict leadership and high standards of conformity. *See also* HUMAN MOTIVATION, 99–100, 102, 103; SCIENTIFIC MANAGEMENT, 22.

Significance Theory X is an application of management expert Frederick W. Taylor's scientific management principles. Taylor's key assumptions about people were that (1) the chief thing people want from their jobs is money; and (2) people are basically simpletons who require strict guidance to perform well. A study by N. Z. Medalia published in the *Journal of Abnormal and Social Psychology* in 1955 suggests that when the worker is an authoritarian personality type, he or she is more productive when working for a Theory X manager. A similar study by A. D. Calvin published in the *Journal of Social Psychology* in 1957 found a 100 percent improvement in the output of workers of comparatively low intelligence under Theory X leadership in contrast to their output under democratic leadership. American scholar Robert Dubin reported in *Leadership and Productivity* in 1965 that Theory X methods are more appropriate for assembly line and continuous flow technologies (i.e., fully automated processes), but that nonauthoritarian leadership is more appropriate for "whole unit technologies." Whole unit technologies are the social worker, the highway patrol officer, and the sanitation inspector, for example. The possibilities of psychological repression are pronounced in Theory X and lead to the bureaupathic behavior described by Victor A. Thompson in *Modern Organization* (1961). Such behavior is explained as defensive reactions developed by individuals to protect their psyches from the frustration of not being able to achieve their personal goals within the organization. Whatever its liabilities, however, the Theory X organizational structure is the conventional and classical one in American public administration. It represents a strict hierarchy with close supervision.

Human Motivation: Theory Y (102)

A people-oriented philosophy of management which holds that people have the capacity to direct their behavior toward organizational goals. Theory Y was proposed in 1960 by management theorist Douglas M. McGregor, who believed strongly that the basic motivating force in a man or woman comes from within. Theory Y assumes that an effective organizational climate has looser, more general supervision than is present in Theory X. The Theory Y manager uses greater decentralization of authority, relies less on coercion and control and more on a democratic leadership style, and emphasizes participative decision making. Theory Y is based on the following set of beliefs: (1) work is as natural to humankind as play or rest and, therefore, is not avoided by human beings; (2) self-motivation and inherent satisfaction in work will be forthcoming in situations where the individual is committed to organizational goals; hence, coercion is not the only form of influence that can be used to motivate; (3) commitment is a crucial factor in motivation; it is a function of the rewards coming from it; (4) the average person learns to accept and even seek responsibility, given the proper environment; (5) contrary to popular stereotypes, the ability to be creative and innovative in the solution of organization problems is widely, not narrowly, distributed in the population; and (6) in modern organizations human intellectual potentialities are only partially realized. Theory Y implies that, if management can make it possible for people in an organization to satisfy their needs and realize their potential by removing artificial barriers that frustrate need satisfaction, the organization will be more effective. McGregor and other organizational humanists maintained that, if an organization is to be healthy and capable of creatively responding to and managing change, an atmosphere conducive to individual growth is essential. The Theory Y manager creates opportunities, releases potential, removes organizational obstacles, encourages growth, and provides guidance. The theory relies on self-control and self-direction. *See also* HUMAN MOTIVATION, 99–101, 103.

Significance Theory Y–oriented management works best in science-based organizations that must operate under conditions of environmental turbulence. Research has shown that Theory X, on the other hand, seems more applicable to programmatic endeavors, such as certain kinds of manufacturing and processing, characterized by stable conditions. The success of any management theory, however, depends on the appropriateness of the theory to the task at hand and the individual's motivation pattern. The tendency to label Theory X "bad" and Theory Y "good" is inappropriate. Theory Y has its critics. Among the doubts expressed about Theory Y are these: (1) Despite the evidence presented by Abraham Maslow and Frederick Herzberg, not all employees are looking for self-actualization and more responsibility. Many workers just want to do their job and go home. (2) Theory Y errs in downplaying the enormous importance of economic rewards to most workers. (3) Participative management is basically manipulative. Managers use consensus-building techniques to win employee support for the course they have already decided on. (4) Hierarchy is not the great evil Theory Y suggests. It provides an orderly ladder for the upwardly mobile employee to climb toward increasing responsibility and authority. (5) The quality of group decisions may be considerably below that of decisions suggested by gifted staff people and bright people in the chain of command. (6) Managers who may have worked hard and stood in line for years to attain power are not about to share decision making with their employees. (7) Theory Y is blatantly utopian and attempts to fly in all kinds of weather, regardless of worker skills and personality, the job to be done, and the technology employed. Clearly Theory Y's prescriptions do not fit all management situations. But its central precepts—a whole view of the human personality, the need to make work worthwhile, and the potential which lies in self-actualized human beings—have left an indelible mark on public administration in the United States.

Human Motivation: Theory Z (103)

A Japanese approach to management that emphasizes participative management from employees who are committed to their work through cultural tradition, shared socioeconomic values, and communal forms of decision making. Theory Z is characterized by personnel policies that reflect high levels of trust, lifetime or long-term job security, and holistic career planning. The term was popularized by William G. Ouchi in his 1981 bestseller, *Theory Z*. With Theory Z has come new attention to the phenomenon of *organizational culture*. Symbols and myths replace bureaucratic methods of giving orders and closely supervising workers, thus leading to increased productivity and mutually supportive relationships at the workplace. In its simplest form, the assumption of Theory Z is that people respond conscientiously when they feel wanted, needed, and trusted. *See also* HUMAN MOTIVATION: THEORY X, 101; HUMAN MOTIVATION: THEORY Y, 102; ORGANIZATION THEORY, 176–179.

Significance Theory Z has taken its place alongside Theory X and Theory Y as a descriptive philosophy of management. Whereas Theory X places a strong emphasis on task orientation, and Theory Y just as strongly emphasizes people, Theory Z is transformation oriented. It assumes that the highest potential for the organization lies in a consciously fostered relationship between the organization and each of its employees. Theory Z postulates that productivity is dependent upon trust, intimacy, and flexible relationships among institutional actors. This view of the cultural properties of an organization represents an integration of humanistic and neoclassical organization theory. It occupies an increasingly prominent place in management literature, due in large part to timing. Given lagging productivity in the private sector, loss of public trust in governmental institutions, poor scholastic achievement scores, and a variety of other indicators of widespread organizational problems in the United States, the prescriptive framework of Theory Z has been very favorably received.

Iron Law of Oligarchy (104)

The principle that one dominant class inevitably succeeds to leadership in an organization. The iron law of oligarchy, or rule of the few, was introduced by French political theorist Robert Michels in 1915.

The idea was the result of Michels's analysis of leadership patterns in democratic governments and in other organizations, such as trade unions. He maintained that society cannot exist without a dominant class, and historically never has. In the French Revolution, for example, the small group that served as the agent of political change eventually became an impediment to change by perpetuating its own power and displacing the official goals of the masses it represented. The iron law of oligarchy says that the overthrow of *any* elite by the masses would eventually lead to such oligarchical leadership. Another dominant group would raise itself to the rank of the governing class. Michels said the principal cause of oligarchy is the technical indispensability of leadership and that, since leadership is essential to the survival of an organization, democratic rule is a useful concept only in the abstract. Contributing to the reign of the power elite in an organization is the gratitude of those led toward the leaders and the resulting passive acceptance of the unofficial goals of the oligarchy. A similar phenomenon in contemporary democracy is the widespread and uncritical acceptance of bureaucratic expertise by the public, and the passive acceptance by most people of highly organized interest groups as being representative of public opinion. The iron law of oligarchy refutes the possibility of the existence of an ideal democracy. *See also* BUREAUCRATIC EXPERTISE, 128; CITIZEN PARTICIPATION, 131; ELITE, 41; INTEREST-GROUP LIBERALISM, 56.

Significance   The iron law of oligarchy is often cited in analyses of citizen participation and interest-group involvement in the formation of public policy. Hierarchical organizations, particularly bureaucracies, discourage rule by the masses. They focus much of the decision-making process at specific access points in the organization. These access points are often guarded by powerful elites or special interest groups, which themselves have great impact on policy formation. General public acceptance of interest-group goals is given in U.S. society and is called interest-group liberalism. Successful leadership by elite groups has important implications for the effectiveness of movements toward increased citizen participation in policy making and implementation. Efforts to involve large groups of citizens in particular policy areas not only have had limited success in the United States, but may even enhance the power of elite groups by giving them a democratic screen for their activities. The iron law of oligarchy, whether applied to the ruling few in ancient Rome or in the modern United States, is a useful concept for explaining the tendency toward conservatism in government bureaus. Bureaucratic planning replaces open competition—by planning prices, planning taxes, planning which services and goods to produce, planning how to create more demand for them, and planning how to educate the personnel who will accomplish the work of the bureaus of the future. The drive toward planning means that managerial control passes into the hands of professional administrators, who as a class may be synonymous with the new oligarchy.

Legislative Oversight (105)
The process by which a legislature monitors the structure and process of policy implementation at the administrative level. Legislative oversight occurs at all levels of government although congressional oversight is most frequently cited. Oversight activities can be formal or informal and can be initiated by individual legislators or by collective legislative effort. Any legislative activity that impacts bureaucratic behavior in policy administration is considered legislative oversight. The federal law that spells out the oversight function is the Legislative Reorganization Act of 1946. It assigns each standing committee in Congress the responsibility to "exercise continuous watchfulness of the execution by administrative agencies of any laws, the subject matter of which is within the jurisdiction of such committee." The Administrative Procedure Act of 1946, the Freedom of Information Act of 1966, and the Civil Service Reform Act of 1978 all assist oversight efforts by providing for methods of agency review and by making necessary records accessible. Congress also performs an oversight function when it changes the enabling statute of an agency by writing in certain prohibitions, or when it transfers the functions of one agency to another. One way of incorporating oversight is by sunset legislation, which forces a review of agency activities at specified periods of time. If the review is not done, the sun sets on the program; that is, it is no longer funded. Other oversight activities include the legislative veto power over agency rules and regulations, and the involvement of legislative staff personnel in the policy implementation process. *See also* GENERAL ACCOUNTING OFFICE (GAO), 274; SUNSET LEGISLATION, 81.

Significance Legislative oversight experienced a resurgence during the Watergate era of the middle 1970s. The conditions that led to the congressional investigations of the CIA and FBI were different, however, from the normal environment of legislative review. Formal and regularly scheduled oversight activity has not assumed priority status at the federal level. There are a number of reasons for this. One is that members of Congress's constituency caseloads frequently have first priority on their time. Another is that congressional rewards tend to be in policy *making*, not reviewing. A third is the amount of technical expertise needed to analyze effectively what has been called the impenetrable maze of bureaucracy. Members of Congress also maintain an intricate balance of loyalty to interest groups, mutually advantageous connections with the executive branch, and a reluctance to offend key claimants of an agency. Consequently, legislative oversight is neither systematic nor comprehensive, and its goals appear to be beyond achievement under the current priority system of Congress. There are, however, *informal* modes of oversight which serve useful purposes. A constituent complains to his or her congressional representative that he or she cannot get social security disability benefits, for example. In following through with this case, a representative has access to information about agency procedures and the effect of legislation and administration on the public. Useful oversight material is provided. Since one goal of congressional members is to survive and get re-elected, they will presumably provide oversight when the electorate is suffering from poor execution of a law.

Lindblom, Charles E. (1917–) (106)
Yale University political economist, author, and leading advocate of incrementalism in the formulation of public policy. Charles Lindblom published a classic critique of rational-comprehensive decision making in 1959, "The Science of Muddling Through." In it he noted that the science of policy analysis assumes intellectual capacities and information that men do not possess. Lindblom contrasted the *root* method of rational-comprehensive decision making with the *branch* method, which he called a model of successive limited comparisons. The latter assumes that a historic chain of decisions exists which the administrator can use as a basis for future choices. In *The Intelligence of Democracy: Decision Making Through Mutual Adjustment* (1965), Lindblom presented in detail the benefits of muddling through, basing them on a process he termed "partisan mutual adjustment." For Lindblom, muddling through (1) focuses on policies that differ only marginally or in a limited way from existing policies, rather than totally reassessing given policies; (2) limits alternatives and consequences available for comparison, thus simplifying the policy-making process; (3) does not insist that a solution to a problem be "right" or "ethical," only that it be pragmatic, feasible, and the result of consensus among competing interest groups (in regard to this, Lindblom wrote: "It is not irrational for an administrator to defend a policy as good without being able to specify what it is good for."); and (4) deals with solving current problems rather than creating what might be "sweeping social policy phantasms." The idea of partisan mutual adjustment was first discussed in a book Lindblom wrote with

fellow Yale professor Robert A. Dahl in 1953. In *Politics, Economics, and Welfare,* Lindblom and Dahl rejected the grand planning strategies of socialism and liberalism as inappropriate to governmental administration in a pluralist society. There is greater social value in having interest groups evaluate social policy than in having social scientists evaluate it, because interest groups will resolve conflict better. Each interest group knows what it wants and can be expected to protect its own survival. Partisan mutual adjustment is therefore the hidden hand in incrementalism. It is safer for democracy, because it draws information from sources outside the agency designing the policy, and thereby lessens the chances of bureaucratic imperialism. The agency's acceptance of compromise in policy formulation introduces rationality at the proper point—not at the point of grandiose social planning, but at the point of the distribution of power. *See also* DECISION MAKING, 92–95.

Significance Charles Lindblom's stature in political science is illustrated by the fact that he was president-elect of the American Political Science Association (APSA) for 1981–1982. The incrementalist paradigm he advanced is uniquely comprehensive, including elements of pluralism, satisficing, bounded rationality, organizational drift, limited cognition, and decentralized authority. Lindblom's leading critic is policy analyst Yehezhel Dror, a professor at the Hebrew University in Jerusalem. Dror maintains that when the results of past policies have been unsatisfactory, those results count for little in deciding what to do next, since incremental changes in them cannot produce significantly better results.

Miles's Law (107)

"Where you stand depends on where you sit." Miles's Law states that an administrator's role is substantially shaped by his or her position in the grand organizational design. The Secretary of Defense, according to Miles's dictum, will not advocate a drastic cut in military spending. The Secretary of Agriculture will be more concerned with farmers' income than with consumers' cost of living. The Secretary of the Treasury will be a defender of fiscal prudence. Miles's Law was stated in early 1949 by Rufus E. Miles, Jr., at that time chief of the labor and welfare branch of the division of estimates of the Bureau of the Budget. The occasion of the law's first statement was a job offer made to one of Miles's examiners from an agency whose budget the examiner reviewed. The examiner in the past had been particularly critical, within the confines of the Bureau of the Budget, of the agency now offering him a position at a grade higher than he held in the bureau. Being unable to match the raise, Miles wished the examiner luck and said he hoped they would still be friends after Miles cut the agency's budget as the examiner would have done. Miles predicted to an associate that after three or four months the examiner in his new job would become as critical of the Bureau of the Budget and as defensive of his agency as he had been the opposite within the bureau. The associate remonstrated that the examiner was much too objective and fair minded for that kind of turnabout. It did take about two months longer than Miles estimated, but the examiner turned into a strong advocate of his new agency's financial needs. Miles then said to his associate: "You see, it depends on where you sit, how you stand." The associate turned that remark into Miles's Law, later shortened to "Where you stand depends on where you sit." It spread by word of mouth among Washington's administrative *cognoscenti* during the next decade. See also BOREN'S TESTIMONY, 9; MURPHY'S LAW, 108; PARKINSON'S LAW, 109; PETER PRINCIPLE, 111.

Significance Miles's Law does not describe reprehensible behavior. Miles himself said he would have been surprised and "quite frankly, disappointed" if the former examiner had not become his new agency's strong advocate in its external relationships. The basic lesson of Miles's Law is that there is no such thing as pure objectivity in the arena of budgeting or public policy making. Every administrator has a function to perform, and assigned responsibility markedly influences one's judgment. A closely related corollary of this principle of human behavior is that no person can totally rise above his or her institutional perspectives when asked to serve as a member of a task force expected to exhibit statesmanship and a long-range view of the public good. "In-house" structural analyses conducted by the Public Health Service, the Office of Education, and the Bureau of the Budget cannot produce significant results because the persons assigned to such self-studies cannot separate their judgments from the effects any proposed reorganization may have on their internal fiefdoms. This also is a manifestation of Miles's Law. A third implication of Miles's Law is that a single line of communication may not give an administrator the truth about what is going on. "Unbiased" counsel probably does not exist. Any single line of communication is bound to be influenced by the desire of the communicator to look good, or at least not to look bad. The communicator will want to influence the administrator's decisions in a manner favorable to the communicator, and increase his or her power vis-à-vis other components of the organization. Miles's Law leaves the administrators with the responsibility of counteracting its extreme manifestations and the dead weight of its ordinary manifestations. One way to lessen its impact is a system of flexible personnel transfers without threat to the employee's status or salary. This tends to refocus loyalty from excessive concern for the defense of a personal empire to a stronger commitment to the administration's program goals. Miles wrote retrospectively in 1978 that where you stand depends not only on where you sit, but on how firmly planted you are in the seat.

Murphy's Law (108)

"If anything can go wrong, it will." Murphy's Law was originally stated by Air Force Captain Edsel Murphy in 1949 while engaged in experimental crash research at Edwards Air Force Base in California. Frustrated by a strap transducer that was malfunctioning because a technician had wired it incorrectly, he remarked, "If there is any way to do it wrong, he will." A reliability and quality assurance manager named George E. Nichols overheard the remark and assigned Murphy's Law to the statement and its associated variations. Shortly after the incident, Air Force Colonel J. P. Strapp indicated at a press conference that the fine safety record of the project during several years of simulated crash force testing was the result of a firm belief in Murphy's Law and a "consistent effort to deny the inevitable." Manufacturers' advertisements then made widespread reference to Murphy's Law, and it became a proverb of management. Among the many corollaries of Murphy's Law are the following: (1) All constants are variables. (2) In any given miscalculation, the fault will never be placed if more than one person is involved. (3) Any wire cut to length will be too short. (4) A dropped tool will land where it can do the most damage. (This is also known as the Law of Selective Gravitation.) (5) If a project requires n components, there will be n-1 units in stock. (6) An item selected at random from a group having 99 percent reliability will be a member of the 1 percent group. (7) Interchangeable parts won't. (8) Components that must not and cannot be assembled improperly will be. Murphy's Law inspired not only Klipstein's corollaries but two additional books of corollaries by Arthur Bloch. Murphy's Law spawned an entire approach to management called "Potential Problem Analysis." In this approach, before any action is taken the following categories are thoroughly explored: potential problems and possible causes; probability (in percentages); preventive actions; residual probability (in percentages); and contingent actions. Murphy's Law is the basis of contingency planning. See also BOREN'S TESTIMONY, 9; PARKINSON'S LAW, 109; PETER PRINCIPLE, 111.

Significance   Murphy's Law has become axiomatic language for explaining problems of control in bureaucracies. Public administrationist Anthony Downs, for example, adapted Murphy's Law to several laws of his own. The most notable of these is the Law of Imperfect Control: "No one can fully control the behavior of a large organization." Public administrationist Dwight Waldo believed Murphy's Law helped to produce a new era, the era he calls the "Revolution of Lower Expectations." This era of lower expectations has altered Murphy's Law in some circles from "If anything can go wrong, it will" to "Things will go wrong." According to this view, energy, ecological, and inflation problems are so unmanageable that Murphy might be called an optimist.

Parkinson's Law (109)

"Work expands so as to fill the time available for its completion." Parkinson's Law was enunciated by British administrative theorist, C. Northcote Parkinson, in 1957. Parkinson's popularity as "the administrative theorist of the masses" has been rivaled only by Lawrence J. Peter and the "Peter Principle," which appeared twelve years later. Although the essay in which Parkinson's Law first appeared, "Parkinson's Law or the Rising Pyramid," was intentionally satirical, it also offered valuable insights into the pathologies of bureaucratic organizations. Parkinson himself became a role model for other writers in the field of management, because he took information that might have been dull administrative analysis of organizations and made it entertaining and "best selling." Parkinson's Law was primarily a commentary on organization size. Based on statistical analysis, it suggested that administrative size grows at a fixed annual rate (approximately 5.75 percent), which is totally unrelated to the actual work load of the organization. Parkinson's Law states that executives see their status in terms of the numbers of workers under them. If they can put more and more people there, it is a sure indication of success. At the end of his essay, Parkinson presented this law in mathematical form. He said that in any public administrative department not actually at war, the staff increase may be expected to follow this formula:

$$x = \frac{2k^m + 1}{n}$$

The component k is the number of administrators seeking career aggrandizement through the appointment of subordinates; l represents the difference between the ages of appointment and retirement; m is the number of man-hours devoted to answering minutes within the department; and n is the number of effective units being administered. The component x is the number of new staff required each year. Parkinson noted that to find the percentage increase, mathematicians must multiply x by 100 and divide by the total of the previous year, thus:

$$\frac{100(2k^m + 1)}{\%yn}$$

The component y represents the total original staff. This figure according to Parkinson will invariably prove to be between 5.17 percent and 6.56 percent. Parkinson's Law did not claim to have political value. No attempt was made to inquire whether departments *ought* to grow in size. Parkinson said that his law was "a purely scientific discovery." *See also* BOREN'S TESTIMONY, 9; MURPHY'S LAW, 108; PETER PRINCIPLE, 111.

Significance Parkinson's Law was the result of a serious inquiry by C. Northcote Parkinson into the reasons why the British Admiralty staff of 8,118 in the year 1935 came to number 33,788 in the year 1954. Parkinson was equally taken by the fact that the Colonial Office had increased from 372 administrators in the year 1935 to 1,661 in the year 1954, during a period of imperial decline. The colonial territories were not much altered in area or population between 1935 and 1939; yet the increase in purely administrative personnel numbered 78. The territories were considerably diminished by 1943, certain areas being in enemy hands, yet an additional 367 administrators were employed. From 1943 until 1954 the British Empire shrank steadily in size, but the size of the Colonial Office administrative staff increased by another 844 persons. A rational explanation of these increases, and similar ones in U.S. administrative agencies, is that they reflected changes in—increases in—scope of agency responsibility. Parkinson demonstrated they did not. Instead they represented stages in an inevitable increase that had nothing to do with the scope—or even the existence—of agency responsibility. Parkinson's Law states that the number of officials and the quantity of work are not related to each other. The rise in the total of those employed is governed by a law that would be much the same whether the volume of work were to increase, diminish, or even disappear.

Participative Management (110)

A process by which workers are brought into organizational decision-making processes to varying degrees, primarily on matters that directly affect them. Participative management is a product of the human relations movement in management theory and is growing as a result of studies done in the 1960s which demonstrated that the more input workers have about what they do and how they do it, the more productive they will be. The goal of participative management is to increase the organization's output, while simultaneously meeting the needs of individual employees. The strategy worked well for such organizations as the McCormick Company, the Glacier Metal Company of Great Britain, and BEA Associates of New York. Each of these companies set up committees of employees who made decisions concerning job design, promotion, salary, and retirement plans. Those persons who used the files, for example, decided how to set them up. An organization may pay people for their judgment as well as their labor, so that creative approaches to management prevail. The participative management approach appears to work best in smaller organizations where subordinates are skilled professionals. It also works well in situations where organizations are in a state of change. Workers who have difficulty coping with change find change easier to accept if they have helped define their new working conditions. *See also* GROUP THEORY, 53; HAWTHORNE STUDIES, 54; HUMAN MOTIVATION: THEORY Y, 102.

Significance   Participative management is based on studies such as those completed at the University of Michigan's Survey Research Center in 1969 which showed that *all* of a sample of 1,533 workers interviewed ranked interesting work and personal authority far ahead of good pay and job security. An explanation for the survey's results can be traced back to Abraham Maslow's theory of human motivation and the hierarchy of human needs. People need not only income from their work, but some sense of status and recognition, as well as feelings of self-worth. Most of the advantages of participative management fall in three categories: (1) subordinate input can improve the quality of decisions; (2) participative management leads to acceptance of and commitment to organizational goals; people tend to support what they help create; and (3) participation promotes teamwork within the organization—it tends to erase the "tunnel vision" workers have if they do not have the whole picture. The disadvantages of participative management are (1) often there is not enough time to have the many meetings required to get everyone involved; (2) participation sometimes leads to conflict and antagonism between workers and managers; and (3) participative management can produce confusion of roles. Once a worker has been "given an inch," he sometimes "wants a mile." The disadvantages illustrate the key issue involved when a manager decides to allow his or her subordinates to participate in decision making: communication. People must be aware of the degree to which they will be participating in management decisions, as well as their role in the total organizational environment. Without effective communication, participative management practices will not achieve their aim, which is to allow workers to become mentally and emotionally involved in their job.

Peter Principle (111)

"In a hierarchy, every employee tends to rise to his level of incompetence." The Peter Principle was stated in 1969 by Laurence J. Peter and Raymond Hull in their best-selling book of that title. Following in the tradition of C. Northcote Parkinson and his "Parkinson's Law," Peter and Hull postulated that things go wrong in the world because hierarchical organizations constantly promote people to work at their level of incompetence. Greater efficiency could be achieved if everyone were demoted one level, so that everyone would operate at his or her level of competence. Work is accomplished by those employees who have not yet reached their level of incompetence. The Peter Principle was based on its authors' feigned discovery of a new science, the science of *hierarchiology*. The term *hierarchy* was originally used to describe the system of church government by priests graded into ranks. Its contemporary meaning, however, includes any organization whose members or employees are arranged in order of rank, grade, or class. Their study of hierarchies convinced Peter and Hull that in any human organizational undertaking—government, politics, business, industry, trade-unionism, the armed forces, religion, and education—the Peter Principle controls. As one wins promotions, moving from one level of competence to a higher level of competence, each individual eventually receives a final promotion. He or she is not promoted further because the level of incompetence has been reached. Thus Peter's Corollary states: "In time, every post tends to be occupied by an employee who is incompetent to carry out its duties." The phenomena of "percussive sublimation," commonly referred to as "being kicked upstairs," and "the lateral arabesque" are not exceptions to the Peter Principle, but are examples of "pseudo-promotions," according to Peter and Hull. The Peter Principle was an effort to explain occupational incompetence. It defined the cause as an inherent feature of the rules governing the placement of employees. *See also* BOREN'S TESTIMONY, 9; MURPHY'S LAW, 108; PARKINSON'S LAW, 109.

Significance The Peter Principle was based on a scientific analysis of hundreds of case histories. Three examples will illustrate the findings. (1) An army general was the idol of his men. He led them to many well-deserved victories. His hearty, informal manner, his racy style of speech, his scorn for petty regulations, and his undoubted personal bravery did not matter very much, however, when he received his next and final promotion. His new position required dealing with politicians and diplomats rather than ordinary soldiers. He would not conform to the necessary protocol. He could not turn his tongue to conventional courtesies. He quarreled with dignitaries and took to lying, for days at a time, drunk and sulking, in his trailer. He had been promoted to a position he was incompetent to fill. (2) An automobile mechanic had been a zealous apprentice and an outstanding journeyman mechanic. He showed exceptional ability in diagnosing obscure faults, and endless patience in correcting them. He was promoted to foreman of the repair shop. But as foreman his love of things mechanical and his perfectionism became liabilities. He would not let a job go until he was fully satisfied with it. He meddled with the work of his employees. He was seldom at his desk, usually being found up to his elbows in a dismantled motor while the man who should have been doing the work stood watching. The shop was overcrowded with work, and customers were unhappy. The man was a competent mechanic, but an incompetent foreman. (3) A maintenance foreman in the public works department of a small city was a favorite of senior officials at City Hall. They all liked his unfailing affability. The superintendent of works praised his good judgment and pleasant and agreeable manner. The foreman was not supposed to make policy, so he had no need to disagree with his superiors. The foreman then succeeded the superintendent on the latter's retirement. The new superintendent continued to agree with everyone. He passed to his foreman every suggestion that came from above. The resulting conflicts in policy and the continual changing of plans soon demoralized the department. Saying "yes" to everyone, the new superintendent actually did the work of a messenger. The man was a competent foreman, but became an incompetent superintendent. The Peter Principle is based on the fact that when there is a job opening in a hierarchy, it usually will be filled by the most competent person available just below the position to be filled. One does not know until the promotion has taken place if it produces incompetence.

Proverbs of Administration (112)

The title of a 1946 article in the *Public Administration Review* authored by Herbert A. Simon. "The Proverbs of Administration" launched a major attack on Gulick's POSDCORB (planning, organizing, staffing, directing, coordinating, reporting, and budgeting) and its associated components. Simon believed them to be inconsistent, conflicting, and inapplicable to many of the administrative situations facing public managers. In a 1947 book, *Administrative Behavior,* Simon expanded on the "Proverbs" article in building a case against the premises of scientific management. He argued that the defect of the premises— that is, the principles or proverbs of administration—is that "for almost every principle one can find an equally plausible and acceptable contradictory principle." The proverbs or maxims Simon attacked are those which predicted increased administrative efficiency by (1) specialization; (2) arranging the group into a hierarchy of authority; (3) limiting the span of control; (4) grouping the workers, for purposes of control, according to (a) purpose, (b) process, (c) clientele, or (d) place. Each of these proverbs was demonstrated by Simon to be mutually contradictory. For example, he pointed out that the principle of narrow span of control is contradictory to the maxim that efficiency requires keeping the number of supervisory levels in an organization to a minimum. With devastating logic, Simon paired widely accepted principles and demonstrated that often implementing one would negate another. *See also* BARNARD, CHESTER I., 122; POSDCORB, 180; SCIENTIFIC MANAGEMENT, 22; SIMON, HERBERT A., 114; TAYLORISM, 25.

Significance "The Proverbs of Administration" effectively discredited the classical school's claim to scientific validity. Among the structuralists of the 1930s, best represented in Luther Gulick and Lyndall Urwick's *Papers on the Science of Administration* (1937), there had been little doubt that their principles would stand the test of time. Indeed some of their principles do continue to influence how governmental agencies are organized. But Simon's work, along with that of contemporaries and coauthors Donald Smithburg, Victor Thompson, James D. Thompson, and James G. March, set a new course for public administration following World War II. Having successfully questioned the premise that organizations can be laid out and administered in a fully rational way, Simon went on to build on the theoretical foundations of Chester I. Barnard and other advocates of a systems approach for examining the various facets of administrative behavior. The enduring significance of the proverbs episode in the history of American public administration is that it put organization theory and research on a firm scientific footing. Simon insisted that the methodology of logical positivism be followed rigorously, and must include (1) value neutrality; (2) logically derived operational hypotheses; and (3) controlled empirical testing of hypotheses. Logically convincing conclusions or generalizations extracted from simple observation are not enough.

Satisficing (113)

The process of finding a decision alternative that meets the decision maker's minimum standard of satisfaction. *Satisficing* was coined by James G. March and Herbert A. Simon in their 1958 book *Organizations*. They argued that while economic man selects the best alternatives from those available, his cousin, administrative man, satisfices—looks for a course of action that is satisfactory. If maximizing means getting the most out of something, satisficing means getting only enough to meet the immediate need or selecting the solution that is least upsetting to stability. The three fundamental satisficing techniques are (1) use only existing agency resources that one's superiors would expect to be used in the process of making a decision; (2) arrange compromises among the various affected elements of the organization; and (3) avoid formulating explicit goals and policies in order to avoid the unnecessary conflict that such explicitness may generate. *See also* BOUNDED RATIONALITY, 88; DECISION MAKING, 92; SIMON, HERBERT A., 114.

Significance Satisficing is a form of incremental decision making that relates to the advantages and disadvantages of incrementalism. The major advantage of satisficing is that it usually promotes a decision that will work. It provides satisfactory relief from the perceived difficulties without threatening undesirable unrest within the agency and among the legislators, executives, and interest groups who involve themselves in the agency's affairs. The chief disadvantage of satisficing is that it promotes drift—action without direction. While satisficing may reflect realism, it leaves unanswered such questions as what standards will be used to determine what is satisfactory. American public administrationist Louis Gawthrop argues that satisficing is irresponsible in the face of complex problems requiring major innovations in public policy. The radical changes sometimes necessary to avoid catastrophe are not possible in the satisficing model.

Simon, Herbert A. (1916–) (114)

American administrative theorist and economist who dismissed the formal principles of administration as mere proverbs and called on public administrators to focus on behavioral issues, such as the decision to participate and the limits of administrative rationality.

Simon is a multidiscipline scholar who holds the Richard King Mellon Chair in computer science and psychology at the Carnegie-Mellon University in Pittsburgh. He first ventured into public administration in 1938 with a pioneering study on measuring the results of government programs. Following World War II, he launched the behavioral revolution in public administration with his *Administrative Behavior*, published in 1947. The revolution had actually begun in 1946 with Simon's iconoclastic piece in the *Public Administration Review* entitled "The Proverbs of Administration," in which he pointed out the ambiguities and contradictions in the Gulick-Urwick principles stated a decade before. Simon methodically attacked each principle of the classical school's synthesis. *Specialization* could be by place or by function, he said, and the principle of specialization does not help at all in choosing between the two. *Unity of command* is in conflict with the principle of specialization. Specialization asserts that confusion is reduced when tasks are accomplished by specialists. This leads automatically to a situation in which the specialists at the headquarters consult with the specialists in the field on matters of common concern without going through the official hierarchy. The result is a *dual* chain of command which promotes the advantages of the principle of specialization. It also violates the advantages of the principle of unity of command. *Span of control* conflicts with both the principle of specialization and the principle of unity of command. In a large, complex organization, whether the span of control is increased or decreased will, under certain circumstances, have either desirable or undesirable consequences. "What is the optimum point?" Simon asks. The principle also throws no light on the problem of whether an organization should be centralized or decentralized. *Organization, purpose, process, clientele,* and *place* each compete with the other as an organizing device. The one selected as the basis for establishing organization may be in conflict with one of the others. Public health administration, for example, might be organized on the basis of purpose, particular clientele served, or place located. Which organizing device would be most effective is not explained by the principle.

After Simon's devastatingly effective attack on the proverbs or principles of administration, he suggested that organizations are primarily *processes* of decision making. To understand organizations it was necessary to understand the various elements and factors involved in making decisions. Decisions are made *in the mind*. Mental choices are decidedly limited because complete and absolute knowledge of all the data in a given situation is seldom available. This was Simon's basic quarrel with the structuralists of the 1930s; that is, their underlying premise that organizations could be laid out and administered in a fully rational way. Every decision maker operates within a "bounded rationality," he said, within unknowables, internal forces, and external developments that may be beyond the control of management. That fact of life requires systems that are open, adaptable, and living in flux with their environments. Public administration's concern with the strictures imposed by bounded rationality should be at the point of decision making, since organizations are first and foremost decision-making networks. Their ability to generate and analyze information flows can compensate for bounded rationality, although limitations on knowledge can never be removed fully. Agencies must *satisfice* by accepting partial solutions rather than pursue illusory, perfect, or optimized solutions. See also BOUNDED RATIONALITY, 88; PROVERBS OF ADMINISTRATION, 112; SATISFICING, 113.

Significance Herbert Simon led an attack on the principles of administration that was logically successful but that had limited practical effect. POSDCORB may have been proverbial, but it was *useful* to administrators in a way that Simon's emphasis on administrative decision making was not. Ironically enough, since about 1960 Simon has moved more and more toward the position that a science of management may be possible after all. His position from the beginning was that it was impossible for managers to achieve a high degree of rationality in making decisions because the amount of information they needed to evaluate was too great. That position was modified by the computer revolution. The computer, with its enormous capacity to process and organize information for managers, may give them the ability to make entirely rational decisions. Simon wrote not only about computers that prepare tax bills and payroll checks, speed up the design of roads and bridges by performing complex engineering calculations, and analyze the budget by breaking down the per-unit cost of operations. He also wrote about computers that can be programmed to think, innovate, and behave like managers. By 1973, Simon had solved the problem of bounded rationality by a cybernetic prescription of employee roles in formal and highly centralized organizations. Decisions were imposed by computer-output analyzing information coordinators. Human relations specialist Chris Argyris joined the computer issue with Simon at this point in the pages of the *Public Administration Review*, where a debate between Argyris and Simon took place during 1973. Argyris accused Simon of fomenting a rational-man theory, which would lead to more hierarchical, less humane organizations. He said Simon was a contemporary structuralist. Simon replied that Argyris suffered from a preoccupation with power. He accused Argyris of being against any kind of structure at all. Argyris replied that he was not against structure, but he was against management information systems which reduced the ability of administrators to use intuition. The extent to which Herbert Simon has become a rational-man theorist is indeed a matter of debate.

Span of Control (115)

The extent to which one person can extend his or her supervisory powers over other individuals or administrative units in an effective manner. The effectiveness of an administrator's span of control depends on many factors, including type of work, the personalities of the superior and of supervised individuals, the physical distance between supervisor and subordinates, and the staff and auxiliary help available to the supervisor. *See also* ADMINISTRATIVE REORGANIZATION, 119; FUNCTIONAL CONSOLIDATION, 143; UNITY OF COMMAND, 118.

Significance The importance of span of control as an administrative concept relates to the basic problem of efficient management in the public service. Most supervisors, including the president, the governors, big-city mayors, city managers, and department and agency heads are responsible for efficient supervision of what amounts in many cases to an unmanageable number of subordinates. Rather than reducing the number of individuals reporting to them, the president and most governors have sought help by strengthening their staff and auxiliary agencies. Although many presidents have come into office with the firm expectation of reducing their span of control to make it more effective, they have discovered that most agencies have powerful friends in Congress and among pressure groups that are opposed to change in the status of agencies. Although the figure is arbitrary, most management specialists advocate that not more than twenty units or individuals should report to and be supervised by a single executive. Many administrative reorganizations in national, state, and local governments are aimed at reducing the span of control for a chief executive or for top level administrators.

Strategic Planning (116)

The process of making and implementing decisions concerning the use of resources to achieve an organization's goals and fulfill its mission. Strategic planning deals with the alternative uses of resources rather than the immediate control of how targeted resources are spent. It defines the structure of the organization and the basic nature of organizational services, products, and activities. Like long-range planning, strategic planning is future oriented. It does not deal with future decisions, however, but with the futurity of today's decisions. It allows for reaction to change or environmental factors, be they internal or external. Long-range planning suggests only the time frame for the strategic plan, which is normally five years.

Significance Strategic planning forces an organization to define its philosophy, mission, role, and goals. It is the responsibility of an organization's governing board to do such planning with the assistance of online management. Strategic planning is rooted in the need of an organization to stay in touch with those it seeks to serve, to assure that the services being provided are those that are needed.

Stress Management (117)

A collection of skills that helps public managers maintain productivity and job satisfaction in the face of complex organizational and community pressures. Stress management's primary goal is to attain individual health and organizational well-being through applications from medicine, psychology, organization development, and public administration. Stress can be described as a body's response to change. It is a physical and chemical reaction to demands that are too high or too low. Too little stress results in low productivity. Too much stress also results in low productivity, with concomitant vulnerability to illness. Stress can be desirable and healthy when kept in balance with measured rates of change, hence the term *stress management*. The tools of stress management are (1) *medical,* which includes examinations, physical fitness programs, good eating habits, relaxation, and the individual's assumption of responsibility for personal health; (2) *psychological,* which includes employee counseling, alcohol and drug abuse programs, hot-lines, and crisis intervention; and (3) *organization development,* which includes seminars on what stress is and what causes it, how to recognize signs of extreme stress in co-workers and subordinates, what normal stress responses are, and how to assess stress-producing organization norms. Stress management identifies four major causes of job stress: (1) work overload and underload—too many demands with tight and competing deadlines, or too few demands so that depression results; (2) role ambiguity—lack of clarity about what is expected by others; (3) role conflict—as when a co-worker, the boss, and a constituent have different but simultaneous demands on the individual; and (4) politics—person-to-person communication problems, intergroup conflict, conflicts of values or political views, and sexual harassment.

Significance Efforts to achieve stress management have resulted in organizational awareness that employees need different challenges as they progress through apprentice, specialist, and generalist stages of their work life. Stress management data indicate that 15 to 20 percent of the work force will experience a mid-life crisis shortly before or after age forty, when radical reassessment, depression, loss of drive, or impulsive job or lifestyle changes may occur. Organizations themselves also go through such life stages. When a crisis occurs, both individuals and organizations go through predictable periods of shock, denial, withdrawal, anger, resignation, and, finally, acceptance of the new circumstances. The public manager typically applies stress management skills when faced with events such as geographic relocation, change of administration, funding cutbacks, reorganization of priorities or work groups, strikes, and reductions in work force. The primary significance of stress management is that major changes and disruptions can be anticipated and their negative effects minimized by the individual. This can be achieved by (1) exercising daily; (2) eating regularly and moderately; (3) avoiding excessive drinking and drug taking; (4) doing things one enjoys; (5) taking time to relax; (6) thinking about what is really important; (7) thinking positively; (8) managing time; (9) setting goals; and (10) planning for the future. Stress management incorporates the notion of self-responsibility with skilled training in self-care, adaptive behavior change, and control over one's environment.

Unity of Command (118)

A basic principle of personnel management that provides for clarity in the relationship between those who issue orders and those who are subject to obey orders. Unity of command, as practiced within a hierarchical personnel structure, means that no person is subject to orders from more than one superior. Most supervisory officials issue orders to those within the sphere of their jurisdiction and, at the same time, are responsible to those officials who are above them on the supervisory ladder. *See also* HIERARCHY, 147.

Significance The typical military organization tends to maximize the principles of hierarchy and unity of command. In applying the principle of unity of command to civilian agencies, however, difficulties arise because of the great variety of tasks to be performed, and the undesirability of trying to foster the strict discipline that characterizes the military. In the federal service, unity of command has been encouraged by giving the President power to appoint and remove top level administrators and to hold all individuals serving in the executive branch accountable through the hierarchical structure. The principle is weakened, however, by the existence of various independent agencies and commissions, by the difficulties involved in trying to remove personnel, especially individuals hired under affirmative action programs and those with veterans' preference, and by the tendency for informal chains of command to develop within administrative units. Unity of command is applied even less to administrative units on the state and local levels, where elective officials often contest with each other and with appointive officials for decision-making power. Administrative experts generally support the unity of command principle and advocate policies that will help make it effective, such as integrating units that perform similar functions, establishing a hierarchy of power (from top to bottom) and accountability (from bottom to apex), and vesting authority for making decisions in a single individual.

4. Bureaucracy and Administrative Organization

Administrative Reorganization (119)
Changes made in the organizational patterns and procedures of governmental agencies aimed at improving their operations through greater efficiency. By-products of administrative reorganization include greater economy, increased productivity, and clearer lines of authority and responsibility. Typically, reorganization plans are aimed at (1) eliminating waste and duplication of services by integrating agencies that carry on the same or similar functions; (2) reducing the number of agencies reporting to a chief administrator by consolidating many diverse units into fewer larger units; (3) providing staff and auxiliary services to help the chief administrator with advisory and housekeeping functions; (4) delineating clear lines of authority and responsibility so that decisions can be made more effectively and accountability can be assigned for each such action; (5) eliminating elective positions and multiheaded boards that engage in routine administrative functions but are not extensively involved in policy making; (6) encouraging long- and short-range planning services to help decision makers; and (7) providing for continuing review of personnel, management, and budget procedures. *See also* ADMINISTRATION, 1.

Significance Reorganization movements typically have been based on the assumption that administrative reorganization would provide the reforms necessary to make government a more vital force in improving the human condition. Such changes have been instituted on all levels of government—national, state, and local. In most cases, they have resulted in strengthening the role of chief executives and chief administrators, including presidents, governors, mayors, and city and county managers. Some reorganizations have captured the public spotlight, such as the reorganization of Georgia's state administrative system by Governor Jimmy Carter, an action that later contributed to his successful bid for the presidency. In 1939, and then under the Reorganization Act of 1949, the president was granted the power to carry on continuing studies and to institute "reorganization plans" that became law within sixty days unless "vetoed" by either house of Congress. The initial act and subsequent renewals have made it possible for presidents to act forthrightly to streamline executive operations without the long delays of the past occasioned by congressional inaction. Several state legislatures have also delegated reorganization powers to the governor while retaining the veto power over gubernatorial actions. Reorganizations in local governments have usually involved changing high level positions from elective to appointive. Opposition to reorganizations typically comes from interest groups adversely affected by the administrative changes, from legislators who have developed close working relationships with existing units and personnel, and from agency personnel who have a vested interest in the status quo. Administrative reorganization plans are often presented as ways of improving the efficiency of government, but as scholars such as Herbert Kaufman have pointed out, they are often in fact politically motivated "power plays." Although the legislative veto approach has been used successfully in many reorganization efforts, in 1983 the Supreme Court declared the legislative veto unconstitutional in violation of the separation of powers (*Immigration and Naturalization Service v. Chadha*, 462 U.S. 919: 1983).

Auxiliary Agency (120)
Any administrative unit that has as its main function the supporting and servicing of other units. Auxiliary agencies can be distinguished from staff agencies in that the latter are mainly concerned with providing know-how and advice to decision makers. Auxiliary units on the other hand are responsible for providing technical services and performing routine housekeeping tasks. These include such services as personnel management, central purchasing, maintaining buildings, and accounting. Some agencies, such as the Office of Management and Budget (OMB), provide both staff and auxiliary services. *See also* GENERAL SERVICES ADMINISTRATION (GSA), 144; OFFICE OF MANAGEMENT AND BUDGET (OMB), 166; OFFICE OF PERSONNEL MANAGEMENT (OPM), 229.

Significance   Auxiliary agencies function as a key control mechanism for department heads or chief executives on all levels of government. Economy is also a major consideration. Centralized personnel management and purchasing, for example, provide for economies of scale and lower per-unit costs than would result if each operating unit tried to carry out its own programs of recruiting and hiring personnel and purchasing supplies. Uniformity also reduces friction among units and permits the standardization of many operations.

Axiomatic Theory (121)

An approach that seeks to explain the nature and function of organizations. Axiomatic theory, developed by Jerald Hage and elaborated in the *Administrative Science Quarterly* in December 1965, identifies variables or formal characteristics common to all organizations. These are (1) complexity; (2) centralization; (3) formalization; (4) stratification; (5) adaptiveness; (6) production; (7) efficiency; and (8) job satisfaction. The first four are organizational means; the last four are organizational ends. Axiomatic theory uses these variables to form seven propositions about how organizational means and ends influence each other. The major theme is the idea of functional strain, or the concept of organizational dilemma. An increase in the effect of one variable results in a decrease in the effect of another. The theory, as set forth by Hage, attempts to specify which variables are in opposition to others, and why. The seven propositions are used to derive twenty-one corollaries, which in turn provide twenty-nine hypotheses, on which axiomatic theory is based. These corollaries and hypotheses are used to codify research and to analyze problems of organizational change.

Significance   Axiomatic theory, with its means-ends distinctions, clarifies much of the conceptual confusion involved in structural-functional analysis. The theory provides precise definitions that clarify such concepts as structural incompatibility, dysfunction, and equilibrium within organizations. The theory is useful in analyzing a number of organizational problems, such as rate of change, centralization versus decentralization, and morale. It also provides the means for improving organizational performance. If greater efficiency is desired, for example, the theory suggests a greater formalization of rules. If greater job satisfaction is desired, the theory suggests decreasing the stratification of rewards. Axiomatic theory provides a partial answer to whether particular social means are appropriate for meeting stated social ends.

Barnard, Chester I. (1886–1961) (122)
American executive and administrative theorist who broke away from the legal-rational approach to organization theory in the late 1930s, arguing that authority is not imposed from above but is granted to supervisors by employees. Barnard had a rich and varied career as a chief executive. From 1927 to 1948, he was president of New Jersey Bell Telephone, a large public utility; during World War II he headed the USO, a nonprofit organization; and from 1952 to 1954, he was president of the Rockefeller Foundation, a large philanthropic organization. Barnard was the first major administrative theorist to develop the concept of the decision-making process. Decision making, in Barnard's view, involves searching for strategic factors that meet the organization's purposes. Barnard said that *coordination* was the chief function of the executive. He said that discussions of administrative coordination led most managers to talk about issuing orders, preparing budgets, and staffing the organization. Barnard took a different approach. He emphasized the idea of organizational purpose. Every organization possessed some unifying purpose, just as New Jersey Bell's purpose was to provide telephone service. The individual employees, by themselves, without an organization, could not accomplish that purpose. The organization came into being when individuals who were in a position to communicate with one another decided to contribute their actions to a common purpose. Barnard did for organizations what John Locke did for constitutions. He set the source of organizations' power in the people who comprised them. From this principle came the idea that the exercise of authority is a two-way street. Top administrators could employ their formal authority to influence subordinates, but at some point subordinates had to be willing to be influenced. Barnard wrote of a *zone of indifference*, which Herbert Simon later renamed a *zone of acceptance*, to suggest that managers would be well-advised to limit their orders to what they were sure subordinates would accept. From this hypothesis followed the observation that only those orders that would be obeyed should be issued. *See also* ORGANIZATION THEORY, CLASSICAL, 176; ORGANIZATION THEORY: HUMANISM, 177; ORGANIZATION THEORY, NEO-CLASSICAL, 178.

Significance Chester Barnard stood directly opposite Henri Fayol. Barnard said simply that *all organizational authority flows from the bottom up;* from the worker to the foreman, from the client to the bureaucrat, from the child to the parent. The conclusions of *The Functions of the Executive* were controversial when Barnard published them in 1938, and they are controversial today. F. J. Roethlisberger thought it remarkable that the Bell System tolerated such deviant behavior on the part of one of its chief executives. Barnard's views are in stark contrast to the orthodox belief that executives acquire official authority from a specific grant of power from a higher office, relevant to their responsibilities, to which obedience is assured through the forces of command and discipline. Barnard insisted that formal authority of this sort existed only in the abstract. In real organizations, he said, authority is always attached to a communiqué to do this or not do that. If the communication channels are snarled, and the order never received, then authority does not exist. Subordinates ignore communiqués for a number of reasons: because they are physically unable to carry them out; because the orders conflict with their personal interests; or because they believe that the orders are inconsistent with their own perception of the true purposes of the organization. In an organization where purpose is legitimized through the cooperation of its members, authority depends entirely on an effective system of communication. Barnard made the executive the trustee of the organizational purpose, and this idea is his chief contribution to organization theory. *Persistence of cooperation,* he said, depends on the ability of the executive to preserve the purpose of the organization. A good executive promotes persistence of cooperation—Barnard's primary administrative value—by fusing the organizational purpose to the personal needs of the employees. The executive must make certain that organizational rewards contain noneconomic incentives, such as affection and a sense of belonging, and, most important, the executive must maintain among the members of the organization a willingness to communicate. Only by keeping communication channels open can the executive transmit the purpose of the organization and learn the needs of the employees. Chester Barnard was a brilliant contributor to the effort to transform public administration into a behavioral science. He was one of the few highly successful practitioners in U.S. administrative history to put his thoughts about administration "on paper."

Board (123)
A multiheaded administrative organization. A board or commission typically consists of three or more persons who are collectively assigned responsibility for carrying out some governmental function. Although "board" and "commission" are often used interchangeably, the former more typically describes a group that exercises policy or decision-making functions, whereas the latter is more usually assigned regulatory or auxiliary responsibilities. Examples of each include a board of supervisors, the National Labor Relations Board (NLRB),

the Federal Trade Commission (FTC), and the Nuclear Regulatory Commission (NRC). See also AUXILIARY AGENCY, 120.

Significance Boards and commissions have become commonplace in the administrative structures of government at all levels. The use of multiheaded in contrast to single-headed directorships is one of the key issues facing organization specialists. In theory, a board is regarded as preferable to a single head when the administrative unit's operations include quasi-legislative and quasi-judicial functions, and a single director is more desirable if the unit's operations are mainly administrative and enforcement in nature. Both types are used with little emphasis on the application of theory to practice. The advantages of boards include (1) where terms of office overlap, continuity of policy is encouraged; (2) bipartisan representation can be applied to boards; (3) in dealing with problems of the economy, various competing groups can be represented; and (4) more effective policies may be developed as a result of group deliberation. Single-headed agencies, as contrasted with boards, have the advantages of fixing responsibility, avoiding conflict and stalemate, and having unity of purpose. Some efforts have been made to meld the two types by assigning policy-making and adjudicatory functions to a board while vesting full administrative responsibility in the chairman of the board. Several federal agencies, including the Federal Trade Commission (FTC), utilize this compromise approach.

Brownlow Committee (124)
The popular name for President Franklin D. Roosevelt's Committee on Administrative Management, which issued an influential report in 1937. The Brownlow Committee was named for its chairman, public administrationist Louis Brownlow. The other two members were public administrationist Luther Gulick and political scientist Charles Merriam. The Brownlow Committee was asked to assemble a staff and apply state-of-the-art principles of administration to the federal government. The committee recommended (1) the establishment of an Executive Office of the President, the core of which would be the White House staff and the Bureau of the Budget, with the latter moved to the Executive Office from the Treasury Department and given expanded budgetary and management powers; (2) the consolidation of all line agencies, including the independent regulatory commissions, into twelve cabinet-level departments; and (3) the alteration of the work of the Civil Service Commission, the General Accounting Office (GAO), and the Natural Resources Planning Board to improve mechanisms for personnel administration, fiscal

Bureaucracy and Administrative Organization

management, planning, and congressional audits. The recommendations of the Brownlow Committee were largely implemented by the Reorganization Act of 1939. In the act, Congress recognized a permanent shift in authority for managing the departments of government by allowing the president to submit reorganization plans to Congress, which were to be effective unless Congress by concurrent resolution disapproved the plans in their entirety. Congress restrained its own power by defeating a motion to not allow any reorganization plan to become effective unless *approved* by Congress, and in not permitting itself to modify any organization plan. Thus in the period from April 1939 to December 1940, President Roosevelt submitted five reorganization plans to Congress, and all became effective. A series of executive orders established professionally staffed personnel offices in each major federal agency and created the Executive Office of the President. The latter was actually a collection of managerial offices, including the Bureau of the Budget; the National Resources Planning Board; the Liaison Office for Personnel Management (to serve as a conduit between the Chief Executive and the Civil Service Commission); and the Office of Emergency Management. The Brownlow Committee saw the creation of the Executive Office of the President as its major objective, assuring that "the President will have adequate machinery for the administrative management of the executive branch of the government." The position of the chief executive was so strengthened by the work of the Brownlow Committee that its report is often called the birth of the modern presidency. *See also* ADMINISTRATIVE REORGANIZATION, 119; HOOVER COMMISSION, FIRST, 149; HOOVER COMMISSION, SECOND, 150.

Significance   The Brownlow Committee did not represent the first impulse for comprehensive administrative reform in the federal government. That distinction belongs to President William Howard Taft's Commission on Efficiency and Economy, established in 1911. The Brownlow Committee was, however, the most influential effort prior to the report of the second Hoover Commission in 1955, and it represented a rite of passage from legislative to executive control of federal government management. The president was overburdened with a mass of petty detail, but was denied the assistance that he needed to control his subordinates; thus he could not delegate the work he should have delegated. Brownlow argued that to remedy this situation it was not necessary to give the president any powers the Constitution did not originally give him. It was only necessary to create in the Executive Office of the President the physical and organizational facilities that any chief executive must have under modern conditions if he or she is to discharge the responsibilities of the office. Another member of the Brownlow Committee, Luther Gulick, who was Director of the Institute of Public Administration and Eaton Professor of Municipal Science and Administration at Columbia University, used the occasion of the committee's research effort to draw together "the essential papers" then extant on "the phenomena of administration." These papers were published in 1937 as *Papers on the Science of Administration*. They included an original piece by Gulick himself, entitled "Notes on the Theory of Organization," and referred to it as "a memorandum prepared as a member of the President's Committee on Administrative Management, December, 1936." The *Papers* and Gulick's "Notes" became seminal pieces in the study of public administration. The Brownlow Committee had spin-off influences unprecedented in U.S. administrative history.

Bureau (125)

A major unit that operates within a department or agency. Each bureau is typically assigned responsibility for some specialized activities. Each bureau chief is responsible to the secretary or director who heads the department or agency in which the bureau is located. *See also* DEPARTMENT, 136.

Significance   A great many bureaus are found within the administrative structure of the thirteen major departments that function under presidential direction and control. Examples of well-known bureaus include the Census Bureau in the Department of Commerce and the Federal Bureau of Investigation (FBI) in the Department of Justice. Although there have been many efforts to develop a standard nomenclature for subunits in each major department, the administrative structure remains a conglomeration of bureaus, offices, divisions, sections, and other units. Although each bureau chief is technically responsible to the secretary or director, many have developed close working relationships with Congress and with key congressional committees. The result is that the lines of responsibility and authority are not always clear-cut, and bureau chiefs may pursue policies and programs that are not compatible with the major objectives of the organization or of the administration.

Bureaucracy (126)

A system of authority relations defined by rationally developed rules. Bureaucracy as a term was first used in 1745 by Vincent de Gournay, a French physiocrat, to describe the Prussian government. It was a derogatory reference to a type of government in which power resided with officials. It thus represented an addition to Aristotle's three forms of perverted government: tyranny, oligarchy, and democracy, which were the dark sides of kingly rule, aristocracy, and constitutional government. Bureaucracy was developed by the German sociologist Max Weber (1864–1920) as an "ideal type" of social system. For Weber, bureaucracy is typified by a rational and effective organization that operates on the basis of (1) rules by which tasks are organized; (2) a division of labor which produces specialization; (3) hierarchy, meaning superior-subordinate relationships; (4) decisions by technical and legal standards; (5) administration based on filing systems and institutional memory; and (6) administration as a vocation. See also AUTHORITY, 87; BUREAUPATHOLOGY, 129; HIERARCHY, 147; RED TAPE, 181; WEBER, MAX, 187.

Significance Bureaucracy in the contemporary world refers primarily to government agencies that are characterized by day-to-day policy implementation, routine, complex procedures, specialization of duties, rights of authority and status, and resistance to change. Bureaucratic behavior is often objectionable to citizens because it denotes delay, red tape, pettiness, ritualistic attachment to rules, and concentration of power in persons neither elected by nor responsible directly to the people. The pathological aspects of bureaucracy, however, are largely the personal behavior patterns of individual bureaucrats and do not refer necessarily to bureaucracy as a form of social organization. Administrative units are necessary for governance. Civil servants who carry out the legally prescribed missions of government agencies are instructed to do so with maximum efficiency and minimum use of coercion. Yet a bureaucracy's legislative mandate is frequently worded in such a general way that bureaucrats also have a considerable amount of discretionary power. This is true whether the society is capitalist or socialist, democratic or authoritarian. In U.S. democracy a premium is placed on guarding against the development of an irresponsible bureaucracy by means of congressional oversight, presidential direction, the power of the purse, and judicial review.

Bureaucrat, Internal (127)

An application of Freudian psychology to public administration which advanced the idea that bureaucrats view agency goals through "psychological spectacles." The internal bureaucrat was explored by political scientist Harold Lasswell in his 1930 book, *Psychopathology and Politics.* Lasswell's study was a frontal assault on the value underpinnings of the Weberian-Wilsonian-scientific management school of thought. Lasswell's primary objective was to understand the personality traits of persons with public authority and to categorize the different types. Whereas obedience to legal authority and "dehumanization" had characterized the bureaucrat previously, Lasswell raised a number of questions related to the internalized psychological forces identified by Freud. What personality types are drawn into bureaucracies? What are the crucial elements in determining whether a bureaucrat will neglect details for general policy or have a passion for details, accuracy, and a delight in routine? Which bureaucrats will gain influence over subordinates? How do bureaucrats react in crisis-stress situations? What are the real patterns of power in hierarchical organizations? Lasswell addressed these and other questions through the study of psychiatric case histories and life histories of ill persons who were exercising or had exercised public authority. The internal bureaucrat emerged as one who frequently exercises power on the basis of an internal hidden agenda. Lasswell concluded that formal patterns of organization as described by organization charts are unrealistic. In fact, informal organization may be more significant than formal organization. The bureaucratic processes cannot be described through legal authority and directives, since these take into account only external behavior and not the internal dynamics of the human mind. The idea of the internal bureaucrat centered on the requirement of gathering data on nonrational and personal phenomena to understand public administration. *See also* BUREAUPATHOLOGY, 129; GROUP THEORY, 53; HAWTHORNE STUDIES, 54.

Significance The internal bureaucrat was an idea whose time did not come for thirty years after Lasswell did his pioneering study. It seemed so revolutionary at the time it was presented—in 1930—that its full impact was not felt for decades. The work implied a theory of values far removed from the traditional emphasis on input-output efficiency as the value goal of administration. The contention that administrative decisions reflect the outcome of contending internal forces based on conscious or unconscious perceptions of the self is still a curiosity to many. Yet the recent work of psychohistorians seems to render the Freudian categories a powerful and serviceable explanation system for human behavior, administrative and otherwise. The problem is that the Freudian categories themselves seem to be a mystery religion and impossible for the uninitiated to understand. They are really not so difficult. Freud's clinical experience convinced him—and Lasswell—that each individual's behavior is shaped by the interplay of three basically conflicting forces, which Freud called the *id,* the *ego,* and the *superego.* The id seeks to maximize pleasure and minimize tension and pain. It has no moral component or ethical implication. The superego is the moral component of a person's subconscious and seeks to regulate or control the id. It does so according to the ideals of the society which have been transmitted to the individual through the socialization process. The ego reflects "reality" and, according to the manner in which it perceives the external world, it seeks to balance in a harmonious way the relationship between the id and the superego. There is always a war going on in a person's subconscious, therefore, and human behavior is largely dictated by the subconsciously determined terms of relative peace. Many of us simply do not know why we act the way we do. Much of the time we act irrationally. Translated to administrative behavior, this means that scientific management assumptions of predictable behavior within organizations, and the "institutional mechanics" approach of political science, may be decidedly unscientific. *Scientific* public administration seeks to deal with illogic as well as logic, and with the self as well as the external manifestations of the self.

Bureaucratic Expertise (128)

The know-how of experts that gives them special influence in their organizations and in society. Bureaucratic expertise is one of the foundations of bureaucratic power when it is brought to bear on programs for which the agency is responsible. Political scientist Francis Rourke has suggested that the influence of experts rests on five major components. They are (1) full-time attention by experts to a problem or subject-matter area, giving rise to both demand and opportunity for professionalism in public service; (2) specialization in the subject; (3) a monopoly on information in the subject area, which, if successfully maintained by only one staff of experts, makes them indispensable in any decision making involving "their" subject; (4) a pattern of increasing reliance on bureaucratic experts for technical advice; and (5) increasing control by bureaucratic experts of bureaucratic discretion. In addition to these components of bureaucratic expertise, there is the pervasive ability of experts to employ a language and concepts unfamiliar to most other people. This use of specialized language, or jargon, has become a common phenomenon among experts both in and out of government. It poses a problem for the layperson who tries to understand complex developments and issues. By using jargon, bureaucratic experts make it difficult for others to challenge them on their own territory. If possible opponents cannot understand what the experts have proposed, how can they argue against it? This specialized language resource of bureaucratic experts has been enhanced by the fact that frequently proposals put forward by experts have yielded positive and beneficial results. The combination of obscurity of means and clarity of results has helped consolidate the position, prestige, and influence of experts in government agencies. *See also* ADMINISTRATIVE DISCRETION, 86; BUREAUCRACY, 126; PLANNING, PROGRAMMING, BUDGETING SYSTEMS (PPBS), 283.

Significance Bureaucratic expertise is a powerful element in government, but it is not without its limitations. While a monopoly of information is desirable from a particular agency's point of view, for example, it is rarely achieved in everyday practice. No agency controls all governmental sources of information on any given subject. Government itself does not control all information sources in society, and information—itself a source of power and influence—is the subject of intense interagency competition. Similarly, not every important decision of an agency revolves around technical criteria or data. Even when an issue involves technical data, top-level administrators, for political or other reasons, may prefer a decision that is not the "best" according to technical criteria. Finally, in recent years the obscurity of means which previously was a source of strength for experts has contributed to growing public disenchantment with "big government," bureaucracy, and experts in general. With the increasing desire for broader public involvement in decision making there has come greater unwillingness to "take the experts' word for it," and a more insistent demand that experts make clear to the general public just what it is they are doing, proposing, and advocating. Bureaucratic expertise has nevertheless been an important factor in the formulation of public policy by defining the alternatives from which higher level officials choose the course to be followed. To the extent that responsible policy makers permit bureaucratic expertise to define available alternatives, they strengthen the experts' influence.

Bureaupathology (129)
A set of behaviors sometimes engaged in by bureaucrats. Bureaupathology hinders the accomplishment of organizational goals because it is self-serving and has little to do with the real work of the organization. It involves personal behavior patterns characteristic of positions of authority in either hierarchical or nonhierarchical organizations. The behaviors can only be exercised in a downward flow, not by subordinates over superiors, or by clients over officials at any level. Victor A. Thompson believed "bureaupathetic" behavior is exhibited by insecure people who are protecting their psyches from the frustration of not being able to achieve their personal goals within the organization. The extent to which the bureaucratic structure prevents people from activating the motivation mechanism

within themselves is the extent to which bureaupathology exists. Even a "normal" person can be affected by the anxiety and insecurity an organization can generate. If job satisfaction does not exist, the affected person, if he or she is in a position of authority, will express a strong need for control. The more insecure the bureaupath becomes, the more he or she will try to control the situation, thus creating more tension in a cycle of self-defeating behavior. The cycle of bureaupathetic behavior can be broken by taking the authority figure out of the dilemma, which frequently is the root cause of his or her feelings of insecurity. This is the gap between the authority position and its rights of review, veto, and affirmation. The person in authority often does not perceive himself or herself as having the specialized ability or skills required to solve most organizational problems. Therefore, he or she must satisfy the demands of superiors by relying on the specialized skills of subordinates, while having only a dim understanding of those skills. Hence strong controls are exerted, subordinates feel resentment, and bureaupathology is illustrated once again. *See also* BUREAU-CRACY, 126; GOAL DISPLACEMENT, 145; ORGANIZATION DEVELOPMENT (OD), 169.

Significance Bureaupathology is a helpful concept because it points out that criticisms of bureaucracy as a form of social organization are sometimes misplaced. Bureaucrats may behave pathologically, but there is no necessary correlation to bureaucracy as a rational and legal system, as Max Weber would be the first to point out. There are healthy bureaucracies and there are sick bureaucracies. Bureaucracy as an idea has had a difficult time since the early nineteenth century when Honoré de Balzac described it in his novel *Bureaucracy* (1836) as "a gigantic power manipulated by dwarfs," and as "that heavy curtain hung between the good to be done and him who commands it." In one manifestation, bureaucracy refers to a red-tape-bound body of civil servants, inefficient, negative, bored, impolite, and unhelpful to citizens seeking service. In another guise, it is a body of all-too-efficient exercisers, often abusers, of power arbitrarily deciding matters without due process. Both contain the essence of bureaupathology. On the other hand, a bureaucracy can be a formal, rational organization of relations among persons vested with administrative authority and the staffing of administration with qualified, full-time, salaried civil servants. The pejorative meanings of bureaucracy almost always refer to the phenomenon of bureaupathology. Human beings transfer their personal disorders to their institutions, which had also helped to cause the disorders in the first place.

Centralization (130)

The tendency for political power to move from smaller, weaker, more local units of government toward larger, stronger, and more general units. Centralization in the U.S. system has involved a shifting of power, responsibility, and programs over two hundred years of history from local units toward the states, and from the local and state units toward the national government. The result of the tendency toward centralization has been a vastly expanded national government carrying on a great variety of programs, many of which were once the sole prerogative of state or local governments. The centripetal forces enhancing the power of the national government have often been unleashed by economic and social crises and war. Beginning with the John Marshall Court, the Supreme Court has been a major factor, encouraging centralization through a liberal interpretation of the Constitution and a strong preference for a broad interpretation of national powers. Cooperative federalism based on the grant-in-aid system has found state and local governments inviting the national government to share state powers in exchange for dollars, thus encouraging a legal centralization and a political decentralization involving mass citizen participation.

Significance   Centralization in the U.S. system has been an inescapable product of growing nationalism and interdependence, and the acceptance by the American people of an expanded role for government in solving problems. The American experience is similar to that of most federal systems of government. The tendency for power to gravitate toward the central unit can almost be considered a "law" of politics. Although this trend has been reversed for short periods, it has always proved dominant, and continues today. President Dwight D. Eisenhower, for example, attempted to reverse the flow of power by inviting the states and local units to take over full control of cooperative programs in which the national government played a decisive role. The antipathy of state leaders to increasing taxation to support such takeovers led to a failure of the decentralization movement. President Richard M. Nixon tried to overcome this problem with a revenue-sharing program that would provide the states and local units with funds to carry out the decentralization, but this program also failed. Although many conservative candidates for public office continue in their campaign speeches to long for a return to the "good old days" of state and local predominance and weak national power over economic and social affairs, the trend toward centralization is unlikely to end, even when such candidates are elected, because of the changes in modern life brought about by new technologies and their impact on society and the role of government.

Citizen Participation (131)

The direct involvement of citizens in the processes of policy formation, program implementation, and administrative decision making. Citizen participation represents a recently revived interest in the doctrine of participatory democracy promoted by Thomas Jefferson in the early history of the United States. Jefferson and French political philosopher Alexis de Tocqueville provided early examples of the theory that individual citizen participation is essential to the survival of a democracy, and that democracy is undermined when citizens are unable to influence government actions. This has been called the "bottom-up rule." A new interest in citizen participation began in the 1960s at the time creative federalism was promoting decentralization of government program responsibility. Decentralization was illustrated in legislation establishing the model cities and community action programs, which also reflected the citizen participation emphasis. Other contributing factors in the development of citizen participation were the perceived failure of the bureaucracy to meet policy needs at the local level and the preachment that the amateur knew more about policy needs at any level than the professional administrator. Citizen participation is distinguished from regular means of indirect citizen participation, such as voting or interest-group activity, in that most citizen participation is at the regional or local level. Common forms are (1) the citizen committee as an advisory group; (2) the citizen committee as a governing group; (3) the neighborhood government; and (4) the citizen as staff member of advisory boards and commissions, sometimes called "paragovernments." Actual citizen participation can mean giving advice, or in some contexts actually making and controlling decisions in an administrative framework. Analysis of citizen participation indicates a fairly large discrepancy between theory and practice. Decentralizing control does not guarantee increased citizen participation or a more democratic process. Participants tend to be the same middle-class citizens who were already involved through interest groups and who have values closely aligned with those of the bureaucracy. There are also informal dimensions undermining citizenship participation as a substantive policy-making tool. The decentralization of authority can be a way of abdicating responsibility and a way of legitimizing the use of citizens as scapegoats for policy failures. See also COOPTATION, 34; INTEREST-GROUP LIBERALISM, 56; PLURALIZATION, 67.

Significance Citizen participation in public administration raises issues of accountability, efficiency, and administrative discretion. On the accountability question, the more decentralized the policy making the more difficult it is to pinpoint responsibility. In terms of efficiency, access to a bureaucracy through hearings, commissions, or task forces requires financial outlays and impinges on rational-comprehensive planning. The growing complexity of programs and the need for specialization is in direct conflict with the demands of citizen participation. Administrative discretion also creates a paradox alongside the goals of citizen participation. As authority is decentralized to allow for citizen participation, administrative discretion increases. Discretionary authority diminishes the prospect that citizen participation will be as effective as it would be under a more structured bureaucratic system.

Classification of Cities (132)
An action by a state legislature to categorize cities within the state according to population or population densities so that the state may pass laws and delegate charters to them according to size. The classification of cities originated as a means for circumventing state constitutional requirements that the legislature impose its will on cities only by general law applicable to all cities. Laws that identified specific cities by name were consequently invalidated by the courts. Classification was invented as a means of legislating in particular, especially for the largest city in the state which typically was placed in a class separate from the others.

Significance Classification of cities was a state legislative reaction to the home rule movement which sought to grant a measure of independence to cities in developing their policies and programs. The courts, however, continue to examine state legislation for cities to ensure that it is reasonable and appropriate for the group or class for which it is applicable. In some states, attempts have also been made to dictate the form of city government for each class by developing standard charters for each. Some cities may be permitted to carry on certain types of activities that are barred to others. In other cases, the legislature dictates specifics to each class, such as salaries to be paid to city officials, whether offices are to be filled by election or appointment, and whether and how a city can borrow money to meet its obligations. Classification of cities demonstrates that federalism does not exist within states and that unitary systems prevail in state-local relations.

Crozier, Michel (1922–) (133)
French sociologist, organization theorist, and author of the influential book *The Bureaucratic Phenomenon,* published in 1964. Crozier is

director of the Centre de Sociologie des Organizations in Paris and has been a visiting professor of sociology and public administration at Harvard University. *The Bureaucratic Phenomenon* explores the cyclical nature of bureaucratic rule making. Rules are created to reinforce the ineffective rules that are already established but that have not achieved compliance. This self-perpetuating cycle Crozier calls "bureaucratic pathology." It might be described as the shadow side of Weber's ideal-type bureaucracy. Crozier conducted two investigations that constituted the database for his conclusions. His first subject was a clerical agency of the French government that employed some 4,500 people. The second was a government cigarette industry that had a complete monopoly on the market. Crozier found there was no psychological commitment to either organization, the workers were isolated from one another, managers solved conflicts by establishing more rules, the hierarchical levels of the organization were separated, and there was little face-to-face contact between and among members of either organization. For the managers, rules eliminated the necessity for personalization. For the workers, rules were perceived as a means for preventing closer supervision, resulting in what Crozier called a "silent conspiracy" against organizational change. Each time a manager enforced a new rule, it reinforced the workers' tendency to take less initiative in their work, which in turn created pressures on managers to create more rules. This self-generating pathology Crozier attributed to (1) impersonal rules developed for every possible situation, hence overregulation; (2) overcentralization of decision making at the top of the organization; (3) the isolation of the hierarchies of the organization from one another; (4) peer groups that encouraged the acceptance of the communication void; and (5) power struggles between people and groups for definition and regulation of areas of organizational uncertainty. Any person who was able to gain control in an area of uncertainty became very powerful in the organization. *See also* BUREAUPATHOLOGY, 129.

Significance Michel Crozier's work introduced the concept of bureaucratic pathology and the effect of culture on the internal structure and processes of an organization. For example, the French preference for privacy and aloofness caused workers in the lower echelons of an organization to resist organizational change, even when such changes could benefit them. Crozier attributed this to a psychological attitude he called *bon plaisir,* which is the proclivity for wanting a place in a given organizational structure. A literary corollary of this phenomenon is in Albert Camus' novel *The Stranger,* where Mersault refuses a promotion because it would not really change his life. This hopelessness stultified any desire for achievement or organizational enthusiasm. It is a tribute to Crozier that he saw beyond what might have been superficially interpreted as organizational apathy. Although Crozier's studies were based on French bureaucracies, his descriptions are applicable to any closed model organization where power is centralized at the top and which lacks the ability to correct its own behavior. Crozier said that delayed organizational change ultimately promotes rapid revolutionary change. When it finally comes, change is comprehensive.

Cybernetics (134)

A modern theory of organization that treats organizations as self-regulating through a communication and control process which triggers adaptive mechanisms within the organization when feedback recommends their application. Cybernetics comes from the Greek word for *steersman*. It was coined in the 1940s by an eclectic group of scientists at Harvard University and the Massachusetts Institute of Technology (MIT). Concerned about the increasing fragmentation in their fields, they stumbled on what they felt to be a common set of problems for medical scientists, biologists, physicists, psychologists, sociologists, anthropologists, economists, engineers, and mathematicians. The problems, according to the group's historian, MIT mathematician Norbert Wiener, were "about communication, control, and statistical machines, whether in the machine or in living tissue" (*Cybernetics*, 1948). The scientists were astonished by the parallels between rapid computing machines and an ideal model of the human nervous system. They drew a model of how all systems—living and mechanical—attempt to control their actions. When an organization, for example, desires to pursue certain objectives, the differences between the objectives and the actual policies of the organization are used as a new input to *steer* the organization toward its chosen objectives. Control engineers call this process *feedback*. The organization engages in a constant scanning process to check its progress toward its objectives. It collects information on its current position and sends this information to a central processing unit, the organization's memory, which compares the new message with its knowledge of previous actions. The central processing unit then issues new instructions to tell the organization how to close in on the objective. The central processing unit is programmed to move the organization smoothly toward the objective and to avoid oscillations caused by oversteering. A thermostat operates in exactly the same way. The cybernetic principle in public administration is the study of how organizations as man-machine systems use communication

Bureaucracy and Administrative Organization

to ensure, at least temporarily, their survival. *See also* ENTROPY, 137; MANAGEMENT INFORMATION SYSTEM (MIS), 58; OPERATIONS RESEARCH, 62.

Significance   Cybernetics has been called the science of messages. The set of assumptions used in cybernetics allows the management scientist to think about the man-machine symbiosis, which is the basis of the modern organization. Symbiosis means the union of two specifically different systems—a human and a life-imitating machine, for example—that join together to accomplish a specific mission. Cybernetics maintains that information destroys entropy. The entropic process is a way of saying the universe is running down: ashes to ashes, dust to dust. Everything eventually dies and returns to sameness. The natural state of affairs is disorganization. A few cells, animals, and organizations survive nature's uncompromising push toward deterioration and disorder by enormous acts of will. In particular, organizations survive because they have the ability to discriminate in collecting information. Cybernetics says that only by learning how to process information can a system steer its way to survival. As entropy is a measure of the tendency of a system to disintegrate, its information-processing capacity is a measure of its organization. A developed system uses information to collect and transform resources so that it approaches a state called *negative entropy*, where its natural tendency to run down is arrested.

Decentralization (135)
The process of dividing and distributing authority and responsibility for programs to administrative subunits. Decentralization typically involves reassigning decision-making responsibilities on a geographical basis to field service operational units. It may also involve reassignment of tasks based on subject matter specializations. *See also* CENTRALIZATION, 130; FIELD SERVICE, 141.

Significance   Decentralization of decision making often contributes to the effectiveness of administrative operations because it permits some measures of adaptation to local conditions and needs. It also spreads decision-making responsibilities among a number of officials who, because of the more limited scope of their activities as contrasted with a centralized administration, can gain greater expertise and understanding of problems. Criticisms of decentralization typically involve the charges that dispersing responsibility weakens accountability, that operations are carried on unevenly depending on the personnel heading each of the subunits, and that decentralized operations are more expensive by their very nature.

Department (136)
A major agency assigned responsibility to carry on diverse governmental administrative functions. Departments are used in national, state, and local governmental operations and are typically headed by a secretary or other elected or appointed official, such as an attorney general or a superintendent of public instruction. In the national government, departments are headed by individuals who collectively comprise the president's cabinet. Currently, cabinet departments include agriculture, commerce, defense, education, energy, health and welfare, housing and urban development, interior, justice, labor, state, transportation, and treasury. In the states, typical major departments include commerce, conservation, education, health, justice, natural resources, and state, with a few states including departments of energy and environment. In city governments, major departments usually include assessing, city clerk, civil defense, community development, finance, fire, parks and recreation, police, public works, sanitation, streets, transportation, and water. Typical county departments include animal control, civil defense, county clerk, drain commissioner, extension services, health, mental health, parks and recreation, planning, prosecuting attorney, register of deeds, road commission, sheriff, social services, treasurer, and veteran's affairs. Departments on all levels are divided into subordinate units, such as bureaus, offices, divisions, sections, and other units based on the nature of their activity.

Significance Departments are the main operational units and perform most of the administrative tasks on all three levels of government in the United States. In the national government, however, many important functions are carried out by independent agencies, some of which are not subject to the direct authority and supervision of the president. Independent regulatory commissions, such as the Interstate Commerce Commission (ICC), and government corporations, such as the Tennessee Valley Authority (TVA), are examples of agencies that function outside of the thirteen major cabinet departments. The departments of the Army, Navy, and Air Force have retained their titles although they were integrated into the new Department of Defense in the 1947 Reorganization Act. Management analysts have called for integrating all federal functions within the major departments so that the president can exercise authority equal to his responsibilities as chief administrator of the executive branch.

Entropy (137)
The degradation of the matter and energy in the universe to an ultimate state of inert uniformity. Entropy in organization theory refers to the energy and resources an organization imports or does not import from its environment. It is also a measure of disorder in an organizational system, as in a thermodynamic system. Entropy may be positive or negative. *Positive entropy,* or energy loss, is the natural movement of an organization toward disorganization and death. *Negative entropy,* or energy conservation, arrests an organization's inevitable decline. Just as complex physical systems move toward simple random distribution of their elements, and biological systems run down and perish, organizational systems frequently fail to replenish the internal energy required to produce outputs. If an organization imports and transforms available energy or resources in its environment and turns the resources into outputs, it delays the entropic process and maintains equilibrium. Equilibrium occurs as the organizational system attains the state of the most probable distribution of its elements. The state of equilibrium is called *homeostasis.* If an organization attains negative entropy, which is the importing of more energy from its environment than it expends, it can store energy to survive during periods of crisis. A closed organizational system is likely to experience positive entropy. An open organizational system is likely to experience negative entropy. Many inner-city ghetto schools, for example, have become closed systems and are experiencing positive entropy. See also ORGANIZATIONS, CLOSED MODEL, 174; ORGANIZATIONS, OPEN MODEL, 175.

Significance The tendency toward entropy is frequently determined by the structure of an organization. Organization theorists have learned that heavily layered organizations impede internal and external communications. They close up exchange processes in the environment and thus promote positive entropy. Tight adherence to unity of command, narrow span of control, excessive rule making, and highly specific job descriptions all contribute to reducing the energy transformation of jobs at all organizational levels except the top. This diminishes the front-line supervisor's power, increases alienation in the ranks, and lowers the agency's performance. The resulting loss of dynamism is the organization theorist's definition of positive entropy and organizational disease. Organizations with dynamic feedback loops, however, typically have negative entropy. They receive *inputs* from the environment in the form of resources such as equipment, supplies, and the energies of employees. The organization then *throughputs* the resources and transforms them to yield *outputs* in the form of products and services. The feedback loop is what actually produces an open system and negative entropy. It provides negative feedback from output back to input so that the system can correct its mistakes. Its positive relationship with the environment is maintained in this way. The irony of the open system, however, is that there is a proven tendency in large organizations to try to reduce dependence on an uncertain environment by bringing much of the environment within their own systems. Manufacturing corporations absorb competitors, and they integrate vertically by developing or acquiring sources of their inputs and wholesale and retail distribution outlets. Government agencies seek autonomy in selecting employees, purchasing supplies, and evaluating their own program outputs. Open systems tend to try to reduce risks by evolving toward closed systems and may suicidally engage in positive entropy in the process.

Executive Office of the President (EXOP or EOP)   (138)
A collection of agencies that are physically housed close to the office of the president, and that, with the executive residence staff, form the president's institutional support base. The four central units of the EXOP are (1) the Office of Management and Budget (OMB); (2) the Domestic Policy Staff (formerly the Domestic Council); (3) the National Security Council (NSC); and (4) the White House Office (WHO). The Executive Office of the President was established by President Franklin D. Roosevelt in 1939, shortly after passage of the Reorganization Act of that year. The President's Committee on Administrative Management (the Brownlow Committee) had strongly recommended establishment of such an office in its report of 1937. In transmitting the Brownlow Committee report to Congress, President Roosevelt wrote, "The plain fact is that the present organization and equipment of the executive branch of the Government defeats the constitutional intent that there be a single responsible Chief Executive to coordinate and manage the departments and activities in accordance with the laws enacted by the Congress." Two years later President Roosevelt transferred the Bureau of the Budget, now the Office of Management and Budget, from the Treasury Department to the EXOP and set up the White House Office. The nine agencies making up the Executive Office of the President today are the (1) White House Office (WHO); (2) Office of Management and Budget (OMB); (3) Council of Economic Advisers (CEA); (4) National

Security Council (NSC); (5) Office of Policy Development; (6) Office of the United States Trade Representative; (7) Council on Environmental Quality; (8) Office of Science and Technology Policy; and (9) Office of Administration. Except for the Office of Administration, each of these agencies has policy concerns that cut across the entire government, or a major segment of it, and regularly occupy the President's attention. Executive office agencies gather information for the President, advise him, monitor the execution of his decisions by the operating departments, and facilitate interagency coordination. *See also* BROWNLOW COMMITTEE, 124; *specific agencies in Index.*

Significance The Executive Office of the President has undergone qualitative as well as quantitative change since 1939. The Brownlow Committee had stipulated the following role for presidential assistants: "These assistants, probably not exceeding six in number . . . would have no power to make decisions or issue instructions in their own right. . . . They would remain in the background, issue no orders, make no decisions, emit no public statements. . . . They should be possessed of high competence, great physical vigor, and a passion for anonymity." The qualitative change attendant to "the swelling of the Presidency" is that presidential assistants do indeed issue orders in the modern White House. One of the organizational disabilities of the Executive Office concept as it has evolved in recent years is the denigration of department heads by powerful presidential assistants who preempt their decision-making authority. The White House staff is now so large that it itself is difficult to coordinate. Cabinet members not infrequently receive contradictory instructions on the same day from different members of the central staff, each purporting to speak for the president. Each new president since Dwight D. Eisenhower has committed himself, as President Jimmy Carter did, to "a Cabinet administration of our government." They have promised, as President Carter promised, that "There will never be an instance while I am President when the members of the White House staff dominate or act in a superior position to the members of our Cabinet." Yet the promises eroded before the requirements of the president to hold his own in the political marketplace. By mid-1979, for example, President Carter had obtained the resignations of the cabinet members who had had the most friction with his assistants. At the same time he designated a chief of staff ". . . to relieve the President of the necessity of dealing with matters that can be decided at a lower level." In the Iran-*Contra* affair investigated by Congress in 1987, cleavages and outright conflicts occurred in the Reagan Administration between cabinet officials, especially the Secretary of State and the Attorney General, and presidential aides in the Executive Office.

Executive Privilege (139)

The doctrine that, under the separation of powers sanctioned by the Constitution, the president and officials of the executive branch can withhold information from and refuse to appear before Congress or the courts. Although not specifically stated in the Constitution, the doctrine of executive privilege began to evolve under the related doctrine of inherent powers early in U.S. history when President George Washington refused to divulge information concerning the Jay Treaty to a committee of Congress. In 1974, the Supreme Court for the first time established a legal basis for limiting executive privilege by unanimously ordering President Richard M. Nixon to release recorded tapes with alleged criminal information on them to the courts and Congress (*United States v. Nixon*, 418 U.S. 683). This decision led eventually to President Nixon's resignation. In the opinion of the Court, the constitutional power of executive privilege does exist, but, like all powers, it is limited.

Significance The doctrine of executive privilege challenges the right of Congress to obtain information under certain conditions, especially when the information may be used in impeachment proceedings. The doctrine also questions the right of the courts to hear and decide cases involving executive department officials when such judicial activity may clash with the power of the president to function as head of one of the three coordinate branches of government. In the *Nixon* case, Chief Justice Burger wrote that the interest in preserving confidentiality "is weighty indeed and entitled to great respect," but that it could be outweighed by other interests, including "demands of due process of law in the administration of criminal justice." Although the power of the president to refuse to appear before congressional committees remains unchallenged, the question of whether other executive department officials should enjoy the same privilege has never been fully resolved.

Ex Officio (140)

A Latin term which means "by virtue of the office" or "because of the office." Many individuals hold position "ex officio" on boards, committees, councils, and other government bodies because of their other appointive or elective positions. Their membership is thus automatic and is not subject to the same procedures for gaining membership that apply to regular members. The Secretary of State, for example, is an ex officio member of numerous boards and committees that function in the upper decision-making levels of the national administration. *See also* APPOINTMENT POWER, 191.

Bureaucracy and Administrative Organization

Significance The ex officio device is utilized on all three levels of government in the United States to involve upper level officials in collective deliberations and decision making. Some interagency and coordinating committees and boards, for example, consist mainly or exclusively of ex officio members. Often, in mixed boards, the ex officio members wield the most power in decision making because their agencies will be directly involved in implementing the decisions made. The device has proved to be extremely useful for coordinating the activities of diverse agencies carrying out unified policies or programs.

Field Service (141)
Administrative operations conducted on a decentralized basis by geographically distributed units. Field service units function under the general guidelines and operational supervision of the headquarters or central unit, typically located in Washington, DC for federal agencies and in state capitals for state agencies. Field service units usually administer programs through direct contact with the general public or with the agency's clientele public. In most field service operations, major decision making, personnel management, and budget administration remain under the control of the central unit. *See also* DECENTRALIZATION, 135.

Significance Field service operations account for most activities carried on by the executive branch of the national government. Only approximately 10 percent of the civilian personnel employed by the federal government, for example, are located in Washington, DC, with the remaining 90 percent assigned to field service offices in the fifty states and abroad. Advantages that relate to field service operations include the ability to resolve problems where they arise and to adapt programs to local conditions and needs. Field service directors can also achieve some measures of specialization in carrying out their tasks because of the distribution of responsibility, and their units can have a better understanding of problems within their local setting. Disadvantages involved in field service operations include the possibility that "politics" may influence the distribution of benefits among various units, resulting in an uneven and unfair administration of programs. Also, the distribution of responsibility through decentralized operations can lead to a weakening of accountability, and the dispersal of administrative activities can increase their cost.

Force-field Analysis (142)
The factors operating either for or against proposed organizational change. Force-field analysis, as suggested by social psychologist Kurt Lewin, incorporates a listing of factors that would encourage worker cooperation in a proposed organizational change, and other factors causing resistance to that change. Administrators then analyze the relative strengths of the two sets of factors. Lewin indicated two different ways to gain acceptance of change. One is to increase the pressure for change to the point where the pressure would simply overpower any resistance. The danger of this approach is that the resisting factors are not eliminated. They may eventually build up enough pressure to rebound, very much like a coiled spring. Lewin called this dramatic flareup of resistance after opposition had apparently been subdued the "coiled spring effect." The other and more appropriate way to gain acceptance of change is to attempt to eliminate, rather than subdue, the opposing factors. Lewin cited the example of dealing with female factory workers during World War II on the matter of wearing safety glasses. A force-field analysis indicated the workers objected to wearing the glasses because they were heavy and unattractive, and because there was no self-determination involved in the new policy. The other side of the force-field listed "protect eyes," "cooperate with company," and "follow rules" as positive factors for change. To gain acceptance of the policy by trying to eliminate the opposing factors, the company (1) found lighter, more comfortable frames and substituted them at a minimal cost increase per frame; and (2) announced a contest for each woman to decorate her glasses in whatever way she thought appropriate, thus giving each individual a chance for self-expression. The wearing of safety glasses in this case gained positive acceptance through force-field analysis. *See also* HAWTHORNE STUDIES, 54; ORGANIZATION DEVELOPMENT (OD), 169; PARTICIPATIVE MANAGEMENT, 110.

Significance   Force-field analysis is an alternative to giving up when there is resistance to change. Most managers are not allowed to give up, so there is a human tendency to overcome resistance with superior power. That frequently becomes a negative act because of the coiled spring effect. Force-field analysis suggests reducing the resistance—after its reasons have been identified—which usually requires less effort and creates far more goodwill. The process of charting the force-field situation can be very revealing to a manager. Force-field analysis provides a methodology for dealing with resistance to change in a consistent and rational way.

Functional Consolidation (143)
The merging of two or more administrative units that perform similar tasks into a single major agency. Functional consolidation has been one of the main approaches used by management and organization specialists to streamline governmental administrative operations on the national, state, and local levels. *See also* ADMINISTRATIVE REORGANIZATION, 119.

Significance By applying the principle of functional consolidation, administrative reorganization specialists seek to reduce confusion and make governmental operations more directly accountable to elected leaders. As new economic and social problems arise, Congress, state legislatures, and local policy-making bodies tend to create new administrative units to cope with them. The result is much overlapping of jurisdictions, duplication of efforts, and confusion in the lines of authority and responsibility. Functional consolidation is then typically applied to pull together these diverse units performing similar tasks. The (Hoover) Commission on Organization of the Executive Branch recommended in 1949 that all operating units in the executive branch be functionally consolidated into twenty-two major departments so that the president could effectively direct and supervise their operations. This recommendation, however, was rejected by Congress. Many states have also been advised to consolidate their diverse administrative structures by bringing them together within a number of major departments, with ten to twenty usually suggested. The constitutions of several states seek to encourage functional consolidations by restricting major departments to twenty or fewer. Some efforts have also been made on the local level to pull operational units together to save money and increase efficiency. Some cities, for example, have combined their fire and police departments into a single department of public safety. Most attempts at functional consolidation, however, meet with failure because entrenched interests in the legislative body, within the units being consolidated, and in pressure groups that constitute the clientele of the units, strongly resist efforts to consolidate.

General Services Administration (GSA) (144)
A major "housekeeping," "overhead," or auxiliary agency that services the entire U.S. government in general and the executive branch of the national government in particular. The General Services Administration is charged with establishing policies, programs, and practices that will provide for efficient and economical management of property and supplies utilized by federal agencies. Included in its

property and records management assignment are (1) the construction and operation of federal buildings; (2) the purchase, use, and disposal of federal property; (3) the management of transportation, traffic, and communications; (4) the stockpiling of strategic materials; and (5) the operation of an automatic data-processing system that services the entire federal government. Established in 1949 as an independent agency, the GSA is directed by an Administrator of General Services who is appointed by the President with Senate consent. See also AUXILIARY AGENCY, 120.

Significance   The General Services Administration provides a variety of services that keep the federal government operating on a day-to-day basis. The GSA was created on the recommendation of the first Hoover Commission, which sought to overcome the inefficiency and added expense of operating separate units to provide property management, record keeping, and transportation. Its centralization of these functions has added to the general effectiveness of the federal bureaucracy, although some critics charge that its management functions contribute to government waste and mismanagement by promoting bigger government. In its operations, the GSA is often said to resemble a large corporation doing business as a conglomerate in a number of different fields. Some of its little-known functions include operating a Consumer Information Center, staffing a number of Federal Information Centers that serve as clearinghouses for information about the federal government, and operating Business Service Centers that provide advice and assistance to those seeking government contracts for business ventures. Also included in the GSA's efforts to provide information are the publication of the *United States Government Manual*, the *Statutes at Large*, and the *Federal Register*, three major sources of information about the continuing operations of the national government.

Goal Displacement **(145)**
The tendency of bureaucracies to adhere to rules as ends in themselves, with bureaucratic methods and procedures taking precedence over the objectives for which the agency was created. Goal displacement was first described by U.S. sociologist Robert K. Merton. Merton said the ideal type of formal organization is bureaucracy. Max Weber was almost exclusively concerned with what the bureaucratic structure *attains:* precision, reliability, and efficiency. The same structure may be examined from another perspective, and that is the limitations of organizations designed to be precise, reliable, and efficient. The bureaucratic structure exerts a constant pressure on public officials to

be methodical, prudent, and disciplined. If the bureaucracy is to operate successfully, it must attain a high degree of reliability of behavior and an unusual degree of conformity with prescribed patterns of action. In order to ensure discipline, leaders of the bureaucracy encourage sentiments of devotion to one's duties and methodical performance of routine activities which are often more intense than is technically necessary. Merton described this as a "margin of safety" imposed on the bureaucrat to conform to patterned obligations. This emphasis leads to a transference of sentiments from the *aims* of the organization on to the particular details of behavior required by the rules. Adherence to the rules, originally conceived as a means, becomes transformed into an end in itself. The result is goal displacement whereby "an instrumental value becomes a terminal value." See also BUREAUCRAT, INTERNAL, 127; BUREAUPATHOLOGY, 129; NEO-WEBERISM, 165.

Significance Goal displacement, excessive rigidity, red tape, impersonal treatment of clients, and unreasonable resistance to change are all signs of a sick organization. Merton calls them *bureaucratic dysfunctions* and characterizes them with the term "trained incapacity." Trained incapacity refers to that state of affairs in which one's abilities function as inadequacies or blind spots. Actions based on training and skills that have been successfully applied in the past may result in inappropriate responses *under changed conditions*. Merton noted that inadequate flexibility in the application of skills, will, in a changing milieu, result in more or less serious maladjustments. As public administrationist Howard E. McCurdy points out, however, Weber's ideal-type model is designed to operate this way. A bureaucracy, by design, is an organization that cannot correct its behavior by listening to its errors. The "feedback loop," the method by which all organizations listen to the impact of their policies and make adjustments in them, is deliberately made weak in a bureaucracy. By training bureaucrats to be skeptical of complaints, the organization assures that its rules will be applied impersonally. By helping bureaucrats to be impersonal, it lends them the tenacity to exercise the full powers of the organization in promoting the predetermined goals. In time, bureaucrats come to identify the disciplined application of the rules with their own self-interest and their desire for promotion and status. The ultimate manifestation of goal displacement is that bureaucrats interpret any challenge to the existing rules as a threat to their own security. Goal displacement passes through a process of sanctification in which bureaucratic procedures are invested with attitudes of moral legitimacy. They are then established as values in their own right, and are no longer viewed as merely technical means for expediting administration.

Government Corporation (146)
A government agency that carries on business, banking, insurance, or other kinds of functions that normally are part of the private sector. Government corporations are usually owned and controlled solely by the government that created them, but some divide ownership, with as much as almost one-half of the stock owned by private individuals or companies. Corporations, unlike other agencies, produce much of their own revenue, a characteristic that adds much flexibility to their operations. The independence and flexibility enjoyed by national government corporations, however, was considerably reduced by the Government Corporation Control Act of 1945, which subjected them to budget and audit controls and to civil service laws. Corporations established by the national government carry on enterprises such as the production and sale of electric power. The Tennessee Valley Authority (TVA), for example, produces energy by hydro, oil, and nuclear generation for sale in seven southern states. Other national corporations ensure private deposits held by banks, savings and loans, and credit unions. The best known government corporation is the United States Postal Service, which was created in an attempt to remove the Post Office Department from politics, reduce its costs, and improve its services. Its operations, however, remain controversial because postal services are intrinsically inefficient. Corporations are generally run by an administrator who is responsible to a board of directors. Some are independent agencies, whereas others operate within major departments. On the state and local levels, corporations, often called "authorities," carry on a variety of functions and services. These include operating turnpikes, airports, local transportation facilities, harbors, and utilities. *See also* INDEPENDENT AGENCY, 151.

Significance The basic organizational idea behind the government corporation device is that an agency that produces and markets a product or service can be run most effectively by using private enterprise methods. Critics, however, often oppose them because they view such activities as a socialistic interference with free enterprise capitalism. Their critics also regard them as unfair competition for private companies operating in the same fields because they do not have to pay taxes, and because they receive various kinds of support from other government agencies. Supporters argue that government corporations typically fill a vacuum created by the failure of private enterprise to meet human needs. They also emphasize that government corporations can provide needed competition for private companies, and they can function as a "yardstick" to measure and compare output and costs. Despite their controversial nature, more than one hundred national government corporations continue to carry on diverse activities and provide a variety of products and services to the public.

Hierarchy (147)
An administrative organizational system in a bureaucracy based on the principle of interlocking responsibility and control that integrates all personnel. In a hierarchy, each member is placed in a particular niche based on a ranking of roles and a system of status. Accountability flows upward from the broad lowest levels of the hierarchy and is ultimately focused at the apex of the structure. Power and control flow from the apex down through the various levels in the hierarchy. For each individual, those who rank higher are called *superordinates,* and those who rank lower are *subordinates.* The perfect hierarchical structure would take the shape of a pyramid, and the armed forces probably come the closest to achieving that organizational design. *See also* ACCOUNTABILITY, 85.

Significance The principle of hierarchy is universally applied to all organized groups. Hierarchies, however, vary greatly from extremely rigid, such as in the army or navy, to relatively flexible, as in a college or university. The type of structure can be important both in terms of the organization's operations and in the impact that the status of an individual within the hierarchy can have on his or her self-characterization. In a democratic society, a flexible, decentralized structure that encourages individual initiative is generally preferred to a rigid structure based on strict hierarchical principles. The latter encourages power, centralization, conformity, and impersonality in its operations, characteristics that are highly regarded in an authoritarian society. Yet, in all hierarchical arrangements, no matter how strict and pyramidal in nature, personal relationships can overcome structural rigidities. Despite the possibility of abuse, the hierarchical principle remains a key to governmental operations in the United States on all levels and provides the means by which a democratic society can keep its bureaucrats accountable.

Home Rule **(148)**
The power vested in local units of government—mostly cities—to carry on their affairs with a minimum of external legislative or administrative control. Home rule implies that local units have the power to write and adopt a charter, to change the charter, and to adopt ordinances and make administrative decisions that have the force of law. State home rule laws vary, but all permit a measure of freedom for cities and an increasing number of counties and home rule towns and townships. Most home rule provisions are incorporated in state constitutions, but some are granted by state legislative actions that take the form of statutes. When a city is granted home rule status, it typically elects a commission to draft a charter which will constitute a "constitution" for the city government. The charter specifies the powers of the city government, the formal structure that will exercise these powers, and how decisions will be made. In some states, the people are not permitted to write their own charter but have a choice among several offered by the legislature (optional plan). In other cases, the legislature, by general law or by special act, grants a charter to a local unit without seeking the formal approval of the voters. *See also* DILLON'S RULE, 305.

Significance Despite home rule provisions in state law, the system remains essentially unitary in nature, although constitutionally sanctioned autonomy for local units can incorporate many features of federalism. Ultimately, however, the state retains its authority over local government. For example, local ordinances or actions that conflict with state law can be rendered inoperable by the state courts. Under a famous precedent established by Judge John F. Dillon, an authority on the powers of local government, cities can exercise only those powers granted to them by state law, those that can be reasonably implied from the granted powers, and those considered essential for the city's operations. Wherever any doubt exists in this delineation of powers, Dillon's Rule provides that the issue must be resolved in favor of state control. Thus, despite home rule provisions in many state constitutions and laws, local governments remain creatures of the state and subject to its ultimate authority. Despite these exceptions, home rule can and does extend a broad scope of self-determination to the people of local units of government, thus strengthening democracy at its roots. The main problem, typically, is in determining what constitutes a *local* problem that should be handled *locally*. The resolution of such issues is influenced by the attitudes of legislators and judges concerning the role of local government in the U.S. system.

Hoover Commission, First (149)

The first Commission on Organization of the Executive Branch of the Government, created by Public Law 80-162 in 1947. The first Hoover Commission, named for its chairman, former President Herbert Hoover, was a Republican response to the New Deal and World War II. These historical periods had produced a swollen bureaucracy with vastly increased governmental functions as viewed by the Republican Party which had last controlled Congress in 1930. With the Republican capture of Congress in 1946, the majority party laid down five goals for a reorganization commission to pursue: (1) find ways to cut government costs; (2) eliminate duplication and overlap; (3) consolidate similar functions; (4) abolish unnecessary functions; and (5) define and limit executive branch activities. The last goal was a reflection of the fact that, although there was a new Republican majority in Congress, the president, Harry S Truman, was a Democrat. The legislation establishing the Hoover Commission did not have a dissenting vote in either house, because it had a distinctive tripartite, bipartisan emphasis. The president of the United States, the Speaker of the House, and the president pro tempore of the Senate (the last two Republicans) would each appoint four members of the commission—two from their own branch, and two from private life. Their appointees would have to include two Republicans and two Democrats. One of House Speaker Joseph Martin's appointees was Herbert Hoover, who was elected chairman of the Commission by his fellow commissioners. The first Hoover Commission utilized twenty-four task forces, composed of prestigious citizens, to arrive at its conclusions. These task forces in turn hired research help from such organizations as the Brookings Institution, which conducted a transportation study, and the Council of State Governments, which researched federal-state relations. The first Hoover Commission, in contrast to the Brownlow Committee, represented a cross section of many powerful interests in the nation. *See also* ADMINISTRATIVE REORGANIZATION, 119; BROWNLOW COMMITTEE, 124; HOOVER COMMISSION, SECOND, 150.

Significance The first Hoover Commission avoided questions of policy. Rather than try to deal with deep philosophical issues concerning the roles that government should or should not be undertaking, the commission confined itself to structural questions and outdated processes. This tactical decision was dictated by the fact that different parties controlled the executive and Congress. Despite this self-imposed limitation, the commission's 1949 report was remarkably successful. Public administrationist J. D. Williams notes that 72 percent, or 196, of the first Hoover Commission's 273 recommendations were adopted, 111 by administrative action and 85 by legislative action. Among the commission's important recommendations was the adoption of a performance budget. It observed that the federal budget for 1949–1950 contained 1,625 tightly printed pages, with about 1.5 million words. Exactly what all this detail meant in terms of work proposed and accomplished was far from clear. Accordingly, the commission recommended that "the whole budgetary concept of the Federal Government should be refashioned by the adoption of a budget based upon functions, activities, and projects," and be designated the "performance budget." The term "program budget," came to be used by many people to describe this type of budget. Thus a proposal first made by the New York Bureau of Municipal Research in 1913 saw the light of day 37 years later when President Truman sent to Congress the first budget entirely prepared on a performance basis in January of 1950. Other important recommendations of the first Hoover Commission reduced the president's span of control, delegated preaudit responsibilities from the General Accounting Office (GAO) to the line departments, and strengthened the hand of departmental secretaries vis-à-vis their bureau chiefs. As chairman of the commission, Herbert Hoover proved that he could be more effective in reorganizing government administration than he had been in his role as chief executive.

Hoover Commission, Second (150)

A federal government reorganization commission created by Congress in 1953 and chaired by former President Herbert Hoover. The second Hoover Commission was composed of four Senate appointees, four House appointees, and four presidential appointees, with six members from government and six members from private life. This was the same membership division the first Hoover Commission had in 1947, except the first Hoover Commission had the additional requirement that half of the commissioners would be Democrats and half would be Republicans. The second Hoover Commission had no bipartisanship requirement. With Republican Dwight D. Eisenhower in the White House and a Republican-controlled Congress, the Republicans established the second Hoover Commission essentially to undo much of the administrative structure set up during the New Deal. Although the first Hoover Commission had been established in 1947 by a Republican Congress, the eightieth, it had to deal with a Democratic president, Harry S Truman. The Republican Eighty-third Congress had no such obstacle in 1953, so it authorized the second Hoover Commission to wade into policy matters and search out government functions that competed with private enterprise.

According to public administrationist J. D. Williams, the different purposes of the first and second Hoover Commissions are illustrated by the following quotes from Chairman Hoover. In 1948, Hoover stated, "Major functions of the government are determinable as needed by the Congress. It is not our function to say whether it should exist or not, but it is our function to see if we cannot make it work better." In 1955, "We are trying to strengthen the philosophical foundations of our country." The second Hoover Commission had seven Republicans and five Democrats among the twelve commissioners. The commissioners could also be classified as nine conservatives and three liberals. *See also* ADMINISTRATIVE REORGANIZATION, 119; BROWNLOW COMMITTEE, 124; HOOVER COMMISSION, FIRST, 149.

Significance The second Hoover Commission recommended in 1955 that many government programs that competed with private enterprise be scrapped. Among these programs were crop loans, housing loans, and Rural Electrification Administration (REA) loans. The commission's management philosophy was to stress the use of interdepartmental committees for coordination purposes and to centralize legal services. It favored dismemberment of foreign aid agencies. It recommended accrual accounting rather than cash flow accounting for federal fiscal management. In terms of public personnel administration, the second Hoover Commission revitalized the faltering politics–administration dichotomy, which was then under intellectual attack. The commission recommended that no more than 800 presidentially appointed political executives should fill top positions in the federal government. It proposed a new upper-echelon administrative class of approximately 3,000 persons to be called the "senior civil service." These officials would be politically neutral career managers and would be transferable from one post to another. The abilities of the person would outweigh the requisites of the position. This was an idea adopted from Western European career systems and assumed that public administrators could and should be transferable from agency to agency. Although the professional senior civil service idea died a quiet death in the late 1950s, it was resurrected in 1978 and became a part of the Civil Service Reform Act of that year. Despite some 314 recommendations for reorganization of the federal government, the second Hoover Commission saw only about 64 percent of them put into effect. The major reason was that by the time the commission finished reporting in 1955, Congress was back in Democratic hands. Whereas all ten of Eisenhower's reorganization plans were sustained by the Republican Eighty-third Congress (1953–1954), he lost three of his five plans in the period from 1956 to 1959. The federal government stayed in the housing business, the crop-supporting business, and expanded its efforts to help young people acquire an education. The New Deal was not repealed. A reorganization commission, even one as prestigious as the second Hoover Commission, could not accomplish what Congress itself had not been able to accomplish; that is, to reduce the role of government in modern life.

Independent Agency (151)
A government administrative agency that is not organizationally within an executive departmental hierarchical structure. The term *independent agency* applies particularly to federal administrative units that operate outside the thirteen major cabinet departments. Although independent regulatory commissions carry on their operations free from presidential direction and supervision, other independent agencies are under the chief executive's control. Some independent agencies are headed by a single individual and others by a group, whereas all of the regulatory commissions are multi-headed. Also, whereas most independent agencies are organized like regular executive departments, the regulatory commissions have a unique organizational design to enable them to carry out their missions in regulating private businesses. As a result of these features, most organizational experts distinguish between independent agencies and the regulatory commissions, although a few lump them together as a single administrative genre. Examples of federal independent agencies include the Central Intelligence Agency (CIA), the Tariff Commission, the Veterans Administration (VA), the Civil Rights Commission, the General Services Administration (GSA), and the Office of Personnel Management. *See also* HIERARCHY, 147; INDEPENDENT REGULATORY COMMISSION, 152.

Significance Independent agencies in the national administration have been established over a period of many years to confront a great variety of problems and carry on a diverse set of missions. The latter include such activities as setting up a seven-state regional dam, flood control, an energy-producing system (Tennessee Valley Authority [TVA]), collecting intelligence about other governments, and engaging in "stabilization" and "destabilization" campaigns abroad (Central Intelligence Agency [CIA]). The "independence" of the independent agencies varies greatly: some enjoy a high measure of de facto freedom from presidential surveillance, whereas others operate under close scrutiny and direction from the president. Still others, such as the Tariff Commission, are more closely linked to Congress than to the president. Many independent agencies have been established by

Congress outside the major departments of the executive branch in response to interest-group demands and, in some cases, because Congress has wanted to maintain greater control over the agency's operations than departmental status would permit. In other cases, Congress has given agencies independent status to protect them from partisan influence. The result is that the independent agency structure has impinged severely on the hierarchical principle of organization in the executive branch, because administrative "independence" means above all freedom from the constraints rooted in hierarchy.

Independent Regulatory Commission (152)
An agency created by Congress to regulate a specific area of business or commerce that is carried on across state lines or with foreign countries. Independent regulatory commissions have been empowered to make and issue rules and regulations, to administer their implementation, and to adjudicate disputes that grow out of interpretations and applications of these rules. In this way, they perform all three basic functions of government: quasi-legislative, quasi-executive, and quasi-judicial. For this reason, they are sometimes referred to as "the fourth branch of government" since under the U.S. separation of powers system they do not fit logically into any of the three major branches. The commissions include (1) the Consumer Product Safety Commission, which issues consumer product safety rules to reduce the risk of injury to consumers; (2) the Federal Communications Commission (FCC), which controls interstate and foreign communication by radio, television, telephone, telegraph, and cable; (3) the Federal Energy Regulatory Commission, which regulates the production and interstate transmission and sale of electricity and natural gas; (4) the Federal Maritime Commission (FMC), which controls rates and services of carriers engaged in foreign and domestic off-shore commerce; (5) the Federal Reserve Board, which sets national monetary and credit policies and supervises the twelve district federal reserve banks and member banks throughout the nation; (6) the Federal Trade Commission (FTC), which restricts the use of unfair business practices and promotes fair competition in interstate and foreign commerce; (7) the Interstate Commerce Commission (ICC), which regulates services, rates, and the general business operations of interstate carriers, including railroads, buses, trucks, oil pipelines, intercoastal and inland waterway carriers, and express companies; (8) the National Labor Relations Board (NLRB), which determines bargaining units for workers and controls unfair labor practices by management; (9) the Nuclear Regulatory Commission (NRC), which licenses and regulates nuclear power plants and

controls the development of nuclear power by the military; and (10) the Securities and Exchange Commission (SEC), which regulates the buying and selling of securities, such as stocks, bonds, and options. All of the commissions are headed by five-member boards except the Federal Communications Commission and the Federal Reserve Board, which have seven-member boards, and the Interstate Commerce Commission, which has an eleven-member board. State and local governments have also created regulatory bodies that usually operate on an independent basis free from direct control by the executive, legislative, or judicial branches. *See also* INDEPENDENT AGENCY, 151.

Significance The complexity of problems spawned by a modern economy have led Congress to create the independent regulatory commissions to control and regulate the private companies operating in various sectors. Purposes underlying the creation of the regulatory commissions were those of removing regulation from politics, of developing continuity of policy, and of acquiring expertise in the making of technical decisions. In many cases, however, the commissioners appointed for that purpose have tended to reflect the views of the private interests they have been appointed to regulate. Also, the problem of achieving political neutrality is more difficult in practice than in theory, since most appointees are politically active up to the point when the president nominates them and the Senate considers their confirmation. Under the *Humphrey* rule (*Humphrey's Executor* [*Rathbun*] *v. United States*, 295 U.S. 602: 1935), the president's removal power was restricted by the Supreme Court so that members of the independent regulatory commissions can be removed from office prior to the expiration of their term only for "inefficiency, neglect of duty, or malfeasance in office," as specified by Congress. The Court thus held that President Franklin Roosevelt's firing of Humphrey for political reasons was invalid, because commissioners must be considered to be politically neutral. In another attempt to provide continuity, Congress has provided that commissioners have long, overlapping terms of office so that no president will be able to dominate policy in the economic regulatory fields. Despite their shortcomings, most observers agree that federal regulatory commissions are more effective than state or local agencies in dealing with economic affairs, because in comparison to federal agencies the state or local agencies seem more prone to becoming captives of the economic groups they are supposed to control. One reason why this problem exists on all levels is that the expertise needed by commissioners can only be gained through many years of experience in the field, with the result that most commissioners are chosen from the regulated industries.

Bureaucracy and Administrative Organization

One commission, the Civil Aeronautics Board (CAB), was eliminated in applying the principle of "deregulation." This action has proved controversial in the case of the nation's airlines, and other independent regulatory commissions have continued to control fares and services.

Intergovernmental Relations (IGR) (153)
The ongoing administrative, political, and legal relationships existing among all levels of government within the U.S. federal system. Intergovernmental relations (IGR) go beyond the necessary framework of traditional federalism to include all the combinations of relationships occurring among units of government. It also includes the nongovernmental agencies and institutions that have impact on local policy making and program implementation. Intergovernmental relations is synonymous with "new-style federalism," which has been predominant in the United States since World War II. This approach, sometimes called "marble-cake" federalism, emphasizes cooperation at all levels of government in the making and implementation of public policy. "New-style" federalism differs from "old-style," or "dual" federalism, which focused on the legal criteria by which one level of government should prevail over another. Although there were intergovernmental relations as early as 1803, it has been in the last forty years that intergovernmental relations has been acknowledged as an activity beyond the framework of traditional federalism. The activities that distinguish IGR from the formal contacts required of all governments within a federal system are the continuous, day-to-day informal contacts necessary to accomplish shared program objectives. Domestic policies are frequently the product of intergovernmental relations policy formation and include especially the policy areas of transportation, education, and public housing. However, policies formulated through intergovernmental relations are not necessarily products of consensus and total cooperation. Legal arguments and jurisdictional conflicts remain in the system as various levels of government exert their claims under the structure of formal federalism. Studies of intergovernmental policy making have found that IGR activities are characterized by a wide range of political relationships, including policy making by consensus, group bargaining agreements, manipulative conflict, and totally unproductive conflict. Since the key relationships in making and implementing policy are those between people, rather than those between formal positions in IGR, the individuals engaged in intergovernmental negotiations determine the course of policy development. Two important policy development areas are intergovernmental fiscal

relations, or fiscal federalism, and intergovernmental administrative relations. Fiscal federalism involves governments helping each other financially. Fiscal federalism has taken on additional significance in the last thirty years as state and local governments have had to rely more and more on national funding for the delivery of public service programs. The growth of fiscal federalism and the special skills needed in administering grant money have created a vertical hierarchy of administrative specialists that cuts across all levels of government in the federal system. This hierarchy in turn has created a need for intergovernmental *administrative* relations to meet the demand of elected officials for accountability and the need for a highly specialized administrative link to run programs. The concept of narrow, vertical administrative links through all levels of government has been described as "picket-fence" federalism. *See also* CIRCULAR A-95, 30; FEDERALISM, 47; FEDERALISM, FISCAL, 49.

Significance Intergovernmental relations represent a major development in contemporary public administration. The history of the development over the last twenty years is helpful in understanding both fiscal and picket-fence federalism. In 1959, the federal government established the Advisory Commission on Intergovernmental Relations (ACIR), made up of representatives of national, state, and local governments, as well as the public. The original intent of ACIR was to strengthen relations between the various levels of government, but it has become an influential force in making policy recommendations for intergovernmental programs as well. Since ACIR's establishment, intergovernmental relations have become the focal point of almost all national efforts to strengthen the federal system. In 1969, the president issued a circular through the Bureau of the Budget, the celebrated Circular A-95, which established consultation procedures among federal, state, and local officials. Two years later the president established the Office of Intergovernmental Relations under the office of the vice president to consolidate efforts in the area of intergovernmental relations. The rapid growth of intergovernmental relations following these two events, and the concomitant growth of administrative specialization and discretion, have strengthened the institutions of federalism at all levels of the federal system.

Line and Staff (154)

The division in the field of public administration between those agencies and individuals engaged mainly in implementing policy, and those concerned primarily with providing advice and assistance to top administrators. In a sense, division into line and staff poses a false

Bureaucracy and Administrative Organization

dichotomy in that line agencies carry on various kinds of staff functions, and in many cases staff agencies do lend assistance to line agencies in carrying out their functions. Yet, a basic difference of emphasis does exist. Line agencies, for example, deal directly with the public or their more limited clientele publics, whereas staff agencies typically are charged with aiding the chief executive and line officials in developing and implementing policies. Typical staff functions include planning, budgeting, personnel, policy development, and policy coordination. Line agencies carry on two basic missions: (1) implementation of policy, and (2) giving advice to superiors on substantive programs. In the national government, the thirteen cabinet departments constitute the major line agencies, and those found in the Executive Office of the President are the main staff agencies. State and local governments also divide responsibilities between staff and line agencies, but in local governments most staff functions are fused into line operations. *See also* AGENCY, AUXILIARY, 120; OFFICE OF MANAGEMENT AND BUDGET (OMB), 166.

Significance   Members of the president's cabinet illustrate how line and staff functions can be vested in the same individual offices. Although their main responsibility is that of directing and supervising the day-to-day operations of their departments, they are also deeply involved in staff functions. The latter include advising the president on substantive policy, engaging in management and budgeting, selecting personnel to fill top positions, and planning future departmental policies and programs. State and local line agencies in many ways reflect the federal line departments because the local agencies provide much of the financing for carrying on the operations of the state agencies. Staff agencies utilized by the governors also resemble those that aid the president, since a chief executive's responsibilities are quite similar regardless of the governmental level. Whereas line agencies operate on a modified hierarchical principle, staff agencies are largely the products of pragmatic needs. Also, whereas line agencies operate with a division of labor, clear lines of communication, and superior-subordinate relationships, staff agencies operate as organizational superstructures. The result is that open conflicts develop frequently between line and staff officials over the definition and implementation of policy. For many years, public administration experts focusing on macroadministrative management held that operations could be made much more effective by beefing up the staff and auxiliary agencies to aid the chief executive. Most modern presidents have expanded their staff facilities in response to this advice, but the results have not always justified the expansions in budgets and personnel.

Local Government: City-county Consolidation (155)
The integration of all local governmental units within a county to form a single government. The fractured nature of local government, especially in metropolitan areas, led to the adoption of city-county consolidation as an approach aimed at reducing duplication and overlapping of functions and jurisdictions, decreasing costs, and improving services. Such consolidations may involve the merger of several cities, townships, towns, school districts, and special districts with the county. More commonly, city-county consolidation involves the merger of a major city and its suburbs with legal boundaries similar to those of the county. Boston, Chicago, New Orleans, and Philadelphia, for example, are potential candidates for consolidation because they have city and county boundaries that are actually or substantially the same. City-county consolidation includes the merging of the units into a single government with a unified policy-making institution and integrated departments and agencies providing such services as police and fire protection, operating recreational facilities, housing programs, and road maintenance. *See also* LOCAL GOVERNMENT, 156–162.

Significance City-county consolidation is one of several approaches that seeks to simplify and improve local governmental operations, area planning, and the administration of services. About twenty U.S. cities and their counties have succeeded in consolidating their operations, including Baton Rouge, Louisiana, Nashville, Tennessee, and Indianapolis, Indiana. Many other attempts have been made but failed. Although consolidation is a logical and rational plan to eliminate duplication and streamline services, political, social, and economic factors make it difficult to achieve. Often it has become a political battle between the people of the city versus those living in the suburbs, with the latter strongly resisting efforts to consolidate. Advantages of consolidation of units include (1) increased efficiency; (2) lower costs based on economies of scale; (3) a better matching of resources with program needs; and (4) the psychological-attitudinal gain from ending competition between units and fostering a common loyalty. Disadvantages include (1) a reduced level of services to some areas following consolidation; (2) creation of a large bureaucracy with resulting problems; (3) a reduction of flexibility that had existed among diverse units; and (4) a dependence on county government structures that developed mainly as administrative units of the state rather than as service organizations. Regardless of the pros and cons of city-county consolidation, it is a phenomenon that is likely to continue to gain adoptions because of the growing financial pressures on taxpayers and voters in metropolitan areas.

Bureaucracy and Administrative Organization

Local Government: Commission Form (156)
A plan of local government centering on elected commissioners who both legislate and administer public policy. The commission form of government has also been called the Galveston Plan, named for its point of origin: Galveston, Texas. In 1901, Galveston was devastated by a tidal wave and flood. At that time the city was governed by the weak mayor–council form of government, which proved to be unable to cope with the destruction and the huge task of rebuilding the city. The government collapsed. The governor of Texas appointed five area businessmen to administer the city, and the governing methods they developed became the commission form of government. The Galveston Plan had the following characteristics: (1) a commission of five members who have complete control over a local government; (2) one commissioner is designated mayor and the other commissioners head the administrative departments of the city; (3) the five commissioners shape policy as well as administer it; (4) the commissioners are nonpartisan elected officials; (5) commissioners represent the entire city, not individual districts; and (6) governing is done collectively. There is no single head of the government. The commission form is an alternative to both the weak mayor–council form and the strong mayor–council form of government. Both the weak mayor–council form and the strong mayor–council form involve splitting the responsibilities for governance between a mayor and a council. The mayor is a figurehead in the weak mayor–council form, with little or no control over top administrators, who are popularly elected. In the strong mayor–council form, the elected mayor has the primary responsibility for administering the government, while the council makes broad policy. The commission form brought the mayor and the council into a single body—the commission—and called for a sharing of responsibilities. The mayor has no more responsibility than the other members of the commission. *See also* LOCAL GOVERNMENT, 155, 157–162.

Significance The commission form of government was hailed from its inception as a way of removing local affairs from the political arena and putting them into the hands of neutral business people and community leaders. The commission greatly simplified the organization of government and was thought to have economic advantages for that reason. It was popular in cities with a population of 25,000 or less, and reached its peak of popularity in 1917, with about 500 cities using it. By 1974, only 220 municipalities still had commissions, however, although it continued to be used by a majority of county governments in the United States. Criticisms leveled against the commission form of government include (1) it lacks a single source of effective leadership, that is, no one is in charge; (2) there is no system of checks and balances because the same body that develops policies carries them out and evaluates them; (3) in larger cities a five-person commission proved too small to represent the varying interest groups of the city; (4) business management methods do not always work in public administration contexts; and (5) commissioners typically can give only part-time service since most of them have other responsibilities. The commission form of government filled a need at a particular time in U.S. administrative history. Larger and more complex jurisdictions required a more professional approach to administration, however, and the council-manager plan eventually replaced the commission as the most widely used form of municipal government.

Local Government: Council-manager Form (157)
A form of local government centering on the city manager, an experienced administrator who undertakes full-time responsibility for the supervision of municipal affairs. The council-manager form of government was attempted for the first time in 1912 in Sumter, South Carolina. Since then it has been adopted by more than half of the medium-sized cities in the United States, cities with populations between 25,000 and 250,000. The city manager is appointed by an elected council, is responsible to it, and holds his or her position at the council's discretion. The manager is the ultimate authority in administrative matters, however, and the council does not intervene. The manager's position is a nonpolitical one in that he or she does not run for office, campaign for any incumbent councilperson, or for any candidate for a council position. The manager does, however, greatly influence policy matters before the council, for he or she is a "professional expert," and the manager's advice to the council is given great weight. The efficiency of the city's administrative operations is the manager's responsibility, for which he or she will be held accountable by the council. Under the council-manager form of government, the mayor plays a public relations role and presides over the council. The mayor does not exercise administrative responsibility nor interfere in the manager's administrative area. About half of the mayors in the council-manager system are selected by their council colleagues, and the other half are elected by the voters. The cardinal feature of the council-manager form of government is that neither council nor mayor competes with the manager in the administration of city affairs, nor do they exercise any administrative functions. *See also* LOCAL GOVERNMENT, 155, 156, 158–162.

Significance   The council-manager form of government marked the high point of the early twentieth-century movement toward the integration of administrative responsibility. By 1915, local government had undergone many basic changes, and a wide variety of administrative patterns had resulted. In addition to the council-manager plan, the strong mayor–council form of local government was popular from the 1880s through the 1920s. By 1917, almost 500 U.S. cities had adopted yet another plan for unified direction and control of local government: the commission. Although the combined legislative-executive-collegial approach of the commission form soon disappeared from the municipal governmental scene, it is still utilized on a large scale in county governments in the United States. All three "good government" reform plans—council-manager, strong mayor–council, and commission—were local manifestations of a nationwide movement toward a strong executive. Beginning in the early 1880s, the center of gravity of the U.S. system gradually shifted from legislative bodies, many of which were corrupt and controlled by corporations, labor leaders, and other special interests, as well as reinvigorated executives. Belief in the virtues of fragmented government had steadily been eroded in the post–Civil War era. The Progressives believed the center of governmental power should be located in the executive branch. They regarded the enhancement of executive power as the surest means to provide clear and responsible leadership. Forceful presidential leadership emerged at the national level, and at the state level of government governors evolved from figureheads to real leaders and public managers. The terms of governors were extended from two to four years, many state constitutions were amended to provide that governors be allowed to succeed themselves, governors were allowed to exercise the item veto on budget bills, and a "short ballot" campaign led to a reduction in the number of elected officials outside of the effective authority of the governor. The spillover of the strong executive movement at the local level was the council-manager plan. The influential city manager paralleled the powerful governor and the forceful president in a recovery of the "doctrine of energy" advanced earlier by Alexander Hamilton and the Federalists.

Local Government: County-manager Plan (158)

A form of local government that can replace traditional county government with a system patterned after the council-manager plan of city government. Under the county-manager plan, an elected county board, which operates as the county's legislative body, hires a professional administrator to function as the chief executive official of the county. While the board makes policy and oversees the administration of state laws and county ordinances, the manager has authority to hire and fire personnel, to direct and supervise the county administration, to implement the budget, and to report regularly to the county board. The board holds the manager responsible for carrying out these duties with skill and effectiveness and may hire and fire managers at will. *See also* LOCAL GOVERNMENT, 155–157, 159–162.

Significance The county-manager plan was first adopted in 1930 in Durham County, North Carolina. Since then, about one-fifth of the more than 3,000 counties in the United States have adopted the plan. It is generally considered effective where adopted, especially in a comparison with the traditional system it replaced. The latter suffers from (1) an absence of a focus for administrative responsibility; (2) a long ballot which is used to elect numerous county officers who are responsible only to the voters; (3) some overlapping of authority and duplicating of functions; and (4) the widespread use of the spoils system. The county-manager plan reduces the long ballot to the election of a single member of the county board, focuses administrative authority and responsibility in the manager, and installs a merit personnel system. Despite its successes, the county-manager plan is unlikely to be adopted in most counties until state constitutions are amended to provide for county home rule. Opposition to the plan comes mainly from entrenched political interests within most counties, and from those who argue that the county should remain only a decentralized unit of state administration, and not become an additional unit for local self-government.

Local Government: Functional Consolidation (159)
A cooperative arrangement established by several units of local government to meet the needs of their citizens. There are two main forms of functional consolidation that involve local governments. One of these—the special district—is a local government unit that cuts across political boundary lines to offer special services not offered by the existing units, such as cities, towns, and counties. In special district government, taxes are levied to support the special programs, which include such functions as fire protection, parks, water and sewage systems, mosquito abatement, and education. Each unit that has joined a special district government typically levies and collects the taxes for it. The second basic form of functional consolidation involves merely a contractual arrangement rather than the setting up of a new governmental unit. This often means that the major city in a metropolitan area offers to provide common services to its suburban

governments if they are willing to contract for them. *See also* LOCAL GOVERNMENT, 155–158, 160–162.

Significance   Functional consolidation offers a means for improving services to citizens, especially those in the highly urbanized metropolitan areas. Some metropolitan areas currently have a dozen or more independent police forces, for example. By consolidating the police function, efficiency could be increased and the cost-benefit ratio improved. In rural areas with weak tax bases, functions such as health services and fire protection often can be financed only through a cooperative program. As inflation has increasingly reduced local governments' abilities to cope with problems individually and to continue to supply adequate services, functional consolidation has become more popular. Local pride often stands in the way of functional consolidations, but economic pressures can overcome these psychological attachments.

Local Government: Mayor-administrator Plan   (160)

A form of city government in which the executive branch is headed by a mayor who appoints a chief administrative officer (CAO) to direct and supervise the administrative operations of city government. Under the plan, the administrator is appointed by the mayor, typically for an indefinite term, with some cities requiring council approval of such appointments. In turn, the administrator appoints and removes supervisory employees, oversees the operations of the city's personnel system, administers the budget, coordinates the work of city agencies, and serves as an administrative adviser to the mayor. Because the administrator handles city administrative chores, the mayor is freed up to provide leadership, present policy proposals to the council, build public support for city programs, and fight political battles when necessary. *See also* LOCAL GOVERNMENT, 155–159, 161, 162.

Significance   The mayor-administrator plan is a modification of the strong mayor–council form of city government used mainly in large cities. It is an effort to combine the best features of the strong mayor system with those of the council-manager plan. Unlike the manager plan, however, the mayor-administrator plan provides that the administrator is directly accountable to the mayor rather than to the council. The main weaknesses of the mayor-administrator plan become obvious when the mayor and the council become entangled in a political dispute and the administrator is caught in the middle. The system in effect postulates the existence of two "mayors," one for policy and one for administration. As a result, the "administrative mayor" can build a political base with the council and in the major city departments that may make it difficult for the "policy mayor" to hold him accountable. Like other forms of city government, the success or failure of the system often depends on the general environment of the city and on the personalities of the two key individuals.

Local Government: Strong Mayor–Council Form (161)
A form of local government that enhances the power of the mayor by giving him or her wide appointing and removal powers, and institutionalized opportunities for taking policy initiatives. The strong mayor–council form of government developed in the 1880s as a counterbalance to the weak mayor–council form, which, according to reformers, did not give the mayor the basic tools necessary for effective municipal leadership. The strong mayor, still found in many large U.S. cities, makes a large number of appointments of high level officials and members of municipal boards and commissions. None of these appointments requires confirmation by the council. The budget considered by the council is initially formulated and then presented by the mayor. The execution of the budget in the postappropriation stage is entirely the responsibility of the mayor and his or her fiscal advisors. The mayor is also authorized to present a legislative program to the council, thereby assuming policy leadership. The mayor can veto any legislation passed by the council. In addition, the mayor is an ex officio member of the most important municipal boards and commissions. Since the council is largely divested of any significant administrative power, it concentrates on legislative proposals, broad policies, and revenue-taxation matters. It typically holds public hearings on the mayor's budget and approves it after modifications. *See also* LOCAL GOVERNMENT, 155–160, 162.

Significance The strong mayor–council form of government provided impetus for increased professionalization in municipal administration. Since the mayor tended to be a "political animal" and was the product of political campaigning, His Honor not infrequently was short on administrative experience and managerial competence. Administrative operations were often turned over to professional public managers who were responsible for coordinating municipal agencies, formulating the budget, administering the personnel system, and representing the mayor in the daily business of running a city. The result was more efficiently administered municipal programs and services. The strong mayor–council form of local government was a key factor in many local governments being able to accommodate the vast influx of people from rural areas and the absorption of large numbers of foreign immigrants during the period 1880–1930. Strong mayors tended to dominate municipal affairs by establishing powerful political machines based on patronage and spoils, especially in cities with partisan elections. Despite the presence of professional administrative officers, high-level decision making was still sometimes based on nonprofessional intuition or partisan political advantages. Whatever its shortcomings, however, the strong mayor–council form of government resolved to a large extent the problem of fragmented municipal power which had plagued local government from the earliest days of the nation. The responsibility of governance could be pinpointed in one office: the mayor's. The strong mayor–council form of government is still widely used in larger U.S. cities.

Local Government: Weak Mayor–Council Form (162)

A form of local government almost universally practiced in American towns and villages prior to the Civil War and still in wide use. The weak mayor–council plan of government features a dominant city council which in early U.S. history paralleled dominant legislative power at the state level. Both were reflections of a widespread mistrust of executive power, which was a holdover from colonial experiences with British governors acting as agents of the Crown. Chief executives, inheritors of the suspicion visited upon executives at all levels of government, saw their prestige wane as legislative bodies gained new influence in the period from 1789 to 1865. The concept of the chief executive as "representative of the people" was not widely accepted in the United States until the Progressive Era of the late nineteenth century. Both the council and the mayor in the weak mayor–council plan are limited by the popular election of large numbers of local officials *in addition to* the election of the council. Like governors, mayors in this form of government have few administrative powers and lack even a limited veto power. The weak mayor cannot hire or fire municipal personnel and is authorized to appoint only a few local officials. Even these appointments often require the consent of the council. The municipal budget is formulated by the council, and the responsibility for administering it is frequently vested in the council. The weak mayor typically has no popular base of support, since he or she was selected by members of the council. The executive authority of the mayor is further weakened in some cities by the frequent council practice of dividing its members into administrative committees and assuming responsibility for the operations of municipal departments. Councils frequently appoint department heads and hold them accountable to the council rather than to the mayor. The fragmentation of administration is also emphasized by the popular election of members of various local boards and commissions. Responsibility is more dispersed under the weak mayor–council form than under any other plan of local government. See also LOCAL GOVERNMENT, 155–161.

Significance   The weak mayor–council plan of government effectively accomplishes what it was designed to do: prevent the rise of powerful executives and distribute power among many power centers. This was the political philosophy of the framers of the constitution, and its rationale applied at the local level meant that mayors emerged largely as symbolic figures. Thomas Jefferson and his followers believed the center of gravity in society should be in small, local governments close to the people. For many years the triumph of Jefferson's ideas over those of the Federalists effectively meant a "no executive" type of government. The people as a whole frequently served as the legislative body when they were convened in town and township meetings for the purpose of enacting ordinances and resolutions and adopting budgets. An interim citizen group of "selectmen" was responsible for the administration of policies once they were adopted by the town meeting. Executive decision making and the management of local affairs by the selectmen was collegial in nature, and there was no single executive on whom the community could pinpoint responsibility. The weak mayor–council form of government is an extension of this principle of participatory democracy. The strong executive leadership ideas fostered by Alexander Hamilton did not emerge again on the local level until the public demand for reform and accountability helped usher them in during the 1870s. Although the weak mayor plan is the most widely used form of city government today, its lack of executive leadership and its emphasis on checks and balances makes it difficult for cities using the plan to cope with the great variety and complexity of problems confronting them.

Matrix Organization (163)
An organizational form whereby teams of specialists from formal organizational units are created for purposes of achieving a specific objective while being supported by administrators who coordinate activities rather than function as superiors. Matrix organizations are also known as program or project organizations, utilizing styles of matrix management, also called program, project, or systems management. Matrix organization is an extension of public administrationist Luther H. Gulick's principle of organization by purpose. But

rather than creating a formal permanent organization, a project-oriented suborganization is developed in order to solve a specific problem. Each matrix organization is headed by a project manager who recruits and coordinates the work of necessary specialists, and who reports to the senior executive in the regular permanent organization. Matrix organizations are nonhierarchical in that the project manager exerts no formal control over the specialists. Matrix organizations are usually temporary in nature and are dissolved on completion of a specific project. They are typified by a "unit of vision" among participating personnel because of the unique focus of their task. The need for matrix organizations developed as a result of the impact of technology on public administration, the emergence of large-scale organizations, and the application of systems analysis to organizational theory. Government agencies have found this form of organization useful for many kinds of projects involving rapidly changing and complex technologies. Aerospace projects are perhaps the best-known examples of matrix management, particularly the *Apollo* spacecraft program, which employed George Low as the program manager. Low's job was to coordinate and direct all aspects of the program, including the supervision of industrial contractors. Altogether he managed twenty subsystems and five division chiefs. Low believed the program was successful because (1) the matrix organization form allowed him to maintain an overall perspective on the system; (2) successes and failures in the project were visible, enabling him to judge whether or not objectives were being accomplished; (3) people were willing to accept authority that was not permanent; and (4) urgent deadlines added impetus to the completion of the project. Although matrix organizations were once associated predominantly with scientific research organizations, they have increasingly been adapted to all public agencies that experience the effects of rapid technological change. *See also* ORGANIZATION THEORY, 176–179.

Significance Matrix organization is one of the most important new developments in management science. A leading advocate of matrix management, James E. Webb, former administrator of the National Aeronautics and Space Administration (NASA) during the *Mercury-Gemini* era, believes that traditional organizational forms do not have the flexibility to adjust to rapid technological change, or to solve complex problems creatively. Webb does recognize the value and necessity of permanent, traditional organizational forms which provide ongoing routine functions such as budgetary processes, purchasing, public relations, and evaluation. Organization development expert Wendell French believes there are several unanswered questions about matrix organizations. One is about the psychological effects on experts who never work with permanent groups and who are perpetually forming and dissolving horizontal working relationships. Organizational humanist Chris Argyris has predicted that organizations will increasingly combine hierarchical and matrix management, whereby authority is based less on power or role, and more on the possession of relevant information and expertise.

National Security Council (NSC) (164)

A staff agency in the Executive Office of the President that advises the chief executive on the integration of domestic, foreign, and military policies relating to national security. The National Security Council was established by the National Security Act of 1947, as amended in 1949, when the Council was placed in the Executive Office. The NSC is chaired by the president, and its statutory members include the vice president, the secretaries of state and defense, and the chairman of the Joint Chiefs of Staff as military advisor and the director of central intelligence as intelligence advisor. Other officials serve at the request of the president. The Council's main task is to develop and assess the objectives, commitments, and risks facing the United States in any critical situation and to make recommendations to the president on a course of action. *See also* EXECUTIVE OFFICE OF THE PRESIDENT (EXOP OR EOP), 138.

Significance The National Security Council was designed to function as the nation's highest advisory body on national security matters. In practice, however, each president determines when and how the NSC will be used. When a serious crisis erupts anywhere in the world, the president may summon the NSC into immediate session, or may consult other sources of advice such as personal friends or cabinet officials. When meeting with the NSC, the president is free to accept or reject its advice. President Ronald Reagan made extensive use of the National Security Council staff in secret operations that involved arms sales to Iran and the diversion of funds from this operation to provide aid for the *contra* rebels in Nicaragua in violation of federal law. This activity led to a major congressional investigation in 1987.

Neo-Weberism (165)

A counterattack on the general thrust of the new public administration, led by Victor A. Thompson and elaborated in his book, *Without Sympathy or Enthusiasm: The Problem of Administrative Compassion* (1975). Neo-Weberism states simply that public service is professional, impersonal, and equal. It is also universalistic and noncompassionate. Public service cannot be compassionate because the organization tool that advances it is a consciously adopted design for goal accomplishment. It is a system of roles and rules. Compassion is an individual gift, not an organizational one. The client is part of a problem category, not a historical person. He or she is an applicant for welfare, a speeder, or a cardiac case, for example. In this transaction, he or she is not a person. The transaction is impersonal and *this fact actually facilitates the expert solution of his or her problem.* Interpersonal emotions do not interfere with the instrumental application of the specialist's expertise. The client's individuality, that is, his or her identity, is ignored. The proponents of Neo-Weberism point out that the modern administrative norm, first described by German sociologist Max Weber (1864–1920), is the rule that everyone in the same problem category should be treated equally. This norm made efficient administration possible. It was a necessary prerequisite of modern mass democratic government. The rule of law in this sense is an administrative necessity in an industrial country. The rule of law, like efficiency, is incompatible with deviation from universalistic rules and regulations. Administrative compassion, then, and the other qualities the new public administration represents, should be thought of as special treatment, as stretching the rules, as the modern version of "rule of men" rather than "rule of law." The neo-Weberians are extremely clear in their understanding of the civil servant's function. As Thompson said, "A screwdriver does not choose among goals or among owners. It does what it is told." *See also* BUREAUCRACY, 126; NEW PUBLIC ADMINISTRATION, 18; WEBER, MAX, 187.

Significance Neo-Weberism is firmly rooted in Max Weber's contention that the civil servant must be "faithless" in the sense of his or her lack of concern for values, ends, or consequences. It is the politician, in Weber's thought, who must be aware of the consequences of his policies and conduct. In his famous "Politics as a Vocation" speech at the University of Munich in 1918, Weber outlined the unique attributes of the politician that set him conspicuously apart from the bureaucrat: "To take a stand, to be passionate . . . is the politician's element, . . . some kind of faith must always exist." The politician's "genuinely human and moving" dilemmas of means versus ends are not the concern of the civil servant. The latter invests his honor in executing conscientiously the order of the politician as the policy-making authority. Weber's Munich speech is perhaps the classic justification for the separation of policy and administration. The excesses of German National Socialism in the 1930s and early 1940s can be understood in part in terms of blind adherence to Weberian doctrine. The Nuremberg Principle resulted.

The Public Administration Dictionary

The guiding rule established in international law when the Nazi war criminals were tried for their crimes was "Following orders from a higher authority is no defense against criminal prosecution for an unlawful act." A civil servant is more than a mindless minion of the organization.

Office of Management and Budget (OMB) (166)
An agency in the Executive Office of the President that annually reviews all proposed federal expenditures in order to draft the government's budget for the president's review and transmittal to Congress. The Office of Management and Budget is the former Bureau of the Budget (BOB), established in the Treasury Department in 1921, and moved to the Executive Office of the President in 1939. The Bureau of the Budget was renamed the Office of Management and Budget by President Richard M. Nixon in 1970. OMB's important role is derived from the president's power, which he has delegated to it. This is the power of "legislative clearance," that is, the determination of whether an agency's budget proposals are "in accord with the President's program." OMB also reviews each bill passed by Congress and sent to the president for approval or veto. It canvasses the views of concerned agencies about appropriate action and assures that the president is aware of those views when making decisions. OMB is charged to improve administrative organization, management, and coordination wherever possible in the executive branch to meet the president's responsibilities as chief executive. In carrying out these functions, OMB staff members walk the corridors of the principal agencies of the federal government and deal with them daily by telephone and memorandum. Thus, OMB is a rich source of intelligence to the president about what is going on in the executive branch at all levels of policy generation and program management. *See also* BUDGET, 261; BUDGET CYCLE, 263; EXECUTIVE OFFICE OF THE PRESIDENT (EXOP OR EOP), 138.

Significance The Office of Management and Budget is a key administrative agency not only because money is the lifeblood of government programs, but because budgeting is virtually the only comprehensive decision-forcing process in the executive branch. Most other decision making is fragmented, episodic, and fluctuating in scope and intensity. The BOB-OMB organization has benefited from a tradition described by one close observer as "neutral competence." The organization has used its resources to serve both the long-term institution of the presidency and the short-term, incumbent president. Higher positions in OMB have been filled for the most part by promotion, so that incumbents tend to be experienced in OMB's work and socialized in its standards. OMB's prestige has attracted some of the ablest civil servants in the federal government. They provide an institutional memory that is otherwise lacking in those around a president, whose vision is circumscribed by a four-year political calendar. Since 1960, however, OMB's influence has declined with the growth and specialization of the White House staff. Powerful White House aides frequently have bypassed OMB in dealing directly with the executive departments. They tended to allow OMB to handle only procedural mechanics and to advise on only noncontroversial legislative proposals of agencies and enactments of Congress. The low point of BOB-OMB history was the Nixon years in which OMB directors and deputy directors were political activists who made political speeches, advocated Nixon policies at congressional hearings, and defended massive impoundments of appropriated funds until the courts ruled them illegal. The Carter and Reagan administrations retained the political associate director positions established under Nixon and generally continued the politicization of the agency.

Ombudsman (167)

A special official in the government appointed to hear complaints from citizens concerning their grievances with the bureaucracy. Although the ombudsman typically possesses no decision-making power and cannot directly overrule an agency decision, the office can be used to mediate, bring pressure, persuade, cajole, and otherwise seek to bring about a reasonable solution to an administrative problem. Typically, the ombudsman is a person of considerable prestige, able to bring public opinion to focus on the problem if necessary. The individual who heads an ombudsman's office must also be knowledgeable about bureaucratic systems and enough of a psychologist to understand why people act the way they do in certain situations, and how their conduct can be modified. Without such qualifications and skills, an ombudsman might prove to be helpless in tackling problems involving public officials who have power while he has none. *See also* DUE PROCESS OF LAW, 306.

Significance The office of ombudsman originated in Scandinavia in the twentieth century and has since been adopted in many other countries for use in national, provincial, and local governments. Known as "defender of the citizen's rights" and the "people's watchdog," an ombudsman may receive and resolve thousands of complaints in a single year. The office is a natural outgrowth of modern bureaucracy and its propensities to commit administrative abuses, with ordinary citizens often the victims. Typically it is the legislative body that creates an ombudsman to function as the means of ensuring that its policies in the form of law will not be applied and enforced in a ruthless, unjust, unfair, or inequitable manner. Like the courts examining an administrative action to ensure that it meets the requirements of due process of law, the ombudsman is concerned with both substantive and procedural abuses by administrative officials and agencies. The creation of the office rejects the ancient doctrine that the sovereign can do no wrong. As a result of campus turmoil during the 1960s and 1970s, many universities in the United States established an ombudsman's office to deal with student complaints. Although some state and local governments have set up an ombudsman's office, the national government has no central system for dealing with citizen complaints other than the members of Congress. Although many observers have suggested that a national ombudsman's office be created to relieve Congress of its heavy workload in trying to correct administrative abuses, such suggestions are unlikely to bear fruit because such activities greatly aid congressmen in their re-election efforts.

Organization (168)

A goal-seeking group of individuals who use a structure designed to help achieve its objectives. Organization is concerned in particular with the ways in which personnel are organized to carry out their basic mission. In public administration, organization and personnel are the two basic factors subject to modification and change. If one devises the best possible organizational arrangement for carrying out an agency's tasks, but personnel are listless, apathetic, and unmotivated, agency operations will suffer. If, on the other hand, an agency has dedicated, ambitious, and highly efficient personnel, but they must try to carry out their duties in an outmoded, inefficient, and convoluted organizational milieu, again the agency will probably fail in its basic mission. Organization, like personnel, is a critical factor in the operations of all political and administrative systems. Organization effectiveness deals with such subjects as the location of responsibility, the application of the principles of hierarchy, the role of line and staff, how accountability of each employee can be ensured, the coordination of efforts, and the most efficient use of personnel through specialization based on a division of labor. The lines of responsibility and accountability should flow smoothly from the lowest levels to the highest, and power and authority should be focused at the top and flow through the different echelons to the lowest ranks. The most effective organizations are those based on some coherent principle or operational characteristic. These might include (1) clientele, such as the Department of Labor or the Bureau of Indian Affairs; (2) specialized purpose, such as the Department of State or the Central Intelligence Agency (CIA); (3) skills or functions, such as the Office of Management and Budget (OMB); (4) geographical area, such as the Tennessee Valley Authority (TVA); and (5) major purpose, such as the Environmental Protection Agency (EPA). All agencies in the national administration are based on one or several of these patterns, and some incorporate all of them. *See also* ADMINISTRATIVE REORGANIZATION, 119; HIERARCHY, 147.

Significance The importance of organization in carrying out policies and programs adopted by Congress has led that body to undertake frequent reorganizations of the executive branch with the objective of achieving greater efficiency at less cost. Because political considerations so often intervened in the efforts of Congress to organize the national government more efficiently, Congress in 1949 turned major authority and responsibility for determining organizational changes over to the president, although retaining the "veto" power over presidential actions. Each president since 1949 has submitted numerous reorganizational plans, and very few have been vetoed by Congress. Because of the growing emphasis on organization, scholars have developed organization theory which seeks to explain the nature and functioning of complex groups. The emphasis is placed on structure and design and on decision processes carried on within organizations. The study of organizations draws heavily from the pioneering work done by the sociologist Max Weber in his studies of complex bureaucratic organizations. Organization will continue to be one of the central focuses of the study of public administration because it is critical to governmental operations.

Organization Development (OD) (169)
A behavioral science approach to organizational change which assumes a process of continuous self-renewal within organizations. Organization development involves employees in both problem analysis and the generation of solutions in a climate of trust and openness. The underlying philosophy of organization development is (1) employees are capable of diagnosing problems they live with; (2) employees are capable of suggesting viable solutions to organizational dilemmas; (3) the climate must be right to elicit employee suggestions; (4) implementation of reforms will be smoother if employees are involved at the analysis stage; and (5) the best remedy for entropy is continuous self-renewal. Organization

development requires management to pay a great deal of attention to such maintenance activities as team building and harmonizing interpersonal relations. The most successful of the techniques used to do these things are transactional analysis (TA) and sensitivity training (T-groups). Their common goal is to reduce defensiveness, promote adult kinds of behavior, and generate a willingness to confront rather than dodge problems. Organization development seeks to build into an agency a problem-solving capability which offers a creative response not only to a current problem, but to any problem that may arise. It is planned change. *See also* ENTROPY, 137; HUMAN MOTIVATION, 99–103; ORGANIZATION DEVELOPMENT, 170–172.

Significance Organization development ideas can be applied only if managers deeply value employee ideas, solicit them, and listen. Organization theorist Victor Thompson stated the case for organization development. He believed that involving larger parts of the organization in the search process would increase chances of acceptance and implementation of problem solutions. Not only must managers genuinely value employee ideas in the OD model, they must *recognize* existing or upcoming problems to assign to employee task forces. Managers frequently find it useful to bring an outside consultant on board to aid and abet the self-analysis that proceeds from problem identification. The consultant is primarily a feedback monitor, making sure feedback flows back to his or her client (that is, the manager) and to and through each team at work on the problem. The underlying psychological assumption in the organization development model is that involvement leads to commitment.

Organization Development: Managerial Grid (170)
A two-dimensional scheme for describing managerial style on the basis of whether the manager is production-oriented or people-oriented. The managerial grid was devised by organization development consultants Robert R. Blake and Jane F. Mouton in 1967, using questionnaire responses. Blake and Mouton gave descriptions of the types of managers who may be found at five points on the classifying grid: at the four extremes and at the center. Concern for people was one axis of the grid; concern for production was the other. Along each axis, a score of one is the lowest, and nine is the highest. Four extremes of management styles were labeled: (1) 1,1—*Impoverished Management:* "Don't make waves. Do as little as possible to keep the boss happy"; (2) 9,9—*Team Management:* "Yes sir! This is the finest staff anybody could want to work with. They really work as a team to accomplish team goals!"; (3) 1,9—*Country Club Management:* "Why

should I worry about progress? My people know what they are doing and are very happy"; and (4) 9,1—*Task Management:* "The job's the thing. Accomplish the objective even if all the troops are lost in the battle." Blake and Mouton theorize that every managerial technique, approach, or style can be placed somewhere on the managerial grid. They offer not only a diagnosis, but also a prescription. Their goal is an organization that scores a nine on the production and a nine on the people scale. In such an organization Blake and Mouton believe there is mutual trust among organization members and that organizational goals become members' goals. Efficiency and satisfaction combine to enhance effectiveness in the model of the managerial grid. *See also* ORGANIZATION DEVELOPMENT, 169, 171, 172.

Significance The managerial grid is used for managerial training and for identifying various combinations of leadership style. It is a useful device for helping managers to see how they manage—for production results or for people. The grid does not tell the student why a manager falls into one section or another of the grid, however. Blake and Mouton's model implies that combinations other than 9,9 are less desirable. As a result, training programs aim at the "ideal" (9,9) pattern, which is a pattern of equal concern for production and for people. There have not been many research studies of the effectiveness of the managerial grid approach. Those that do exist suffer from a number of difficulties, chief among which is that the information obtained tends to be anecdotal and subjective. Individuals were asked in one study to describe changes that had occurred more than a year earlier.

Most programs based on the managerial grid approach have been carried on without control groups. Indeed, most managerial grid analyses of organizations are not evaluated at all. The relatively few rigorous studies that do exist have generated mixed, and often contradictory, conclusions. Nevertheless "grid organization development," as the idea was first called, remains an excellent packaging concept. It is a method for explaining and developing training programs to focus sensitivity training and organizational development on the leadership concept. Blake and Mouton suggest many types of activities which might help leaders improve. Among these are *laboratory-seminar groups* to create an awareness of managerial qualities; *teamwork* in specifying the desirable characteristics of leaders; *intergroup action* among teams for discussion, analysis, and generalizations about growth experiences; and *goal setting* for specific, measurable progress in leadership development.

Organization Development: Sensitivity Training**(171)**
An effort to train selected executives in new attitudes about "authentic" behavior in interpersonal relationships within the organization. Sensitivity training attempts to teach administrators how to let down their guards associated with hierarchical and competitive positions in the authority structure and how to clarify their own identities as human beings interacting with other human beings. Sensitivity training as a form of organization development activity seeks to transform the psychological atmosphere of the whole organization. The training takes the form of one or two weeks intensive exposure to "T-groups" (the "T" for "training" or "laboratory training"), which are led by a member of the human relations school of administrative management. The group leader takes a nondirective role, encouraging group members to engage in interpersonal dynamics characterized by extreme candor. T-groups are the same as "encounter groups," which also flourished in the troubled 1960s. See also ORGANIZATION DEVELOPMENT, 169, 170, 172.

Significance Sensitivity training has produced a paucity of reliable evidence to support its claims. The evidence that exists seems to indicate that, although many participants value the T-group experience and alter their behavior back on the job, the new behavior may either improve or lessen their effectiveness in organizations. The effects of the T-group experience usually fade after a few months. The participants' organizations are not changed. The first major organization development (OD) effort undertaken in the federal government was launched in the State Department in the mid-1960s. The program was called ACORD, for Action for Organization Development Program, and it provided sensitivity training and team development workshops for high-level department officials, including ambassadors. Twenty of the most prestigious T-group trainers in the nation were employed in the program. It was terminated after only two years. Its stated objectives "were, at best, achieved only to a marginal extent," according to Michael H. Harmon in his paper, "Organization Development in the State Department: A Case Study of the ACORD Program." Despite this experience, OD programs were subsequently initiated in over half the bureaus and agencies of the federal government. Sensitivity training became a part of the program of the Federal Executive Institute, the government's training center for senior government officials.

Bureaucracy and Administrative Organization

Organization Development: Transactional Analysis   (172)
A theory of human behavior that attempts to describe what happens when any two people interact. Transactional analysis (TA) wasoriginally developed by psychiatrist Eric Berne in his 1964 book, *Games People Play*. One of his associates, Tom Harris, developed the idea more fully in his 1969 book, *I'm O.K.—You're O.K.* Transactional analysis theorizes that everyone has three typical modes of behavior: the parent ego state, the adult ego state, and the child ego state. The theory also uses certain names for some of the characteristics of human interaction situations. Among these are *strokes, games, transactions,* and *life positions*. The *child* ego state is that body of experience stored in a person's brain that relates to childhood experience. It includes feelings of frustration, inadequacy, and helplessness. The child ego state is called the "felt concept of life" in TA. The *parent* ego state comes from a person's observation about the way his or her mother and father or other "big people" in one's early life behaved. Because of the little person's dependency, "they" were right. The parent ego state is referred to as the "taught concept of life" in TA. One's parent is the part of a person that lectures, moralizes, and lays down the law. The *adult* ego state is that part of a person that figures things out by collecting and looking at facts. He or she estimates probabilities, explains reasons, and suggests alternatives, rather than reacting emotionally. The adult ego state is described as the "thought concept of life" in TA. *Strokes* are defined as the special rewards human beings look for in interaction situations. Positive strokes may be words of praise, compliments, or smiles. Negative strokes come in the form of critical comments, avoidance, or failure to return telephone calls. *Games* are defined as routines people use to get strokes. We play roles, adapt emotions, and act in ways which experience has taught us will get the kind of strokes we like. Games reinforce psychological positions and strengthen the "I'm not O.K." and/or "You're not O.K." feelings people have. *Transactions* are exchanges of words and related behavior between two people. When we see each person involved in an exchange as having a parent, an adult, and a child, we are able to draw a diagram of what happened in the transaction, hence the term *transactional analysis*. *Life positions* summarize our characteristic behavior toward other people. They are based on our assumptions about ourselves. Life positions are classified as (1) *I'm not O.K. and you're O.K.* This is a conclusion based on early negative feelings about oneself. This person will defer or relinquish rather than feeling capable of contributing to a conversation or a problem-solving situation. (2) *I'm O.K. and you're not O.K.* This is a distrustful life position. It usually results from a person being

mistreated by grownups when he or she was small. He or she looks forward to growing up and being able to exercise control and power over others. When this person communicates, he or she will probably try to control the situation and dominate the conversation. (3) *I'm not O.K. and you're not O.K.* This is a despairing outlook on life. It is totally negative in perspective. The person with this approach is likely to be withdrawn and resentful. (4) *I'm O.K. and you're O.K.* This is a rationally chosen life position. It represents an adult decision and is likely to be made by a self-actualizing person who communicates by attentive listening and reflective posture. Transactional analysis has proved to be a powerful technique for analyzing communication activities in interpersonal relationships. *See also* HUMAN MOTIVATION, 99–103; ORGANIZATION DEVELOPMENT, 169–171.

Significance Transactional analysis is used in public administration contexts as a technique of organization development. It is a communications mechanism that allows organizational team building. It permits managers to address the security, love, and self-esteem needs of employees as identified in the Abraham Maslow hierarchy of needs. TA also speaks to the satisfier elements of Frederick Herzberg's two-factor theory of human motivation. Transactional analysis helps the manager to help workers free themselves from personal hangups to be more productive. The self-analysis that characterizes TA encourages employees to engage in organization problem solving, which is not unlike personal problem solving. Transactional analysis recognizes the simple fact of organizational and interpersonal relationships, that if *I'm* not O.K., there's no way *you* can be O.K.

Organization Man (173)
A description of an individual adaptation to organization life involving a total surrender of individuality to the organization. Organization man as an adaptation model was first described by William H. Whyte in his book, *The Organization Man,* published in 1956. In the course of doing research on corporations in the early 1950s, Whyte discovered what appeared to be a new work ethic taking the place of the Protestant work ethic. He termed his finding the *social ethic* and identified its three major beliefs: (1) the group is the source of creativity; (2) "belongingness" is the ultimate need of the individual; and (3) the application of science to achieve belongingness is an important pursuit of personal and organizational life. The results of the social ethic, Whyte suggested, were total conformity and sacrifice of individuality to the organization in a religious acceptance of organizational paternalism. The ethic rationalized the organization's

demands for allegiance. In return for the individual's allegiance, the organization provided security, protection, and initiation rites for the individual and members of his or her family, with the organization becoming an extended family. Profit sharing, health plans, and stock options were some of the benefits Whyte saw as promoting commitment to the organization. IBM and AT&T are cited as corporate examples of the organization man phenomenon. Whyte suggested that the role of organization man went beyond the company door and that suburbia became the setting for the polishing of the organization man value system. Home location preference, club membership, social activities, the characteristics of married life, and the socialization of children were all strongly influenced by the demands and desires of the corporate family. Since the organization was considered a closed system, a candidate for entry into it often had to take personality tests to determine compatibility and the ability to adapt to the company personnel standard. Whyte included an appendix in his book on how to cheat on personality tests to gain access to the organization. He saw the organization man model as having important negative influences on the development of the organization as a social structure. Yet he said, "The fault is not in the organization . . . it is in our worship of it." The problems Whyte saw included (1) excessive organizational conformity robs organizations of their one dynamic feature, the people in them; (2) the organization man model promotes a delusion of total compatibility between individual and organizational goals; (3) the social ethic is premature in promoting cooperation without an understanding of the eventual goals of cooperation; and (4) the organization man model is self-destructive in that it promotes neuroses in a futile pursuit of "normalcy." Whyte suggested alternatives to this pattern, some of which are topics of current theories on human motivation. He saw job enrichment and techniques of fitting the group to the individual, rather than molding the individual to the group, as ways in which creativity could be encouraged without sacrificing the spirit of cooperation he recognized as essential to successful organizational life. *See also* ADMINISTRATIVE MAN, 2; GROUP THEORY, 53; JOB ENRICHMENT, 224.

Significance   Organization man can be found in public agencies as well as private corporations. As Whyte points out, the organization man could just as easily be the new professor in a university, the doctor in a clinic, or a professional in a government agency. The groundwork that made the organization man syndrome possible can be traced to the human relations theories of human motivation. The prescription of the human relations approach was to make organizations better by making them nicer. Chester Barnard, for example, stressed the importance of *esprit de corps* as the way to gain member commitment to organizational goals. Management scientist Elton Mayo, famous for the Hawthorne studies, believed that organizations should be cooperative bodies and should avoid conflict. Mayo said that motivation of employees in organizations was best achieved by nurturing a commitment to the organization. The organization man concept suggests, however, that organizations change people, and over time organizations alter personalities. Career civil servants are not exempt from this tendency. Studies of "total organizations," such as prisons and schools, have shown that over a period of time a person does change and will go through an adaptation process to survive within the institution. Although prisons and schools differ from bureaucracies in that their members are forced in some way to be there, some theorists argue that the same phenomenon occurs in bureaucracies. Sociologist Robert K. Merton in his essay on the bureaucratic personality states, for example, that the drive of the bureaucracy to routinize procedures transforms bureaucrats into mere servants of the routines. In criticizing the organization man, Whyte does not argue against surface uniformity or the need to cooperate. He wants to preserve individualism within organizational life so that creativity can be maintained as well.

Organizations, Closed Model (174)
A concept used to describe organizations in which organizational interests supersede the interests of individuals, and in which efficiency, task specialization, and obedience to authority are stressed. The closed model of organizations is described by such adjectives as bureaucratic, hierarchical, vertical, formal, rational, and mechanistic. Schools of administrative thought associated with the closed model are scientific management, classical organization theory, and the POSDCORB ideas of Luther H. Gulick. The prototype of the closed model was German sociologist Max Weber's "ideal-type" bureaucracy, although the basic assumptions about the appropriate location of authority in the upper echelons of the organizational structure are found in the writings of English political theorist Thomas Hobbes. The identifying characteristics of the closed model of organizations are (1) a surrounding environment that is relatively predictable and unchanging; (2) a pyramidal structure in which the repository of power, authority, and expertise is at the top, producing vertical lines of interaction; (3) a clear division of labor, including well-defined roles that join rank and prestige, task specialization, and routinization of procedures; and (4) commitment to values of efficiency and to service of organizational goals. Weber's classic rationale for such an

organization was that it has the capacity to counteract "the irrationality and lunacy inherent in human nature and society" as well as the excesses of charismatic leadership. For Weber, bureaucracy is an island of rationality in an essentially nonrational social sea. The closed model's disabilities, such as goal displacement and red tape, are justified by the "higher morality" of social justice and progress for the masses. The closed model assumes a theory of human behavior as described by organization theorist Douglas McGregor as Theory X, which claims that the average person is lazy, prefers authoritarian leadership, and is unable to contribute to the solution of organizational problems. *See also* GOAL DISPLACEMENT, 145; ORGANIZATIONS, OPEN MODEL, 175; ORGANIZATION THEORY, CLASSICAL, 176.

Significance The closed model of organizations subjugates personal goals to commonly agreed on organizational goals. Because of its pyramidal structure, it allows the employment of manipulation techniques, ranging from the physical force employed by the Third Reich under Adolf Hitler's leadership to the production line sanctions of the 9,1 manager on Robert Blake and Jane Mouton's managerial grid. The ideal of the closed model is that common goals, lines of authority, and obedience all work together to create an organization that hums like a well-oiled machine. Critics of the closed model point to common organizational dysfunctions and pathologies symptomized by excessive rigidity, impersonality, and dehumanization. Advocates of the alternative *open* model say top-heavy organizations cannot always detect their own weaknesses, and those persons at the top do not always know best. Experience has taught organization theorists that the closed model works best in organizations that manufacture products. Routinization and established lines of authority conserve human energy. When tasks are uniform and well defined, it is unnecessary to reinvent the wheel perpetually. As one observer wrote of closed organizations, "It is far easier to convert one heretic than to reverse the course of a large organization." The prevalence of closed models in U.S. organizational life is explained in large part by the necessity to control the joint action of a multiplicity of persons.

Organizations, Open Model (175)

A concept used to describe organizations that are structured horizontally rather than vertically, that share authority and expertise, that are task-oriented as well as responsive to environmental pressures, and that emphasize the importance of human relations and personal goals. The open model of organizations is described by such adjectives as "collegial," "competitive," and "natural." Schools of administrative thought associated with the open model are organizational humanism, organization development, and human relations. Contrary to common belief, the open model predates the closed model first advanced by German sociologist Max Weber as "ideal-type" bureaucracy. The open model was written about by French philosophers Claude Henri de Rouvroy Saint-Simon and Auguste Comte in response to the despotism of Napoleon Bonaparte. They predicted that organizations would someday become forces for human liberation. English political philosopher John Locke also said that power is relational in that subordinates grant authority to their superiors. Identifying characteristics of the open model are (1) it functions most effectively in unstable environments; (2) authority and expertise are distributed throughout the organization; (3) loyalty is directed to the entire organization rather than to a department or subunit; (4) interaction is relational rather than role- or task-oriented; and (5) prestige is based more on actual job performance than on assigned rank. In the open model, manipulation of people occurs through education, cooptation, persuasion, peer group pressure, and the ancient art of "buttering up." Represented in the open model is the view of humans as described by organization theorist Douglas McGregor as Theory Y, which assumes that people like to work and that work provides meaning in life. *See also* HUMAN MOTIVATION: MOTIVATION-HYGIENE THEORY, 99; ORGANIZATION DEVELOPMENT (OD), 169; ORGANIZATIONS, CLOSED MODEL, 174.

Significance The open model of organizations assumes that every individual member of the organization has personal goals, such as achievement or recognition, that can operate in the service of broad organizational goals. The building blocks of this foundational idea were provided by organization theorists and psychologists Elton Mayo, Chester Barnard, Abraham Maslow, Frederick Herzberg, Warren Bennis, and Kurt Lewin. Since the open model functions best in unstable environments and in times of rapid social change, the upheavals of modern American life create the conditions for open model applications. Open organizations are more able to consider suggestions from outside sources, such as interest groups. They tend to possess a more accurate view of the organizational reality which economist John Kenneth Galbraith called "bureaucratic truth." Max Weber saw bureaucracy apart from society and citizen. The open model posits the interlocking nature of bureaucracy and society. Organizations *are* society, and there can be no means-ends justification for the dehumanizing characteristics of bureaucratic practices. The open model is not without its dysfunctions and pathological aspects, however. Persons working in open organizations can suffer from role ambiguity and often expend a great deal of energy analyzing the meaning of social behavior. Organizational democratization sometimes produces enervating consensus-building processes as well. Proponents of the open model admit that tensions between the organization and the individual are inevitable, and few believe the open model can be practiced in all organizations under all conditions. Some routinization and standardizing are essential components of organizational effectiveness.

Organization Theory, Classical (176)
The view of organizations as social systems in which power and authority flow from the top downward through a hierarchy, and accountability flows from the bottom upward. Classical organization theory states that the mission or goal of an organization can rationally be broken down into specific tasks, which lead to the accomplishment of that goal. The arrangement of work constitutes rules so that the organization can operate on a continuous basis. The members of the organization know what tasks they are responsible for doing. Once the various tasks that relate to the organization goal are identified, functional specialists can be hired to handle these tasks with a high degree of efficiency. The various functional specialists in an organization are coordinated and directed by bosses within the hierarchy, thus producing the familiar superior-subordinate relationships within the organization. The view of authority from above defines classical organization theory. *See also* BUREAUCRACY, 126; HIERARCHY, 147; ORGANIZATION THEORY, 177–179.

Significance Classical organization is believed by its proponents to have several benefits over organizations arranged along collegial or honorific lines. Chief among classical organization theory proponents is German sociologist Max Weber (1864–1920). Classical organization theorists tend to believe in the historical inevitability of the increasing dominance of legal-rational organizations. Even Weber, however, who thought bureaucracy to be the best example of a legal-rational organization, worried in 1909 about the dehumanizing of people in the bureaucracy itself. The primary weakness of classical organization theory is its underestimation of the human factor in administration. It accepts the simplistic view that people in a hierarchical relationship to others will carry out orders. As neoclassical organization theory discovered, sometimes they will, and sometimes they will not.

Organization Theory: Humanism (177)
A view of organizations that is concerned with the quality of life of individual workers within the organization. Organizational humanism began with the recognized dehumanizing tendencies of the scientific management movement of the early 1900s. In humanism's link to scientific management, however, both were concerned with workers' productivity and such related matters as absenteeism and turnover. The humanists demonstrated in the 1950s and 1960s that happy workers were more productive workers "Happiness" was usually called "job satisfaction" in the research studies and was unrelated to monetary and promotional rewards. Satisfaction was rooted in interpersonal relations in the small face-to-face group of fellow workers and their immediate supervisor. Humanism stated that a satisfaction-generating and productive atmosphere was not a bureaucratic one, but one that fostered democratic participation by the workers in decision making for the group. The supervisor was not autocratic and directive, as in scientific management, but informal, consultative, trusting, and concerned for team members' welfare. Organizational humanism had a normative commitment to the individual's opportunity for self-actualization and to the equality of persons. The primary spokesperson for the movement—also called the human relations movement—made clear the conviction that the large formal organization with its hierarchical authority structure is repressive. These and other ideological elements of the human relations movement were prominent in the formation of the new public administration in the late 1960s. *See also* ORGANIZATION DEVELOPMENT (OD), 169–172; ORGANIZATION THEORY, 176, 178, 179.

Significance Organizational humanism has been severely attacked by modern researchers. Accumulated evidence now seems to indicate that the conditions that make some workers happy make other workers unhappy, and that happy workers are not necessarily more productive workers. The grounds of criticism of the human relations school have been summarized by James W. Fesler as follows: (1) Most of the research providing the empirical proof of human relations school doctrines was conducted by "true believers." (2) The sweeping contrast of the "bad" hierarchical organization with the "ideal" humanist organization was overdrawn and rested on assertion rather than scientific study of large organizations. (3) In humanism's commitment to development of the whole person, the job was treated as if it were the whole life. Many people obtain important satisfactions apart from the job, and a high overall level of happiness is often achieved despite only moderate satisfaction with the job's sociopsychological attributes. (4) Humanism's normative commitments blocked out awareness that a qualified leader needs to lead and not just be one of the boys. Organizational humanism nevertheless survived and prospered in the form of organization development. Its emphasis continues to be on authentic interpersonal relationships within the organization.

Organization Theory, Neoclassical (178)
A view of organizations that systematically deals with the human element in them while maintaining emphasis on a hierarchy as the major way of coordinating individual efforts. Neoclassical organization theory deals primarily with the concept of power in organizations. Classical organization theorists see power as a unidirectional authority relationship going through the hierarchy from the top down. Neoclassical organization theorists see power as a human relational concept. The bosses might give orders, but the informal organization below has power to determine the extent to which those orders are obeyed. Relational power was explored by the leading proponents of the neoclassical school: Mary Parker Follett, Elton Mayo and Fritz Roethlisberger, and Chester Barnard. Mary Parker Follett was a political philosopher and social critic whose 1920 book, *The New State,* launched her on a career of human relations analysis in administrative contexts. She maintained that in organizations many of the important relationships involve resolution of conflict. Follett saw that the three basic ways of doing this were through (1) domination; (2) balance of power; and (3) integration. *Domination* means one interest bullies the other. The boss uses the power of the hierarchy to force subordinates to act in accordance with his or her wishes. This, in turn, leads to lack of cooperation and repressed behavior. Conflict resolution by domination is generally the way conflict is managed in classical organization theory. *Balance of power* is a bargaining situation where compromise is the main way of resolving conflicts. The boss, who has the formal power to make the decision, compromises with the subordinate, who has specialized knowledge of the problem under consideration. But bargaining allows resentments and basic antagonisms to remain below the surface. *Integration* means in Follett's view that decisions regarding conflicts are resolved through full and free contributions by all participants. If people can be honest with each other and not have to worry about taking positions to enhance their bargaining positions, problems can be solved more successfully. The "law of the situation" applies. People can be led to respond to the requirements of objective situations rather than to the internal dynamic of the organization's hierarchy. Cooperative behavior would theoretically ensue. Elton Mayo and Fritz Roethlisberger were

professors at the Harvard Business School who conducted the Hawthorne experiments at the Hawthorne (Chicago) plant of the Western Electric Company from 1927 through 1932. They discovered the "Hawthorne effect" which is stated by neoclassicists as the observed fact that people respond favorably when they perceive that others are trying to help them. The Hawthorne researchers also found informal organizations flourishing within, and sometimes creating situations contrary to the needs of, the formal organization. In one notable experiment involving fourteen men in a bank wiring observation room, the researchers showed that the informal work group, not management, controlled production. The group enforced their norms. They brought pressure to bear on "chiselers" and punished "rate-busters." The third spokesperson for the neoclassical school, Chester I. Barnard, was president of the New Jersey Bell System. His 1938 book, *Functions of the Executive,* described people in organizations as occupying a zone of indifference. Herbert A. Simon later called the same phenomenon a "zone of acceptance." This means that each subordinate in an organization is willing to accept certain demands made by the boss. Each employee has a perceptual zone in which he or she accepts the boss's orders as legitimate and carries them out. The subordinate is thus "indifferent" to the orders. If an order is outside the zone of indifference, however, the subordinate might not accept the order as being legitimate and could refuse to carry it out. Barnard saw an important function of management as expanding the employee's zone of acceptance by offering incentives such as more money, improved working conditions, and recognized informal social groups, and by providing opportunities to show distinction in one's work. Neoclassical organization theory maintains that individuals contribute to, or withhold their talents from, an organization in return for a range of satisfactions the organization might provide. *See also* HAWTHORNE STUDIES, 54; HIERARCHY, 147; ORGANIZATION THEORY, 176, 177, 179.

Significance Neoclassical organization theory never questioned the existence of a hierarchy. It accepted the goal of efficiency and the belief that workers should be molded to fit the needs of the organization. Neoclassical organization theory rested on the pillars of classical organization theory. It added the recognition, however, that informal organizations exist within formal organizations, and that these informal organizations are power relationships among people. In the 1940s and 1950s, the human relations movement became a popular offshoot of the neoclassical school. Often "human relation" was, in the words of one observer, "a combination of the glad hand, the back slap, and the big smile." Too often it involved replacing the stern, autocratic boss with a more mild-mannered type of leader who would pretend interest in his or her subordinates. In 1952, public administrationist Dwight Waldo referred to the human relations movement as "enlightened paternalism." Neoclassical organization theory left the legacy that money was not the only, perhaps not even the prime, motivator in the world of work. Relationships between and among people were at least as important as money.

Organization Theory: Pluralism (179)
The view that society is characterized by the political warfare of groups seeking to have their interests prevail, and that administrative organizations are themselves the product of conflict and accommodation of interests. Pluralism regards the administrative process as another battleground to which interest groups carry their struggle from the electoral and legislative arenas. The administrative structure is fragmented, just as Congress is fragmented, and the president is just another player. The president is so occupied with policy and political leadership, speaking for the combination of forces which enabled him to attain power, that the president can give only partial and discontinuous attention to maximizing the administrative authority of the position as chief executive. Administrative agencies, therefore, will be responsive primarily to Congress, and especially to congressional committees and their leaders. That is the source of both substantive power and appropriations. The task of administration, therefore, is essentially the same as that of politics: to facilitate the peaceful resolution of conflicts of interest compatibly and to distribute power among groups in the society. The pluralist approach to public administration is classically represented in David B. Truman's *The Governmental Process* (1951) and J. Leiper Freeman's *The Political Process: Executive Bureau-Legislative Committee Relations* (1965). See also HIERARCHY, 147; ORGANIZATION THEORY, 176–178; SUBSYSTEM, 80.

Significance The pluralist model of organization theory charged that the "textbook model" of classical organization theory is an unreal portrayal of the executive branch and is in conflict with democratic values. The classical model is one in which an organization is composed of clearly bounded units and subunits that are so arranged as to provide a hierarchical structuring of authority, often pictured as a pyramid. The pluralist model yields a more realistic description and explanation of what goes on in administration and politics. But as James W. Fesler points out, the fragmentation it describes "and even celebrates" as part of the genius of the U.S. political system affords little or no guidance as to what direction one should move in if he or she had the opportunity to express a preference or exert influence. Although pluralism separates what *is* from what *ought* to be, it does not help those confronted by opportunities to change organizations. The hierarchic model has the operational significance of a belief widely subscribed to. It has been the pattern advocated by every reorganization commission that surveys federal administration. Many of the advances made in administrative organization have been attempts to apply to a pluralistic government the arrangements of the hierarchic administrative model. Yet the advances have been limited by the power groups identified by the pluralist model, forces which do not wish their access to the administrative process blocked by a strengthened hierarchical administration. Efforts to improve government and its administration often emphasize the coordination, rationality, and legitimacy found in the hierarchic model. The pluralist model stands as a warning that, unless there is accommodation of the variety of interest groups, congressional committees, and government agencies that form the pluralist perspective, these efforts for improvement will have limited success.

POSDCORB (180)

An acronym developed by Luther H. Gulick to describe managerial activities common to all organizations. POSDCORB stands for planning, organizing, staffing, directing, coordinating, reporting, and budgeting. In "Notes on the Theory of Organization" (the lead article in a volume Gulick edited in 1937 for the President's Committee on Government Reorganization—called the Brownlow Committee after its chairman, Louis Brownlow), Gulick explained the seven basic functions of executives. These are (1) *planning*—working out in broad outline those things that need to be done and the methods for doing them to accomplish the purpose of the organization; (2) *organizing*—establishing the formal structure of authority through which work is subdivided and defined; (3) *staffing*—recruiting and training a group of people to do the work, and maintaining favorable working conditions for them; (4) *directing*—making decisions and embodying them in general and specific orders and instructions, thus serving as leader of the enterprise; (5) *coordinating*—interrelating the various parts of the work of the organization; (6) *reporting*—informing those to whom the manager is responsible as to the progress of the work, by having the manager and his subordinates keep themselves informed by record keeping, research, and inspection; (7) *budgeting*—controlling the affairs of the organization through fiscal planning and accounting. POSDCORB was greatly influenced by the work of Henri Fayol (1841–1925), a French mining engineer and executive, and by

Lyndall Urwick, a British consulting industrial engineer, who collaborated with Gulick in the preparation of *Papers on the Science of Administration* (1937). See also BROWNLOW COMMITTEE, 124; FAYOL, HENRI, 14; GULICK, LUTHER, 17.

Significance   Gulick's POSDCORB emphasis is more specific than Weber's ideal types in a bureaucracy and more general than Taylor's focus on organizational productivity. POSDCORB aimed at turning "principles" of administrative theory into administrative practice. Its primary concern is how organizations might actually be structured, and what the roles of their executives are. POSDCORB also describes staff activities that are supportive of organizational units not directly involved in the production of the services, or products that constitute the main functions of an agency. *Staff* activity may be contrasted with *line* activity, which refers to units directly engaged in producing the organization's services or goods. Contemporary criticism of POSDCORB emphasizes that, as an analytical tool, it does not include all staff or executive functions carried on within a modern organization. Data processing and evaluation, for example, are two staff activities not included in POSDCORB. Some critics also charge that leadership is undervalued in Gulick's scheme. In the context of the period when it emerged, however, POSDCORB made the classical tradition practical and gave easy-to-understand advice to novice administrators. Despite academic reservations about the inclusiveness of the concept, its continuing influence through government-sponsored training programs has been substantial. POSDCORB served as a convenient starting point for a generation of writers interested in dealing with different aspects of administration. They added to, subtracted from, and amended the acronym to meet their needs. POSDCORB was indeed a seminal idea.

Red Tape (181)

Bureaucratic procedures characterized by mechanical adherence to regulations, excessive formality and attention to routine, and the compilation of large amounts of extraneous information resulting in prolonged delay or inaction. Red tape originated in seventeenth-century England, where it was the practice to tie official documents with a tape of reddish hue. Procedures, rules, and regulations—often referred to as "red tape"—*protect* people's rights as well as cause them annoyance. In the early twentieth century, the Pure Food and Drug Act and the Meat Inspection Act were passed and created what many food processors called "government red tape." The standards set by these acts caused some food processors to lose their livelihood; yet the horrible health conditions abounding in many sausage-processing plants also had something to do with the fact that the standards could not be met. A democratic system designs rules and regulations to protect the individual. When rules and regulations go beyond the protective stage and become excessive, red tape has frequently emerged. See also BUREAUPATHOLOGY, 129; GOAL DISPLACEMENT, 145; NEO-WEBERISM, 165.

Significance Red tape is caused by the natural tendency of human beings in bureaucratic settings to routinize their activities. The very characteristics that Max Weber ascribed to bureaucracies—highly rational and dispassionate service to policy makers and the public—encourage such attention to proper procedures. However, the original public service goals of the organization can easily be displaced. If bureaucrats did not insist that all the paperwork on a given project be executed, for example, they could be called to task by auditors or other evaluators who review their performance. The complex set of requirements for obeying the letter of the law may or may not be at the discretion of the public servant to honor. His or her job may depend on exact compliance. Excessive rule making is frequently the outgrowth of good intentions on the part of legislators to prevent, correct, or eliminate abuses within the system. Often, however, sensitive administrators can act within their discretion to revise policies that are bogged down with red tape. Techniques of administration are means, not ends in themselves. When excessive red tape causes a system to be virtually inoperative, the red tape must be cut, or the goals of the organization will be submerged. In this sense red tape is a self-inflicted wound. It need not be fatal if public managers carefully monitor its inevitable assertion of itself. Those public servants whose lives find their expression and fulfillment in red tape alone represent all that is dysfunctional about bureaucracies.

Regionalism (182)
A redistribution of governmental power from the federal government to interstate regional councils and commissions, and from the states outward for joint administration of programs that were previously under the jurisdiction of individual states only. Regionalism represents both centralization and decentralization, depending on one's point of view. Regionalism has broken down state boundaries over the past twenty years for the following reasons: (1) states are too small to be effective units for administering many federal programs, while the same programs are not wide enough in scope to call for centralized federal administration; (2) officials of the federal

government desire to bring more order, efficiency, coordination, and evaluation to federal programs at the state and local level; and (3) the proliferation of categorical grants, block grants, and revenue sharing involving federal aid to state and local governments increased from $2 billion in 1950 to $68.4 billion in 1977, indicating the need for an innovative solution to the problem of "the federal maze." The solution of regionalism has resulted in the development of (1) federal regional councils made up of officials from the Departments of Health and Human Services (HHS); Housing and Urban Development (HUD); Transportation; Labor; and the Environmental Protection Agency (EPA). Since the establishment of such councils, the time needed for processing grant requests for federal funding of state and local governments has been reduced by half; (2) federal districts to administer multipurpose programs such as urban and rural development, transportation, and solid waste disposal; (3) special purpose regional commissions, such as river basin commissions; (4) the Advisory Commission on Intergovernmental Relations, composed of representatives of national, state, and local governments, and coordinated by a single staff; (5) councils of governments (COGs), currently numbering over three hundred, many of which are regional planning commissions; (6) interstate compacts creating bistate or interstate administrative agencies for a specific purpose, such as the Port of New York Authority; and (7) special regions created by the federal government for administering national security and civil defense programs. In addition to the above instrumentalities of *interstate* regionalism in modern public administration, there is also *substate* regionalism, which breaks down boundaries of cities, municipalities, and counties for purposes of eliminating jurisdictional conflicts and administering grant programs on a regional basis. See also CIRCULAR A-95, 30; INTERGOVERNMENTAL RELATIONS (IGR), 153.

Significance Regionalism represents a new level of government in the U.S. federal system. Its development was occasioned by the federal government's attempt to promote intergovernmental planning for federal program funds under categorical grants, block grants, and revenue sharing in the 1960s and 1970s. Regional administrative (or confederal) groups go by many designations: regional councils, regional commissions, and councils of governments are the most widely used. These groups prospered because they built on the status quo without disturbing its formal organization. Traditional political boundaries remained untouched. Regional communities have been established, governmental interdependencies have been clarified, and some coordinating of federal programs has taken place.

Representative Bureaucracy (183)
A system in which public employees are seen as representatives of various segments of the population rather than as neutral civil servants. Representative bureaucracy is based on the belief that the ratio of each minority at each employment level in a governmental agency should equal that group's proportion in the general population. Representative bureaucracy is related to the concept of social equity in that it is based on the principle that in a true democracy, public service should reflect the racial, ethnic, and sex composition of government's constituencies, so that responsive public policy can be made. It also embraces the principle that a bureaucracy exists not only to provide public service, but also to provide jobs and economic advancement for the public it serves. Public jobs are seen as rights every group in society should share in equally. Representative bureaucracy is in conflict with the merit system, which emphasizes the hiring of people solely on the basis of objectively determined qualifications, and it bears some resemblance to the patronage system. Proponents of representative bureaucracy insist that public employees under merit systems are not neutral people doing nonpolitical tasks. They are policy makers using discretion in allocating public funds and deciding between and among competing interests. Classical political neutrality is seen as a sacrifice of the skills and assets an intentionally diverse group of public servants can bring to an agency. Furthermore, the merit system contains many considerations not really based on merit. Veterans preference points, for example, discriminate against women. The movement for increased representativeness in bureaucracy has accrued four major benefits: (1) increased minority and female employment increases the economic, social, and political status of those groups; (2) recipients of public services benefit because their group needs are better addressed; (3) bureaucracies benefit from increased responsiveness to minority problems and from having a more diverse staff; and (4) the entire democratic system benefits because the bureaucracy is a closer reflection of the population it serves. *See also* EQUAL EMPLOYMENT OPPORTUNITY, 211; SOCIAL EQUITY, 23.

Significance Representative bureaucracy is not a new concept in U.S. public administration. Concern for representatives in public employment was the rationale for the spoils system of President Andrew Jackson, and it was reflected in the civil service reform movement of the 1880s as well. The Pendleton Act of 1883 outlined a proportionate representation plan among the states for filling civil service positions in Washington, DC. The plan helped southern states gain representation they would not otherwise have had. The representativeness sought today is not geographical, however; it is aimed at affirmative action for minorities and women. In a number of major cities roughly half the population is black, and the overwhelming majority of victims of crimes is black as are the suspects. Yet the majority of police officers is white. Advocates of representative bureaucracy say a police force can deal more effectively with the public if it has roughly the same racial mix. Police officers are not seen as neutral public servants performing mechanical tasks, but as individuals who exercise discretion in their work and whose relationships with clientele groups are affected by their color. School teachers are also seen as public employees having a high degree of discretion in dealing with their "clients," and whose race and sex affect relationships. Two frequently raised objections to representative bureaucracy are (1) it provides less technically competent public employees than merit systems provide; and (2) it discriminates in reverse.

Secretary (184)

The title assigned to the top administrator in twelve of the thirteen major federal departments and to several high state officials. On the federal level, only the Attorney General of the United States, who heads the Department of Justice, does not carry the title of secretary. The secretaries are part of the cabinet where they function as advisers to the president. Their terms of office are indefinite in that they serve only at the pleasure of the president. In the states, the secretary title is assigned typically to the secretary of state and to the heads of a few other major departments, such as commerce and labor. *See also* DEPARTMENT, 136.

Significance Secretaries are delegated powers by the president to direct and supervise the administrative functions carried on by their respective departments, with additional authority over such matters as budget and personnel. In their appointments, most are chosen for political reasons as well as for their experience, background, and proved competence, but training in the subject matter of their department is not essential. Each secretary is directly responsible to the president under provisions of the United States Constitution. In the states, the secretary of state is a constitutionally elected officer not usually responsible to the governor, although the secretaries of other major departments are typically appointed by and are responsible to the governor.

Special District **(185)**
A unit of local government that is designed to carry out some particular function such as education, air pollution control, flood control, fire protection, the provision of public utilities, public transit, hospital care, mosquito abatement, street lighting, reclamation, and burial. Special districts are the most numerous of all U.S. governments. They are created and given their authority by the states in which they operate. The boundaries of special districts are flexible and may overlap entire municipalities or counties, unincorporated land, and other special districts. Such overlapping is based on the legal assumption that a particular district must provide a service not provided by any of the multipurpose governments or any other special district. Where intergovernmental cooperation has lagged or the geographical scope of the service area is so extensive that a single agency is preferable, a regionwide special district may be established under state law and with federal approval. A school district, for example, may encompass a large number of cities as well as overlap numerous special districts performing other specific functions. Intercounty water districts may bring water great distances into several counties and the cities within those counties. Special districts have the right to sue and to be sued, to acquire real or personal property, to exercise the right of eminent domain, to adopt a seal, and to tax.

Significance Special districts have increased in number and in importance in the recent history of the United States. There were approximately 8,000 special districts in 1942; thirty years later the number had risen above 20,000. Special districts are created for a variety of reasons. (1) *To avoid a state-imposed ceiling on taxation or debt,* as in an irrigation district in the West. There are large capital costs involved in irrigation. Many of these districts have the power to tax, while others have the power to make "assessments." (2) *To provide a service more efficiently than the regular local unit of government can provide it.* This is most frequently the case in rural areas where a fire and water district is needed. (3) *To change the power structure of public institutions.* Special districts are often governed primarily by special interest groups whose representatives sit as a board of directors either elected by the people of the special district or appointed by officials of other governmental units in the district. School districts frequently create a politics of their own, separate from the politics of the corresponding city or county. Special districts are most common in California, because of the need for water and irrigation districts, and in Illinois, where the prevalence of special districts is a factor in the survival of the Chicago political machine. Townships, counties, and, in some cases, cities are declining in importance relative to the growth of special districts.

United States Government Manual (186)

The official handbook of the organization of the three branches of the national government. The *United States Government Manual* describes all executive and administrative units, including departments, agencies, boards, commissions, and committees, in terms of their organizational structure, their powers, and their duties. Detailed descriptions of Congress and its working structure and the federal court system are included in the *Manual*. Charts of major agencies, recent publications by the federal government, and a list of discontinued agencies and name changes are also found in each *Manual*. The *Manual* is published annually by the United States Government Printing Office. Similar kinds of information can be found in organizational manuals published by each state.

Significance The *United States Government Manual* is a "structural encyclopedia" of the federal government and its operations. Its comprehensive and official nature make it a valuable reference tool for the citizen, the student, the political scientist, the librarian, and the public administrationist. Each new annual volume of the *Manual* can be purchased from the Government Printing Office for a nominal sum.

Weber, Max (1864–1920) (187)

German sociologist and intellectual father of the bureaucratic model of organization theory. Weber advanced a theory very similar to the classical model of Henri Fayol, Luther Gulick, and Lyndall Urwick, although Weber reached his conclusions by a different route. Weber was a contemporary of Fayol, Gulick, and Urwick, as well as Woodrow Wilson and Frederick Taylor, but his views did not become widely known in the United States until 1946 and 1947, when translations of his work by H. H. Gerth, C. Wright Mills (*From Max Weber: Essays in Sociology*), A. M. Henderson, and Talcott Parsons (*The Theory of Social and Economic Organization*) appeared. Weber focused an important part of his work on why people feel an obligation to obey commands without assessing their own attitudes about the value of each command. This focus was part of Weber's emphasis on the organization of society as a whole and the role of the state in particular. He wanted to understand the relationship between power—the ability to make people do what they do not ordinarily do—and authority. Weber described authority as *legitimate* power. He said that a subordinate's belief in legitimacy produces a stable pattern of obedience and deference to the source of command in the organizational system. Authority cannot depend on appeals to a subordinate's purely material interests and a calculation of personal advantage, or on affectional motives such as liking or admiration of the superior. Neither can authority depend on ideal motives.

Weber developed three "pure" types of legitimate authority as discussed by James W. Fesler in *Public Administration: Theory and Practice* (1980). (1) *Traditional* authority claims legitimacy on the basis of control patterns that have been handed down from the past and that, presumably, always existed. The immemorial traditions are sacred. Legitimacy is closely related to a citizen's felt obligation of personal loyalty to the individual who has attained chiefship in the traditional way. Change is inhibited by precedent. Those exercising authority are afraid to stretch the traditional ways of doing things because the ensuing change might undercut their own source of legitimacy. Whim is allowed in traditional authority systems, because there is an intensely personal relationship between the rulers and the ruled. If the traditional ruler oversteps the loose, traditional bounds of arbitrariness, however, he or she personally may be deposed; but a successor would be chosen by traditional means, and the system of authority would continue. (2) *Charismatic* authority rests on personal devotion to an individual because of the exceptional sanctity, heroism, or exemplary character of that person. The position a charismatic leader occupies in society is not sanctified by traditional criteria. The charismatic person is not bound by traditional rules and is capable of sparking revolutionary changes. Charismatic authority does not accept any system of rules for organizing society. There is no law, no hierarchy, no formalism except the basic demand of devotion to the charismatic figure. His or her followers are duty-bound to follow the leader's commands, which are supposed to lead to accomplishment of his or her mission. The followers obey because of personal devotion, not because rules force them to obey. The leader intervenes whenever and wherever he or she feels like it, unbound by tradition or law. Charismatic authority is opposed to regularized routines. Both traditional and charismatic authority may legitimately be exercised arbitrarily or by revelation and inspiration. Both types of authority therefore lack rationality. *Weber believed they were responsible for almost all organized action in the world before the Industrial Revolution.* The early modern period demanded the establishment of social organization on a stable basis, but one which was still open to change. (3) *Legal-rational* authority is based on a "legally established impersonal order." Obedience is due "the persons exercising the authority of office under it only by virtue of the formal legality of their commands and only within the scope of authority of the office." The legal-rational system of authority is based on rules—rules rationally developed by people. Such rules can be intentionally changed to cope with changes in the environment in a systematic, more highly predictable way than is possible under either traditional or charismatic authority. The quintessence of legal-rational authority is bureaucracy. The heart of bureaucracy is the system of authority relations defined by rationally developed rules. *See also* AUTHORITY, 87; BUREAUCRACY, 126; HIERARCHY, 147; ORGANIZATION THEORY, CLASSICAL, 176.

Significance Max Weber was one of the most influential figures in modern intellectual history. His ideas on legal-rational authority closely parallel the principles of classical organization theory as developed in the United States. Both emphasized efficiency. Both emphasized administrative regulations establishing fixed and official jurisdictional areas of responsibility as part of a systematic division of labor. Both emphasized the authority to give the commands required for the discharge of the duties assigned. Both emphasized principles of office hierarchy and levels of graded authority in a firmly ordered system of superior and subordinate. Both emphasized that a rational bureaucracy should be composed of officials who were full-time, salaried, appointed careerists, with thorough and expert training for the career, who were selected on the basis of technical qualifications. Both insisted that the human beings who constitute "the bureaucratic machine" should be stripped of their human differences. Given these and other similarities, it is an oddity in administrative history that classical organization theory has been scathingly attacked, while Weber's bureaucratic organization theory continues to command profound respect in widely diverse intellectual circles. It is not as though Weberian theory does not have its weaknesses. One weakness is the unacknowledged conflict between the hierarchic authority Weber emphasizes and the specialized, professional knowledge and technical competence he also recognizes. Weber fails to note that this technical knowledge gives "authority" to subordinates having such specialized knowledge and competence. Another weakness of Weber's theory is the uneasy relationship between bureaucratization and modernization in developing societies. The Chinese critique of bureaucratic forms of organization is a powerful one, based on objections to the Weberian emphasis on technical competence and on a strong Maoist affirmation of political purity. During the Great Leap and the Cultural Revolution periods of Maoist history, the Chinese press was full of examples of highly trained specialists who could not solve the simplest work problems, and of unskilled personnel who, using common sense and political inspiration, were able to come up with vital work innovations. "Specialists in command" was a slogan that came to signify an ideological position in China strangely related to, but very unlike, the Weberian bureaucratic model. A statement much easier to understand was Mao Tse-tung's exhortation in 1933: "This great evil, bureaucracy, must be thrown into the cesspool." Throughout his career, Mao held a sharply critical view of bureaucracy and bureaucrats. For a profound discussion of Weber's theoretical weaknesses, the reader should consult Martin King Whyte's "Bureaucracy and Modernization in China: The Maoist Critique" in the *American Sociological Review*, April 1973.

White House Office (188)
A staff agency in the Executive Office of the President that includes personal assistants who provide the president with information and help in major areas of policy development and execution. The White House Office staff maintains communication with Congress, individual members and committees of Congress, the heads of executive agencies, the news media, and the general public. Presidents typically appoint key members of their campaign staff to White House Office positions, giving a distinct political cast to its operations. Other staff members are appointed because of their expertise in critical policy areas. All serve at the pleasure of the president and may be removed by him at any time. *See also* EXECUTIVE OFFICE OF THE PRESIDENT (EXOP OR EOP), 138.

Significance The president depends heavily on the White House Office staff to help play the many roles as head of state. Individual members are appointed by the president not only because of their ability but also because of their unquestioned loyalty to the president. Often jurisdictional and personal conflicts arise between members of the White House Office staff and members of the president's cabinet, who also offer advice and counsel to the president. In both the Nixon and Carter administrations, for example, conflicts arose between the president's National Security Advisor and the Secretary of State. Conflicts also developed in the Reagan administration between National Security Advisor Vice Admiral John M. Poindexter and Secretary of State George Shultz. The clash led to several attempts by the latter to resign, all rejected by the president. Because the White House Office staff can play such a critical role in policy development, it is sometimes referred to as the "invisible presidency."

5. Personnel Administration

Affirmative Action (189)
A policy that advocates special efforts to hire minorities, women, and members of other disadvantaged groups as a way of compensating for the discriminatory practices of the past. Affirmative action is based on the Civil Rights Act of 1964, the first major legislation in the area. This act prohibited job discrimination on the basis of race, sex, religion, national origin, age, and physical disability, the latter two categories being amendments to the original act. The act also established the Equal Employment Opportunity Commission (EEOC) to administer the law. In 1965, Executive Order 11246 required public and private employers to establish affirmative action programs. The Intergovernmental Personnel Act of 1970 assures that civil service merit systems do not discriminate. It contains six major requirements: (1) All hiring and promoting is to be done on the basis of ability, with open competition existing. (2) All employees are to receive fair compensation. (3) Employees are to be retained on the basis of performance. Provisions will be made for the correction of inadequate performance with dismissal only when these inadequacies cannot be corrected. (4) Training should be concerned with achieving high-quality performance. (5) Applicants are to be fairly treated with consideration for their privacy and constitutional rights. (6) Employees will be protected against political coercion. The Equal Employment Opportunity Act of 1972 tied all the preceding affirmative action legislation together and brought state and local government under the provisions of the Civil Rights Act of 1964. Public employers of over fifteen persons and federal, state, local, and educational institutions having government contracts or subcontracts of $10,000 or more are required, under this act, to have affirmative action

programs. The EEOC may investigate charges and follow up its investigations by bringing suit against offenders. When investigating, the EEOC concentrates on "adverse impact" since "intent to discriminate" and "unequal treatment" are difficult to define. If a hiring procedure is found to have adverse impact on a disadvantaged group, the courts or the EEOC may order a quota system until the fault is corrected or there is payment of back pay to the parties affected. It has been shown that a kind of institutionalized racism and sexism exists in the hiring and promotion practices of government. Affirmative action is an attempt to change this condition. It seeks to institute hiring practices that will result in a work force reflective of the racial and sexual composition of the population, *See also* EQUAL EMPLOYMENT OPPORTUNITY, 211; REVERSE DISCRIMINATION, 243.

Significance Affirmative action programs have had a substantial impact on public personnel administration. There is a continuing ethical dilemma that can be simplified and stated as follows. One side says that some "bending of rules" is necessary and desirable in order to "make up" for past injustices. The opposing side states that no lowering of employment standards should be considered because this would result in inferior service to the public. The bending of rules, however, does not necessarily lead to a lowering of standards. The standards or rules used in the past, especially in the case of test scores, have often been shown to be invalid. *Griggs v. Duke Power Company* (401 U.S. 424:1971) was a landmark case in this area. The Supreme Court ruling in *Griggs* bars employment practices, especially testing, that discriminate against disadvantaged groups when those practices cannot be shown to be related to job performance. The ruling did not preclude testing, but it did open up the question of test validity and cultural bias in testing. Until very recently, few employers had attempted to show that there was indeed a correlation between high test scores and job performance. Neither did the *Griggs* ruling require quotas. Quotas have come into wide use, however, as a result of court rulings subsequent to *Griggs*. This development has led to cases dealing with the problem of reverse discrimination. The best-known case in this area is *Regents of the University of California v. Bakke* (438 U.S. 265:1978), in which Allen Bakke, a white male, sued the medical school of the University of California at Davis for rejecting his application for admission although his qualifications were higher than some minority students who were accepted. The Supreme Court ruled that Bakke's civil rights were indeed violated, and that he should be accepted. At the same time, the Court said that attention could be paid to racial and sexual differences when accepting students. Quotas were not acceptable, but affirmative action was. The

Personnel Administration

Court appeased both sides, and the debate continues. Equal employment opportunity does require some special effort on the part of employers. Affirmative action programs should have qualitative as well as quantitative goals. The changing of attitudes is often a larger part of the qualitative goals. Goals of this kind necessitate the involvement of personnel administrators with community agencies and neighborhood organizations. Disadvantaged applicants must be recruited and personnel practices revised to meet the needs of these applicants. Affirmative action requires thought, consideration, and effort if the intent of the Civil Rights Act of 1964 is to be carried out.

American Federation of State, County, and Municipal Employees (AFSCME) (190)

The largest union of public employees in the United States, with a membership of over 1 million. AFSCME is the largest union in the AFL-CIO, and the sixth largest union in the nation. It was founded on May 17, 1932, by a group of Wisconsin state employees. It merged with other state unions and was granted an international charter by the American Federation of Labor (AFL) in 1936 at the same convention that gave birth to the Congress of Industrial Organizations (CIO). AFSCME's first international constitution, copied from that of the American Federation of Government Employees (AFGE), provides for three organizational levels: the international, the council, and the local union. The international convention is the highest legislative and policy-making authority. The basic operating units are the councils, which coordinate the activities of local unions and provide services to members. There is considerable variation in the way each local union is governed. AFSCME's jurisdiction covers employees of states, territories, commonwealths, counties, districts, school boards, cities, towns, villages, and many other governmental units. Teachers and fire fighters are excluded, not by constitutional limitation but by their choice. The union is dedicated to promoting the welfare of its members and providing them with a voice in the determination of terms and conditions of employment through collective bargaining and legislative and political action. *See also* COLLECTIVE BARGAINING, 203; PUBLIC UNIONISM, 240.

Significance The American Federation of State, County, and Municipal Employees (AFSCME) is the most active union in public employment. It has publicly opposed legislation prohibiting public employee strikes and penalizing those who engage in or lead such strikes. It claims the right of government employees to strike is the ultimate weapon for resolving bargaining impasses. Strikes are called by local unions, with headquarters providing staff assistance and financial aid before and during the strike. AFSCME's interest in the political arena extends beyond the economic interests of its members. The major vehicle of the union's political involvement is its PEOPLE (Public Employees Organized to Promote Legislative Equality) program. It was adopted at the 1968 international convention and provides for participation in the AFL-CIO Committee on Political Education (COPE), intensive lobbying in Congress and in state legislatures, education programs, and work to end restrictions on political activities by public employees. AFSCME is the only public employee organization that has substantial membership in all municipal functions, exclusive of fire protection. One-half of AFSCME members are employed by cities, one-fourth by state governments, one-tenth by counties, and the remaining 15 percent by school districts, universities and colleges, nonprofit organizations, and special authorities. The union remains an organization that public employees can enter and leave at will.

Appointment Power (191)
The exercise of the authority vested in a public official to fill a vacancy in a government office. The appointment power is exercised by chief executives, such as the president, governors of the various states, and mayors, and by the heads of agencies who have been delegated that authority by a chief executive or by the legislative branch. In the national government, presidential appointments of judges, high-level executive branch officers, members of the independent regulatory commissions, and commissioned officers in the armed forces are merely *nominations* that must be followed up by *confirmation* in the Senate by a majority vote. When Congress is not in session, the president may fill such vacancies on a temporary basis (recess appointments), with such appointments expiring at the end of the next session of Congress. The president's removal power is also limited in that federal judges and civil service personnel cannot be removed; the president can remove members of the independent regulatory commissions only for nonpolitical reasons, as specified by Congress. In the states, the governor shares the appointment power with the state legislature, and in the cities the mayor nominates and the city council confirms appointments. Appointment of other officials is made by the chief executive alone or by executive and judicial officials delegated the power by the president, governor, or mayor. Most appointments are made under civil service rules and are based on merit, with some discretion left to the appointing official. In the federal service, limitations have been placed on the appointment powers of

Personnel Administration

administrators by requirements imposed by Congress that give preferential treatment to veterans, disabled veterans, handicapped persons, and, under affirmative action guidelines, to women and minority group members. See also REMOVAL POWER, 242.

Significance The appointment power is one of the most critical exercised by chief executives and heads of agencies. Through it the appointing official can select individuals who are likely to be sympathetic to the goals and objectives of the government and the agency and will lend tangible support to accomplishing them. In addition, patronage appointments may contribute to the president's, the governor's, or the mayor's control over a political party and its support in the next election. The solving of problems and the resolution of public issues may be directly affected by the individuals appointed— their ideological convictions, the wing of the party they support, and their loyalty to the party and to the appointing official. In public administration, the power to appoint and remove personnel helps to determine the effectiveness with which departments and agencies carry out their basic missions.

Arbitration (192)

The process of settling a dispute between two parties by submitting it to a third party empowered by agreement of the disputants to render a binding decision. The arbitrator may be a single individual or an arbitration board or tribunal of three, five, or seven persons. If a board, all members must be impartial or, by agreement of the parties to the dispute, each side may choose an equal number of board members, with at least one impartial member chosen by mutual consent. The parties to the dispute must also agree in advance on the issues to be decided and the procedures that will be followed. Although submission of a dispute is usually a voluntary act on the part of the disputants, some of the states and the federal government have enacted compulsory arbitration laws aimed particularly at avoiding strikes by public employees, by workers in essential industries, and by those in critical industries during wartime. Congress has on occasion passed legislation requiring compulsory arbitration to settle prolonged labor disputes that threatened the nation's well-being. Congress has also provided for binding arbitration since 1969 for federal employees in disputes over new contracts. Many contracts, particularly labor-management agreements, provide for arbitration if other settlement procedures fail. A decision rendered by an arbitrator or arbitration tribunal is final and binding, although it may be appealed to the courts on such grounds as fraud or procedural error. *See also*

COLLECTIVE BARGAINING, 203 IMPASSE RESOLUTION, 221; PUBLIC UNIONISM, 240.

Significance   Arbitration as a means of settling disputes has become increasingly common in the United States and in Western Europe. The arbitration approach is an ancient one. It has been used for centuries to settle disputes in the international arena. The American Arbitration Association, a private organization, provides a panel of technically qualified arbitrators who are available for settling disputes at the request of the parties. Arbitration has helped to settle catastrophic strikes, to relieve the courts of some of the pressure of litigation, and to resolve numerous personal disputes. In addition to provisions for compulsory arbitration found in state and federal laws and in private contracts, pressure from the public, from the media, and from government officials has helped to convince parties to accept the process. Typically, the use of arbitration in labor disputes follows the breakdown of other approaches, such as the use of conciliation and mediation as settlement techniques.

Assessment Center (193)
A term in personnel administration used to describe a process for identifying candidates for promotion and for selecting candidates for development programs in their current positions. Assessment center techniques test the knowledge and skill areas of a group of participants, using a variety of group and individual exercises in a controlled environment. Trained observers make an assessment of the potential of each participant. The assessment center concept arose from a need for early identification of future managers. It was first practiced in the early 1940s by the Office of Strategic Services (OSS) as a means for selecting agents. It was expanded and refined in the private sector in the 1950s by the American Telephone and Telegraph Company (AT&T), which used it to identify supervisors. AT&T tested for three primary characteristics: decision-making ability, creativity, and flexibility. The design of an assessment center typically begins with a task analysis of the position to be filled. The target characteristics of the person filling the position then become the object of the exercises selected to bring out the desired behaviors. If a special skill is required, a special exercise is developed, such as the "irate customer phone call" made in the middle of the night to participants in the J. C. Penney assessment center to test immediate reactions and the ability to resolve conflict. Since intensive research and validation go into designing and evaluating assessment center exercises, specialized consulting firms exist to offer assessment

packages to interested organizations. A frequently used assessment technique is the in-basket exercise, in which the individual participant is required to handle several work-related items under the types of constraints most often found on the actual job. Other exercises include a leaderless discussion, a strength bombardment, fact-finding expeditions, management games, paper and pencil tests, and the interview. The thread common to all the exercises is that they simulate on-the-job activity. The accessors are often line managers one step above the position being filled and fully trained for observing human behavior. They observe, record, and analyze the behavior of the participants on at least a 1:1 ratio. Some large assessment centers rotate managers through the assessor position to give experience in evaluating job performance. See also PERFORMANCE APPRAISAL, 233; TESTING, 249.

Significance The assessment center is used by more than 2,000 federal and state agencies and private companies. Many centers are full-time operations with highly diversified staffs. Most of the studies done on the effectiveness of assessment center techniques indicate a high correlation between evaluation and later performance on the job. Arguments *for* the assessment center include (1) it removes supervisory bias from promotion; (2) it provides standardized exercises throughout an organization; (3) it is close to trying someone out on the job; (4) it can be legally defended under equal employment opportunity codes; (5) it provides an opportunity to demonstrate qualities and skills beyond one's current job; and (6) it can be a valuable developmental training tool. The chief arguments *against* the assessment center are that it penalizes the nonassertive personality and that research has not yet established the validity of the approach to the extent necessary to justify its high cost. Assessment centers are continuing to grow in popularity as an effective way to identify human potential.

Bailey v. Richardson, 341 U.S. 918 (1951) (194)

A controversial Supreme Court decision holding that there is no prohibition against dismissal of government employees because of their political beliefs, activities, or affiliations, and that "the First Amendment guarantees free speech and assembly, but it does not guarantee government employ." *Bailey* represents the high-water mark of the presidential privilege of denying government employment to anyone reasonably suspected of disloyalty. Dorothy Bailey, who was hired into the classified civil service in 1939 as a training officer, was released in 1947 because of a reduction in force. She was reinstated with a temporary appointment a year later, but was subsequently ruled ineligible for federal employment because of her admitted membership in the American League for Peace and Democracy, an alleged communist organization. Bailey was never given the opportunity to confront the person who accused her of being a communist. The only witnesses who appeared at her administrative hearings were those affirming her own vigorously asserted loyalty to the United States. The decision to disqualify her from government employment was based on the Supreme Court's agreement with the arguments of the Fifth Circuit Court of Appeals that the due process clause of the Fifth Amendment did not apply in this case because government employment is not property, and one cannot be deprived of something to which she or he has no right. *See also* SEPARATION FROM SERVICE, 245.

Significance The *Bailey* decision began a movement toward reducing the second-class citizen role of civil service employees. The case became a *cause célèbre* when it became known that during one of the administrative hearings on Bailey's loyalty she was asked "Did you ever write a letter to the Red Cross about the segregation of blood?" The fact that the hearings did not provide for confrontation and cross-examination resulted in major procedural changes that are reflected in today's administrative process. Subsequent to *Bailey* the Supreme Court found a liberty interest for civil servants in *Board of Regents v. Roth* (408 U.S. 564:1972) and a property interest in *Arnett v. Kennedy* (416 U.S. 134:1974). Due process must now be shown before such interests may be terminated in public sector employment. Dorothy Bailey lost her battle for government employment in a time of national paranoia about communist infiltration of administrative agencies, but in time she won the war of equal protection for civil servants.

Burnout **(195)**
A debilitating condition brought about by unrelieved work stress manifested in psychological, behavioral, and physical reactions. Burnout tends to result in increased dissatisfaction and pessimism, depleted energy reserves, increased absenteeism and inefficiency, and greater susceptibility to illness. These negative characteristics are often reinforced in the workplace by difficulty in making decisions, failure of short-term memory, and general impatience, cynicism, irritability, hopelessness, and resistance to new ideas. *See also* COGNITIVE DISSONANCE, 202.

Personnel Administration

Significance The impact of burnout in the workplace can be disastrous. Valuable and well-trained employees can suddenly become dysfunctional. Every public and private personnel system has been challenged by the progressive burnout of valued workers. The victims of burnout are often the best employees who have set extremely high personal standards that conflict with reality. Because burnout is so intangible, its basic nature, causes, and cures are all subject to dispute among psychologists, personnel managers, and others. Suggested cures for burnout include bringing greater realism into training programs, making better use of psychologists and counselors and employing them on a regular basis, cultivating a pleasant work environment, bringing representatives of the work force into the decision-making process, and reducing pressures for greater productivity, since such pressures are often counterproductive. Managers must realize the consequences of their own stress-inducing behavior.

Career Service (196)
A personnel system based on merit and professional standards. A typical career service contains civil service requirements that include recruitment, competitive examinations, classification based on the nature of the position, objective evaluation of work performance, promotion for meritorious service, and protection against arbitrary dismissal. *See also* CIVIL SERVICE, 198; MERIT SYSTEM, 226.

Significance The idea of a career service replaces the once widely held assumption that government jobs should be awarded to those who contributed money or effort toward an election victory, and that most of these jobs were simple enough for the average person to carry out satisfactorily. The career service has been instituted in the national and state governments and in some local units. Although county governments still operate largely on a spoils basis, many city governments—especially the larger ones that operate under the manager plan—have established career services. In the national government, the career service idea has been extended to include college graduates who have been recruited in large numbers through competitive career examinations. This is part of the larger effort to professionalize the federal personnel system. Some federal agencies operate their own career services outside the federal civil service, including the Foreign Service, the Federal Bureau of Investigation (FBI), the Central Intelligence Agency (CIA), and the Secret Service.

Certification of Eligibles (197)
A procedure whereby the hiring officer of a government agency is provided with the names of individuals who meet the qualifications of a specific position. The civil service agency typically certifies three persons as eligible to fill the position, a practice referred to as the "rule of three." Those certified are the individuals who received the highest scores in a competitive written or oral examination, or were judged best fitted for the position by an education/experience evaluation. See also CIVIL SERVICE, 198.

Significance All merit systems provide for certification of eligibles. The procedure is useful because it offers a compromise between appointment strictly on the basis of merit, and the exercise of discretion by the appointing officer. Discretion may include rejection of all three candidates and the certification of the three with the next highest rankings. By certifying three or more, the appointing officer is offered the opportunity of weighing such intangible factors as personality, appearance, and ability to communicate. Although the "rule of three" is commonly applied, civil service systems vary, with some certifying only the person most highly qualified and others certifying as many as six. Affirmative action, equal opportunity programs, and veterans' preference tend to impact the selection process, in some cases prior to certification of eligibles, and in others in influencing the appointing officer's decision. Individuals who are certified but not appointed have their names returned to the eligible list.

Civil Service (198)
A generic concept that describes the civilians employed by a government who are part of the career service. Civil servants are recruited and hired on the basis of merit, are evaluated periodically as to their job performance, are promoted on the basis of their efficiency ratings, and have job security. In the national government, the civil service includes all civilian employees who are part of the "classified civil service." Elective officials, policy-making officers who have been appointed by the elected officials, employees of certain agencies that enjoy their own personnel systems (such as the Federal Bureau of Investigation [FBI], the Foreign Service, and the Tennessee Valley Authority [TVA]), and all persons employed in the judicial branch and by Congress are not part of the federal classified civil service. *See also* CAREER SERVICE, 196; CLASSIFIED SERVICE, 201; MERIT SYSTEM, 226; PENDLETON ACT OF 1883, 232.

Personnel Administration

Significance   The civil service constitutes the core of the bureaucracy of the national government, all state governments, and many of the medium and large city governments. Most townships, counties, and other local units of government continue to operate under the spoils system, although a few have changed over to management plans that incorporate civil service personnel systems. By law, civil service personnel are not permitted to strike, but in most systems they can organize into unions that participate in negotiating pay and working conditions. In state and local units of government, civil service personnel have occasionally gone on strike or have used tactics such as "blue flu" (wherein most members of the police, fire, or other departments take sick leave). Although civil servants who strike are sometimes fired, final settlements between the government and union typically provide for their rehiring. In the 1980s, almost 20 million persons were employed by national, state, and local governments, most of them in civil service merit systems.

Civil Service Reform Act of 1978 (199)
A major act that reformed the federal personnel system. The Civil Service Reform Act of 1978 assigned the functions performed by the United States Civil Service Commission to two new and separate agencies: the Merit Systems Protection Board and the Office of Personnel Management. This reassignment abolished the Civil Service Commission. In addition to this reorganization, the reform act provided for a total overhaul of the system through which federal employees can appeal dismissals or demotions. Previously an employee had three bodies to which he or she could appeal a supervisor's adverse decision: the Federal Employee Appeals Authority, the Appeals Review Board, and the Civil Service Commission. The reform act abolished and replaced these bodies. First, it converted the Civil Service Commission into an independent agency known as the Merit Systems Protection Board, and it gave the Board both appellate and investigatory responsibilities. Second, it established an Office of Personnel Management for personnel policy making. The reform act also created an Office of Special Council, appointed by the president, which has responsibility for investigations and prosecutions in the civil service. *See also* GENERAL SCHEDULE (GS), 218; OFFICE OF PERSONNEL MANAGEMENT (OPM), 229; SENIOR EXECUTIVE SERVICE, (SES), 244.

Significance   The Civil Service Reform Act of 1978 received its most immediate impetus from the abuses the civil service system suffered under President Richard Nixon's administration in the early 1970s. Among the more notorious examples of those abuses was the so-called Malic Manual, named after Fred Malic, a high official in the Office of Management and Budget (OMB), who encouraged the appointing of high-level federal executives on the basis of partisan politics. His manual was a procedural guide for implementing that approach. President Jimmy Carter stated in his 1978 State of the Union address that reform of the federal personnel system was "absolutely vital." President Carter said the reform act itself was designed to "restore the merit principle to a system which has grown into a bureaucratic maze. It will provide greater management flexibility and better rewards for better performance without compromising job security." The "better rewards for better performance" reference is to the Senior Executive Service (SES), also established by the reform act. The members of the SES receive incentive pay for increased productivity in their agencies. In successfully arguing for incentive pay, Civil Service Commission Chairman Alan K. Campbell noted that "The current system provides few incentives for managers to manage or for employees to perform." Even though the Civil Service Reform Act of 1978 tried to put merit principles back into the federal personnel system, merit is still under attack from all sides. The attack comes especially from (1) those who want to include more minorities and women in government; (2) those who want to expand freedom of political expression for government employees; (3) those who seek to bring more professionals into government, professionals who often do not identify with the public service in the same sense that traditional personnel specialists have defined it; and (4) those who support unionism and collective bargaining for federal employees. Nevertheless, the Civil Service Reform Act of 1978 keeps alive the traditional efforts to encourage merit in the public service by financial rewards.

Civil Service Reform League (200)

A national organization formed in 1881 to seek reform of the spoils system in the federal government. The Civil Service Reform League, now known as the National Civil Service League, was an amalgamation of thirteen state associations. The first of these associations had been founded in 1877 as the New York Civil Service Reform Association. The League studied and advocated the British system of public service, particularly the principles of competitive examinations and a "neutral" civil service free from partisan political pressures. It also represented the three dominant objectives of the reform movement; (1) *a negative purpose,* the accomplishment of which—that is, doing away with the spoils system—would eliminate evil in high places; (2) *a moral tone,* which invested public personnel administration with "good" as opposed to "bad" connotations apart from the purposes for which people were employed or the nature of the responsibilities they carried; and (3) *a concern with efficiency,* which the reformers believed the merit system would automatically assure. The Civil Service Reform League's quick success in bringing about passage of the Civil Service Act in 1883, just two years after the League was formed, consolidated its position as a powerful influence in the history of public administration. The League created a period of "government by the good" in which ethics and egalitarianism were highly prized. *See also* CIVIL SERVICE, 198; PENDLETON ACT OF 1883, 232; POLITICS-ADMINISTRATION DICHOTOMY, 70.

Significance The Civil Service Reform League has had a lasting effect on U.S. public administration. Its influence on Woodrow Wilson was enormous. Only four years after passage of the Civil Service Act, Wilson wrote his seminal essay on "The Study of Administration" (1887), from which many scholars date the beginning of American public administration as a self-conscious discipline. The tone of moral rectitude in Wilson's article perfectly reflected the ideals of the League and has remained a continuing undercurrent in the study of public administration. Wilson later became president of the League. The politics-administration dichotomy received its initial legitimacy and acceptance as a result of the thinking that dominated the League. "Politics" was "bad" in the civil service, and "administration" was "good." The Civil Service Reform League ensured the continuing independence of the Civil Service Commission and encouraged its use as a model in the reform of state and local governments. Whether the League's influence in disassociating public personnel administration from the substantive functions of government was a useful service is a hotly debated point. There are those who believe the League's distinction was artificial.

Classified Service (201)

A bureaucracy in which personnel operate in a merit system under the jurisdiction of a civil service agency. In the national government, nearly 3 million individuals are employed in the federal classified service. Those not in the classified service include persons employed in agencies that operate their own personnel systems (for example, the Foreign Service and the Secret Service), elected officials and those appointed by the elected officials, and all employees of the judicial branch and the Congress. *See also* CAREER SERVICE, 196; GENERAL SCHEDULE (GS), 218; MERIT SYSTEM, 226.

Significance   Although most federal employees are in the classified service, Congress has authorized the president to exempt certain positions. In addition, Congress has granted power to the Office of Personnel Management to determine which classified positions should be filled by competitive examination, which by noncompetitive, and which do not require any examination. Those not requiring an examination may be highly sensitive positions in the field of defense, those which require special or unique skills, and common labor jobs. Agencies outside the classified service operate on merit standards typically higher than those established for civil service, as in the case of the Federal Bureau of Investigation (FBI), the Secret Service, and the Foreign Service.

Cognitive Dissonance   (202)
A theory holding that when persons find themselves in a situation where they are expected to believe two mutually exclusive things, the subsequent tension and discomfort generates activity designed to reduce the dissonance or disharmony. Cognitive dissonance was first postulated by Leon Festinger in his book, *A Theory of Cognitive Dissonance,* in 1957. The theory has been particularly useful in public personnel administration in relationship to perceived wage inequities. Employees who see themselves performing the same work as others but being paid significantly less, for example, frequently experience cognitive dissonance. Among the options for tension reduction are asking for a raise, restricting output, or seeking another job. If the employees avoid the stress and do not try to relieve the dissonance, severe mental and physical disabilities sometimes result. *See also* BURNOUT, 195.

Significance   Cognitive dissonance infers a relationship between *cognition*—the process of knowing—and *dissonance*—the lack of harmony or agreement. It signals an environmental condition that a human being does not feel to be right, proper, or reasonable. A healthy person thus signalled will act to change the psychologically uncomfortable situation. The changes can have both positive and negative impacts: positive when, for example, a person changes his or her attitude toward the dissonant element in the environment by gaining new information about it or deciding to live with it creatively; negative when, for example, a person engages in self-deception or denial to rid himself or herself of discrepancies he or she no longer wishes to confront. Either way, cognitive dissonance accurately describes the human personality as a tension-reduction system. The successful manager continually looks for ways to change the cognitive elements in the working environment to control the dissonance always lurking in the human condition.

Collective Bargaining (203)
The process whereby an employer and employee representatives attempt to arrive at agreements governing employee compensation and working conditions. Collective bargaining in the private sector involves a mutual obligation by labor and management representatives to meet at reasonable times, to confer and negotiate in good faith, and to execute a written agreement with respect to wages, hours, working conditions, grievance procedures, and fringe benefits. Neither party is compelled to agree to a proposal nor to make any concessions. In the public sector, the right of federal civil service employees to bargain collectively was granted by Executive Order 10988, issued by President John F. Kennedy in 1962. Although the Lloyd-LaFollette Act of 1912 had established the right of federal employees to organize, before 1962, in the words of one expert, "Federal employee organizations existed on sufferance and by grace, welcomed in some agencies and hardly tolerated in others." Executive Order 10988 greatly strengthened the role of federal employee organizations by stating that "the efficient administration of the Government and the well-being of the employees require that orderly and constructive relationships be maintained between employee organizations and management officials." Agency administrators were required to deal with the employee organizations and to grant them official recognition for negotiation or consultation. Exclusive recognition and contract negotiating rights covering all employees in a bargaining unit were provided for those organizations that had the support of the majority of the employees in the unit. Executive Order 10988 also placed certain limitations on collective bargaining in the public sector in stating that all agreements are to be "governed by the provisions of any existing or future laws and regulations." The effect of this in the federal civil service is that salaries, wages, hours of work, and fringe benefits cannot be bargained, but items such as tours of duty, lunch periods, locker facilities, sanitation, vacation scheduling, rest periods, health services, and training and recreation programs can be bargained. *See also* CIVIL SERVICE REFORM ACT OF 1978, 199; PUBLIC UNIONISM, 240.

Significance The nature of collective bargaining in the public service reflects the fact that, since the early 1960s, public employment has grown faster than any other sector of the U.S. economy. The burgeoning of public employment and the power of numbers meant that the original 1962 executive order establishing the right of public employees to bargain collectively had to be modified in subsequent years. The first change was President Richard M. Nixon's Executive Order 11491 of October 29, 1969, providing for a Federal Labor Relations Council (FLRC) to oversee management-employee relationships in the public service. The 1962 executive order had not established a public administration equivalent to the National Labor Relations Board (NLRB), which has monitored labor disputes in the private sector since 1935. The FLRC thus became the public sector equivalent of the NLRB. Executive order 11491 had been in effect only a few months when the first major strike of federal employees took place. In March 1970, about 200,000 postal employees left their jobs in a wage dispute. Since bargaining for wages was clearly outside the provisions of the 1962 and 1969 executive orders allowing collective bargaining for public employees, the strike and its subsequent method of settlement were unprecedented. The federal government was forced to bargain for the first time with unions representing public employees whose compensation was set by congressional statute. The salaries negotiated were subject to ratification by Congress, which promptly accepted them. Congress then passed the Postal Reorganization Act, including a provision allowing future postal employee compensation to be determined by collective bargaining. The power of public unions, particularly the postal employees, was further illustrated in the Civil Service Reform Act of 1978. The unions had long considered the FLRC a management tool, since it was composed of the chairperson of the Civil Service Commission, the Secretary of Labor, an official of the Executive Office of the President, "and such other executive branch officials as the president from time to time designated." The unions wanted a statutory basis for the public labor relations program, because executive orders can be freely changed by presidents. They got what they wanted in the Civil Service Reform Act of 1978, which enacted into law all provisions of the executive orders on collective bargaining. Title VII of the act changed the FLRC to an independent Federal Labor Relations Authority (FLRA). The new agency is composed of three members serving five-year terms, subject to removal only for cause, and a General Counsel who receives complaints and may prosecute unfair labor practices. Collective bargaining for federal employees is now a settled fact and an important aspect of public personnel administration. The illegality of federal employee strikes, however, was affirmed in 1982 when President Ronald Reagan fired all striking air traffic controllers. An agreement had been reached between the Professional Air Traffic Controllers Organization (PATCO) and the Federal Aviation Administration (FAA), but the 15,000-member union rejected it by a margin of 19 to 1. President

Reagan then entered the dispute and gave the strikers 48 hours to return to work. Some returned, but about 11,500 remained on strike and were fired.

Collective Bargaining Agreement (204)
A contractual arrangement whereby labor and management agree to terms that prescribe wage rates and working conditions for a specified time period. An "agency shop" is a collective bargaining agreement between a company and a labor union that requires all of the workers included in the contract to either join the union or pay it a service fee in lieu of union dues. Another common type of collective bargaining contract involves a *union shop,* in which all newly hired workers must join the union after a specified period of time on the job, usually thirty days. Under federal law, a state can modify an agency shop or a union shop by enacting a "right-to-work" law that provides for an "open shop" in which workers do not have to join a union as a condition of employment. About twenty states have adopted right-to-work legislation. In right-to-work states, located mainly in the South, unions find it extremely difficult to engage in effective collective bargaining. An agency shop and a union shop are to be distinguished from a *closed shop,* an agreement under which management can hire only union members. The closed shop has been prohibited in most fields since enactment by Congress of the Taft-Hartley Act of 1947. *See also* PUBLIC EMPLOYEE UNIONS, 237.

Significance Collective bargaining agreements in their various permutations have become a common part of the U.S. economic system. Each type has its supporters and its detractors. In recent years, the agency shop has been gaining support. The agency shop is a modification of the union shop, and in a sense it represents a compromise between a union shop and an open shop agreement. It recognizes that some workers may have religious, moral, or other grounds for refusing to join a union. Payments to the union in lieu of membership dues are justified on the ground that the union is bargaining to improve wages and working conditions for nonunion workers as well as for its members. Under law, a union under federal jurisdiction as well as under many state jurisdictions *must* bargain for *all* employees. In 1977, the United States Supreme Court upheld the right of public employees to establish an agency shop agreement with the government which employs them (*Abood v. Detroit Board of Education,* 431 U.S. 209). The union shop remains the most common type of labor-management agreement, covering about three-fourths of organized labor. Unlike an open shop, the union shop eliminates "free riders" who benefit from collective bargaining agreements but do not pay union dues. Labor unions have spent much money and engaged in extensive political action since 1947 in their efforts to restore the closed shop, authorized by the Wagner Act (National Labor Relations Act of 1935) but outlawed by the Taft-Hartley Act (Labor-Management Relations Act of 1947). Their efforts have failed, and most labor leaders have come to accept the union shop and the agency shop as reasonable compromises. Forces opposed to compulsory membership in labor unions continue to support the enactment of federal legislation that would establish a national open shop provision based on the right-to-work principle.

Comparable Worth (205)
A controversial concept that provides for equal compensation for people who have dissimilar jobs but whose work activities are of equal value to the employer in that they require similar skills, effort, and responsibility. Comparable worth issues have primarily addressed the situation whereby, on the average, women receive considerably less pay for their work than men. Comparable worth, however, goes beyond the formula of "equal pay for equal work" by claiming that unequal pay for dissimilar jobs of equal worth to an employer is based on sex discrimination in violation of the Fourteenth Amendment of the United States Constitution. The United States Supreme Court first recognized that denial of comparable worth constituted sex discrimination in the case of *County of Washington v. Gunther* (450 U.S. 907: 1981). In this precedent-setting decision, the Court held that female jail matrons who received only 70 percent of the pay received by male guards were the victims of wage discrimination. Although their jobs were dissimilar, the Court agreed that the matrons deserved pay equal to that of the male guards because their jobs were of equal value to their common employer. *See also* AFFIRMATIVE ACTION, 189; FAIR LABOR STANDARDS ACT (FLSA), 46.

Significance Comparable worth goes beyond the better-understood issue of equal pay for the same work to address the problem of consistent underpayment for women in the work force. Comparable worth stresses that people perform different jobs that nevertheless involve the same levels of prerequisites, skills, tasks carried out, responsibilities, and general value to their employer. Business and industry have been the main opponents of the idea of comparable worth, claiming that in the long run both women and business are harmed by the doctrine. The main problem in applying the concept is found in the need to evaluate job requirements and performance in a manner that makes it possible to link people in terms of equal pay when they are performing quite different tasks. Some critics argue that comparable worth is an erroneous notion that resembles comparing apples and oranges and then charging the same price for both. Advocates of the comparable worth doctrine hold that it is the only way in which a fair market wage can be paid for work that has historically been carried out by women. Wage rates, consequently, should be based on the productivity contributions of the employee rather than on gender. Comparability is a broader concept that involves comparisons of the relationship between the work performed by different groups and the pay received. The rates of pay for government employees, for example, both male and female, may be influenced by studies conducted of rates of pay in the private sector. The comparable worth doctrine has been controversial because it involves a claimed sex bias that detrimentally affects a majority of the members of the U.S. work force.

Compensation (206)

Payments to employees for their services. Compensation makes up the largest single category in the operating budgets of state and local governments. Compensation can be direct or indirect. Indirect compensation is commonly referred to as "fringe benefits." Direct compensation generally takes the form of basic wages and salaries. Direct compensation also includes geographic differentials for unusual living conditions or unusually high living costs in certain areas; hazard pay for working with dangerous materials or in hazardous surroundings; and special pay, which includes overtime, night, and holiday pay. The amount of compensation appropriate for a particular position is frequently determined by analyses of three relative groups: (1) employees working at similar jobs in other organizations; (2) employees working at different jobs within the organization; and (3) employees working at the same job within the organization. If government is the employer, pay levels may be legislated by the setting of statutory rates. In the Salary Reform Act of 1962, for example, Congress mandated that federal pay must be "comparable with private enterprise salary rates for the same levels of work." The Federal Pay Comparability Act of 1970 reincorporated the principles of the Salary Reform Act, but empowered the president to establish the rates for the General Schedule (GS), the Foreign Service, and the special medical and nursing schedules in the Veterans Administration (VA). The new General Schedule, which the president promulgates to take effect each October 1, is greatly influenced by a Federal Employees Pay Council, composed of five representatives of employee unions, and an Advisory Council on Federal Pay, composed of three pay and labor experts appointed by the president. *See also* FRINGE BENEFITS, 217; GENERAL SCHEDULE (GS), 218; HUMAN MOTIVATION: MOTIVATION-HYGIENE THEORY, 99.

Significance   Compensation is a necessity of life. The objective of a compensation system is to create a system of rewards that is equitable to the employer and employee alike, so that the employee is attracted to his or her work and is motivated to do a good job. Yet many behavioral scientists feel that compensation *per se* cannot appropriately serve as an employee motivator. Frederick Herzberg, for example, considers compensation as a maintenance, rather than a motivating, factor. Even when other motivating factors, such as achievement and recognition, have been added to the compensation system, basic wages and salaries remain the prime motivators. Over a period of time various experiments have been conducted by states and cities to find some foolproof scheme to permit salary schedules to adjust automatically with changes in cost-of-living or price indexes. Sliding-scale plans have suffered from several drawbacks: (1) original base rates come to be viewed as sacrosanct, making the correction of any inherent inequities more difficult; (2) prevailing pay is not given sufficient independent attention, even though this is the one economic criterion that encompasses the interaction of almost all economic forces; (3) price indexes indicate only changes in prices and do not measure the kind and amount of goods and services that families buy or their total family expenditure; and (4) dependence on cost-of-living changes ignores changes in labor's share of economic gain that may have been secured by increased productivity, organized union bargaining, or other effects.

Consulting (207)

The provision of information, assistance, or analysis in support of ongoing or emerging public sector or commercial activities. Public consulting is done by persons or firms offering a service of advice to governmental units on a fee basis. It includes such activities as developing a wage and salary plan, analyzing an administrative process to improve it, facilitating an organizational development effort, analyzing data for a program, offering new solutions for program implementation, and assisting in the implementation of a management-by-objectives plan. The difference between consulting and *contracting* is that contracting describes a situation where a discrete and specialized task is designed, implemented, and administered by a nongovernmental unit. Examples of contracting are the

Personnel Administration

McDonnel-Douglas Corporation designing and building campuses for the St. Louis Junior College system, the Lockheed Corporation providing a computer system for the state of Alaska, the Philco-Ford Corporation producing a zip code reader for the United States Post Office, and the Judd Brown Corporation building highways for the state of Iowa. *Consulting* deals primarily in basic management needs and the provision of advice.

There are at least five reasons why consultants may be called on in lieu of using personnel already on the government payroll. These are (1) *Limitations on hiring civil servants.* In spite of dramatic increases in the federal budget over the past twenty years, the size of the federal bureaucracy has remained relatively stable. In 1966, for example, Congress enacted the Revenue Expenditure Control Act, which required the executive branch to reduce itself in size to the level of employment existing in 1964. The theory behind the act was that the reduction of, and stabilization of, a personnel ceiling for the executive branch would first cut, and then stabilize, federal expenditures connected with personnel costs. One of the results of the legislation was a dramatic increase in agency use of consultants to accomplish legislatively mandated activities. (2) *Needs for special skills.* The long battle for job security won by government employees through the establishment of elaborate civil service procedures greatly improved the quality of life of thousands of civil servants. An offshoot of such benefits as higher salaries and job security, however, is the reluctance by agencies to hire persons with unique skills or whose training may limit their productivity to one project or type of project. Since government workers cannot easily be discharged, it is considered more cost-effective to hire a consultant than to hire a full-time person to perform a short-term task, even though the consultant's costs include overhead and possible profit charges of a firm. (3) *Evading Parkinson's Law.* One effect of calling in consultants is to frustrate the inevitability of Parkinson's Law, which states that work expands to fill the time available for its completion. Because of the contractual nature of consulting, the tasks are agreed on before work starts and generally are given relatively short life spans. (4) *Rapid project turnaround.* Most firms operate on a 24-hour basis when necessary, and one need only schedule several hours in advance for the appropriate typing, copying, graphics, or staff resources at virtually any given time. Thus, projects with particularly tight deadlines, which would be impossible to complete on time if forced into a nine-to-five schedule, can be expected to be completed on time by consulting firms. (5) *Assumed objectivity.* Consultants are often called on to perform studies because of their assumed objectivity with regard to the political issues in a given area.

Consultants are viewed as disinterested third parties who can weigh issues on their merits rather than in light of political considerations. The degree to which their actual objectivity is greater than that of government employees is, of course, debatable. A consultant's level of impact on a governmental agency is likely to be determined by numerous factors including (1) the type of task being performed; (2) the time constraints on the agency for implementing action; (3) the availability of alternative sources of information and advice, either internal or external, to the agency; and (4) the credibility of the consultant.

Significance Consulting has enjoyed remarkable growth in recent years. In 1966, there were 2,612 consulting organizations in the United States. By 1987, this number had grown to over 6,000. Formal listings do not identify the small firms that are organized informally or the number of individuals who do consulting in their spare time. Another indicator of the size of the consulting industry is dollar volume of activity. In 1986 alone, the federal government spent almost $200 billion in contracts to nonfederal agencies, of which over half went to contracting units in the private sector. The remaining funds were spent on grants to states, cities, and nonprofit organizations, such as universities. Consultants have become a reality in modern government. Their proper utilization is a major responsibility of public managers.

Discrimination (208)

The unequal treatment of people because of their race, color, religion, national origin, sex, or age. Discrimination has usually been either *de facto* (private discrimination or segregation not required by law) or *de jure* (legally enforced discrimination). Both forms have been under attack since the adoption of the Fourteenth Amendment in 1868. The Due Process Clause and the Equal Protection Clause of the Fourteenth Amendment have been invoked by the United States Supreme Court in literally hundreds of cases, as the Court has systematically struck down governmental actions that discriminate. In addition, starting with the Civil Rights Act of 1964, numerous federal laws and executive orders have been promulgated to reduce or eliminate private as well as public discriminatory activity. State and local governments have also joined in the fight against discrimination by enacting state laws and local ordinances that forbid discriminatory practices at every level of social intercourse. Affirmative action policies and programs have been developed in recent years in an attempt to remedy the effects of past discrimination, especially in employment and education. See also REVERSE DISCRIMINATION, 243.

Significance   Since the 1930s, a veritable revolution has occurred in how the nation has dealt with problems of discrimination. Any arbitrary classification of people has been declared by the Supreme Court to be in violation of the Fourteenth Amendment's Equal Protection Clause. All *de jure* and most *de facto* discrimination has been outlawed, either by action of the courts, by legislative bodies, or by executive orders. Public schools across the nation have been desegregated since the Supreme Court's antisegregation holding in *Brown v. Board of Education of Topeka* (347 U.S. 483: 1954; 349 U.S. 294: 1955). Numerous cases and various laws have also been applied to expand the rights of women in economic and social fields. In *Craig v. Boren* (429 U.S. 19: 1977), for example, the Supreme Court invalidated a state law that established different alcoholic drinking ages for men and women. In 1968, the Court held in *Jones v. Mayer* (392 U.S. 409) that all racial discrimination in the sale or rental of property, both public and private, is illegal. Congress has aided the Court in its antidiscrimination campaign by enacting various civil rights laws. Probably the most important of these, the Civil Rights Act of 1964, outlawed discrimination in voting, in public accommodations such as hotels and restaurants, and in employment opportunities. It prohibited discrimination of any kind based on race, color, religion, national origin, and, in the case of employment, sex. Most institutionalized forms of discrimination and segregation have been eliminated through these kinds of actions, but subtle forms of it persist. The affirmative action approach to remedying the effects of past discrimination remains highly controversial, with critics charging that it constitutes a form of reverse discrimination. Although great progress has been made in alleviating discrimination, much remains to be done.

Double Dipping (209)

The receipt each month of military retirement pay plus income from a civilian job or social security benefits. Double dipping is a phenomenon that results from the early retirement program utilized by the military services. After twenty years of service, enlisted men and officers may retire with substantial benefits that include a monthly retirement check, free medical care at military hospitals, free dental care, and shopping rights at base post exchanges. Often military personnel are young enough at retirement to work at civilian jobs for another twenty to thirty years, thus receiving double paychecks for some time. At full retirement the retiree has worked long enough to qualify for social security, or, in the federal service, to qualify for civil service retirement pay. Since military retirement, civil service retirement, and social security are all included in the COLA (cost of living adjustment) system, many retirees receive retirement checks larger than the pay they received while on active duty in the military. Similar double dipping occurs when members of the federal civil service retire and secure private sector employment which makes them eligible for social security. See also SEPARATION FROM SERVICE, 245.

Significance Double dipping has become a serious economic problem as the number of military and civil service retirees escalates while the working population supporting the military and social security retirement programs shrinks. The magnitude of the problem can be determined from the fact that in 1982, for example, lifetime values of pensions averaged $228,000 for the military, $159,000 for the federal civil service, and $37,000 for private sector employees. During the Reagan administration, the president's Private Sector Survey on Cost Control (also known as the Grace Commission) made recommendations to deal with double dipping and related problems. As a result, two pieces of pension reform legislation were enacted by Congress: (1) the Federal Employees' Retirement System Act of 1986; and (2) the Military Retirement Act of 1986. Based on Grace Commission estimates, it is anticipated that these two laws will save U.S. taxpayers about $6 billion annually.

**Employee Retirement Income Security Act   (210)
(ERISA)**
Provides for a program administered by the Departments of Labor and the Treasury to safeguard the rights of workers in private pension plans. Enacted in 1974, the Pension Reform Act established minimum federal standards for the administration of private pension funds. Although employers are not required to set up pension plans under the act, those that do are brought under the federal regulatory power. Under the act, qualifications for admission to private pension plans are stipulated, as is the point at which contributions to an employee's fund begin to "vest" in the worker, bestowing a right to the funds whether or not the worker remains with the same employer. ERISA also provides for minimum levels of employer contributions to pension funds, and requires insurance for situations in which a pension fund collapses. The act also gave permission to banks, savings and loans, and other financial institutions to establish individual retirement accounts for self-employed persons, with special tax

advantages to encourage workers to set aside part of their income for retirement.

Significance   ERISA's enactment by Congress was generated partly by the collapse of a number of private pension funds in the 1960s and 1970s, partly by the experience of individual workers who were eliminated from their programs as they neared retirement, and partly by the need to ensure the stability of the nation's retirement systems for the future. It was the first involvement of the federal government in the private pension field, and Congress appeared to act reluctantly but necessarily to cope with a growing problem. Over 30 million workers are covered by private pension plans today, with others depending exclusively on social security, or on social security plus income from savings and other private sources. Even though social security payments have been indexed by linking them to the Consumer Price Index (CPI), heavy inflation has placed an increasing burden on retired persons. The Pension Reform Act was an attempt to strengthen the retirement system by ensuring that private pensions will serve to supplement the social security system for millions of Americans.

Equal Employment Opportunity (211)

The idea that no person should be denied the opportunity for employment because of discrimination based on race, color, religion, sex, national origin, or physical disability. Equal employment opportunity is basically a redefinition of the merit system. Prior to 1960, little was done in the public or private sectors to correct the discrimination existing in hiring practices. The Civil Rights Act of 1964 began to change this situation. Title VII of the act bars discrimination on the basis of race, color, religion, sex, or national origin. It does, however, permit different standards of compensation, appointments under the merit system, and the use of ability tests as long as there is no *intent* to discriminate. Preferential treatment for minorities was not required. Since the Civil Rights Act of 1964, there have been many court cases that have broadened and challenged the scope of the act. The Equal Employment Opportunity Act of 1972 also brought state and local, as well as federal, employers under the antidiscrimination provisions of the 1964 statute. In 1971, the Supreme Court heard the case of *Griggs v. Duke Power Company* (401 U.S. 424:1971) in which it was alleged that an employer had used selection requirements having an adverse effect on minority hiring. Blacks were relegated to manual labor jobs, and, in order to change jobs, they were required to finish high school and score well on two different tests. The Court ruled that the power company must prove that selection requirements are job related and the tests valid. *Griggs* was used to (1) order termination of employment requirements having adverse effects on minorities, and (2) justify affirmative action programs, validation of tests, pretest tutoring, and temporary remedial hiring ratios. In the mid-1970s, with a more conservative Supreme Court, some changes were made in the *Griggs* doctrine. The case of *Washington v. Davis* (426 U.S. 229: 1976) saw the Supreme Court overrule an appeals court, saying that testing could be used if the employer could show validity—that is, a relationship among the test, the training program, and a person's success on the job. The most controversial case concerning equal employment opportunity was *Regents of the University of California v. Bakke* (438 U.S. 265: 1978), in which a white male sued the medical school of the University of California at Davis for admission because it had rejected his application in favor of minority students less qualified than he. The university had set up a quota of minority students for each entering class in a voluntary effort to correct years of minority discrimination. With many people expecting a definitive decision about equal opportunity, the court pacified both sides by ruling that Davis must admit Bakke, but that special attention could be given to minorities. Affirmative action was legitimized, but the methods used to pursue it were questioned. Race consciousness in recruitment and selection was all right, but quotas were not. *United Steel Workers of America v. Weber* (443 U.S. 193: 1979) strengthened the case for affirmative action by upholding the Kaiser Aluminum Company's voluntary effort to promote equal opprotunity by placing minorities in 50 percent of the slots in its training program. The ongoing battle over the use of quotas can be understood as a conflict between the old belief in the merit system, which is violated if the more qualified person is not hired, and the new philosophy of hiring a possibly less qualified person to make up for discrimination in the past. Public administrationist J. D. Williams believes the merit system is not lost through affirmative action. Instead, the search for qualified people is widened through a combination of merit and equal opportunity. *See also* AFFIRMATIVE ACTION, 189; UNITED STEEL WORKERS OF AMERICA V. WEBER (1979), 251.

Significance   Equal employment opportunity has had a significant impact on all areas of public personnel policy, as well as educational institutions and private businesses. Given the traditional neutrality of the Civil Service, equal employment opportunity directives have had a revolutionary impact on American society. In order to facilitate an integrated work force, for example, housing opportunities have to be nondiscriminatory. Job classifications must frequently be redesigned

Personnel Administration

to accommodate new levels of employees. Recruiting must be done with the cooperation of neighborhoods, churches, and minority schools. The personnel selection process must be broadened to include valid testing and pretest training when necessary. All public employers of fifteen or more people, and any employer with federal contracts or subcontracts of $10,000 or more, are required to have affirmative action plans, which mean equal opportunity for everyone. Employers must specify clearly the qualifications needed for a job, and they must seek those best qualified, at the same time recruiting specific numbers of minorities and women. In recent years equal employment opportunity has focused on age and disability discrimination, problems that still meet substantial resistance.

Ethics in Government Act of 1978 (212)
Legislation intended to promote and preserve the integrity of public officials through mandatory financial disclosure requirements and the prohibition of certain activities by former government employees. The Ethics in Government Act of 1978 was approved as Public Law 95-521, with five titles. Title I established a standby mechanism to appoint a special prosecutor, if needed, and an Office of Government Crimes in the Department of Justice. Title II created an Office of Congressional Legal Counsel to represent Congress in court, so that Congress would not be dependent on the Department of Justice—the executive branch—in trial cases. Title III required public disclosure of financial interests by high-level officers and employees of all three branches of the federal government. Disclosure is neither a net worth statement nor a detailed tax return. Income is reported in broad categories, and good faith estimates are sufficient, a provision described by critics as a weakness in the legislation. The reports are made available for public inspection. Title IV provided for an Office of Government Ethics, a small central coordinating organization designed to provide focus and consistent guidance on conflict-of-interest issues. The office is also responsible for formulating regulations for administering the act, especially for ensuring that heads of federal agencies bring the performance of their personnel into line with the act's provisions. Each agency is required to have an ethics officer who serves as liaison to the office. Title V dealt with prohibited activities by former officers and employees of the federal government. It added new restrictions to Chapter 18 of the United States Code, which already barred former government employees from acting as another party's representative to government in matters where the employee had been substantially involved. *See also* ADMINISTRATIVE DISCRETION, 86; ETHICS, 13.

Significance The Ethics in Government Act of 1978 was the product of post-Watergate concern about the integrity of government officials and the need for citizens to have confidence in government employees. In the wake of the act, and in response to criticism that it did not go far enough in describing ethical standards, Congress also enacted Public Law 96-303, that took effect October 1, 1980, prescribing a Code of Ethics for Government Service. The code states, "Any person in Government service should: I. Put loyalty to the highest moral principles and to country above loyalty to persons, party, or Government department. II. Uphold the Constitution, laws, and regulations of the United States and of all governments therein and never be a party to their evasion. III. Give a full day's labor for a full day's pay; giving earnest effort and best thought to the performance of duties. IV. Seek to find and employ more efficient and economical ways of getting tasks accomplished. V. Never discriminate unfairly by the dispensing of special favors or privileges to anyone whether for remuneration or not; and never accept, for himself or herself or for family members, favors or benefits under circumstances which might be construed by reasonable persons as influencing the performance of governmental duties. VI. Make no private promises of any kind binding upon the duties of office, since a Government employee has no private work which can be binding on public duty. VII. Engage in no business with the Government, either directly or indirectly, which is inconsistent with the conscientious performance of governmental duties. VIII. Never use any information gained confidentially in the performance of governmental duties as a means of making private profit. IX. Expose corruption wherever discovered. X. Uphold these principles, ever conscious that public office is a public trust."

The Ethics in Government Act and the Code of Ethics for Government Service were major efforts by Congress to deal with the basic problems of a progressive loss of faith in government and a widespread belief in the endemic nature of official wrongdoing. Problems relating to ethics in government came to the fore again in 1987 when Congress investigated the covert actions carried on by National Security Council (NSC) personnel relating to secret sales of arms to Iran and the illegal diversion of such funds to aid the *Contras* in Nicaragua. Lies, personal use of government funds, shredding of evidence, violations of the laws enacted by Congress (the Boland Amendment), and other excesses were justified by NSC officials on the ground that the ends sought justified the means used. Actions were undertaken under the president's authority, but the president was not informed of critical decisions so that he could retain "plausible deniability."

Personnel Administration

Executive Order (213)

A formal and legally binding presidential policy directive to be followed by members of the executive branch of the federal government. An executive order is an instrument used by the president of the United States to exercise the limited and delegated authority of the executive branch. Although not considered statutory law, executive orders have the force of law. There is no statute that defines the term "executive order." The earliest executive orders were neither numbered nor issued in any standard format, and there was no requirement for official notice or publication. As the mechanism became more formalized, however, a chronological numbering system came into use in 1907, and all earlier orders were assigned numbers. The Federal Register Act of 1935 required all executive orders of general interest to be published in the Federal Register, with a later act requiring publication of all executive orders. Executive Order 1 was issued by President Abraham Lincoln in 1862. It concerned the establishment of military courts in Louisiana. Since that time, executive orders have been used in a wide range of policy areas, depending on the president's personal values and his perception of his constitutional responsibilities. Beginning in the early 1960s, executive orders were used more and more in controversial social and political policy areas. They were frequently issued as a result of recommendations made by task forces and special committees, which were first introduced by the Kennedy administration as new policy-making groups. Once a president has decided to make an authoritative policy statement, there are a number of factors involved in the decision to use an executive order, as opposed to some other means of proclamation. First, there must be a strong public demand for solution to a given problem. For example, Executive Order 11491 was issued in 1969 by President Richard M. Nixon in response to growing federal employee discontent over the limited provisions for public sector labor relations contained in Executive Order 10988, which had been issued in 1962. Second, the president must consider whether there will be funding for, and enforcement of, the directive. Both factors are crucial to the success of an executive order. Third, the president must consider whether Congress or the courts will effectively address the policy need he has in mind. If they will act, perhaps he does not need to act. Neither Congress nor the courts seemed inclined to deal with discrimination in public housing in the early 1960s. Therefore Executive Order 11063 was issued by President John F. Kennedy in 1962, setting the official national policy of nondiscrimination in federally assisted housing. Executive orders are subordinate to statutory law, to decisional law by the Supreme Court, and even to the legislative intent of Congress. An executive order can be declared invalid by the courts if it conflicts with any of these "laws of higher authority."

Significance   The executive order is an important policy-making tool that is more flexible and adaptive than statutory law. It allows an opportunity to experiment with programs at the federal level without full-scale congressional involvement. The availability of the executive order serves a safety-valve function as part of the overall system of checks and balances. If a critical issue gets bogged down in Congress, the executive order is a mechanism available to fill a policy void until a statutory decision can be made. Some critics object to a president's use of the executive order, considering it a usurpation of legislative power.

Featherbedding (214)

Restrictions placed on management by a collective bargaining contract that requires an employer to hire or keep unneeded workers or to limit output. The objective sought by the union in featherbedding is to ensure the employment of union members. Examples of featherbedding abound. They include such requirements as retaining linotype operators on the payroll even though they and their machines have been replaced by computerization; limiting the number of bricks each bricklayer can lay in a day; requiring paid standby musicians whenever a radio station plays recorded music; the required use of small shovels and narrow paint brushes; the retention of firemen ("coal shovelers") on diesel locomotives; and the arbitrary limitation of class size by teacher unions. Other cases of featherbedding involve deliberate slowdowns of the entire work force of a plant to limit production, and the insistence that only those persons deemed qualified by a union be permitted to perform certain tasks.

Significance   Featherbedding is a product of increasing unemployment resulting from automation (the substitution of automatic machines for human labor) and from economic stagnation and inflation. Job insecurity resulting from the use of machines has been a problem since the early days of the Industrial Revolution when French workers "sabotaged" the machines that threatened them by throwing their wooden shoes (*sabots*) into the works of the new machines. Although the Taft-Hartley Act of 1947 outlawed featherbedding in businesses and industries engaged in interstate commerce, many such practices remain. Featherbedding is difficult to deal with because it is not always easy to distinguish it from safety and other legitimate concerns of unions for their members. Labor leaders also defend it as a natural consequence of free enterprise. They point out that it cannot be distinguished from the actions of professionals, such as medical doctors and dentists, who limit competition by licensing systems, or from the businessperson who restricts production to keep prices high, or from the farmer who is paid under the price support system not to grow crops. Although management regards featherbedding as a serious impediment to production and as an encroachment on its right to determine work assignments, it often accepts featherbedding arrangements to avoid strikes. In the 1980s, new efforts to eliminate featherbedding to increase U.S. productivity and improve the nation's foreign trade posture are balanced by the growing concerns of workers for their jobs and increasing electronic automation of factories and offices.

Federal Executive Institute (FEI) (215)

A federal interagency executive development center created by presidential order in 1968. Currently operated by the Office of Personnel Mangement, the Federal Executive Institute (FEI) is located in Charlottesville, Virginia. Its programs are designed to meet the education and training needs of individual executives and their organizations, and to achieve professional excellence. Enrollment in the executive development programs is limited to supergrade federal executives, normally in the grade of GS-16 and higher, and it particularly attracts persons in the Senior Executive Service (SES). Participants are nominated by their agencies. Although the requirements of the SES are a special focus of the Institute, its programs are also intended to serve executives at comparable levels in state and local governments and in the military services. The basic goals of the Federal Executive Institute are (1) to promote active appreciation of the values of American constitutional democracy; (2) to foster an understanding of, and dedication to, the responsibilities of public servants in a pluralistic and dynamic society; (3) to develop the executive's ability to provide leadership; and (4) to facilitate the acquisition of knowledge relevant to the executive's political, social, and economic environments. There are four main program categories designed to accomplish these goals: (1) the Senior Executive Education Program is a seven-week residential program designed for federal executives who have had extended experience in government; (2) the three-week Executive Leadership and Management Program is designed for executives about to enter the SES; (3) special programs lasting one week or less address current public management issues, such as organization development and team building, for select groups; and (4) special alumni "follow-on conferences" are conducted for alumni about six months after graduation and again several years later. The Federal Executive Institute considers three main areas of study to be central to executive development. These are (1) an organization's internal and external environment; (2) management systems and processes; and (3) management practices and behavior. These concerns are dispersed throughout the programs in a number of different approaches to adult learning. The Institute's pedagogical premises are the need for the individual student to assume the major responsibility for learning, and the need for the learner to apply his or her knowledge to immediate and actual situations. Each program includes self-evaluation activities, forums, workshops, field trips, and individual projects. See also CIVIL SERVICE REFORM ACT OF 1978, 199.

Significance The Federal Executive Institute represents a commitment by the federal government to meet the demands of high executive responsibility at all levels of government. The establishment of the Institute in 1968 was the result of President Lyndon B. Johnson's Executive Order 11348 of 1967 which encouraged the Civil Service Commission to work more actively with agency heads to develop in-service personnel training programs. Regional training centers also developed from this impetus. Education and training centers similar to the Federal Executive Institute for middle-range public managers have been established in New York, California, Delaware, and Tennessee. The Civil Service Reform Act of 1978 reinvigorated FEI programs with its emphasis on the need for executive improvement, its financial incentives for good public management, and its location of rank in the person rather than in the position in the newly created Senior Executive Service. The indifference of some federal agencies to the purposes of the Federal Executive Institute was at least temporarily arrested.

Flextime (216)
A flexible work schedule that allows an employee some degree of freedom in selecting starting and quitting times. Flextime is based on the assumption that in many work situations rigid starting and stopping times are unnecessary and can be adapted into a more flexible system. Flextime consists of a core time, during which all employees are to be present, and a flexible band which is determined by the employee. The core time is generally a period of four to six hours in the middle of the traditional work schedule. It coincides with the periods of greatest activity in the agency or business: from 9:00 A.M. to 3:00 P.M., for example. Flexible time allows workers to

Personnel Administration

determine their starting and quitting times as long as they are present during the core hours. Under flextime, an agency may be open from 7:00 A.M., to 6:00 P.M., with all employees present from 9:00 A.M. to 3:00 P.M., arriving between 7:00 and 9:00 A.M. and departing between 3:00 and 6:00 P.M.

Significance   Flextime was developed in West Germany in the early 1960s to alleviate a serious labor shortage by inducing housewives and mothers into the work force. Its use in the United States began in 1972. The net effect of flextime is a reduction of absences and an increase in productivity. Workers do not need to use sick days and personal leave days to conduct personal business. Employees are able to work in tune with their biological clocks and usually choose times during which they can work most productively. Overtime hours are often reduced with use of flextime, resulting in monetary savings for the agency or business. Flextime encourages employees to acquire additional skills so that job coverage is maintained. This not only contributes to job enrichment, but provides a reserve pool of talent for the employer. In general, flextime improves labor relations because employees are given a larger role in determining their own time schedules, previously a sole prerogative of management. Critics charge that flextime requires much additional planning of work schedules and, over a period of years, leads to abuses of the system by the work force.

Fringe Benefits (217)
Nonmonetary employee benefits and services that are designed to reinforce loyalty to the employer. Fringe benefits are part of a larger reward system including pay and promotion, but fringe benefit packages are considered nontaxable income. An expansive program of fringe benefits challenges money as a job motivator. Current areas of fringe benefit expansion are pay for time not worked, subsidized insurance, subsidized retirement, pension portability, educational benefits, periodic cost-of-living increases to pensioners, yearly physical examinations, longer vacations, group purchasing plans, employee retraining programs, custodial care, optional retirement at age 55, flexible work periods, more generous time off for socially desirable pursuits, counseling for personal investments and family problems, employer-sponsored scholarships, on-the-job training, leisure-time services, packaged vacations, and sabbatical leaves. Fringe benefit programs equal about one-third, and can total as much as one-half, of total compensation costs for individual employees. They have been

increasing at about double the rate of pay increases. *See also* COMPENSATION, 206.

Significance Fringe benefits have become a part of social custom in modern personnel administration. Some employers provide them to keep unions out, or to keep unions weak, or because unions have won the benefits. Fringe benefits are frequently provided as a result of government requirements. These requirements include workers' compensation, unemployment compensation, and social security. A basic policy question many public and private organizations face is whether to follow general fringe benefit practice as it develops, or to become a leader in one or more developing areas of fringe benefits. Since fringe benefit costs are substantial, an organization that initiates a new benefit might have the advantage of developing ways to have employees share the benefit's cost. Personnel administrators frequently emphasize fringe benefits as tax-free pay. Organizations that want to hold their employees over long periods of time and have low turnover have found that employees are more responsive to fringe benefits than to monetary incentives. Management expert Robert M. Fulmer estimates that by 1990 employees will probably have all medical and dental costs taken over by paternal employers. He further predicts that fringe benefits and "human fulfillment" wants will merge to the extent that the American worker in both public and private sectors will emphasize psychological and social needs more than subsistence needs, and that a guaranteed annual wage will allow that development. Fulmer and the Council on Trends and Perspective of the Chamber of Commerce of the United States believe that fringe benefits will mean the eventual end of the wage-salary difference in all U.S. employment. The growth of benefit programs, especially income security programs and short work week provisions, has laid the groundwork for a shift to salary status for workers who have been paid by the hour throughout their employment history.

General Schedule (GS) (218)

The device utilized for position classification in the federal classified civil service. The General Schedule provides a rank and salary designation for each position in the classified service. Ranks range from GS-1 to GS-18, and in 1987 salaries ranged from $9,339 to $84,157 per year. Individuals with only general or clerical skills are appointed at GS-1 through GS-4 levels, whereas college graduates and others with experience in skilled job categories usually receive appointment at GS-5 or GS-7 levels. Those with graduate training and/or extensive experience may receive appointment at GS-9 or

Personnel Administration

GS-11. Key management personnel typically rise to GS-13 to GS-15, and top-level decision makers are found in the GS-16 to GS-18 levels. Each General Schedule class has a pay schedule established by Congress, and annual salary increases are related to experience gained and the rate of inflation. *See also* CLASSIFIED SERVICE, 201; POSITION CLASSIFICATION, 234.

Significance The General Schedule is an application of the principle of position classification. At each level from GS-1 to GS-18, the general nature of positions that fall within that level are spelled out, required skills are specified, and duties to be performed are described. The General Schedule is an attempt to standardize job performance responsibilities and link them with pay schedules. In that way, two individuals performing similar tasks in different agencies receive equal pay for their work. The advantage of such systems is that subjective judgments by superiors in determining pay levels and increases is greatly reduced. The main disadvantage lies in the stagnant nature of the system, in that all individuals in one GS grade are placed on much the same level, a situation that discourages initiative and excellence in job performance. Congress has attempted to keep GS levels equal in pay to similar job categories found in private employment.

Hatch Acts (Political Activities Acts of 1939 and 1940) (219)

Major laws enacted by Congress to protect government employees from partisan political pressures and to limit political contributions and spending. The First Hatch Act of 1939 applied limitations on political activity to federal civil service personnel, and the Second Hatch Act of 1940 extended them to state and local employees working on projects supported by federal funds. Although provisions of the two laws were not made applicable to politically appointed officers, all other "executive officers" were prohibited from taking "any active part in political management or in political campaigns." The Hatch Acts also prohibit political leaders from applying pressure on welfare recipients or from engaging in other forms of political intimidation. Individuals and companies working under contract for the federal government are forbidden to contribute to political campaigns or to candidates for office. No attempt may be made under the Hatch Acts to obtain political support by promising or threatening to deny employment on any project supported by federal funds. Moreover, government employees may not serve as party officials, circulate nominating petitions, solicit campaign funds, work in a partisan campaign, seek election to a partisan office, endorse candidates, transport voters to the polls, count ballots, or serve as a delegate to a party convention. In addition to provisions that attempted to limit political activity, the Second Hatch Act severely limited the size of political contributions and spending in campaigns. Those provisions, however, were repealed by new limitations set forth in the Federal Election Campaign Act of 1972. There have been two notable challenges to the constitutionality of the First Hatch Act. In *United Public Workers v. Mitchell* (330 U.S. 75: 1947), the Supreme Court upheld the removal of civil service personnel from their jobs for taking an active role in political campaigning. In 1973, in *Civil Service Commission v. National Association of Letter Carriers, AFL-CIO* (413 U.S. 548), the Court again upheld the First Hatch Act's provisions aimed at keeping politics out of the federal personnel system. The Supreme Court also found the Second Hatch Act to be constitutional in its application of limits on political activities in a case that involved state government employees working on projects financed in part by federal grants-in-aid (*Oklahoma v. United States Civil Service Commission*, 330 U.S. 127: 1947), but in 1974 Congress repealed it.

Significance The Hatch Acts have contributed much to the long-running campaign to clean up the U.S. electoral system and to establish an efficient personnel system based on meritorious performance rather than political service. Before 1939, civil service personnel were hounded by political leaders and pressured into contributing time and money to campaigns and party service as a condition of retaining their jobs. Others who voluntarily participated often received special considerations for tenure, promotion, raises, and better working conditions from their politically motivated bosses. In many ways, prior to 1939 the civil service operated in a manner quite similar to the spoils system it supposedly had replaced. Critics of the two supreme Court decisions, however, argue that the Hatch Acts have denied basic political rights to government employees. In a democratic system of government, they point out, all citizens should have the basic right to participate in political activity that leads to the selection of the individuals and policies by which they will be governed. Such criticism has led Congress in the 1980s to consider changing the basic provisions that have removed federal employees from partisan activity.

Hay System (220)

A way of conducting studies of job content and salary ranges in public agencies for the purpose of developing salary plans that will be internally equitable and externally competitive with similar positions in both the public and private sectors. The Hay System begins with the completion of questionnaires by employees so that the duties of each position can be accurately defined. Staff members from Hay Associates, a private personnel firm, join with representatives from the agency being evaluated to form a review committee. Quantitative values are assigned to the basic components of the personnel system being studied. The main components are (1) know-how; (2) problem solving; (3) accountability; and (4) working conditions. Following the review committee evaluation, each position is given a numerical rating through the use of the Hay-Guide Chart Profile. The review committee then evaluates the agency's current salary plan in relationship to the new job descriptions. Finally, a new salary plan is drawn up by the committee. The agency may accept all or part of the plan, or it may reject the plan entirely. *See also* PUBLIC PERSONNEL ADMINISTRATION, 238.

Significance The Hay System is basically a job content and salary plan evaluation. As a guide for public personnel systems, its strength lies in its procedures and objectives. Personnel affected by the system participate directly in the process, and every effort is made to make the final evaluation equitable in comparison to other public and private organizations. Critics charge that the system is too subjective and does not provide rewards for employee initiative and leadership. The Hay System has been used in a variety of public agencies over the past ten years.

Impasse Resolution (221)

A term used in collective bargaining to describe techniques aimed at avoiding a strike when negotiations have broken down. Impasse resolution methods used in government are the same as those in industry: (1) mediation; (2) fact finding; and (3) arbitration, either voluntary or compulsory. *Mediation* is the logical first step in trying to resolve an impasse. It is the effort of a third party, usually a single person, to persuade the disputants to come to an agreement. The mediators are frequently supplied by either a state government agency or by the Federal Mediation and Conciliation Service. *Fact finding* is the method most used in an impasse resolution of public service deadlocks. Fact finding is a judicial process, in which a single person, panel, or board holds formal hearings and the parties present evidence supporting their positions. Following procedures specified by law, fact finders then make public reports of their conclusions and recommendations for a settlement. *Arbitration* is also a judicial process, with arbitrators holding formal hearings and weighing the evidence, just as fact finders do. Arbitration may be voluntary or compulsory. Voluntary arbitration occurs when the parties agree to pledge themselves in advance to accept the recommendations of the arbitrators as binding. Under compulsory arbitration, the law mandates arbitration, binds the parties to accept the recommendations of the arbitrators, and forbids strikes. Eighteen states have compulsory arbitration laws. Most apply to police and firefighters, or to other essential public employees, such as prison guards. Impasse is a fact of life in collective bargaining, and the methods of impasse resolution are frequently used. *See also* COLLECTIVE BARGAINING, 203; *UNITED FEDERATION OF POSTAL CLERKS V. BLOUNT* (1971), 250.

Significance Impasse is often declared in contract negotiations because either or both parties believe they can benefit from third party intervention. The methods of impasse resolution also provide both sides with additional channels of communication that may be more effective than face-to-face negotiations. They frequently provide the stimulus that leads to a settlement. Yet, it is also true that the availability of third party mechanisms tends to weaken the collective bargaining process. For this reason it is not uncommon for mediators and fact finders to return the dispute to the parties for a resumption of direct negotiations. Of the three methods used—mediation, fact finding, and arbitration—fact finding has produced a remarkable record of success in states such as New York and Wisconsin. To some extent, this is because fact finders function also as mediators in many cases. Advocates of compulsory arbitration argue that it is necessary to keep disputes from going on indefinitely, and bringing appreciable harm to the public. Compulsory arbitration, however, has historically been opposed by unions in both the public and private sector. Unions in particular resist compulsory arbitration because they believe it discourages honest, good faith collective bargaining. In fact, both parties tend to hold back on concessions, fearing that their positions with the arbitrator will be jeopardized. The unions argue that, under compulsory arbitration, wage and benefit decisions affecting tax rates are made, not by elective officials, but by private parties who often do not live in the community and have no investment in it. Impasse resolution methodologists are now experimenting with two new techniques. One is *final offer* arbitration, whereby the parties each submit their final offers to arbitrators, who have only the option to select one or the other. The other new technique is referral to the voters for decision. For example, the San Francisco city charter now provides that, when an impasse develops, the city's Civil Service Commission must prepare a pay plan based on the union's last demands. This pay plan is then submitted to the voters for a decision at a general or special election within sixty days.

Internship (222)

An employment situation in which an advanced college student gains supervised practical experience while employed in a professional administrative position. An internship facilitates the transition between classroom theory and everyday practice by bridging the gap between the academic and the professional world for a fledgling administrator. There are various types of internships available at federal, state, and local levels. At the federal level, the Presidential Management Intern Program was created by President Jimmy Carter in August 1977, to provide persons completing graduate degrees in public administration with two-year appointments to developmental positions in federal agencies. The purpose of the Presidential Management Intern Program was "to attract to federal service men and women of exceptional management potential who have received special training in planning and managing public programs and policies." Responsibility for administering the program was assigned to the United States Civil Service Commission, now the Office of Personnel Management (OPM). In implementing the president's directive, the OPM has asked for nominations from interested communities, graduate school faculty members, deans and directors, federal managers, and state and local officials. Approximately half of the nation's states are served by some type of public sector management internship program. A survey of state internship programs revealed four basic objectives: (1) meaningful work assignments for academic studies; (2) high-quality work for an agency; (3) a recruitment source for the agency; and (4) the completion of public policy assignments. Program responsibility for state internships rests in a variety of places: (1) the governor's office; (2) personnel or administration departments; (3) a consortium of state colleges; (4) a bipartisan state commission; and (5) individual state agencies. Means of compensating student interns include (1) paid salary or stipend; (2) college credits in lieu of salary; (3) salary plus college credit; and (4) tuition plus college credits. *See also* COMPENSATION, 206; ON-THE-JOB TRAINING, 230.

Significance   The internship is considered by most public managers as an investment in the future, a way of reducing the front-end costs of learning the labyrinthine byways of complex organizations. Public administration professionals have made a major commitment to the idea, because direct benefits often occur to an agency, to the student, and to the school sponsoring the student. The host organization may get a sophisticated project done at low cost. The intern's fresh perspective and classroom talents may occasion an organizational analysis for the agency, not only about its mission, but also about the "skill mixes" of the people it wishes to hire. The intern gains insight into the world of administration, assesses his or her current skill inventory, and perhaps gains or reaffirms a career path. The intern may also secure a job in the host agency after graduation. The school's most concrete gain is perhaps the testing of its curriculum through the feedback that a group of interns may provide. The school therefore tries to achieve the best match between what *is* taught and what *should be* taught. When interns come back to class, they often help other students relate to the real world of administration. If a school's interns do well in the field, they advertise the strength of the school's program and increase the market value of its graduates. An internship program affords students an opportunity to gain on-the-job experience and gives public agencies an opportunity to recruit talented, motivated, and experienced employees.

Job Description (223)

A list of tasks required in an individual position. A job description is normally prepared by a personnel manager as new positions are established. From a job description, a position is classified in terms of its duties and responsibilities, but not in terms of the person filling the position. The development and operation of a classification system, the determination of lines of promotion, and the application of the principle of equal pay for equal work all depend on the adequacy of the information regarding individual positions. Job description information is of three basic kinds: (1) information concerning the duties of the position, including the tasks ordinarily assigned to the incumbent; (2) information concerning the responsibilities of the position, including the degree of supervision under which the work of the position is performed and the extent to which the exercise of independent judgment is required; and (3) information concerning the knowledge and skill necessary for adequate performance of the duties of the position. The fundamental data for a job description are gathered by personnel managers through interviewing organization heads, administrators, and supervisors, and by studying the individual positions. The latter procedure is most frequently done by surveying employees—by asking them to describe their actual duties and responsibilities. The questionnaire method is widely used. A job description analyzes the nature of the work, the knowledge required to do it, its complexity, how it is carried out, what supervision is exercised by others over it, and what responsibility for the work of others is inherent in the position described. See also GENERAL SCHEDULE (GS), 218; POSITION CLASSIFICATION, 234.

Significance A job description for certain positions, such as junior clerk, can be made quite objectively. But in positions where the amount of discretion and supervisory responsibility or level of difficulty of scientific work are in question, the process becomes highly subjective. Beyond the GS-7 level, job descriptions in the federal service tend to be general and not particularly useful. The following description of an Economist (GS-11) position illustrates this point. The position requires ". . . difficult and responsible work requiring considerable training and experience and the exercise of independent judgment." Who judges what the word "considerable" means in evaluating the credentials of an applicant for this position? Can "independent judgment" be accurately predicted? Job descriptions and related position classification procedures obviously must leave some latitude and discretionary authority to personnel managers in most agencies of government.

Job Enrichment (224)

An employee motivation technique that uses job redesign strategies aimed at providing employees with more responsibility, more autonomy, and a greater sense of accomplishment. Job enrichment is based on the work of industrial psychologist Frederick Herzberg and other human motivation theorists who pioneered the concept that superior and sustained employee performance can only occur if the job itself is designed to elicit self-motivation. The job must include opportunities for achievement, recognition, responsibility, and career growth. Herzberg distinguished job *enrichment* from other efforts at job redesign such as job *enlargement* and job *rotation*. But the terms have since come to be used interchangeably, and contemporary job enrichment programs include aspects of both job enlargement and job rotation. There are several aims of job enrichment: (1) to create a natural and complete work unit by abolishing the assembly-line mentality and forming teams to complete an entire task, thus contributing to a sense of accomplishment; (2) to remove unnecessary controls and allow workers more say over how, when, and where the work gets done; (3) to provide feedback to workers as part of the accountability process, to let them know if their performance has improved, deteriorated, or remained the same; and (4) to introduce new and more difficult tasks as workers gain experience, thus allowing career growth. Job enrichment is classified as either horizontal or vertical. *Horizontal* job enrichment is characterized by an increasing variety of functions performed at a given level. As an intermediate step, it serves to reduce boredom and broaden the employee's perspective, thereby preparing him or her for *vertical* enrichment. Vertically enriching jobs enable employees to take part in the planning and control functions previously restricted to persons in supervisory and staff functions. The ideal job enrichment program requires a participatory management system and an organizational structure similar to organization theorist Rensis Likert's concept of linking-pin supervision. Linking-pin supervision uses the team approach with the supervisor having an overlapping group membership with the worker team and the management team. It also requires a thorough analysis of the task and a determination that both the task and the employee can benefit from a job enrichment program. Not all employees can benefit from job redesign. Well-planned efforts may boomerang if apathetic workers choose to seek achievement and recognition outside the job. See also PARTICIPATIVE MANAGEMENT, 110.

Significance Job enrichment represents a potentially powerful strategy for change. It can help public organizations achieve goals of efficiency and high work quality, while simultaneously meeting the needs of employees for a more meaningful work life. Enrichment programs have grown more rapidly in the private sector than in the public sector, however. The problems of job enrichment in the public sector include the difficulty of effecting such programs under civil service rules and the difficulty of achieving a flexible, employee-oriented work system within rigid bureaucratic procedures operating strictly from the top down. A related concern is the need to consider how clients are likely to be affected by job enrichment changes, and what developmental activities need to be undertaken before beginning work on the targeted jobs themselves. Some of the most successful job enrichment programs have involved the Swedish corporations of Volvo and Saab-Scania, and the American Telephone and Telegraph Corporation (AT&T). Findings in all three corporations indicate that quality of work, turnover, and absenteeism improved dramatically under job enrichment programs.

Manpower (225)

The total quantitative and qualitative store of human assets in a society. Manpower, sometimes referred to as "personpower," is an economic and social resource taking into account that human beings are active agents who accumulate capital, exploit natural resources, build social, economic, and political organizations, and carry forward national development. Human resources are an aspect of the wealth of nations. Manpower has always been a vital economic resource, yet as a result of industrialization the understanding of manpower has undergone significant shifts. Industrialization transferred labor to the production and distribution of goods. Emphasis has currently shifted from goods production to services, and from blue-collar to white-collar employment. Consequently, the most rapidly growing occupations over the past twenty years have been those that required the most formal education and training. Manpower development and planning became a priority undertaking for both the public and private sectors in the late 1970s. It is pursued from the standpoint both of economic efficiency and social welfare. The *economic efficiency approach* concerns itself with manpower as a resource contributing to economic growth and overall well-being in the same sense as natural and capital resources. The *social welfare approach* looks on employment as a source of income for workers and their families, and as a determinant of social status in a work-oriented society. Historically, the United States government has played an active role in manpower development, emphasizing the social welfare approach. Through the passage of the Employment Act of 1946, the Area Redevelopment Act of 1961, the Manpower Development Act of 1962, and the Comprehensive Employment and Training Act of 1973, government programs provided education, training, work experience, and employment for the disadvantaged and unemployed. The other dimension of manpower, economic efficiency, is illustrated by a description of manpower planning. Manpower planning is the process by which an organization ensures that it has the right number of people, and the right kind of people, in the right places, at the right time, doing the right things, to serve the purposes of the organization. Through implementation of manpower planning, an organization can continuously provide the level of goods and services required for it to survive. *See also* AFFIRMATIVE ACTION, 189.

Significance Manpower is the power of men and women to produce the goods and services necessary for a society or an organization to survive and prosper. In the United States, manpower policy is an important *public* policy, and many laws have been enacted in an attempt to prepare people for productive employment roles. The success of these policies can ultimately be measured by the degree to which they provide individuals with income and status. Unsuccessful manpower policies produce poverty, malnutrition, racial tensions, a deteriorating physical environment, and the most costly social disease of all, hopelessness. Most ideologies, such as capitalism and communism, contain ideas of how manpower can best be used to achieve the goals of society. In practice, however, even well-meaning ideological guidelines can be converted into dehumanizing actions that serve the narrow interests of an elite group.

Merit System (226)
The recruitment, appointment, retention, and promotion of government employees based on ability, education, experience, and job performance. Most merit systems operate as federal, state, and local career civil service systems that emphasize demonstrated fitness as the key personnel factor. Recruitment and selection of the "best qualified" applicant to fill a vacancy, job tenure, position classification, standardization of pay, and promotion and pay increases based on "performance" evaluations are hallmarks of the system. Various kinds of evaluation techniques and instruments have been devised to measure merit effectively, but none is scientifically accurate. The result is that merit systems cannot be "pure," and, because they are operated by human beings, they incorporate some measure of subjectivity and bias. Whereas civil service was originally aimed at keeping unqualified persons out of government service, with the adoption of the merit system it has become a positive approach. *See also* CIVIL SERVICE, 198; CLASSIFIED SERVICE, 201.

Significance A merit system rejects most of the typical criteria that are used in personnel systems in the absence of demonstrated fitness, such as politics, friendship, kinship, race, and religion. The only relevant question in a merit system is: How effectively can this person do the job? During most of the nineteenth century, the United States government operated on what was known as a "spoils system," with positions handed out to the party faithful after winning elections. In 1883 Congress enacted the Pendleton Act, which established the principle of merit in federal appointments through the creation of a civil service system headed by a Civil Service Commission. Although only 10 percent of federal employees were initially brought under the system, the merit principle prevailed, and over the years since 1883 more than 90 percent of all federal positions have been covered. In addition, many federal agencies operate merit systems outside civil service, including the Tennessee Valley Authority (TVA), the Federal Bureau of Investigation (FBI), the Central Intelligence Agency (CIA), and the Secret Service. After appointment, the main challenge to merit in pay and promotion considerations is the principle of seniority.

Personnel Administration

Merit Systems Protection Board (MSPB) (227)
The central appeals and review board that protects the integrity of federal merit systems and the rights of federal employees. The MSPB, along with the Office of Personnel Management (OPM), replaced the United States Civil Service Commission that had governed personnel matters in the national government since 1883. Created by a Reorganization Plan in 1978 as an independent review board, MSPB's authority and duties are prescribed by the Civil Service Reform Act of 1978, the same law that established the new OPM. Prior to the 1978 actions, an employee could appeal a supervisor's adverse decision to the Federal Employee Appeals Authority, to the Appeals Review Board, and to the Civil Service Commission. The 1978 Reform Act abolished these bodies and replaced them with the Merit Systems Protection Board which functions as an independent agency, exercising both investigatory and appellate functions. In carrying out its duties, the Board—headed by a chairperson—is involved in conducting special merit studies, hearing and deciding charges of wrongdoing, and taking corrective and disciplinary actions against an agency or an individual. An independent Special Counsel of the Board investigates and prosecutes officials and employees who violate civil service rules and regulations. *See also* CIVIL SERVICE REFORM ACT OF 1978, 199; OFFICE OF PERSONNEL MANAGEMENT (OPM), 229.

Significance In carrying out its appellate and investigatory functions, the Merit Systems Protection Board oversees the personnel practices of the entire federal government. Included in its surveillance are not only the classified civil service but various merit systems not included in civil service, such as the Foreign Service, the Federal Bureau of Investigation (FBI), and the Central Intelligence Agency (CIA). Each year the MSPB hears and decides hundreds of difficult cases involving infractions of federal law or of merit rules that have led to removals, suspensions, and demotions. Cases involving alleged discrimination have increased in recent years. In such cases, an employee or applicant for a federal job can ask the Equal Employment Opportunity Commission (EEOC) to review the Board's decision if he or she is adversely affected by it. The centralization of all merit personnel review and appeals functions in a single MSPB has helped to clarify employee rights and simplify the procedures for seeking remedies for abuses.

New York Bureau of Municipal Research (228)
A prototype of numerous municipal bureaus founded by philanthropic funds in the scientific management period of public personnel

administration, 1906–1937, to aid local officials in adopting more efficient administrative techniques. The New York Bureau of Municipal Research was founded in 1906 in recognition that, apart from national defense, almost 75 percent of public expenditures were at the local level. Since the functions of local government at that time were to provide routine physical services, such as garbage collection, fire protection, and water supplies, local government tasks were receptive to improved efficiency via the techniques of scientific management. Municipal research bureaus generated a concern in local government for planning, specialization, quantitative measurements, standardization, and the discovery of the "one best way" to perform a duty. The New York Bureau of Municipal Research is noted in the history of U.S. public administration for its advanced thinking on budgetary concepts. In 1913, for example, it made the revolutionary pronouncement that the budget could be used for more than merely controlling the public's fiscal accounts. Bureau officials urged "a classification of costs in as many different ways as there are stories to be told." The Bureau developed a threefold scheme of classifying expenditures: by administrative units, by functions, and by items. The scheme was ultimately rejected by the city on the grounds that adequate accounting information was not available. Yet the Bureau's arguments became the basis for performance budgeting at all levels of government in the 1940s and 1950s. The Bureau provided a link between the techniques and values of scientific management and everyday administration in the public sector. Bureau employees were enthusiastic developers of quantitatively oriented and detailed job descriptions, productivity measurements, training programs, examinations keyed to job-related abilities, and efficiency ratings. The New York Bureau of Municipal Research and its sister bureaus throughout the nation led the way in applying scientific methodology to administrative requirements in budgeting and personnel management. *See also* CIVIL SERVICE REFORM LEAGUE, 200; POLITICS-ADMINISTRATION DICHOTOMY, 70; PUBLIC PERSONNEL ADMINISTRATION, 238; SCIENTIFIC MANAGEMENT, 22.

Significance The New York Bureau of Municipal Research strengthened the politics-administration dichotomy already part of public administration doctrine at the time of the Bureau's founding in 1906. Public personnel administration was an area where quantitative, "hard-nosed" applications of efficiency theory could readily be tested. The effects of the Bureau's activity were to widen the scope of the merit system at all levels of government and to aid in the development of the city manager profession in the United States. Because of the efforts expended on the development of job descriptions, tests, and

Personnel Administration

measurements, the information basis for position classification was considerably broadened. It was only a matter of time until civil service extended control over public personnel systems through a system of position classification. Civil service regulations applied to fewer than 46 percent of the federal government's nonmilitary employees in the year 1900. By 1930, as a result of efforts by the Bureau and other groups in "selling" the idea of a merit system, almost 80 percent of federal civilian employees were under civil service. The New York Bureau of Municipal Research, firmly supported by other bureaus across the nation, supported the view that the city manager idea would lead to municipal administration which was expert, scientific, and efficient. The city manager would administer the policy formed by the city council in a manner that was removed from, unresponsive to, and even contemptuous of, local politics. The first city manager plan was adopted in 1914 on the basis of the arguments of the politics-administration dichotomy. The International City Management Association remains firm in the belief that public administration is separable from politics.

Office of Personnel Management (OPM)   (229)
The major personnel agency of the national government that administers the merit system for federal employment. The Office of Personnel Management was created by a reorganization plan in 1978 as an independent agency following enactment by Congress of the Civil Service Reform Act of 1978. Many of the functions of the former United States Civil Service Commission were transferred to OPM, and additional authority and duties are specified in the Reform Act. Ten regional offices around the country are used to carry out OPM programs, which include recruiting, examining, training, and promoting of federal employees on the basis of their knowledge and skills. Individuals who are in the civil service or seek employment are considered on the basis of merit regardless of their race, religion, sex, political influence, or other nonmerit factors. In addition, OPM conducts extensive personnel investigations, implements affirmative action programs, encourages employee development and training to improve performance of career personnel, makes incentive awards, and operates intergovernmental programs to improve personnel management in state, local, and Indian tribal governments. *See also* CIVIL SERVICE REFORM ACT OF 1978, 199; MERIT SYSTEMS PROTECTION BOARD (MSPB), 227.

Significance   The Office of Personnel Management, along with the Merit Systems Protection Board, replaced the Civil Service

Commission that had operated as the central federal personnel agency since 1883. Its main role is that of providing leadership in personnel administration by maintaining high standards for individual performance and in stimulating improvements in personnel methods used in all federal agencies. While the OPM makes basic policy and supervises personnel activities throughout the executive branch, each federal department and agency must carry out personnel management on a day-by-day basis. The OPM has continued the strong, independent role under the president's direction that characterized the operations of the Civil Service Commission. Its role, however, has become increasingly complex and controversial because of new problems that have arisen, such as the pressure to keep pay scales abreast of double-digit inflation, the difficulty of meshing policies that forbid any form of discrimination with those calling for special consideration under affirmative action guidelines, and the growing pressures for unionization of federal employees.

On-the-job Training (230)

A method of employee training in which a worker is placed directly in a work situation and learns the job and "tricks of the trade" from a supervisor or experienced worker. On-the-job training consists of an employee carrying out regularly assigned duties while receiving instruction in how to perform them. It is probably the most widely used method of training. Typically, on-the-job training is highly informal and consists of orientation about organizational rules and regulations as well as coaching about ways to correct mistakes the trainee may make in meeting the technical requirements of the job. Sometimes on-the-job training is supplemented by an additional formal training program. The skilled trades have used on-the-job training for many years. In this system an apprentice works under the observation of a journeyman, who offers advice on production techniques and characteristics of materials. The apprenticeship system has now been adapted to white-collar and professional positions, as well as maintaining its usefulness in traditionally blue-collar fields. *See also* INTERNSHIP, 222.

Significance On-the-job training is a method of employee indoctrination that does not require special schooling. The employing organization does not have to use money or expensive, time-consuming programs of formal, "canned" instruction. Neither does the employer gamble on employees who may leave the organization during, or at the end of, the instruction phase of their employment. On-the-job training means an employee does not have to go through a reorientation period from textbook to actual task once formal training is completed. When the employee learns the job, he or she is actually doing it. In many cases the employee is productively involved in the job long before he or she steps up from the "trainee" classification. Some organizations therefore have a tendency to exploit the training period to receive quality work at a much lower cost. Surveys of employees who have participated in various types of management training programs indicate that entry-level personnel strongly prefer on-the-job training to any other form of management training. The reasons most frequently given are "It gives me the opportunity to show what I can do," and, "I can learn what the organization's activities are really about." The surveys also show that on-the-job training for management positions is greatly enriched by in-house seminars, attendance at high-level meetings, access to privileged correspondence, guided reading, and rotation through related jobs. However, the key to success of on-the-job training is a quality trainee-mentor relationship.

Patronage (231)
The power vested in political leaders and elected officials to make partisan appointments and to confer licenses, contracts, franchises, honors, and other benefits on political supporters, friends, and relatives. The term and the practice of patronage originated in England in the fifteenth century. In the United States, patronage powers are wielded on the national level primarily by the president, cabinet members, agency heads, members and committees of Congress, and by federal judges. In the states, patronage awards are conferred mainly by the governors and other elected officials, by members of the legislature, by judges, and by state political leaders. In local governments, patronage is exercised by mayors, especially in strong-mayor systems, by judges, and by elected county officials. Often, on all levels, the official or political leader who dispenses patronage by selecting the appointees is not the one who makes the formal appointment. U.S. senators, for example, exercise broad patronage powers in their respective states under the rule of "senatorial courtesy," whereby the senior senator of the president's party selects the individuals who will be appointed by the president to federal positions in the state. *See also* PENDLETON ACT OF 1883, 232; SPOILS SYSTEM, 246.

Significance Although several of the early presidents had exercised limited patronage powers, an era of unrestrained partisanship in appointments began when Andrew Jackson assumed the presidency in 1829. Charged by political opponents with operating a "spoils system," Jackson defended it as "rotation in office." He held that government jobs were generally so simple that any citizen of average ability could manage them, and that frequent changes of personnel would tend to promote efficiency in the public service and keep employees from becoming infected with arrogance toward the public. The spoils system became entrenched, and patronage appointments reached a peak during the Civil War period. With the passage of the Pendleton Act (Civil Service Reform Act of 1883), patronage powers wielded by federal officials began to progressively decline, although there have been brief periods, such as the early New Deal years of the 1930s, when patronage appointments have increased. State and local patronage systems vary greatly, but the county and a few strong-mayor systems in large cities remain patronage strongholds. Defenders of patronage argue that the system strengthens parties and the political system while permitting executive and other elective officials to surround themselves with appointees they know and trust. Critics point out that appointments based on politics, friendship, or nepotism are likely to be inferior to merit-based appointments, and that other favors and rewards are a form of "honest" or "dishonest" graft and corruption.

Pendleton Act (Civil Service Reform Act of 1883) (232)
A major law enacted by Congress that ushered in a transition in the federal government's personnel system from a politically dominated, corrupt, and inefficient spoils sytem to a merit system based on professional competence. The Pendleton Act established the United States Civil Service headed by a Civil Service Commission (now the Office of Personnel Management [OPM] and the Merit Systems Protection Board [MSPB]) responsible for administering the system in the executive branch. Major changes ushered in by the act included (1) establishing a merit system based on recruitment, competitive examination, political neutrality, and job tenure; (2) permitting the president to expand the personnel placed under the protection of civil service from approximately 15 percent of federal employees in the 1880s to a current figure in excess of 90 percent; and (3) initiating a unique "open" personnel system whereby individuals can move from positions in the private sector to civil service jobs (lateral entry) and back again to private employment, thus providing flexibility and maximizing opportunity and expertise.
See also CIVIL SERVICE, 198; CIVIL SERVICE REFORM ACT OF 1978, 199; MERIT SYSTEM, 226.

Personnel Administration

Significance The Pendleton Act began a process of replacing the spoils system that had been brought into the national government in the 1820s by President Andrew Jackson. By 1883, the voting public was thoroughly disappointed, even outraged, by the blatantly political abuses that typified the federal personnel system. Two other factors—the assassination of President James Garfield by a rejected officeseeker and an effort by the Republican majority in Congress to oblige the public and at the same time ensure that Republican officeholders would remain in their jobs—contributed to the passage of the reform act. The basic principle embodied in the Pendleton Act—that the federal personnel system should be based on merit—served as a beacon which led the states and many local units of government to establish civil service merit systems. Although a number of major civil service acts have been passed by Congress since 1883, including the Ramspeck Act of 1940 and the Civil Service Reform Act of 1978, the Pendleton Act remains the basic personnel law governing the federal bureaucracy.

Performance Appraisal (233)

An evaluation of an employee's progress or lack of progress measured in terms of job effectiveness. Performance appraisal was first used systematically by industrialist Robert Owen in 1800. Owen used "character books" and "character blocks" at his cotton mills in New Lanark, Scotland. The character books recorded each worker's daily reports of production. The character blocks were wooden objects of various colors displayed at each worker's station to signify whether the worker was a "good" or "bad" person. There are two primary reasons performance appraisal systems are used in modern personnel administration in both the public and private sectors: (1) evaluations help clarify what is expected of the employee and, used properly, strengthen and improve employee performance; and (2) evaluations aid the personnel administrator in refining and validating personnel methods and techniques, and they help establish an objective basis for personnel decisions. Types of performance appraisals include person-to-person comparisons, production records, rating schedules, graphic ratings scales, the critical incident method, and open-ended narrative appraisals. Most public personnel administrators use more than one method simultaneously. Most also use a participative approach in the setting of standards, as well as in the evaluation process itself. Without the full understanding, participation, and acceptance of the employees being appraised, the process will have limited value. Public personnel administrators have also learned to develop rating systems for each general category of work, rather than applying the same system throughout the organization. The most reliable systems of performance appraisal reporting are those in which supervisors cite and measure specific performance compared to stated job demands. *See also* PUBLIC PERSONNEL ADMINISTRATION, 238; PUBLIC PERSONNEL SYSTEMS, 239.

Significance Performance appraisal is perhaps the most difficult area of personnel administration. Yet, from management's perspective, it is necessary to allocate resources, reward employees, provide feedback for employees, and maintain fair relationships and communication bonds. The primary difficulties in establishing performance appraisal systems are (1) finding ways to evaluate and report performance which are meaningful and useful in their impact on the work to be done; and (2) finding ways to implement the evaluation process and apply its results, knowing the process itself is a major factor in employee motivation and morale. The experienced administrator regards the appraisal process as an opportunity to discuss openly with the employee his or her progress and the possibilities for improvement. The performance appraisal is most appropriately used for diagnostic purposes, not for punishment by demotion or dismissal. The evaluation interview should always be held separately from a wage increase interview. If not separated, the two purposes can put the manager into conflicting roles. It is difficult for the manager to act simultaneously as performance counselor and wage arbiter. Performance appraisal can be a great asset to an organization. If, however, the manager waters down the evaluation, its significance, or the impact of the employee's input, it can become routine and meaningless drudgery.

Position Classification **(234)**
The clustering of government jobs according to their nature, qualifications required, duties performed, and responsibilities assumed. Position classification is used to provide equal pay for equal work for government employees. In the federal civil service, a General Schedule (GS) is used to classify jobs according to their nature and the pay involved from GS-1 to GS-18, with the pay at the highest level approximately tenfold greater than at the lowest level. *See also* GENERAL SCHEDULE (GS), 218; MERIT SYSTEM, 226.

Significance Position classification is an attempt to deal fairly with all employees by establishing standardized categories with extensive job descriptions for each. One of the objectives underlying the system is that of maintaining morale among employees by providing for equal treatment. Position classification also aids in recruitment and hiring by permitting the use of standardized tests to determine qualifications. Within each classification, promotion to a higher class and merit pay are utilized to encourage excellence in performance. Position classification also provides for clear lines of authority and responsibility and facilitates the operations of a hierarchical and structured organization. Merit systems utilizing some form of position classification are commonplace today in federal, state, and local personnel administration.

Productivity (235)

Efficiency in producing goods or services, or the ratio between the units produced or services provided by an organization (*output*) and the resources consumed in production (*input*) during a specified period of time. Productivity indexes measure the efficiency of an organization over a period of time by comparing the current output-input ratio with that of a previous base. The Joint Financial Management Improvement Program (JFMIP) is dedicated to increasing productivity in federal departments and agencies. Each organization participating in the JFMIP, with the technical assistance of the Bureau of Labor Statistics (BLS), can identify the output measures that are most meaningful for its own operation. Consistent with BLS productivity measures for the private sector, the input factor is limited to labor. Productivity, then, is expressed in terms of output per staff year. Productivity indexes are generally constructed so that they measure efficiency of producing products or services with no change in the level of quality or effectiveness during the period being measured. *See also* ACCOUNTABILITY, 85; COST-BENEFIT ANALYSIS, 35; PERFORMANCE APPRAISAL, 233.

Significance Productivity has become "the very hottest new word" among many of the nation's public administrators. Enthusiasm for the concept is facilitated by the fact that at the abstract level everyone is for productivity. It seems to be a simple and uncomplicated concept—but it is not. One of the problems facing the public productivity movement is the assumption that everyone shares a common definition of the term. Most authors who write about productivity discuss it from perspectives rooted in such diverse subject areas as measurement, labor relations, training and development, management, budget, and finance. Academicians and practitioners specializing in each of these areas tend to have different interests, views, and opinions from their counterparts in each of the other areas. Consequently, they define productivity in different ways. There is no commonly shared definition. Productivity tends to be intertwined with the concepts of efficiency, savings, cutbacks, measurement, effectiveness, and performance. The result is considerable confusion. The difficulty with measuring most government services is that the measures of the amount of work being done do not adequately reflect the "real" service being provided. Output indicators such as the number of tons of paving materials used—or the number of potholes patched—are useful measures of work accomplishment, but they indicate nothing about the effectiveness of the service, that is, the resulting condition of the streets. The "number of clients treated" in a health and rehabilitation program does not necessarily indicate how many people are actually helped. The measurement of efficiency requires that product *quality* be considered. How meaningful can the "cost per ton of waste collected" be unless it considers the quality of the output? A reduction in unit cost achieved at the expense of a reduction in service quality would not be a true efficiency improvement. Has the service become degraded, through excessive spillage? Has a shift from backdoor to curb collection taken place? Similarly, increases in the "number of arrests per police officer" may not mean increased efficiency, if the percentage of arrests failing to lead to conviction because of police error is going up. Productivity equations must include quality factors as well as numbers.

Progressive Discipline (236)

A concept in public personnel administration referring to the initial use of the least severe measure of disciplinary action needed to correct unacceptable behavior. Progressive discipline provides for an increase in the penalty with each subsequent offense. Some first offenses are severe enough to curtail this process and result in an application of the most severe form of discipline available. The various steps which can be used to discipline are informal talk or counseling; oral reprimand or warning; written reprimand or warning; suspension or disciplinary layoff; demotion or transfer; and discharge. (1) *Informal talk or counseling* is used for minor first-time infractions. A friendly discussion will often clear up the problem. The supervisor explains what is expected from the employee and allows the employee to express his or her views. The discussion is documented. If desired results are not forthcoming, the next step is taken by the supervisor. (2) *Oral reprimand or warning* is generally used for second offenses or more severe first-time rule violations. The employee is told the interview is an oral reprimand. Previous violations are mentioned. The employee is told that his or her behavior could lead to serious disciplinary action if not corrected. The employee is left with the feeling that he or she must improve in the future. The interview is documented. (3) *Written reprimand or warning* is a letter or memorandum written to the employee listing prior incidents, specifics on what behavior is expected, how the employee is not meeting the expectations, what will happen if the behavior is not corrected, and a period of time for correcting the behavior. A copy of the letter is placed in the employee's file. (4) *Suspension or disciplinary layoff* occurs if the behavior is not corrected. The employee is suspended or laid off for one to thirty days. This is the final step that attempts to correct behavior before discharge. This step may also be used pending investigation of a serious charge that may result in dismissal. (5) *Demotion or transfer* is generally not used as a disciplinary step in rule violation. It is used for failure by the employee to perform at an acceptable level. (6) *Discharge* is the most drastic form of disciplinary action. It is reserved for the most severe offenses and is taken after other corrective efforts have failed. The employee is notified of the supervisor's intent to recommend dismissal. *See also* SEPARATION FROM SERVICE, 245.

Significance Progressive discipline is corrective in nature, not punitive. It is a reasoned approach that ties the severity of the discipline to the severity of the offense. The employee can be less severely disciplined for minor offenses, and it is possible to keep a relatively good working relationship between the supervisor and the employee. Employees are a valuable resource and, most often, it is worth the effort to retain them by attempting to correct unacceptable behavior. Challenges to discipline by the employee are usually based on "just cause." Just cause means the employer had or did not have justifiable reason to take the action that he or she took. Just cause does not exist if either the employee did not commit the violation, which means any discipline was unjustified, or the discipline was excessive, or the employee indeed committed the violation but should not be disciplined because the organization had not disciplined the offense in the past. The proper use of progressive discipline reduces the impact of such challenges as these.

Public Employee Unions (237)

Labor organizations of federal, state, and local governmental employees that engage in collective bargaining with agency heads and other governmental leaders. Public employee unions can operate only on an "open shop" basis, with union membership strictly voluntary. Collective bargaining by these unions involves such matters as working conditions, job security, and pension rights, but most public employees are not permitted to bargain collectively for wages and are prohibited by law from striking. The largest public union, the American Federation of State, County, and Municipal Employees (AFSCME), bargains on behalf of over 1 million workers and maintains an affiliation with the AFL-CIO. Other large public employee unions on the federal level include the American Federation of Government Employees (AFGE) and the National Association of Retired Federal Employees, the latter with a membership of almost a half million. Many state and local unions of public employees have also been formed in recent years. In many cases specialized groups, such as a state police unit, have become organized and engage in collective bargaining. Even some federal and state management officials who are too high in the bureaucracy to be eligible for union membership have organized "professional associations." The largest public employee unions on the local level are the teacher unions, headed by the National Education Association and its network of state and local associations. *See also* COLLECTIVE BARGAINING, 203; PUBLIC UNIONISM, 240.

Significance   Public employee unions evolved slowly for many years following the enactment of the Wagner Act in 1935—labor's Magna Carta—but the pace has greatly accelerated in the 1970s and 1980s. Developments leading government employees increasingly to form and join labor unions include heavy inflation, the threat of losing many jobs as the result of budget balancing and administrative reorganizations, and growing public hostility toward public employees. Nearly two-thirds of federal employee unions are white-collar workers, and most state union members are either white-collar workers or professionals. The most aggressive local unions are those whose employees are teachers in local schools, as reflected by the waves of teacher strikes in many states each fall. Although strikes by public employees are outlawed on all three levels of government, local unions and associations of police, firemen, teachers, and garbage collectors have often refused to report to work without a contract. Strike prohibitions are often circumvented by such tactics as those used by police units, referred to as "blue flu"—wherein most officers call in sick. Public employees suffer from insecurity about their jobs and working conditions particularly when changes in administrations occur as a result of elections. Most candidates for major offices have contributed to this psychological problem by making public employees bureaucratic scapegoats, largely or partly responsible for whatever has gone wrong. Public employee unions at all levels have generally performed more effectively as pressure groups and through lobbying than in negotiating collective bargaining agreements.

Public Personnel Administration (238)

Managing and developing policies for the body of persons in public employment. Public personnel administration (PPA) deals with "people problems" in the environment of public merit systems. Merit has not always been the environment of PPA, however, as the following analysis of the evolution of the field illustrates. Public administrationist Nicholas Henry divides the development of public personnel administration into six phases. Phase 1 (1789–1829) was the *Guardian Period*. This was the period of "government by gentlemen," to use Leonard D. White's term. President George Washington set the moral tone of the early federal bureaucracy by appointing men to office who were reputed to be persons of character as well as competence. Character was synonymous with merit, and merit from 1789 through 1829 meant a respected family background, a high degree of formal education, and substantial loyalty to the president. The public servant was a member of the establishment. Roughly 65 percent of the top-level federal appointees during the guardian period were drawn from the landed gentry, merchant, and professional classes, making the public service highly elitist in nature. Phase 2 (1829–1883) was the *Spoils Period*. Administrative historian Leonard D. White attributes the name of the period to a remark by United States Senator William L. Marcy of New York, who in 1832 commented that American politicians "see nothing wrong in the rule that to the victor belong the spoils of the enemy." The rationale of the spoils system was that if presidents were to emerge from the class that earned its own living—as Andrew Jackson had emerged in 1829—then politics had to be made to pay. This "democratization" of the public service meant that it became a system subject to bribes and graft. Appointive power was transferred from the gentry to political parties. Phase 3 (1883–1906) was the *Reform Period*. Reform of the spoils system was encouraged by two major developments in the year 1881: (1) the merger of thirteen state reform associations to form the National Civil Service Reform League; and (2) the assassination of President James A. Garfield by a dissatisfied officeseeker. In 1883, Congress passed the Civil Service Act (Pendleton Act), which created a bipartisan Civil Service Commission (replaced in 1978 by the Office of Personnel Management and the Merit Systems Protection Board). The Civil Service Commission was charged with the duty of filling government positions by a process of open, competitive examinations. In Phase 4, the *Scientific Management Period* (1906–1937), public administration in general and PPA in particular were decisively influenced by developments in business administration. Business administration at that time was dominated by the time-motion, scientific management school represented by Frederick W. Taylor and Frank and Lillian Gilbreth. The ultimate value of this period was *efficiency*, which was compatible with the concepts and structure of the civil service. During the reform period, efficiency had been associated with morality and lack of corruption and was "neutral." Public personnel administration in the scientific management period that followed combined goodness, merit, morality, neutrality, efficiency, and science into one conceptual whole. Phase 5 (1937–1955) was the *Administrative Management Period*. The New Deal brought a new view of government into focus and into practice. Government should be active, aggressive, and positive in trying to solve public problems. *Management* became the new goal of public personnel administration. This view implied that there was something more to PPA than mere efficiency. People in public service were perceived as having a political as well as an administrative function. The traditional politics-administration dichotomy was questioned, with "management" serving as something of a codeword to express this new dimension of PPA. Phase 6 (1955–present) was the *Professional Period*. As a result of the work of the second Hoover Commission, whose report was issued in 1955, public personnel administration entered a new phase of professionalism. The report indicated a new awareness of professional education as a contributing factor to government effectiveness. Although the report represented the high-water mark of the administrative management period, it also viewed management itself as a profession. Administrative management was perceived as an area of research and learning that was needed for good government regardless of the specialization of an agency. Public personnel administration today continues this "professional" approach. *See also* BROWNLOW COMMITTEE, 124; HOOVER COMMISSION, FIRST, 149; HOOVER COMMISSION, SECOND, 150; POLITICS-ADMINISTRATION DICHOTOMY, 70; PROFESSIONALISM, 20.

Significance   Public personnel administration accurately reflects the growth and development of public administration. In some ways, PPA *is* public administration in that the main conceptual battles fought over the years—for example, the spoils system, the politics-administration dichotomy, efficiency in government, civil service laws and regulations, and the characteristics of professionalism—have all been fought on personnel territory. Public personnel administration has developed to the point that there are now personnel directors in almost every agency of government. Rather than being staff appendages, these directors are a part of the centralized managements of the agencies themselves. People, it has been generally recognized, are the key to effective government.

Public Personnel Systems (239)
Organized arrangements established for the purpose of providing and maintaining public employees within government bureaucracies. Various types of public personnel systems currently function on all three levels of U.S. government. Public personnel systems are classified by public administrationist Frederick C. Mosher as (1) the political appointee system; (2) the general civil service; (3) the professional career system; and (4) the collective system. Each might be found operating simultaneously with one or more of the others in the same agency. The *political appointee system* is composed of "political executives" without tenure who are outside the civil service system. There are only about 6,500 of these policy-making positions in the federal service, and they have been called "the true nexus between politics and administration." The most noteworthy characteristics of political executives are their lack of job security and their high level of rank. The *general civil service system* is composed of white-collar, generally nonprofessional personnel who have tenure and who are administered according to traditional civil service practices. Its chief characteristic is the emphasis placed on the *position:* the description of its duties, responsibilities, requirements, and qualifications. The civil service system values the notions of neutrality, merit, and being removed from "politics." *Professional career systems* are made up of white-collar professional and paraprofessional personnel who are tenured, although not always in a legal sense. The main feature of professional career systems is the emphasis placed on the *person*, rather than on the position. High value is attached to professionalism, specialization, and expertise. The *collective public personnel system* refers to the unionization of government employees. This is a collective bargaining system composed primarily of blue-collar workers whose jobs are administered under the terms of agreements between management and the union. See also CIVIL SERVICE, 198; MERIT SYSTEM, 226; PROFESSIONALISM, 20; PUBLIC UNIONISM, 240.

Significance The four basic types of public personnel systems represent fundamental value differences in the practice of public personnel administration. The typologies also represent some stereotyped thinking about groups of men and women in the public employ. In 1966, the cabinet included six college professors and only two members with significant political experience. At the assistant secretary and deputy agency administrator level, political scientists Dean E. Mann and Jameson W. Doig found that 90 percent of this group in the Kennedy administration were college graduates rather than political hacks. The education level has risen with every administration since that of Franklin D. Roosevelt. Mann and Doig concluded that only 10 percent of their sample of 108 assistant secretaries were appointed by reason of service to party. Although this may be true at the federal level, however, the political appointeee system at the state and local levels is much less "executive" in tone. Here the political appointments are more an effort to pay off political debts. The governor of Oregon controls fewer than a dozen patronage jobs, while the governors of New York and Illinois have the power to make thousands of patronage appointments. The majority of these positions are below executive level, with clerical and lower positions going to party loyalists. The national government, the fifty states, and most of the larger cities depend mainly on the operations of civil service systems. Collective public personnel systems, however, have become quite typical on the state and local levels as police and fire units and many white-collar public employees have resorted to unionization to cope with new economic conditions. Public personnel systems have been a historic focus for the study of public administration. The concepts they represent have provided the substance for the subfield of public personnel administration.

Public Unionism (240)
A movement of public employees to form unions and associations that collectively bargain for public employee rights. Public unionism has progressed much more slowly in the United States than unionism in the private sector, but it had a period of rapid development in the 1960s and 1970s. Private sector unions were already a major social force in the late 1880s, but federal employees were not allowed to join unions until passage of the Lloyd-LaFollette Act of 1912. Presidents Theodore Roosevelt and William Howard Taft had issued executive orders in 1902, 1906, and 1909 severely limiting lobbying activities by federal employees. The Lloyd-LaFollette Act repealed these "gag orders" and gave federal postal employees not only the right to join unions and to petition Congress individually or collectively, but the right to receive in writing the reasons for all proposed demotions and dismissals. The framework for present-day public unionism was established by Executive Order 10988, issued by President John F. Kennedy in 1961. It established a clear-cut policy allowing all public employees to organize, to have their organizations accorded official recognition, to be consulted in the establishment of personnel policies and procedures, and, under specific conditions, to negotiate agreements with agency management on working conditions. The order continued the prohibition against strikes by federal employees. In 1969, President Richard M. Nixon issued Executive Order 11491, setting up both a multilateral collective bargaining system and a

Personnel Administration

Federal Labor Relations Council to decide major policy issues, authorize binding arbitration, and settle negotiation impasses. The principles of Executive Order 11491 were codified as Title VII of the Civil Service Reform Act of 1978. *See also* COLLECTIVE BARGAINING, 203; HATCH ACTS, 219; PUBLIC EMPLOYEE UNIONS, 237.

Significance Public unionism had a startling period of success beginning in 1961. Increases in public employee union membership exceeded 250 percent in the period 1961–1980, while government employment rose only 70 percent. Public unionism matched the equal rights movement as the dominant new development in managing public employees in the modern era. The largest union, composed almost entirely of government employees, is the American Federation of State, County, and Municipal Employees (AFSCME), an affiliate of the AFL-CIO. It is the single largest union in the AFL-CIO, with a 1987 membership of 1.1 million. It is also the sixth largest union in the nation, with a jurisdiction covering employees of states, territories, commonwealths, counties, districts, school boards, cities, towns, villages, "or other public authority, or any governmental subdivision, or any quasi-public agency, or any nonprofit or tax-exempt agency of a public, charitable, educational, or civic nature." AFSCME was founded in Wisconsin and was granted an international charter by the American Federation of Labor (AFL) in 1936. In 1959, Wisconsin became the first state to recognize the right of state employees to organize and bargain collectively. Another strong public employee union is the American Federation of Government Employees (AFGE), which was founded in 1932 and confines itself to organizing federal employees. It had a 1987 membership of 200,000. The two largest independent public employee unions, both of which are influential beyond their size, are the National Federation of Federal Employees (NFFE, with a 1987 membership of 52,000) and the National Association of Government Employees (NAGE, with a 1987 membership of 195,000). NFFE left the AFL in 1931. Today it serves "all civil employees of the federal government and of the District of Columbia except postal employees and those exclusively eligible to membership in any other existing national or international organization affiliated with the AFL." Founded in 1961, NAGE was originally a veteran's fraternal group in the Boston Navy Yard, but is now an independent union of civilian federal government employees with locals and members in military agencies, the Internal Revenue Service (IRS), the U. S. Postal Service, the Veterans Administration (VA), the General Services Administration (GSA), the Federal Aviation Administration (FAA), and other federal agencies, as well as state and local agencies. Its activities include direct legal assistance, information services, legislative representation, employment protection, and insurance coverage. Many observers consider NAGE to be the most influential union in federal employment. Altogether, about 1.9 million federal civilian workers are represented by recognized unions—almost 70 percent of total federal civilian employment.

Recruitment (241)
The process that ensures that an adequate number of qualified persons will apply for vacant positions in organizations. Recruitment is understood by some public administrators to include those policies that bring a potential public servant to the point of application. Others include application, examination, and placement as components of the overall government recruitment process. Recruitment may also include shifting an employee from one position to another within an agency or between two different agencies. Public personnel administrators believe a genuine merit system cannot be achieved without an effective and inclusive recruitment system, which includes open competition for available jobs regardless of one's political affiliation. The preamble of the Intergovernmental Personnel Act (IPA) of 1970 mandated recruitment, along with selection and advancement, on the basis of ability, knowledge, and skill. Initially, the merit system was designed to depoliticize the hiring of public servants, but its expectation was that good public employees would come forward on their own. As a result of the scientific management movement, a greater concern for developing an aggressive recruitment policy came about, whereby good candidates would be encouraged to apply. Older practices—such as examination fees, filing dates, limiting advertisements to post offices, and ignoring universities—were discarded. The modern approach to public personnel recruitment includes procedures commonly used in the private sector, such as utilizing the media, using mailing lists from vocational and educational institutions, circulating pamphlets, and developing a government career directory. *See also* AFFIRMATIVE ACTION, 189; MERIT SYSTEM, 226.

Significance Recruitment to the public service has had to face strong negative forces. One is a prevalent negative attitude toward "bureaucracy." Another is the inability of the public sector to compete with the salary scales of some private businesses. As a result of the Federal Salary Reform Act of 1970, however, federal salaries were set competitively with those in the private sector. There have also been self-imposed federal employment restrictions based on educational level, age, citizenship, residence requirements, credentials, and veterans' preference. Other barriers such as race and sex considerations have also been imposed. The Civil Rights Act of 1964 and the Equal Employment Opportunity Act of 1972 spawned affirmative action programs that encouraged the federal government to recruit actively from minority groups. Under court order, government examinations have been improved to measure more adequately a person's potential and ability, with less reliance on his or her educational credentials. One such test is a nonverbal aptitude test emphasizing one's ability to carry out a specific task and deemphasizing the white middle-class bias some critics charge is built into written tests. The importance of effective recruitment is illustrated by the fact that payroll costs for all levels of U.S. government, without benefits or pensions, currently come to over $90 billion each year. Some personnel specialists believe a new public personnel administration is evolving to spend these funds more wisely. Some forecast the end of traditional recruitment and selection procedures, with greater reliance being placed on internships, oral interviews, character and job reference checks, and intuition. These elements constitute what might be termed the quest for "true merit" in public service.

Removal Power (242)

The power exercised by executive and administrative officials to dismiss a public official from office. As a general rule, chief executives—the president, governors, and mayors—can remove any administrative official they have appointed. Exceptions to this rule include judges, civil service and merit system personnel, and members of independent agencies and commissions. Federal judges are appointed for life and can only be removed through the impeachment process. State and local judges appointed to fill vacancies typically remain in office for the duration of the term to which they have been appointed and must then stand for election. Members of independent agencies and commissions can be removed only for cause, including misfeasance or malfeasance in office. Civil service personnel can be separated from the service only for reasons and through processes provided by law. The removal power of most governors and mayors is weaker than that of the president because many state and local administrative officials are elected to office, and because in many states and cities the governor and the mayor share removal powers with the state senate and the city council, respectively. *See also* APPOINTMENT POWER, 191; SEPARATION FROM SERVICE, 245.

Significance The exercise of appointment and removal power is a key to efficient administration. Appointment powers make it possible for executive and administrative officials to surround themselves at the managerial levels with loyal officials and employees who are sympathetic with the objectives and operational methods of the appointing officials. Removal powers are important because they permit such officials to retain and enforce the system. Most such appointees serve at the pleasure of the chief executive, who can remove them for any reason, including political ones. Some presidents, for example, have been known to request, upon their appointment, letters of resignation from each cabinet officer and from other high level federal officials. Later, if the appointed official failed to measure up to expectations, the president simply would take out the resignation letter, date it, and publicly accept it, with regret of course. In an effort to limit the president's removal power, in 1876 Congress enacted the Tenure of Office Act declaring that the Senate's concurrence was needed in removing any executive official appointed with the Senate's consent. In a famous case in 1926, the Supreme Court declared the Tenure of Office Act unconstitutional on the grounds that it had limited the president's removal power unconstitutionally (*Myers v. United States*, 272 U.S. 52: 1926). In a subsequent case, however, the president's removal power was limited. In *Humphrey's Executor* [Rathbun] *v. United States*, 295 U.S. 602 (1935), the Supreme Court held that members appointed to independent regulatory commissions, such as the Federal Trade Commission (FTC), could be removed by the president prior to the expiration of their term of office only for "inefficiency, neglect of duty, or malfeasance," as specified by Congress. The trend at all governmental levels today is in the direction of strengthening removal powers of executive and administrative officials to make government more responsive and more responsible to the voters.

Reverse Discrimination (243)
The belief that racial quota systems designed to correct the racial imbalances of past discrimination are a violation of Title VII of the Civil Rights Act of 1964 and the Equal Protection Clause of the Fourteenth Amendment. Those who charge reverse discrimination state that the Civil Rights Act proscribes *preferential* treatment based on race and other factors, and that the suspension of merit registers, so that minority hiring quotas can be imposed, is preferential treatment. The most celebrated reverse discrimination case decided by the Supreme Court was *Regents of the University of California v. Bakke* (438 U.S. 265: 1978). Although not a public employment case, *Bakke* directly raised the related question of how far a public institution, in this case a state medical school, may go in using racial

Personnel Administration

quotas to build a racially diversified student body and, beyond graduation, a racially diversified corps of doctors. The faculty of the medical school at the University of California at Davis had reserved sixteen places out of one hundred in each new entering class for minority students. Racial minorities could therefore compete for all one hundred seats, with sixteen reserved for them, while white applicants could compete for only eighty-four. During a four-year period under this arrangement, sixty-three minority students were admitted at Davis under the special admissions program and forty-four under the general admissions program. For two years a white applicant, Allan Bakke, was rejected, although he had combined scores higher than those admitted under the special program. He charged racial discrimination by a state agency. By a five to four vote, the Supreme Court ordered Bakke admitted, holding that quotas in the fashion used were unlawful. The court did, however, permit public institutions to consider race among other selection factors. Reverse discrimination in this case meant that a white male was successful in his charge that "the system" had subjected him to racial discrimination. See also AFFIRMATIVE ACTION, 189; DISCRIMINATION, 208; EQUAL EMPLOYMENT OPPORTUNITY, 211.

Significance Reverse discrimination has divided the Supreme Court and public personnel policy makers as no other issue in recent times. The *Bakke* decision clearly undercut the spirit of affirmative action. Justice Lewis F. Powell said for the Court, "It is far too late to argue that the guarantee of equal protection to *all* persons permits the recognition of special wards entitled to a degree of protection greater than that accorded others." The *Bakke* case told government officials that they may be race conscious in recruitment and selection, but that quotas would not be allowed. Yet the very next year the Supreme Court modified its position. In 1979, it said in *United Steelworkers of America v. Weber* (443 U.S. 193: 1979) that the Kaiser Aluminum Company could promote equal employment opportunity and "eliminate traditional patterns of racial segregation" by instituting a training program to correct an imbalance in its skilled craft positions. Of 273 skilled workers in a Louisiana plant, only 5 were black. Since the local work force was 39 percent black, Kaiser, in conjunction with the Steelworkers Union, started a training program that would have a 50 percent black and a 50 percent white enrollment. The Supreme Court rejected the contention of Brian Weber, a white male who was refused admission to the training program, that he was therefore a victim of reverse discrimination. The pendulum of what constitutes reverse discrimination continues to swing back and forth as public institutions seek to define what constitutes justice for all.

Senior Executive Service (SES) (244)
A senior federal executive incentive pay program incorporated in Title IV of the Civil Service Reform Act of 1978. The Senior Executive Service is made up of over 9,000 career and noncareer executives whose grade and rank are assigned to them as persons rather than to their positions. In return for high performance within national administrative agencies, 5 percent of the SES are eligible for substantial annual incentive bonuses. Another 1 percent may be designated by the Office of Personnel Management as "distinguished executives," eligible to receive double bonuses on top of their base salaries. The president is granted the authority to identify all SES positions that should, by nature of job responsibilities, be nonpartisan and to appoint career executives to these positions. The remaining SES positions can go to career or a limited number of noncareer appointees. See also CIVIL SERVICE REFORM ACT OF 1978, 199; COMPENSATION, 206; FEDERAL EXECUTIVE INSTITUTE (FEI), 215.

Significance The Senior Executive Service (SES) signifies a return to the values of the administrative management period of U.S. public administration. After years of debate, Congress finally adopted a recommendation of the second Hoover Commission that a Senior Civil Service be established in the European tradition. Rewards in the SES are to come through a shift from a "rank-in-position" personnel system to a "rank-in-person" plan under which promotions and salary increases go to those who perform well rather than to those who merely spend a predetermined time in grade. The fact that the president can appoint a number of the SES increases presidential influence over administration and policy by reintroducing vestiges of the spoils principle. In his request for the SES, however, President Jimmy Carter stressed the need to make career managers' jobs politically more, rather than less, neutral and to reward the SES for maintaining neutrality. This was in response to the "Malek Manual," named after a senior official in the Office of Management and Budget (OMB) under President Richard M. Nixon. Malek encouraged the appointment of high-level federal executives on the basis of partisan politics and produced a guide about how to achieve political control over large sections of the federal bureaucracy.

Separation from Service (245)

The phrase used in the federal classified service to denote termination of employment. Reasons why a federal employee is separated from service include (1) resignation, taken at the initiative of the employee; (2) retirement, which is voluntary up to age 70; (3) being laid off as part of a reduction in force; (4) being fired for moral turpitude, conduct unbecoming a public employee, or for misfeasance, malfeasance, or nonfeasance on the job; and (5) dismissal for failure to measure up to work standards during a probation period or after receiving tenure. Dismissal procedures for federal employees are long, arduous, and difficult, but employees can be separated from service for failure to perform satisfactorily. The head of an agency has the power to fire as well as hire agency personnel, but both must be done according to prescribed rules. Civil service regulations stipulate that an employee can be dismissed from service "for such causes as will promote the efficiency of said service." See also AFFIRMATIVE ACTION, 189; TENURE, 248; VETERANS' PREFERENCE, 252.

Significance The main reason for separation from service for federal employees is resignation. Lagging salary scales for public employees contrasted with those offered by private companies have encouraged a large turnover in recent years. Retirements have also increased in recent years, as many of those who came into federal service during World War II and in the postwar period of expanding government programs have reached retirement age. Reductions in the work force resulting from budget cuts or from shifts in emphasis concerning government's responsibilities and objectives have also taken a toll. Often, employees will be transferred from one agency to another to avoid layoff as part of a reduction in force. In reductions, consideration is given to such factors as veterans' preference, seniority, and general competence. Conflicts have arisen in recent years over what weight should be attached to these factors and what emphasis should be given to affirmative action considerations. To avoid discriminatory treatment, each federal employee has a right not to be dismissed until informed in writing of the reasons for dismissal, and until the employee has had an opportunity to respond. If the dismissed person is a veteran, an appeal resulting in a hearing may be taken to the Merit Systems Protection Board which, along with the Office of Personnel Management, replaced the Civil Service Commission in 1978. In addition, all government employees are given security checks and any judged to be a "security risk" may be dismissed. Some federal employees are union members and have a right, under Executive Order 10988 issued by President John F. Kennedy in 1962, to engage in collective bargaining concerning discharge procedures.

Spoils System (246)
A government personnel system based on the principle of rewarding members of the winning political party with jobs in the public service. The spoils system got its name from the old Roman slogan that "To the victor belong the spoils." The spoils system became entrenched in the American political system after President Andrew Jackson established it when taking office in 1829. For Jackson, the spoils system meant (1) political selection of federal job holders; and (2) rotation in office. He believed that the government officials of his day were out of touch with the common people and should be replaced. Moreover, for Jackson, government jobs involved basically simple tasks that ordinary individuals could handle without special training. Party job holders could also function as campaign workers in subsequent elections. When the voters tired of a political party, they could vote it and the multitude of federal job holders out of office, to be replaced by members of the winning party. This form of rotation in office was heralded as the embodiment of the most basic principles of democracy. By 1883, however, sentiment had turned against Jacksonian Democracy and its spoils system, and Congress enacted a major civil service reform act aimed at recruitment and appointment of federal personnel based on merit. Although many top-level positions in the national government are filled by political appointment today, most vestiges of the spoils system as defined by President Jackson have disappeared. County government, however, remains a stronghold of the spoils system, and a few of the larger cities retain the practice of political appointment. In *Elrod v. Burns* (427 U.S. 347: 1976), however, the Supreme Court challenged the continuation of the spoils system in holding that a county sheriff's dismissal of an employee not engaged in policy making and not holding a confidential position was invalid. *See also* MERIT SYSTEM, 226; PATRONAGE, 231.

Significance Some political scientists continue to defend the spoils system as an essential ingredient of the two-party system of democratic government. In taking this position, they point out that large numbers of people are not likely to work diligently for a political party unless they are given a chance to participate directly in government following a victory at the polls. Supporters also emphasize—just as President Jackson did—that the only way to avoid building a massive bureaucracy that remains aloof and out of touch with the people's interests is to set up a system that provides for rotation in office. The only practicable way to implement this is through a spoils system. Opponents, however, point out that government is a very complex institution in today's world, with just about as many occupational specialities represented in the public service as in the private sector. Necessary competence and expertise cannot be secured through rapid rotation in office, with appointments based largely on political considerations. Since most party workers are employed in the private sector, typically at higher salaries than government can offer, the spoils system would not work under contemporary conditions. Opponents also point out that the civil service system on all levels of government has produced millions of competent, dedicated employees who help to keep government effective in meeting social and economic problems.

Staff Development (247)

A planned set of experiences designed to improve the skills and job performance of individual workers. Staff development begins the day an employee starts a new job. It includes orientation to the organization and initial training in the basic routines and tasks of the job. Most staff development, however, is the ongoing assessment of, and planning for, individual growth in the organization. It is grounded in the human relations approach to management. It assumes that all employees can continue to grow and learn new skills, and that they willingly accept more responsibility. Staff development was particularly emphasized in the 1970s as an alternative to employee obsolescence in a time of rapidly changing technology, and as a way to address job satisfaction as an element of productivity. Staff development programs are conducted primarily on the job. The methods used include (1) on-the-job coaching; (2) guided experience and special assignments; (3) conferences, seminars, clinics, and meetings; (4) case discussion groups, role playing, critical incident games, simulations, and in-basket exercises; (5) task force or research teamwork, sometimes called the "junior board" approach; and (6) self-development, involving home study courses, college courses, reading programs, and club or professional association membership. Some personnel needs can be met only through formal off-the-job programs, often including organization funding for external courses, seminars, and conferences. Staff development activity is frequently aimed at management development through three types of programs. (1) *Presupervisory programs* concentrate on the development of human relations and leadership skills not necessarily required in a technical position. These programs are often part of an individual career development plan in which a target position is identified and the necessary skills for that position become the objectives of the training. (2) *Middle management programs* concentrate on management theory and decision making as functions of management beyond the supervisory level. (3) *Executive development programs* involve on-the-job coaching, sensitivity training, simulations, games, and individual projects to give a more complete perspective on executive-level decision making. The leading example of an executive staff development program is the Federal Executive Institute in Charlottesville, Virginia. *See also* ON-THE-JOB TRAINING, 230.

Significance Staff development has become an important aspect of public organization development. The changing approach to employee motivation in recent years has caused a new focus on individual job satisfaction as a requirement for motivation and productivity. The federal government has placed increasing emphasis on staff training and development, beginning with the Government Employee Training Act of 1958, and continuing with the Civil Service Reform Act of 1978. Staff development programs at the state and local level have grown more slowly than at the federal level, but some of the programs now in place are quite sophisticated. The state of Michigan, for example, uses assessment center techniques for diagnosing employee strengths and weaknesses, with the resulting information used for the structuring of individualized staff development programs. Some staff development programs fail, usually because (1) the purposes and objectives of the program are not clearly defined; (2) the program is too narrowly focused on a functional area; (3) too much emphasis is placed on off-the-job development activities; (4) the focus is on preparation for promotion rather than development of skills; and/or (5) lack of support from top management.

Tenure **(248)**
The right to continue to hold an office or a position in public employment without fear of arbitrary dismissal. The tenure for elective offices is a definite time period, although reelection to consecutive terms can provide for a lengthy tenure in the same office. Politically appointed administrators have an indefinite tenure in that they are subject to dismissal by the chief executive or other appointing official at any time. Public employees are granted tenure after completing a probationary period, but continuing employment may be ended by various means available that provide for separation from service. Tenure guarantees that the loss of one's job in the public

Personnel Administration

service is not due to political, personal, or other arbitrary reasons. See also MERIT SYSTEM, 226; SEPARATION FROM SERVICE, 245.

Significance Tenure is the key to the operations of an effective merit system. The concept of tenure is most extensively developed in the field of teaching where public school teachers enjoy legal and customary protections against arbitrary disciplinary actions and the threat of dismissal. Federal employees in the classified service enjoy many of the same benefits that school teachers have won, and many state civil service employees do also. One of the main ingredients of a collective bargaining agreement for public employees is the establishment or strengthening of tenure rules. Yet, the right to tenure is not and cannot be absolute. So long as disciplinary or dismissal actions undertaken against tenured personnel meet the test of due process (i.e., fair, just, and reasonable actions based on law), they are likely to be upheld by executive authority and by the courts.

Testing (249)
The science of measuring or evaluating a sample of behavior, knowledge, or ability as a basis for predicting future behavior. Testing may be carried out through written, oral, or performance tests. The essence of these is to extract a cross section of a real-life situation in which the behavior of the candidate may be evaluated by observation or review. In public personnel administration, testing is characterized (1) by standards of *objectivity*, which disregard extraneous factors, such as race, religion, politics, sex, residence, and chronological age; (2) by *validity*, which insists that written tests actually measure what they purport to measure, with statistical correlations between test results and criteria of efficiency on the job; and (3) by *reliability*, which refers to the consistency with which a test serves as an accurate measuring instrument. Reliability is determined by such methods as giving the test to the same group at two separate times and correlating these test scores, and by giving the test only once but dividing the items and correlating scores on the two halves. See also RECRUITMENT, 241.

Significance Testing in the field of public administration relates mainly to personnel selection. Here it reduces the elements of chance and caprice that might otherwise be present in the selection process. A merit system cannot exist without carefully validated and standardized tests that measure general ability, special abilities or aptitudes, achievement, health and physique, and personality and emotion. Highly sophisticated testing instruments are available to personnel departments in modern organizations, which also test educationally disadvantaged people for motivation. Disadvantaged but highly motivated people, for example, can sometimes perform better at routine jobs than more experienced people with higher intelligence. Some of the better known examples of federal testing include the Professional and Administrative Career Examination (PACE) and the Foreign Service Examination. Many appointments to the federal service, however, are not based on competitive tests but on an evaluation of credentials, such as education and experience (unassembled test).

United Federation of Postal Clerks v. Blount, (250)
404 U.S. 802 (1971)

A United States District Court decision, affirmed by the Supreme Court, that denied the claim that public employees have a constitutional right to strike. The court in the *Blount* decision rejected the union argument that a federal antistrike statute was invalid because it was a violation of employee rights of association and free speech. The union also claimed that statute was a denial of equal protection of the laws, since private workers are allowed to strike. The court reasoned that under the common law there is no basic right to strike for either private or public employees, and the United States Constitution is silent on the issue. Although Congress had granted the right to strike to private employees in the National Labor Relations Act of 1935, it did not grant the right to public employees. In the absence of such a statute, public employees could not strike because they do not have a "fundamental right" to do so. Equal protection of the law applies only in the case of fundamental rights, the court declared, and a strike does not fall into that category. The Supreme Court in effect gave its approval to the district court's decision by refusing to hear it on appeal. *See also* COLLECTIVE BARGAINING, 203; IMPASSE RESOLUTION, 221.

Significance The 1971 *Blount* case was the first decision rendered by the federal judiciary on the question of strikes by public employees. Although bills are frequently introduced in Congress to legalize federal employee strikes, and although the judiciary cannot prohibit the enactment of such laws, the *Blount* decision remains a legislative, as well as a judicial, standard. Eight states, however, have laws granting public employees a limited right to strike (Alaska, Hawaii, Minnesota, Montana [nurses only], Oregon, Pennsylvania, Vermont, and Wisconsin [only municipal employees and teachers]). The limited right to strike usually means that work stoppages are not permitted before exhausting all statutory impasse resolution procedures, and that strikes that represent a clear and present danger to public health, safety, and welfare are subject to court injunction. The current trend in state legislation regarding strikes by public employees not only bans them but provides severe penalties. The record shows conclusively, however, that public workers will strike despite penalties such as dismissal, fines, and imprisonment. In 1974, for example, of 384 strikes by public employees, 348 occurred at the local level, 34 at the state level, and 2 at the national level. The final settlements typically provided for the return to work of those who had been fired, and other penalties were often mitigated in the agreements ending the strikes. Public employee strikes are realities whether or not there are laws or judicial decisions permitting them. The emotional issue of whether public employees have a right to strike runs deep. This issue again gained public attention in 1982 when President Ronald Reagan fired striking air traffic controllers who failed to report for work during a 48 hour ultimatum period. Polls revealed that a large majority of the U.S. people supported the president's action.

United Steelworkers of America v. Weber, (251)
443 U.S. 193: 1979
Decided that a voluntary affirmative action program can be used by a private employer to give preferential treatment to members of minority groups without violating the Civil Rights Act of 1964. Specifically, in *United Steelworkers of America v. Weber,* the United States Supreme Court decided by a 5–2 vote that, under terms of a collective bargaining agreement, a private employer can provide exclusive on-the-job craft training for minority employees even though white male employees have greater seniority claims on the openings in the training program. Brain Weber, a white male with six years seniority at the Gramercy, Louisiana, plant of the Kaiser Aluminum Company, complained that two of five blacks selected for a special craft training program had less seniority than he, which constituted a violation of Title VII of the Civil Rights Act of 1964. Weber claimed reverse discrimination. The Supreme Court held that Kaiser's voluntary affirmative action plan was permissible because of the legislative intent of Title VII. The applicable language is, "It shall be an unlawful employment practice for any employer, labor organization, or joint labor-management committee controlling apprenticeship or other training or retraining, including on-the-job training programs, to discriminate against any individual because of his race, color, religion, sex, or national origin in admission to, or employment in, any program established to provide apprenticeship or other training" (Section 703). Despite the apparent applicability of the language, in the *Weber* case the Court said it must, in the context of the entire act,

interpret the *intent* of the language and the legislative body and decide accordingly. See also AFFIRMATIVE ACTION, 189; REVERSE DISCRIMINATION, 243.

Significance The *Weber* decision permits the continued use of the highly controversial personnel practice of maintaining a double seniority list. Some agencies and companies maintain one list for white employees and another list for black employees for personnel selection purposes. While a white employee may have greater seniority than any individual on the list of black employees, the top-ranking persons on the latter list may be selected for available slots in training or other advancement programs. The *Weber* decision was assailed in *Commentary* and the *Harvard Law Review* for "egregiously misreporting the intent of Congress" and for going "too far in approving quotas in excess of parity." Proponents hailed the decision as a victory for continuing efforts in the affirmative action area, with one writer in the *Nation* stating that if Brian Weber had been successful "affirmative action, in all aspects, is dead." The *Weber* case affirmed the Supreme Court's current commitment to a group theory of society in which affirmative action is understood to be a remedy for wrongs perpetrated against minority groups in the past. Quota systems are a means of compensating for discrimination or unequal treatment, services, or facilities. This view contends that all members of the same group were treated in the same manner in the past and that they must be given the same additional help today. One way to expiate past wrongs is to give preferential treatment in hiring, training, and promoting, until parity has been established. The contrary view is the argument from merit, which says the individual and not the group is the basic unit of society. In this view, the group affiliations of an individual ought to be irrelevant to an individual's ranking in the meritocracy. Merit is measured in terms of individual talent and should be the only determining factor for receiving society's rewards, including jobs. The *Weber* decision intensified this debate.

Veterans' Preference (252)

Special treatment accorded to verterans by a civil service system. Veterans' preference is given only to those who served in active military service for a specified period of time. Benefits for veterans in or seeking employment with the federal service include (1) five points added to a passing score on a competitive examination, ten points for disabled veterans; (2) for some jobs, the waiving of age, physical, and educational requirements for veterans; (3) restricting applications for some positions to veterans; (4) extending veterans' preference in some positions to wives, widows, children, and mothers of disabled or deceased veterans; and (5) providing special treatment for veterans threatened by layoff or a disciplinary dismissal. Most civil service systems on the national, state, and local levels offer some or all such favorable treatment. See also TENURE, 248.

Significance Veterans' preference is largely the product of a grateful people thanking those who served in the armed forces of the United States. Like educational and other benefits for veterans, it also helps in recruiting personnel for a voluntary military force. The impact of veterans' preference has been to fill most civil service positions with veterans or their relatives, with the result that the principle of merit based on competitive examinations and on-the-job performance has been weakened. Efforts to mitigate the impact of veterans' preference on merit systems have been vigorously fought by veterans' organizations and other related interest groups. Increasingly, veterans' preference has clashed with affirmative action programs since both attempt to provide for special treatment based on what has happened in the past.

6. Financial Administration

Accounting (253)
A bookkeeping function that collects, classifies, records, aggregates, preserves, and analyzes financial data. Accounting is a major element of the budgetary process and of the manager's responsibility. It centers on an orderly arrangement for the control of expenditures and for their proper relationship to receipts. The accounting process is divided into three categories: (1) *recording,* the assembling of a permanent record of activities that can be referred to in case of dispute; (2) *reporting,* a detailed presentation of activities; and (3) *auditing,* a system of independent evaluation. Accounting also includes a data processing system and an internal control system. The oldest type of accounting is cash accounting. Receipt transactions are recorded at the time funds are received from various sources. Disbursements are recorded when checks are issued or paid. Cash accounting thus shows the immediate cash position of an organization and serves as a strong management control device. Other types of accounting are (1) *encumbrance,* which records "expenditures" when purchase orders are written or contracts entered into; (2) *accrual,* which records "revenues" when taxpayers incur a tax liability or when the government incurs a liability to pay for goods and services; and (3) *cost,* which shifts from reporting the status of appropriation balances to the actual cost of providing goods and services when the resources are used, not when they were acquired. *See also* AUDITING, 256; BUDGET, 261; GENERAL ACCOUNTING OFFICE (GAO), 274.

Significance Accounting maintains and strengthens the day-to-day direction of an agency's operations. It reduces waste and inefficiency. It assures that resources are used in accordance with legislative intent.

Without a good accounting system and comprehensive financial reports derived from the accounting data, no agency could function effectively. Accounting serves primarily to help carry out management policies with maximum effectiveness by providing complete information about costs in relation to program objectives. These data are used in the auditing process as well. Accounting as a way to measure benefits is much more difficult in governmental accounting than in commercial accounting. In commercial accounting, the benefit is to the company in terms of revenue inflow from customers. In governmental accounting, the benefit is to the public served in terms of social needs or national security. Governmental accountants, therefore, emphasize *control:* control of a sum of money devoted to a specific public purpose, as in fund accounting, or control of an actual transaction designed to accomplish a limited goal, as in budgetary accounting. The General Accounting Office (GAO), an independent agency established by the Budget and Accounting Act of 1921, supervises the accounting systems used by federal agencies and departments and ensures that methods of reporting result in full disclosure of receipts and disbursements. The GAO audits all national government expenditures as an agent of Congress.

Ad-valorem Taxation (254)

Levying taxes on goods, services, or possessions based on the value of the items or *property* being taxed. *Ad valorem* (a Latin phrase meaning "according to the value of") taxes include three basic types: (1) taxes on wealth, primarily physical property; (2) income taxes; and (3) excise, sales, or transaction taxes. Of the three, the tax on wealth or property is the oldest. Historians believe the property tax was first used by the Greeks around 600 B.C. The Romans prepared the first assessment roll and called it the *census.* The property tax continued in use by various societies until about A.D. 500, at which time it disappeared for about six hundred years. All land was owned under the feudal system during this period, and farmers paid rent in the form of a portion of their crops instead of paying taxes. The property tax came into use again in the waning years of the medieval period, and it began at that time to include the taxing of personal property as well as land. Because personal property was difficult to assess, in that time as well as modern times, it was dropped and then added again several times in subsequent history. The ad-valorem tax system consists of a tally or exhaustive list of all taxable property, its legal description, its owner, or to whom it is to be assessed, and the property's assessed value. The assessment may be its full cash value, or cash equivalent, or it may appear as a statutory portion or percentage of the cash value. Some taxing authorities provide for a form of assessment relief for certain individuals such as handicapped persons, veterans, senior citizens, or persons with excessively low income. Some property, such as church property, is entirely exempt from taxation. When revenue is needed by a taxing authority to perform essential government services, a taxing rate, usually in the form of a voter-approved millage, is established. The taxed amount for each item of property is simply the assessment multiplied by the approved rate. *See also* FISCAL POLICY, 272; MONETARY POLICY, 280; PROPOSITION 13, 74.

Significance Ad-valorem taxation is based on the ancient idea that land ownership is the proper yardstick to measure wealth and one's social responsibility. Taxation experts say it continues to be a valid gauge. A tax system that taxes "according to the value of" implies that the tax will be levied according to one's ability to pay. In the eyes of many this is an equitable arrangement for gaining the money to do the people's business. Those who support revisions of the current ad-valorem system tend to be motivated more by the need to generate revenue than by philosophic differences with the concept. The Proposition 13 movement is not opposed to the idea of ad-valorem taxation, but believes property taxes should be restricted substantially below their current levels.

Appropriation (255)

A grant of money by a legislative body to carry out a governmental function or program. Appropriations provide that the money be spent for a public purpose and in the manner authorized by law. Before an appropriation bill can be considered, the legislative body must pass an *authorization* measure that establishes the program and estimates the amount of appropriation needed for funding it. Typically, authorization bills go to the substantive committees in each chamber, whereas the appropriation bills are considered by the appropriations committees. Thus a bill to aid farmers must first go to the Agriculture Committee in each chamber and be approved by both houses of the legislative body and by the chief executive before budget bills can be submitted to the specific Appropriations Committee. With the adoption of the executive budget system, both the president and the governors of the various states present their respective legislative bodies with an annual budget proposal plus requests for *supplemental* (authorization of additional funding for specific purposes for the *next* fiscal year after the major appropriation bill has been passed) and *deficiency* (a special appropriation to make up the difference between an appropriation for the fiscal year and the amount actually needed to carry on the program for the full *current* fiscal year) appropriations. *See also* AUDITOR, 257; BUDGET, 261.

Significance The two-step process of authorization followed by appropriation ensures that the measure under consideration will be evaluated in terms of both substance and cost. The role of appropriations committees and legislative chambers in funding programs is extremely important. For one thing, very little can be done by government in the contemporary world that does not require substantial financial support. Whether a program succeeds or fails will often depend on the level of financing accorded it. For example, an authorization measure may pass the legislative body by an overwhelming vote, indicating strong support for the program, but the appropriations committees may greatly weaken it by refusing to give it meaningful support, or they may kill the program completely by refusing to recommend any appropriation to their respective houses. Often, important appropriations bills are "negotiated" in a conference committee consisting of members from both chambers, with each group voting separately on compromises. The appropriation function demonstrates the power of the chief executive and budget agency in developing budget proposals. However, the "power of the purse" vested in the legislative body and its appropriations committees is based on the constitutional requirement that every expenditure of public money be made "according to law."

Auditing (256)

A process of analyzing an organization's accounting records, systems of data processing, and internal financial control. Auditing includes (1) procedural checks on the accuracy of the accounting system in use; (2) study to determine accuracy in the operation of the system, including the validation of inventories and existing equipment; (3) an inquiry into whether proper legal authority exists to carry on activities being performed; (4) determination of the adequacy of the internal control system; (5) checking for possible fraud, waste, and mismanagement; and (6) evaluation of the overall effectiveness of agency programs. Auditing's basic objective is to verify that all financial transactions have been properly handled and recorded in compliance with legal provisions. Auditing is commonly divided into preaudit and postaudit phases. Preaudits are executive branch functions to determine the compliance of subordinate officials or agencies with the provisions of appropriations bills. In the national government, preaudits carried out by General Accounting Office (GAO) personnel take

Financial Administration

place prior to the payment of an obligation and involve close examination of payment vouchers. Postaudits occur after payments are made. They focus on document verification and the discretion used by officials to ascertain if they have made errors of judgment or if they have authorized illegal expenditures. Postaudits typically take place many months after payment, because of the large volume of transactions in federal agencies. They are also selectively done, with the auditing agency, the GAO, giving priority to postaudit requests of congressional committees and individual members of Congress. The GAO is not sufficiently staffed to postaudit every agency's operations every year. *See also* ACCOUNTING, 253; AUDITOR, 257; BUDGET CYCLE, 263; GENERAL ACCOUNTING OFFICE (GAO), 274.

Significance Auditing is a check on the accuracy and honesty of officials making and implementing budgets on all levels of government. Despite its obvious utility, auditing has some negative aspects, particularly in the preaudit phase. Preaudits tend to reduce the level of responsibility officials will assume; they promote red tape, they foster interagency friction, and they are costly. Postaudits are sometimes very narrowly conceived, focusing only on catching financial irregularities rather than researching the efficiency of agency operations and the wisdom of spending decisions. However, auditing is increasingly moving into a new phase called *operational, performance,* or *management* auditing. Operational auditing includes a thorough review of management policies and administrative practices, as well as traditional financial auditing. It has a positive function in that it attempts to identify opportunities to reduce costs, increase efficiency, and improve program effectiveness. All phases and interpretations of federal auditing are ultimately the responsibility of the GAO, which some students of finance believe to be in a conflict-of-interest situation regarding preaudits and postaudits. If the GAO as an agent of Congress has the power to make both a preaudit authorization and a postaudit check, can the president reasonably be held responsible for executive spending activities? Can a postaudit be meaningful if carried out by the same agency that earlier had authorized the expenditures in a preaudit? Congress continues to say yes, and auditing continues to be one of Congress's most important checks in a checks-and-balances system.

Auditor (257)

The agent of a legislative body who examines the expenditures of public funds to determine that they are being spent or have been spent in the manner and for the purposes specified by the legislative body in making the appropriation. In the national government, the Budget and Accounting Act of 1921 established the General Accounting Office (GAO) to function as the fiscal watchdog for the Congress. The GAO is headed by the Comptroller General who is appointed by the president with the Senate's approval for a fifteen-year term. The Comptroller General functions as the chief financial adviser to the Congress. The GAO is empowered to validate all payments to ensure that they meet the intent of Congress, and to audit the accounts of all government agencies with a few exceptions, such as those of the Federal Reserve and certain intelligence operations. In most states, the auditor is elected directly by the voters and is accountable to them at periodic elections. At the local governmental level, the auditor (often called comptroller) is appointed to the office to examine expenditures and to determine whether they conform with state and municipal law. *See also* AUDITING, 256; COMPTROLLER GENERAL, 265.

Significance Auditors perform a critical function in a democratic system by ensuring that expenditures of public monies are carried out according to law. The auditing function is one of the many checks and balances built into the system to prevent serious abuse and misuse of power, and to help maintain public confidence in government. Fiscal responsibility is impossible to achieve without an effective auditing system. Yet, many problems exist at all three levels of government. Preaudit validating of expenditure vouchers, for example, renders postaudit checks either invalid or meaningless since the same people are involved in both functions. Government controls can never be effective when officials are empowered to check on the validity of their own actions. Public administrationists have often recommended that executive officials be authorized to conduct the preaudit authorization of expenditures, leaving the postaudit action in the hands of the auditing agency. Those opposed to this change argue that once expenditures have been made it is too late in a postaudit to ensure that the intent of the legislative body is complied with. The problem of correcting errors after the fact, they argue, is greater than the problems involved in double auditing by the same agency. Nevertheless, the goal of most administrative experts is to set up effective auditing systems throughout government that focus on determining the validity of accounts and payments *after* the expenditures have been made.

Backdoor Financing (258)

A process whereby legislative committees in Congress bypass the appropriations committees by providing agencies with spending or

Financial Administration

obligating authority in substantive legislation. Backdoor financing is an aspect of the rivalry existing among legislative committees such as Agriculture, Armed Services, Education and Labor, Public Works and Transportation, and the House Appropriations Committee. The rivalry is rooted in concern for program priorities and concern for committee power. Often a legislative committee strongly favors a program that is regularly short-changed by an appropriations subcommittee, and ways are sought to liberate the program from financial dependence on the subcommittee. The legislative committee versus appropriations committee contest is based on the rules of each house. Each house can appropriate funds only for activities that it has separately and previously authorized in substantive, enabling legislation. Enabling legislation establishes policies and programs and directs particular agencies to execute them. In theory, every administrative agency is bound by two kinds of congressional enactments—the enabling statutes and the currently operative appropriations acts. Enabling statutes may be "permanent" legislation, effective until amended or repealed, as is the case with the antitrust laws, or they may be temporary legislation, effective only until the expiration date stated in the legislation. Such statutes often specify dollar ceilings on appropriations. The House Appropriations Committee's bills and the appropriation acts themselves cannot exceed the stated ceilings, although they may provide amounts far short of the ceilings, even to the point of including no funds at all. Backdoor financing seeks to erode the House Appropriations Committee's comprehensive control of expenditure authorization. Backdoor spending occurs under four kinds of authority which is contained in substantive legislation initiated by the regular legislative committees. They are (1) *Contract authority* whereby an agency is authorized to enter into contracts in advance of appropriations. Technically, this is authority to obligate—not to spend—money. But when the time for payment approaches, the appropriations committees have no choice but to honor the contractual obligations by appropriating money for their liquidation. (2) *Borrowing authority* whereby agencies are authorized to "spend debt receipts," that is, to borrow money directly or indirectly from the Treasury, which in turn borrows from the public. Then the agency obligates and spends the money without ever having to seek appropriations. (3) *Mandatory entitlements* whereby citizens such as veterans and welfare clients and state and local governments are guaranteed specified individual payments if they meet eligibility standards, or they are assured automatic increases of the amounts when economic conditions change, as measured by a "triggering" formula. (4) *Permanent appropriations* whereby provisions are incorporated into substantive legislation to pay the interest on the public debt, social security benefits, and annual amounts due state and local governments under general revenue sharing. This legislation requires no further appropriation action. The result of these and related backdoor financing practices is that most federal annual spending is outside the appropriations process. The appropriations committees have no role in authorization. In 1974, Congress attempted—with little success—to curb backdoor financing in the Congressional Budget and Impoundment Control Act. *See also* BUDGET CYCLE, 263; CONGRESSIONAL BUDGET AND IMPOUNDMENT CONTROL ACT OF 1974, 266; FISCAL POLICY, 272.

Significance Backdoor financing is the result of a fragmented appropriations process in Congress that begins when the president's budget arrives in January of each year. Consideration of the executive budget begins in the House of Representatives. By constitutional mandate, revenue measures must start there. By custom, appropriations measures start there, too. In the traditional process the first surgery on the budget document was the severance of revenue estimates and recommendations, which are the concern of the Ways and Means Committee, from expenditure estimates and appropriation recommendations, which are the concern of the House Appropriations Committee. Never again were the revenue and expenditure sides united in the legislative process. Since the revenue committees in both houses—the House Ways and Means Committee and the Senate Finance Committee—are *legislative* committees, the contest between legislative and appropriations committees began early. It was exacerbated by the fragmentation of the House Appropriations Committee itself, which in 1979 was divided into thirteen subcommittees—each responsible for drafting an appropriation bill for a particular set of agencies and programs, and each subcommittee virtually an autonomous fiefdom. The *legislative* committee of jurisdiction and the *appropriations* subcommittee of autonomy therefore engaged in fierce skirmishing over agency funding, with backdoor financing the result. Intercommittee rivalry in the Senate is reduced by the fact that Senate Appropriations Committee members are also members of legislative committees. The fifty-five members of the House Appropriations Committee cannot be members of other standing committees, except the Budget Committee and the Small Business Committee. What the Congressional Budget and Impoundment Control Act of 1974 did to control the legislative-appropriations committee rivalry was to require that legislative committees report by May 15 of each year "any bill or resolution which, directly or indirectly, authorizes the enactment of new budget authority" for the fiscal year beginning the following October 1. Thus legislative committees cannot skirt the

Financial Administration

appropriations process by delays in passing enabling legislation. The act calls for remarkable self-discipline and efficiency by the legislative committees. The apparent victory of the appropriations committees is further illustrated by the act's provision that any bill or resolution permitting backdoor spending must provide that it is "to be effective for any fiscal year only to such extent and in such amounts as are provided in appropriation Acts."

Block Grant (259)
A lump sum of money given by the federal government to a state or local government to be used in a general policy area. The block grant was designed to consolidate previously fragmented, although functionally related, categorical grants into larger grant programs. The first block grant was the Partnership for Health Act of 1966, followed by the Omnibus Crime Control and Safe Streets Act of 1968, and the Comprehensive Employment and Training Act (CETA) of 1973. The Housing and Community Development Act of 1974 remains, however, the major piece of legislation using the block grant concept. This act consolidated ten categorical urban development programs. The merged categorical grants were the previously separate urban renewal, model cities, neighborhood development, land acquisition, open space land, public facility loan, basic water and sewer facilities, advanced planning grant, code enforcement, and neighborhood facility programs. At the same time the act consolidated the categories, it also delegated substantial program and priority direction to local communities. The grant recipient had a great deal of discretionary power, but not quite the latitude of revenue sharing. Under the Housing and Community Development Act of 1974, there are certain federal requirements for recipients of block grants. The community must identify its community development needs, formulate a plan to meet those needs, devise a housing assistance plan, and be in conformity with civil rights laws and citizen participation requirements. State and local governments must carefully plan how they will use the grant, and report how the money is allocated and spent. On the other hand, the grantor cannot question the uses of the money unless they violate statutes. Thus there are many procedural requirements in block grant programs, but little control over substance. *See also* FEDERALISM, FISCAL, 49; REVENUE SHARING, 287.

Significance Block grant legislation is a compromise between the categorical approach to federal funding of state and local needs, and revenue sharing. The block grant approach has had many well-founded criticisms. One is that federal reliance on self-reporting leads to situations in which "illegal, as well as trivial, quixotic, and inequitable uses of block grant funds may go undetected and unpunished." Another is the Brookings Institution contention that while national lawmakers and administrators are attuned to the needy, state and local officials are more attuned to the middle class. The emphasis of block grant programs therefore shifted from programs for the poor to mixed patterns of spending, from social services to short-term capital improvements. Brookings suggested that future block grant legislation build in formulas and requirements that favor the needy. An example of this is a requirement of the Housing and Community Development Act of 1974 favoring aid for older houses and computing "population lag," which means more money for the older, presumably needier, cities of the North and Midwest.

Borrowing Power (260)
The grant of authority, usually made by a constitution, that enables a government to meet its financial obligations when its expenditures exceed its income. In the national government, the Constitution in Article I, Section 8, assigns Congress the unrestricted borrowing power. Congress, however, has imposed an arbitrary debt limit for the national government, but Congress has always increased that limit whenever new debt was incurred or needed. State constitutions on the other hand severely restrict state borrowing. In some cases, this approach involves a blanket prohibition of state debt. In others, it permits the state to incur indebtedness only for a few constitutionally approved purposes. States can, however, get around such limitations by the adoption of constitutional amendments in which the voters agree to permit the state to borrow for a specified purpose. The borrowing power of local governments is strictly regulated by state constitutional and statutory limitations. Debt limits on local governments typically restrict total debt to a percentage of the assessed valuation of their taxable property. *See also* PUBLIC DEBT, 285.

Significance From the beginning of the nation's history, the borrowing power of state and national governments has been an essential financial tool to encourage economic expansion and provide for necessary improvements. Many of the states became deeply indebted during the eighteenth and early nineteenth centuries, with frequent defaulting on bond payments. As a result, many of the states adopted tough constitutional limitations on borrowing that continue to limit their operations today. In the national government, the adoption of the Keynesian economic approach following World War II has led to numerous federal deficits as fiscal policy has been used by all

Financial Administration

presidents—Republican and Democratic alike—to move the nation out of serious economic downturns. These deficits have become progressively larger, and the national public debt has grown to huge proportions—now approaching $3 trillion dollars. New campaigns to limit the borrowing power of all governments have resulted, with an increasing loss of financial flexibility for all. By the 1980s, the idea of a balanced budget and an end to the unlimited use of borrowing power by government dominated the thinking of the mass public and became a major plank in the platform of both major parties and of most candidates for office. Despite these efforts to discredit government's borrowing power, the need remains for flexibility in coping with serious economic problems and in authorizing capital outlays for major projects that cannot be financed in a fiscal year.

Budget (261)

A proposed action plan for government, defined in financial terms, that gives direction to the execution of policies and programs. A public budget is (1) a fiscal statement describing the revenues and expenditures of all governmental units; and (2) a mechanism for controlling, managing, planning, and evaluating the activities of each governmental unit. A budget is political in content. It represents government's ranking of many activities. It reflects the relative strengths of competing groups and the nature of the compromises reached among competing values. A budget announces the direction in which government intends to go in the near future, usually in the next fiscal year. Political scientist Allen Schick has identified three distinct purposes for which budgets have been used: control, management, and planning. These purposes correspond to three historical periods in this century during which certain types of budgets were dominant. The United States is currently in a fourth period, with budgets now used for evaluation purposes. Although a dominant type is found within each of the four periods, some previous budget techniques were used in each succeeding period. The *control function*, the first of the primary budgetary functions, was emphasized from about 1900 through the middle 1930s. The line-item budget was widely used in this period. The control period was featured by the establishment of central budgeting offices. At the federal level, the Budget and Accounting Act of 1921 created the Bureau of the Budget (BOB), which in 1970 became the Office of Management and Budget (OMB). Prior to 1921, each agency presented its budget requests to Congress, whereas after 1921, in the new "executive budget," requests from executive agencies were funneled into the Budget Bureau, which functioned as a central clearinghouse. This system facilitated control by the president and by the Congress over requests for money and for expenditures once the requests had been approved. The Budget and Accounting Act of 1921 made the president responsible for formulating the national budget, with the Budget Bureau functioning as the chief staff agency to help him accomplish the task. The *management function* was emphasized from the middle 1930s until the late 1950s. *Performance budgets,* also called *program budgets,* largely replaced line-item budgets in this period. They were designed to answer the question of how well—that is, how efficiently—programs were being administered. This was the first use of the budget as an evaluation device. The *planning function* was emphasized from the late 1950s through the late 1960s in a budget process known as planning, programming, budgeting systems (PPBS). The overall purpose of PPBS (also called PPB) was to create greater rationality in the budgeting process by requiring administrators to plan long-range organizational goals, to establish programs to attain those goals, and to budget specific projects within those programs to make them effective. The *evaluation function* emerged during the 1970s and is represented by zero-based budgeting (ZBB). This sytem requires all spending for each program and agency to be justified anew each year. ZBB questions the need for a program at any funding level, and it rejects the incrementalist principle by which new budgets are constructed on the basis of last year's funding level. *See also* BUDGET CYCLE, 263; LINE-ITEM BUDGET, 278; PERFORMANCE BUDGETING, 282; PLANNING, PROGRAMMING, BUDGETING SYSTEMS (PPBS), 283; ZERO-BASE BUDGETING (ZBB), 291.

Significance A budget was once considered to be little more than a document showing sums of money to be spent for particular purposes in a given period of time. Budgeting, or the process of creating the budget, was treated as an isolated, routine, administrative duty. The relationship between budgeting and other managerial functions was thought to be minimal. The primary concern and purpose of budgets was to ensure that money was spent only for what had been approved. This accounting approach to budgets has yielded today to a much broader role for the budget maker. A budget has come to be the single most important managerial tool available to the manager. It is a work plan and an evaluation instrument that gives direction to the execution of public policies.

Budget and Accounting Act of 1921 (262)

The basic legislation that established a rational budget-formulation process in the executive branch of the federal government. The

Financial Administration

Budget and Accounting Act of 1921 was a major reform of the process by which national spending programs are formulated, authorized, executed, and audited. For much of U.S. history prior to the act, agencies' requests for funds were simply "packaged" by the Treasury Department and transmitted to Congress without change. There was no unified executive budget. Agencies put together their asking figures, went to legislative committees of jurisdiction, and wangled what appropriations they could get. From 1885 to 1920, the appropriation requests for almost half the federal budget were distributed in the House of Representatives among seven substantive committees, rather than being considered by the Appropriations Committee. In 1920, the House restored full jurisdiction to the Appropriations Committee, but a more sweeping reform of the budgetary process was prevented by President Woodrow Wilson's veto of the bill, which a year later became the Budget and Accounting Act of 1921. President Wilson opposed the independence of the legislative auditor that the law would, and finally did, create. The act created a new bureau in the Treasury Department, the United States Bureau of the Budget (after 1970 the Office of Management and Budget), to receive agency estimates and prepare the president's budget. It established the General Accounting Office (GAO) in the legislative branch as the independent auditor of executive accounts. The president appointed its head, the Comptroller General of the United States, for a fifteen-year term. The Comptroller General could be removed only by a joint resolution of Congress or by impeachment. He could not be reappointed. A major feature of the Budget and Accounting Act was that it did not limit the GAO to postauditing. It gave the GAO the power to "prescribe the forms, systems, and procedure for administrative appropriation and fund accounting in the several departments and establishments, and for the administrative examination of fiscal officers' accounts and claims against the United States." The act specified that control of agency accounting systems and the preaudit were also responsibilities of the General Accounting Office. *See also* AUDITING, 256; BUDGET, 261; GENERAL ACCOUNTING OFFICE (GAO), 274; LINE-ITEM BUDGET, 278.

Significance The Budget and Accounting Act of 1921 was the product of reformist pressures to establish a consolidated executive budget. The act's sponsors believed that financial corruption in government could be eliminated by the establishment of public financial bureaus under the chief executive. With the executive budget came additional innovations such as competitive bidding for contracts, centralized purchasing, standardized accounting procedures, and expenditure audits. Each of these innovations related directly to the idea that the budget was a useful device for controlling public administrators and ensuring morality in government. The line-item budget was identified with the reform movement as well. The first director of the Bureau of the Budget, Charles G. Dawes, was a typical spokesperson for the reform position. In 1923 he wrote, "The Bureau of the Budget is concerned only with the humbler and routine business of government . . . it is concerned with no question of policy, save that of economy and efficiency." The "economy and efficiency" theme went back to the origin of the movement that had resulted in the Budget and Accounting Act. This was the report of the Taft Commission on Economy and Efficiency, whose 1913 report had called for an executive budget that would include functional categories beyond the traditional listing of personal services and things to be bought. The line-item budget was made to order. It emphasized skilled accountancy, the objects needed to run an office or program and their costs, incremental policy making throughout government, dispersed responsibility for management and planning, and a fiduciary role for the budget agency. Public administrationist Nicholas Henry points out the following item as an example of the technical definitions stressed in line-item budgeting: "pencils, 112, with 1/2 inch erasers, wood, No. 2 grade lead, 6″ × 1/4″." Following passage of the Budget and Accounting Act such phrases as "watchdog of the treasury" and "balanced budget" were common, indicating the prevalent mentality of control and tight management. The control turned out to be too tight and too inflexible. The General Accounting Office (GAO), for example, assumed powers more appropriately lodged in the executive branch than in an agency of the legislative branch. Given the fact that an agency's spending officers were personally liable for expenditures that GAO could later disapprove, these officers often asked the GAO for advance opinions. The GAO thus increasingly preaudited expenditures before they were made. As a result, the GAO not only delayed actions but became less an auditor; that is, it forsook the function of an evaluator after the fact and became more a participant in the very transactions it was supposed to audit later. This situation was corrected in the Budget and Accounting Procedures Act of 1950.

Budget Cycle (263)
The formal steps followed in the preparation, appropriation, execution, and auditing of an agency's financial plan that involves detailed proposals for spending and revenue raising during the ensuing fiscal year. The budget cycle in the federal government begins as much as two years, and as little as nine months, before the beginning of a new

Financial Administration

fiscal year, which runs from October 1 to September 30. The deadline in the budget cycle calls for the president to submit an executive budget to Congress in mid-January of each year. The executive budget is for the entire federal government, as mandated by the Budget and Accounting Act of 1921. Prior to 1921, Congress dominated financial decision making at the federal level by operating under a constitutional provision that specified that "no money shall be drawn from the Treasury, but in consequence of appropriations made by law." A series of federal deficits and other events led to the executive budget, whereby a single office, the Office of Management and Budget (OMB) in the Executive Office of the President, has primary responsibility for preparing the Budget of the United States. The *preparation* phase involves formal and informal exchanges between OMB and all federal agencies. OMB issues instructions for agency budget requests in the spring, formal estimates are submitted by the agencies in the early fall, a presidential review takes place in November, and the budget is transmitted to Congress in January. The *appropriation* phase of the budget cycle is accomplished as Congress enacts numerous and separate appropriation bills. The *execution* phase carries out the programs for which appropriations have provided the resources. The OMB acts for the president in establishing a schedule for granting an agency permission to spend in the execution phase. Some of the appropriated funds may be reserved, that is, not immediately apportioned to the agency. Apportionments by the OMB are normally provided on a quarterly basis, with reserved funds being released late in the fiscal year. The *auditing* phase of the budget cycle is accomplished by the General Accounting Office (GAO), an agency of Congress that audits administrative agencies by assuring that obligations created and money paid out were done legally. The GAO asks such questions as Was the expenditure authorized? Were proper procedures followed, such as competitive bidding, where required? The auditing phase is not sequential as are the preparation, appropriation, and execution phases of the budget cycle. It is an ongoing process that may include examination of present and planned activities, as well as those already completed. *See also* BUDGET, 261; GENERAL ACCOUNTING OFFICE (GAO), 274; OFFICE OF MANAGEMENT AND BUDGET (OMB), 166.

Significance The budget cycle is repeated every year. It is the process in which public administrators devote large amounts of time to obtain from other administrators, from the chief executive, and from the legislature, the financial support crucial for the expansion or continued existence of particular programs, or even of the agency itself. The budget cycle, perhaps more than any other administrative activity, focuses on an organization's internal administrative knowhow. Because resources are scarce and there is competition—usually cutthroat rather than genteel—for those resources, difficult decisions about funding must be made. Money is the most negotiable form of resources. It translates eventually into programs. Without money the mere *authorization* of a program has no effect. The phrase frequently heard in Washington is: "The program is authorized but not funded." This means simply that program authorization has been made by a congressional "committee of substance," but that an appropriation bill has not been passed to give the program money. It is suspected that authorizing committees sometimes pass statutes granting an agency authority to operate a program they really do not want, knowing that, when funding is sought in the budget cycle, the specific appropriations committees will be the "bad guys" and say "No!"

Central Purchasing (264)

Vesting authority in an auxiliary agency to buy, maintain stocks, and distribute supplies and materials to other agencies. Central purchasing replaces the system in which each administrative unit purchases its own supplies. In some cases, each unit is given a budget for supplies which it purchases from the central unit through a credit transfer system. In the national government, the central purchasing function is carried out by the General Services Administration (GSA), which also handles centralized property and records management. *See also* GENERAL SERVICES ADMINISTRATION (GSA), 144.

Significance Central purchasing has become one of the accepted principles of efficient administration. Its main advantages include (1) centralization of responsibility for supplies; (2) lower costs through large purchases; (3) standardization of equipment and record keeping; and (4) reduction of corruption. Its main disadvantages include (1) loss of effectiveness through requirements for uniformity and standardization; (2) waste that can occur when stockpiled materials become obsolete; and (3) the potential danger of politicization of supply purchasing. Many private corporations as well as most governments employ central purchasing as a routine operation.

Comptroller General (265)

The federal official who heads the General Accounting Office (GAO), which is responsible for auditing the accounts of all federal agencies. The Comptroller General of the United States serves as financial adviser to Congress. The office is filled through appointment for a

Financial Administration

fifteen-year term by the president with Senate consent. The main powers exercised by the Comptroller General are those related to directing and supervising the validation of payments by federal agencies and other units to ensure that they are within the intent and limits of Congress as specified in its appropriations acts. In addition, the Comptroller General is charged with carrying out legal, accounting, auditing, and claims settlement functions, and with making recommendations aimed at improving federal financial operations. *See also* AUDITING, 256; GENERAL ACCOUNTING OFFICE (GAO), 274.

Significance The Comptroller General exercises important powers in overseeing and participating in the financial activities of the entire United States Government. Because the "power of the purse" is the key power exercised by Congress, the GAO's role under the leadership of the Comptroller General can be decisive in translating the will of Congress into decisions and actions. Because the Comptroller General has great flexibility in making decisions, the holder of the office has often been accused of injecting personal and political views into his role as director of the GAO. Accountability to the Congress is weakened by the fact that, typically, the 535 members of the two houses of Congress differ greatly in their views about financial matters. Occasionally, conflicts between the Comptroller General and the president have flared and become public, particularly when they have involved major presidential programs to which the Comptroller General has exhibited open hostility by refusing to validate key payments. Validation is a "preaudit function of approving or refusing to allow payments *before* they are made." Many financial experts have criticized this system, preferring in its place a "postaudit" system in which executive officials make the initial validation for payments, followed later by a GAO auditing of the accounts to ensure that payments conform with congressional intent.

Congressional Budget and Impoundment Control Act of 1974 (266)

A federal statute creating budget committees in each house of Congress and a new Congressional Budget Office to provide Congress with a mechanism for monitoring the impact of the budget on the nation's economy. The Congressional Budget and Impoundment Control Act of 1974 was corrective legislation in that, previous to its passage, only the president, through the Office of Management and Budget (OMB), had an opportunity to view the total federal budget. Major responsibility for considering the budget's economic impact rested with the president. Congressional appropriations committees and those concerned with taxation examined the budget only as it was reflected in numerous separate appropriation and revenue bills. Under the 1974 legislation, a maximum spending figure is set for the total budget and for each of several broad funding categories. This helps to assure that members of Congress are aware of the potential impact which each appropriation bill has on spending totals. Not only did the Budget and Impoundment Control Act establish a budget committee in each house of Congress and a Congressional Budget Office to improve Congress's analytical base for economic planning, it also required that on two prescribed dates every year, Congress must vote explicitly on the budget as an entire package and on budget priorities. All subsequent decisions concerning the budget must relate to these two votes. The act also established a timetable for scheduling different phases of action by Congress on the budget. Appropriation bills, for example, cannot be considered by either house until authorizations have been passed and the first concurrent budget resolution has been adopted. Congress is not allowed to adjourn under the act until it has ironed out all differences on budgetary matters. Finally, some patterns of spending that had developed apart from the regular appropriations process, known as "backdoor spending," were abolished or brought under a measure of control and oversight, and the president's capacity to impound funds appropriated by Congress was limited. *See also* BUDGET, 216; BUDGET CYCLE, 263; IMPOUNDMENT, 275.

Significance The Congressional Budget and Impoundment Act of 1974 substantially revised the budgetary process in the United States. It has been called "the most significant legislation in the field since the Budget and Accounting Act of 1921." It represented a unique effort by Congress to consider total federal expenditures and revenues together to determine their effects on the economy. In the act, Congress tried to focus directly on national budget priorities in the light of national goals and the performance of individual policy programs. In performance since 1974, the act has been considered a success by most observers. Complaints by such organizations as the National Urban Coalition that the methods through which an agency gets money are characterized by secrecy, lack of a comprehensive review procedure, and inadequate decision criteria have been ameliorated in part. Yet the essence of the budgetary process continues to be political. Close observers such as political scientists Aaron Wildavsky, Richard F. Fenno, Jr., and Jesse Burkhead agree that a budgeteer must first be a politician in securing an agency's funding. Politics requires the use of strategies, and the politics of the budgetary process is no exception. In Wildavsky's words, "What really counts in helping an agency get the appropriations it desires? Long service in

Washington has convinced high agency officials that some things count a great deal and others only a little . . . as several informants put it in almost identical words, 'It's not what's in your estimates but how good a politician you are that matters.' " Although the Congressional Budget and Impoundment Act of 1974 establishes a more rational and comprehensive process for budget making, and makes Congress a more equal partner in policy determination, the political rules of the game for successful agency administrators have not changed.

Council of Economic Advisers (CEA) (267)
A three-member staff agency that advises the president on economic matters concerning the nation's economy. The Council of Economic Advisers was established by Congress in the Employment Act of 1946 to formulate proposals "to maintain employment, production, and purchasing power." It consists of three outstanding economists appointed by the president, with the advice and consent of the Senate, who serve at the president's pleasure. Located in the Executive Office of the President, the Council confers regularly with the president concerning current problems of the economy. One of its main functions is to help the president prepare an Annual Economic Report to the Congress on the state of the economy and what policies and programs are recommended for congressional consideration to cope with existing problems. *See also* KEYNESIANISM, 57.

Significance The enactment of the Employment Act of 1946 and the creation of the Council of Economic Advisers indicated that the United States would pursue Keynesian economic policies to try to achieve stability and growth. This meant that, rather than permitting the economy to be governed by nongovernmental forces such as the interaction of supply and demand in the marketplace, government would play an active role in promoting expansion and full employment through positive policies and programs. This has meant that the Council is charged with responsibility for keeping its finger on the economic pulse of the nation so that it can amass the data needed to make effective decisions. The Council's position as a leading advisory agency emphasizes the leadership role which the nation has assigned to the president for keeping the nation's economy healthy. The success or failure of a president's reelection campaign may well depend on the success or failure of his economic policies. These in turn may be influenced or determined by the advice the president receives from the Council of Economic Advisers. The Council has played a key role in recommending policies to combat seven post–World War II economic recessions. Its influence depends on the president and on its acceptance as a professional group of advisers who have the ability to fine tune the economy. Most of its advice to the president relates to the use of fiscal policy by the federal government. Its lack of a direct linkage with the Federal Reserve Board of Governors has meant that on occasion incompatible monetary and fiscal policies have been pursued by the government. This situation may arise when the Federal Reserve Board believes that inflation is the main enemy while the Council of Economic Advisers views unemployment and economic stagnation as the most serious problems. In such cases, the "Fed" has pursued a "tight money" policy to fight inflation, whereas the Council and the president have sought to stimulate the economy through deficit spending.

Earmarked Revenues (268)
Provisions found in statutes or constitutions that provide for certain types of public funds to be placed into segregated accounts and spent for stipulated purposes. Because the spending of earmarked revenues is often related to their collection, the process is often based on the benefit theory of taxation. The income from excise taxes on gasoline, for example, is earmarked by most states for highway improvement and maintenance. In the national government, as another example, the income from excise taxes on firearms and ammunition is spent on wildlife management. In many states, one-half or more of the total revenue is earmarked for specific purposes, which may include such broad categories as education and crime prevention.

Significance The earmarking of tax revenues in the states has become so widespread that state general fund budgets have become extremely vulnerable. When a state is forced to dip into earmarked funds to meet pressing demands in the general fund budget, vociferous protests from outraged members of groups benefiting from the earmarking are likely to develop. Advantages of earmarking include (1) the likelihood of dependable support for certain critical tax programs by those who benefit from them; (2) the ease of justifying new or higher taxes on the basis of specific needs; and (3) the ability to finance major projects over a long period of time, as, for example, the building of the interstate highway system by using mainly federal gasoline excise taxes. Disadvantages of earmarking include (1) a great reduction in flexibility in using tax revenues for addressing social problems; (2) the difficulty of providing for tax cuts when programs are dependent on a constant flow of funds at certain levels; and (3) encouragement and strengthening of interest groups by "paying them off" through richly financed programs that benefit their members. Evidence indicates that the trend toward earmarking funds, especially in state governments, will continue to expand.

Economic Indicators (269)
Standard measurements of national economic activity that provide information on where the economy has been, where it is situated currently, and where it is likely to go. Such information is provided monthly by the Department of Commerce and the Council of Economic Advisers (CEA) for use in making economic policy decisions. The Department of Commerce offers statistical information drawn from a variety of different indicators. Some of the key ones are gross national product (GNP), industrial production, business inventories, money supply, Consumer Price Index (CPI), new construction, employment and unemployment, interest rates, productivity levels, farm income, and international transactions. Indicator information is used both by the president and by Congress as it makes fiscal policy through the Joint Economic Committee. Economic indicators are also used by the Federal Reserve Board in making monetary policy. The use of indicators applies the policy-making procedures prescribed by the Keynesian approach to national economic security. *See also* COUNCIL OF ECONOMIC ADVISERS (CEA), 267; KEYNESIANISM, 57.

Significance The monthly publication of economic indicators by the Department of Commerce permits government policy makers to keep their fingers on the pulse of the national economy. When some of the key indicators take a downward turn, for example, the president and Congress may announce countercyclical fiscal policies to provide a stimulus to the economy. The Federal Reserve Board and the Treasury Department may implement stimulative monetary policies as well. The objective is to avoid a serious recession or an economic slump of major proportions. When the indicators take a sharp upward turn, on the other hand, policies to dampen the economy can be undertaken to avoid overheating and rampant inflation. These decisions are based on information that was largely unavailable before the creation of the Council of Economic Advisers in 1946.

Equalization (270)
The process of reviewing and adjusting property tax assessments to achieve a degree of uniformity among taxing districts. Equalization is aimed at achieving a fair distribution of the tax burden among different assessing districts. Two types of equalization are typical:

(1) adjustment of assessment values among the cities and townships or other local units by a county equalization board; and (2) a general equalization of property tax assessments in all districts by a state equalization board. In both cases, equalization is applied on the basis of the relationship between assessed valuations and the actual market value of property in the district. Equalization applies to all property within a taxing district and should not be confused with the "review" function whereby a board of review within a district examines individual cases of alleged overassessment. *See also* PROPOSITION 13, 74.

Significance While the assessed valuations of property have grown as a result of inflation and soaring property values, the process of equalization has taken on a new importance. Equalization is particularly critical when school and special district tax powers cross district assessment lines. In such cases, some property owners may pay far more than their fair share to support the common activity, whereas others may pay far less, depending on how their local assessor values their property. The problem may even involve serious inequities when some of the taxing districts have an elected assessor and others use an appointed assessor. State constitutional and statutory limitations on the taxing powers of local units—especially those that limit the "millage" or tax rate—have encouraged local assessors to try to match up assessment figures with tax needs. Widespread belief that the property tax is unfair and an overdependence on it to provide income needed by local governments have led to the adoption of constitutional amendments that severely limit assessments for property tax purposes, such as Proposition 13 in California. Although equalization reduces inequities among taxing units, it does not eliminate them, nor does it meet the problems of inequities in individual assessments and of the growing dependence on the property tax as tax revolts vitiate efforts to increase income from other sources.

Federal Reserve System (FRS) (271)
The central bank of the United States charged with the responsibility of developing and administering monetary and credit policies for the nation. The Federal Reserve System, often referred to simply as "the Fed," is a combination public-private banking regulatory system headed by the Federal Reserve Board. Created in 1913, the Federal Reserve System consists of twelve Federal Reserve banks, each located in one of the twelve Federal Reserve districts into which the country is divided. Each Federal Reserve bank is a privately owned "bankers'

Financial Administration

bank," with all member banks in that district required to hold stock in it. Each is headed by a board of nine directors, six chosen by private member banks in the district and three by the Federal Reserve Board in Washington. Each member of the Board of Governors, along with six members elected from the Reserve banks, serve on the Federal Open Market Committee (FOMC). This body makes and carries out policies of buying and selling securities and engages in foreign currency exchanges aimed at protecting the value of the dollar in international exchange markets. Other operations carried on within the Federal Reserve System include those of the Federal Advisory Council, which advises on general business conditions, and the Consumer Advisory Council, which advises in the field of consumer credit. Whereas the Federal Council is composed of twelve members with one selected from each district, the Counsumer Council is composed of twenty-eight members selected from all parts of the country and broadly representative of consumer and creditor interests. Congress has provided that each bank with a national charter must be a member of the Federal Reserve bank in its district, whereas state banks have an option. Most state-chartered banks, however, have joined the Federal Reserve System. *See also* MONETARISM, 61; MONETARY POLICY, 280.

Significance The Federal Reserve System provides the nation with central banking functions that include the transfer of funds, the handling of government deposits, managing the federal debt, supervising and regulating private banks, and acting as the lender of last resort. Its most important function in terms of the nation's economic well-being is that of determining the supply of money and credit in the system. This function is performed regularly by raising or lowering the rediscount rate, by selling or buying government securities in open market operations, and by determining the reserve ratio requirements that each bank must maintain to meet depositors' demands for their money. Policies adopted by the Federal Reserve Board are carried out in thousands of member banks across the country. Federal Reserve banks in each district must generally implement Board policies, but in some areas they are permitted a measure of autonomy in decision making. The nation has increasingly turned to the Fed to come up with policies and decisions that will bring inflation under control, but not at the expense of heavy unemployment. However, in fighting inflation the Board has pursued a "hard" or "tight" money policy, whereas in fighting recessions and unemployment it has followed a "soft" or "'loose" money policy. When the two exist simultaneously—as in the "stagflation" of the 1970s and early 1980s—the Federal Reserve

System is placed in a quandary. Often in the past there has been a lack of harmony between the Fed's monetary policies and the president's fiscal policies, with the former more concerned with inflation and the latter concentrating on trying to solve unemployment problems and restore growth and expansion in the economy. As a result of these pressures, the System has become less politically independent and increasingly willing to try to harmonize its monetary policies with the president's fiscal policies. One school of economic thought—the Monetarists—believe that the quantity of money and credit available in the nation, as provided by the Federal Reserve System, determines the state of the nation's economy.

Fiscal Policy (272)
A macroeconomic concept that assumes a relationship between the total spending level in the economy and the existence of either unemployment or inflation. Fiscal policy is related directly to the gross national product (GNP). Fiscal policy states that when government's direct share of the GNP is big, government budgets have an enormous impact on the status of the country's economy. The federal budget is an instrument of fiscal policy because at the end of World War II Congress permanently committed the federal government in the Employment Act of 1946 to use its budgets and other instruments of national policy to promote maximum employment, production, and purchasing power. The "other instruments of national policy" include the controls the government has on personal consumption by the use of withholding taxes and excise taxes, and controls on investment by the use of corporate taxes, depletion allowances, amortization rules, and subsidies. Fiscal policy may promote full employment, redistribute incomes, or foment inflation. Its main goal, however, is economic stabilization. This involves not only full employment (many consider 4 percent unemployment an acceptable level), but also (1) the maintenance of price stability; (2) steady economic growth; (3) an adequate supply of collectively consumed goods; (4) public activities which involve services for the good of society, such as police protection and national defense; and (5) equilibrium in the international balance of payments. Fiscal policy requires action by standard constitutional processes, which are too slow to fine tune the economy. Fine tuning is attempted through the use of monetary policy, but fiscal policy is an important determinant of monetary policy. *See also* BUDGET, 261; FEDERAL RESERVE SYSTEM (FRS), 271; KEYNESIANISM, 57; MONETARY POLICY, 280.

Significance Fiscal policy represents the deep impact British economist John Maynard Keynes and his disciples have had on federal budgeting in the United States. Keynes said simply that government regulates the economy by the amount of money it spends. Fiscal policy since World War II has involved the use of deficit spending to combat seven recessions and to avoid others. Fiscal policy must always be considered in trying to cope with national economic problems along with monetary policy. *Monetary policy* refers to Federal Reserve Board regulation of the amount of money in circulation and credit available. The Federal Reserve Board can directly influence interest rates, credit availability, and money supply. It can indirectly affect employment, production, and prices. It is more insulated politically than fiscal policy. Good fiscal policy does not always make good politics. Budgeting to meet increased programs and demands, for example, often conflicts with public pressure for a balanced budget. Attempts to control spending to reduce deficits and achieve a balanced budget may be complicated by inflation, labor costs, and employee pensions, while a tight budget may help to bring on a recession, increased unemployment, and less spending for social programs. Fiscal policy is obviously a highly complex and specialized subject which is always subject to multiplier effects. Multiplier effects take into account that any transaction will generate other transactions which may or may not serve the basic federal policy goal. That goal is to regulate spending in order to stabilize the economy, limit inflation, and minimize deficit expenditures. From this goal come practical budget decisions, such as overall size of the budget, the types and timing of spending, the balance of activities or which activities should be emphasized, the size of programs and the degree of control over them, the building or selling of stockpiles, and the tax policy for the nation.

Fiscal Year (273)

A special twelve-month financial period used by government for convenience in record keeping, tax collecting, spending, and general fiscal management. The fiscal year for a government can begin and end at any times chosen by government. In the United States, government fiscal years typically begin on October 1 and end on September 30 (the national government and a number of state governments), or begin on July 1 and end on June 30 (formerly used by the national government, currently by many states and most local units). A few states and local units equate the fiscal and calendar years. The fiscal year always has a title based on the calendar year in which it ends; for example, Fiscal 1987 for the federal government began on

October 1, 1986, and ended on September 30, 1987. Private businesses and organizations often use fiscal year periods other than calendar years, and the submission of tax payments and returns can be adjusted for these under Internal Revenue Service rules. *See also* BUDGET CYCLE, 263.

Significance Financial policies and actions undertaken by government are tied in, through budgeting and appropriations, with specific fiscal years. In studying and evaluating government programs, the fiscal year period is often used as a base rather than the calendar year. In choosing a fiscal year period, the legislative body is concerned with trying to match the availability of funds with the need for them. When the national government changed from a July 1–June 30 to an October 1–September 30 fiscal year in the Congressional Budget and Impoundment Control Act of 1974, for example, it was in recognition of the changes that had occurred in adopting huge budgets and in attempting to finance them out of current revenues. The change was also aimed at giving Congress more time to work out its new legislative budget to be used as a means of keeping the president's budget under a greater measure of control. At the time the change occurred, members of Congress were motivated especially by the hope of achieving a balanced budget. The changeover, however, appears to have had no appreciable effect on reaching that goal.

General Accounting Office (GAO) (274)

An arm of Congress engaged in the auditing of the financial accounts of federal agencies to guarantee executive compliance with the provisions of appropriations bills. The General Accounting Office was established in 1921 by the Budget and Accounting Act. Just one year before, President Woodrow Wilson vetoed legislation that would have established the federal budget system on the grounds that he opposed the creation of an auditing office answerable to Congress rather than the president. But President Warren G. Harding signed the bill into law. The GAO was created to investigate "all matters relating to the receipt, disbursement, and application of public funds." It conducts two major types of audits. One is the comprehensive audit, which focuses on the agency's accounting system and includes a spot check of particular transactions. The other is the more detailed general audit, which examines each of the accounts of the agency and scrutinizes each transaction in those accounts. The results of all audits undertaken by the GAO are transmitted to Congress. Because it is not possible to perform a detailed audit of each agency every year, auditing is either random or selective. If individual members or

Financial Administration

committees of Congress request that an agency be audited, the request is almost always honored. The purpose of the audit is undergoing considerable change. Although the original intent of ensuring honesty in dispensing public monies and in preventing needless waste is still there, and accounting procedures are prescribed to assure that record keeping meets that end, the scope of auditing has been broadened in recent years to encompass studies of whether governmental programs achieved desired results. Officials within the audited agency are subject to prosecution should obligations be incurred for illegal amounts or for unauthorized purposes. The General Accounting Office is headed by the Comptroller General, who is appointed by the president for a single term of fifteen years, with the advice and consent of the Senate. *See also* ACCOUNTING, 253; AUDITING, 256; BUDGET AND ACCOUNTING ACT OF 1921, 262.

Significance The General Accounting Office is one of the most powerful institutions of government. From its creation in 1921 until the late 1940s, it frustrated presidents by exercising not only the postaudit review but the preaudit as well. That is, it passed in advance on the legality of proposed expenditures, a function presidents claimed was an executive, not a legislative, prerogative. In 1948, the GAO joined the Department of the Treasury and the Bureau of the Budget to launch the Joint Financial Management Improvement Program. Under this program preauditing and accounting became executive branch prerogatives, with the GAO setting standards and checking on agency compliance. Under the Budget and Accounting Procedures Act of 1950, the GAO received authorization to conduct onsite audits, which stopped the shipment of tons of agency vouchers to the GAO. A further expansion of GAO's power came in the Legislative Reorganization Act of 1970, which instructed the GAO to undertake cost-benefit analyses as an aid to congressional appraisals of agency budgets. But the primary mission of the GAO continues to be postaudit checks for fraud and embezzlement.

Impoundment (275)

A form of postappropriation control on spending exercised by the president under statutory authority and under the president's constitutional powers. Impoundment is refusal to spend money Congress has appropriated. In the past the president has impounded as a result of disapproving of a funded program, its margin of increase, or its effect on total government expenditures and the economy. Despite the president's constitutional obligation to "take care that the laws be faithfully executed," the president is faced at times with conflicts in the intent of legislation. For example, Congress may tell the president to avoid deficits, stay under a debt ceiling, control inflation, and protect the environment. It may then allot money for large public works projects that will break through the debt ceiling, generate inflation, and impair the beauty of canyons and the countryside. Given the constitutional separation of powers, which recognizes the independence and equality of the presidency vis-à-vis Congress, presidents since Thomas Jefferson have therefore impounded funds. On October 17, 1803, for example, President Jefferson reported in his annual message to Congress that he had set aside $50,000 that Congress had appropriated for buying gunboats for the Mississippi River. Jefferson gave two reasons for ignoring the will of Congress: (1) conditions had changed, since the United States had acquired the territory and pacified the river; and (2) he did not want to waste money on outmoded gunboats when better ones were being designed. A year later he reported that he had allowed the expenditure to begin. Impoundment was used sparingly until the presidency of Franklin D. Roosevelt, who used it dramatically during World War II to stop pork-barrel projects. Roosevelt ordered substantial amounts for dams and highways to be placed in frozen reserves, unavailable for expenditure, for the duration of the war. Since World War II, impoundment has stopped air force expansion to fifty-eight groups from forty-eight; the B-70 bomber; several aircraft carriers; water projects; highway expansion; and rural aid programs; among many other congressionally authorized projects. From 1963 to 1976, the dollars impounded by the president went from $4.5 billion to $12.1 billion. President Richard M. Nixon's impoundments were unprecedented, however, in their scope and severity. They focused on domestic programs that had been sponsored by preceding Democratic administrations and enacted by Democratic Congresses. Among the programs dismantled were those for water-pollution control, rural electrification, agricultural disaster loans, health research, health services, urban renewal, low-rent housing, and other housing assistance. Whereas previous presidents had used impoundment to withhold funds for particular weapons systems, a category in which a president might claim some authority as Commander-in-Chief, or for pet projects of members of Congress, the Nixon "conservative revolution" applied impoundment across the board of all policy areas. This led to enactment of the Congressional Budget and Impoundment Control Act of 1974, which now severely limits a president's ability to impound at all. *See also* CONGRESSIONAL BUDGET AND IMPOUNDMENT CONTROL ACT OF 1974, 266; EXECUTIVE OFFICE OF THE PRESIDENT (EXOP OR EOP), 138; OFFICE OF MANAGEMENT AND BUDGET (OMB), 166.

Financial Administration

Significance Impoundment effectively gave the president a line-item veto of legislation. Unlike the constitutions of forty-two of the fifty states, the United States Constitution gave the president no authority to veto *parts* of appropriation acts. A take-it-or-leave-it authority thus leaves the president constitutionally at the mercy of whatever ill-considered project may be added to an appropriation measure the president would otherwise approve. The Constitution is vague, however, on whether appropriation acts are mandates to spend, or whether they constitute *permission* to spend. Presidents have taken the latter view, interposing their judgment and advising Congress on *how much* of an appropriation ought to be obligated. Until the Nixon impoundments of 1970–1973, impoundment had been used for decades with restraint and circumspection and without precipitating a major crisis. Congress now tends to draft enabling and appropriation acts in such a way as to deprive the president and agency heads of discretion in implementing programs at approximately the levels funded. Congress increasingly votes, "The Secretary shall . . . ," instead of the traditional "The Secretary is authorized to. . . . "

Indexation (276)
The process whereby costs and income are adjusted automatically to reflect changes in a nation's inflation rate. Indexation is typically a contractual system that is based on the Consumer Price Index (CPI) or on some other index of changing price levels that reflects the purchasing power of a nation's currency. Indexing has been developed as a means for moderating the impact of heavy inflation in a national economy. For example, if the inflation rate jumps to 15 percent by a certain point in any year, an indexing system would provide that income from pension plans, salaries, and wages, and other sources included in indexing agreements would also increase by approximately 15 percent. At the same time, costs, such as insurance premiums, loan payments, and interest charges would go up by 15 percent if included in an indexation agreement. The objective of indexation, therefore, is to try to keep income and costs in relative balance by tying them to the factor of the inflation rate. *See also* INFLATION, 277.

Significance Countries experiencing heavy rates of inflation tend to utilize some elements of indexation to smooth out the impact of skyrocketing costs. In the United States, double-digit inflation in the 1970s helped to popularize this approach. In some countries, such as Israel and Brazil, governments have admitted failure in their efforts to control inflation and have called for general indexation as a means of adjusting to the rapidly changing value of the national currency. In the early 1980s, for example, Israel's inflation rate hit an annual rate of almost 200 percent, a rate that would have been catastrophic in its impact had it not been for indexation of most costs and wages. Critics of indexation, however, charge that it does not solve inflationary problems but merely raises the toleration levels of societies that employ it. Moreover, they charge indexation with being a major factor contributing to increases in the rate of inflation. In the United States, indexation is applied selectively to many wages and costs, such as in labor contracts, in insurance policies, and for social security benefits. The indexing of social security payments, critics charge, has not only contributed to the rate of inflation but has jeopardized the funding of the system. Until the means of controlling inflation are determined and applied effectively, indexation will likely remain as a "crutch" used to mitigate the impact of inflation on society.

Inflation (277)
An economic condition characterized by an increasing level of prices and a decreasing value of the national currency in terms of its purchasing power. Inflation typically reflects an increase in the quantity or "movement" of money without a corresponding increase in the quantity of goods and services available. Thus the traditional explanation for inflation is that it results from "demand-pull"—too much money chasing too few goods. Economists have developed additional theories to explain inflation because the phenomenon can and does appear when demand-pull conditions are not present. A second theory seeks to explain inflation as a result of oligopoly (control of the market by a few companies), wherein the lack of competition produces a "profit-pull" condition in which powerful corporations seek to increase their profits by raising prices artificially high. A third theory holds that inflation is the product of rapidly rising costs of production that result in a "cost-push" impact as the prices for labor, raw material, and energy rise. Advocates of cost-push explanations for inflation point out, for example, that two-digit inflation hit the United States following large increases in the cost of imported oil. Whatever its causes, observers agree that mass psychological factors play an important role in keeping inflation going once it gets started. A number of countries have in effect accepted inflation as a continuing way of life and have developed indexation systems as means for adjusting to the phenomenon. *See also* INDEXATION, 276.

Significance　　By the early 1980s, inflation had become a serious threat to the stability of most nations. Even the tightly controlled economies of Communist bloc nations have felt the impact of skyrocketing prices for many imports from the West. Public administrators on all levels in the United States were forced to make continuous budgetary adjustments as prices soared and taxpayers revolted. Through a tight monetary policy administered by the Federal Reserve, inflation was brought under control by the mid-1980s. Surplus stocks of oil led to a global reduction in energy prices that also helped quench the inflationary fires. Although most economists believe that serious inflation can be avoided or cured through the proper use by government of monetary and/or fiscal policy, in some cases the social and political costs involved in balancing budgets and increasing taxes in the form of higher unemployment and economic stagnation make it difficult for elected leaders to take such actions. Studies of how to control inflation without being forced to accept undesirable trade-offs continue, but none has yet produced an empirically sound approach. In the 1970s, the impact of OPEC pricing on world oil prices and, indirectly, on all other prices indicates that the costs of energy may be a key to understanding inflation. Inflation encourages a "buy now" attitude, which assumes that delay in making purchases merely adds to the costs. The willingness of millions of people to go progressively deeper into debt is also a by-product of inflation, since debt is encouraged by the belief that it can be paid off in cheaper dollars in the future. Increasingly, government, giant corporations, the welfare system, and "bureaucrats" have become the public scapegoats blamed for the continuing problem of inflation.

Line-item Budget (278)

A detailed financial plan of specific spending requests an executive presents to a legislative body for approval. In a line-item budget, each budgetary division is listed by *organizational unit*, such as a department or agency, and by *category* of expenditure, such as salaries, purchases, and supplies. Line-item budgeting, also called cash-based budgeting, was widely used in the United States from about 1900 through the middle 1930s. It gave legislative bodies maximum control over administrators. No expenditure (item) approved by the legislature could be changed subsequently by an agency administrator without authorization from the legislature. Administrators, therefore, had little discretion or flexibility in the management of their agency's resources. If money had been allocated for a particular piece of equipment or program, administrators were required to spend it as specified even though conditions had changed and the money might better be saved or spent for another purpose. In the national government, congressional and executive control over the budget was increased and institutionalized by the Budget and Accounting Act of 1921. That historic act established the Bureau of the Budget, now the Office of Management and Budget (OMB), and the General Accounting Office (GAO). The OMB reviews all requests for funds before the president submits the budget to Congress, and the GAO examines expenditures to ensure they were made in accordance with congressional intent. Line-item budgeting favors those managers who "go by the book," meaning they follow a budget precisely with detailed accounting procedures. Although line-item budgeting has yielded to other forms of budgeting at the federal level, it is still widely used in state and local governments. *See also* PERFORMANCE BUDGETING, 282; PLANNING, PROGRAMMING, BUDGETING SYSTEMS (PPBS), 283; ZERO-BASE BUDGETING (ZBB), 291.

Significance Line-item budgeting reflects the scientific management school of thought and emphasizes honesty, efficiency, and inflexibility. If an agency fails to spend all the money it has been allocated, even if there are justifiable reasons, it can expect to be penalized in the next budget. Line-item budgets do not reward administrators who cut expenses in a program or who try to be flexible when suggested by circumstances. The implication of line-item budgeting is that administrators cannot be trusted, for if money remains on a line after the budgeted year, it is probably because the organization's request was inflated. The main advantage of the line-item budget—tight control—is also its main limitation. A line-item budget tells administrators how much money is being spent for each item, but not whether the money is being expended wisely. Individual expenditures are not related to each other or to the agency's goals or programs. Evaluation is extremely difficult in a line-item budget, and there is no direct linkage to public policy goals and objectives. All a line-item budget indicates is the total dollar amount for each individual agency and category. It does not indicate what collective purpose the items are intended to serve. Hence, duplication of effort may be encouraged and remain undetected in line-item budgeting because control focuses on expenditures rather than on planning and evaluation. It also encourages destructive competition among agency heads for the funds available.

Management by Objectives (MBO) (279)

A process whereby organizational goals and objectives are set through the participation of organizational members in terms of results expected. Management by objectives was first discussed by Peter Drucker in his 1954 book, *The Practice of Management*. MBO encourages "self-management" and decentralization. It advocates an integrated approach to total management, stresses the concepts of communication and feedback, encourages organization development and change, and emphasizes policy research and the support of top management. MBO is an attempt to set objectives, track the progress of the appropriate program, and evaluate its results. The organization decentralizes by operationalizing its objectives and letting the individual managers most concerned with the program achieve those objectives in the most effective way possible. MBO has a managerial orientation that stresses common sense. It is concerned chiefly with program effectiveness, and in this orientation it is not unlike performance budgeting. The advantages of an MBO system are that it gives those people closest to the problem some latitude in dealing with it, while simultaneously measuring their performance according to criteria developed by policy makers at the highest level. An MBO system that works permits individual initiatives and innovation by on-line managers; yet their participatory policy making is limited by centrally planned operational goals. *See also* PARTICIPATIVE MANAGEMENT, 110; PERFORMANCE BUDGETING, 282; PLANNING, PROGRAMMING, BUDGETING SYSTEMS (PPBS), 283.

Significance Management by objectives (MBO) became popular at all levels of government in the early 1970s when planning, programming, budgeting systems (PPBS) was largely abandoned. PPBS had what one observer called an "unfortunate association with a passion for uniformity and detail." MBO looked like a flexible alternative. It was ironic that President Nixon's administration embraced MBO, because MBO's distinguishing characteristic was its emphasis on decentralization and on policy implementation by subordinates. The Nixon administration was not known for its trust of bureaucrats beyond the immediate confines of the White House. Frank P. Sherwood and William J. Page, Jr., wrote in a *Public Administration Review* article entitled "MBO and Public Management" in 1976 that "the attitude of the Nixon top management was one of low trust and contempt towards civil service." Nevertheless, by 1975, MBO was popular enough in the federal government that the Office of Management and Budget (OMB) issued Circular A-11, which required the submission of agency objectives with the fiscal year budget estimates. This was a new budgetary format in which OMB was implementing an MBO concept. Many state and local governments also adopted MBO. Management by objectives remains a remarkably successful administrative innovation, made effective by MBO's propensity to decentralize administrative responsibility.

Monetary Policy (280)
The way in which government controls the supply and price of money in the economy, which in turn affects unemployment and inflation. Monetary policy is determined by the Federal Reserve System (FRS), headed by the Federal Reserve Board. The Federal Reserve is the central bank for the United States. By increasing the cost of money, for example, the Federal Reserve can reduce the level of spending. If there is a shortage of money in the economy, it is worth more; if there is too much money in the economy, it is worth less. The Federal Reserve may try to expand money and credit to foster greater employment. It may also contract money and credit to combat inflation. Monetary policy is implemented by three fundamental techniques: (1) *Open-Market Operations*. If the Federal Reserve wants to take money out of the economy, it sells bonds, usually at a favorable interest rate. If it wants to increase money in the economy, it buys bonds. (2) *Discount Rate*. This is the interest rate the Federal Reserve charges member banks for short-term loans. An increase in the discount rate increases interest rates, which makes money more expensive, thereby discouraging people from borrowing. (3) *Changing the Reserve Requirements*. Banks use depositors' money to make loans but are required to keep a certain percent of their money in the bank, usually in the form of government bonds. The Federal Reserve can tighten the money supply by requiring that a greater reserve be maintained in local banks, thus shrinking the amounts available for loans. On the other hand, decreasing the reserve requirement increases the money supply. Monetary policy attempts to fine tune the economy by determining the amount of money and credit available and by rapid applications of investment and credit controls which affect income flows through structures of liquidity and assets. *See also* BUDGET, 261; FEDERAL RESERVE SYSTEM (FRS), 271; FISCAL POLICY, 272.

Significance Monetary policy is differentiated from fiscal policy in that the former is more immediate, less political in nature, and less subject to time-consuming constitutional processes. Monetary policy has a profound effect on society. It substantially regulates companies in the housing industry, which depend on external credit. When banks are forced by the Federal Reserve to restrict loans, higher credit groups have preference, and smaller and newer businesses suffer. Tight monetary policy affects certain sectors of the economy more than others, and certain groups, such as the young and minorities, more than others. Monetary policy is also important for public budgeting because all levels of government borrow and invest. Available credit and interest rates frequently determine if budgeted programs can be approved. Budget justifications and intelligent

Financial Administration

budget reviews are therefore dependent on a calculation of the effects of monetary policy on proposed programs.

Negative Income Tax (281)

A public assistance system that would replace current welfare programs by providing people with a guaranteed annual income through the taxing authority. The negative income tax idea was introduced by economist Milton Friedman of the University of Chicago in his 1962 book, *Capitalism and Freedom*. It was popularized as a major part of the program to fight rising poverty in the United States, proposed by the President's Urban Council in the late 1960s. The council was led by policy planner and later United States Senator from New York, Daniel Patrick Moynihan. The negative income tax is a radical program in that it transfers the basis for public assistance away from such programs as food stamps and aid to families with dependent children, to income level. Income supplements would be given to those people whose income, as reported on a federal tax return, falls below the level Congress determines is necessary to maintain a minimum standard of living.

Proponents of the negative income tax cite four reasons for their support of the idea. (1) It is only supplementary in nature. The amount needed for a minimum standard of living is not guaranteed; therefore, there is incentive to look for other sources of income. (2) Administration of the program can be consolidated into an existing structure, such as the Internal Revenue Service (IRS) or the Social Security Administration (SSA), and would thereby be more efficient than multiple public assistance agencies. (3) It standardizes benefits nationwide. Welfare benefits are currently higher in some states than in others, and higher benefit states attract large numbers of welfare recipients. (4) The program would be less costly than those programs presently in operation. Opponents of the negative income tax question the control it takes away from government over how assistance is utilized. When one gives food stamps, one is reasonably sure food will be purchased. When one gives cash, anything can be bought with it. The negative income tax also encourages a complete restructuring of the tax system. Income analysis would have to be done more frequently than once a year for those persons receiving assistance.

Significance The negative income tax is a proposal of neoconservatives to change the present welfare system while retaining some elements of the tradition of governmental assistance to the poor. It would be self-executing and would eliminate many caseworkers by making aid directly available to those with low incomes. The negative income tax was implemented experimentally in Hawaii, New Jersey, and Massachusetts, but with marginal success. It appears to be too radical an idea for federal policy makers to accept, having been defeated twice in the Senate.

Performance Budgeting (282)
A method of budgeting that collects and arranges individual expenditures into the functions, activities, and projects an organization is to perform. Performance budgeting, also called program budgeting, takes former line items and attempts to see how they relate to the larger purpose of the agency, rather than looking at them as a string of separate expense items. Performance budgeting gives administrators much more personal responsibility for their organization's budget than does line-item budgeting. While administrators must meet an efficiency objective, they are given considerable discretion in the use of appropriated resources. Line-item budgeting sees administrators essentially as clerks. Performance budgeting sees them as managers. Legislators exercise much less direct control over administrative agencies under performance budgeting than they do under line-item budgeting. *See also* BUDGET, 261; LINE-ITEM BUDGET, 278; PLANNING, PROGRAMMING, BUDGETING SYSTEMS (PPBS), 283; ZERO-BASE BUDGETING (ZBB), 291.

Significance Performance budgeting is primarily concerned with efficiency and economy in government, not with whether government effectively responds to public needs. Administrative and managerial skills tend to dominate agency decision making under performance budgeting, with budget analysis focused on precision accounting and control. There is heavy emphasis on work-cost measurement. The development of performance budgeting with its focus on evaluation represented progress from line-item budgeting, with its emphasis on how many typewriters and paper clips are needed. But even performance budgeting does not ask the basic question: Should this particular program be implemented in the first place? A performance budget only assesses the program that has been determined as the one the agency should administer. The possibility remains that even though the program is being run efficiently, it is not the best one to meet the agency's or the government's goals. The result often is wasted money. Performance budgeting does not select the "best" program from among all the possibilities. It only assesses what is already in existence. Program selection as a part of budget making is

Financial Administration

the primary function of another approach to budgeting: planning, programming, budgeting systems (PPBS).

Planning, Programming, Budgeting Systems (283) (PPBS)
An approach to budgeting which assumes that the search for and selection of goals, programs, and projects can be quantified. PPBS administrators identify all the possible alternatives in each budgeting category and then apply cost-benefit analysis to each one. The alternative that shows the most benefit for a given cost, or a predetermined benefit for the least cost, would be the best choice—the "best" choice being the "most rational" choice. Under PPBS (sometimes called PPB), administrators are involved with evaluation at virtually every step of the budgeting process. A great deal of managerial responsibility flows to top administrators. Their expertise as systems analysts and "economic experts" tends to preempt legislative decision making. Under performance budgeting, for example, efficiency analysis is applied to a program *after* the legislature determines which one the agency should implement. In contrast, PPBS administrators have already completed most of the analysis *before* the legislature can determine policy. Thus legislative choices are severely limited by administrators who preselect policy alternatives. *See also* DECISION MAKING, RATIONAL-COMPREHENSIVE, 95; PERFORMANCE BUDGETING, 282; SYSTEMS ANALYSIS, 83.

Significance Planning, programming, budgeting systems (PPBS) had a brief and glorious history in the federal service. PPBS was fully implemented in the Department of Defense in 1961 under Secretary Robert S. McNamara. PPBS was an effort to reduce competition among the armed services, each vying for control over a particular weapons system and each convinced its own program was essential to national defense. PPBS worked so well in gaining overall coordination of defense policy that it was adopted in all federal departments in 1965 by President Lyndon B. Johnson. By 1967, the Bureau of the Budget had implemented PPBS in twenty-one agencies and looked toward its implementation in many others. By 1971, however, the Budget Bureau's successor, the Office of Management and Budget (OMB), had issued a memorandum to all federal agencies indicating they were no longer required to submit a PPBS budget. What had happened in the interim was more than the coming of a new Republican administration to Washington. The basic weaknesses of PPBS had overtaken it. Chief among the weaknesses was the limitation of the rational decision-making model itself. It was difficult for administrators to identity and quantify all possible goals, programs, and projects. Trying to place an accurate and agreed-on dollar amount on the costs and benefits of social programs was virtually impossible. As one observer stated, "How does an administrator determine if a park is worth more or less than a library?" PPBS also ignored three political considerations, which undermined its usefulness and credibility. (1) Elected officials suspected that their control over many key policy decisions had been usurped by PPBS administrators. Legislators believed they were not receiving all the information they needed, and that they had no way to evaluate the data they did receive. PPBS administrators controlled much of the policy-making debate through their computer-simulation models, which turned out the analyses of the various alternatives. PPBS tended to reverse the role of legislators and administrators. The legislature was placed in the position of having to look to the bureaucracy for policy and information. This was not acceptable to most legislators. (2) Many of the planning projections in PPBS were for periods of five to seven years. Legislators tended to think and work within the shorter spans of their own terms in office or until the next election. (3) PPBS ignored the political importance of individual politicians and groups. The most rational or cost-effective program according to PPBS might not be the most politically feasible one, especially if it failed to reflect the political strength of legislators or constituencies. Political realities or values could not be neglected. Despite the weaknesses of PPBS, however, its advocates did bring planning and rationality to the budget process. They made people aware of the need to evaluate critically various policy and program alternatives. PPBS employed techniques, such as cost-benefit analysis, that are still used for assessing the relative merits of policy choices.

Progressive/Regressive Tax (284)

Two contrasting approaches to taxation that differ mainly in the application of tax rates and the incidence (where the burden really falls) of the tax. A progressive tax provides for rates that increase as the tax base (the value of the property or the amount of income being taxed) increases. In a regressive tax, on the other hand, tax rates remain constant or decline as the tax base increases. For example, a progressive income tax might provide for rates that progressively increase from 10 percent to 70 percent as income (and tax-paying ability) increases, whereas a regressive tax might retain a constant 20 percent rate regardless of the amount taxed, or it might be reduced to 10 percent for all income over a stipulated amount. A progressive tax, however, might be turned into a regressive one if, for example, there are substantial exemptions of income from taxation, such as permitting stock dividends, capital gains, and interest income to be partly or wholly exempted from the tax, or if such income is taxed at a lower rate.

Significance Most of the political battles fought over taxes relate not only to whether or not taxes are needed, but to the issue of whether they are basically progressive or regressive in nature. As a rule, regressive taxes are easier to adopt or increase because progressive taxes tend to arouse the ire of those elements in the community that are politically most adept at protecting their interests. While progressive taxes are based on the principle of "ability to pay," (tax-paying responsibility increases as income increases), many but not all regressive taxes are based on the "benefit" theory (income from taxes should be spent to benefit the taxpayers directly) of taxation. Typical progressive taxes include the individual and corporate income taxes, estate and inheritance taxes, excise taxes on luxury goods, and gift taxes. Examples of regressive taxes include sales, value-added, personal and real property, and excise taxes. The most regressive kind of tax is that which places levies on necessities, such as a sales tax on food and medicine. Although most business taxes are progressive at face value, many are regressive in practice because businesspersons are able to shift the incidence of the taxes to consumers. The question of incidence, or who bears the ultimate burden of a tax, is often the critical issue in tax battles because the incidence of most taxes can be shifted.

Public Debt (285)

The cumulative total of budget deficits, including accrued interest, of all governmental units within a country. In the United States, the public debt includes the total national debt, plus the total indebtedness of the fifty states and all of the thousands of local units of government. It does not, however, ordinarily include the vast number of claims against the government—for example, future social security benefits payable. Although state and local debt has increased more rapidly than the national debt in recent years, the major portion of the nation's public debt is owed by the national government. Each fiscal year deficit is added to the total debt, which by the late 1980s approached $3 trillion for the national government. In a typical fiscal year, the greatest share of income comes from individual income taxes, followed by the corporation income tax. Social security payments rate first place for expenditures, with defense expenditures a close second. Interest on the national debt has increased tremendously, with a rapidly growing portion paid to foreign investors. State and local debt, on the other hand, has been kept under some measure of control by constitutional provisions, statutory limits, revenue sharing from the national government, and direct voter participation in making many fiscal decisions. Although the United States Constitution contains no limitations on the size of the national debt, Congress has unsuccessfully attempted to institute a greater measure of frugality by imposing—and periodically raising—a statutory debt limit in specific amounts. State and local governmental income comes mainly from property, income, and sales taxes, and major expenditure categories include education, welfare, highways, and health, in that order. The rapid increase in state and local debt in recent years is largely the result of the failure of income to keep pace with soaring costs. See also BORROWING POWER, 260; FISCAL POLICY, 272.

Significance The growth in the public debt over the years since the Great Depression has reflected the turbulent and crisis-filled times the nation has experienced. Three wars, seven major recessions, a number of social revolutions, environmental programs, and soaring energy costs have all contributed to the growing deficits. Keynesian economic theories, for example, have called for massive deficit spending by government during economic recessions to avoid the threat of a major depression. The national debt increased from about $16 billion ($132 per capita) in 1930 to nearly $43 billion ($367 per capita) in 1940 as a result of deficit spending to meet the emergency needs of the Great Depression. By 1950, the debt was increased to $257 billion ($1,697 per capita) to pay for World War II and its aftermath. During the 1950s, the debt remained fairly stable as a result of three balanced budgets during the Eisenhower presidency. The Vietnam War in the 1960s contributed to the deficits that typified the federal budget in nine of the ten years of that decade, with the national debt rising to $370 billion ($1,806 per capita) by 1970. By 1980, the debt had risen to over $800 billion as a result of the massive deficits of the Nixon, Ford, and Carter administrations. During the 1980s, Reagan administration deficits exceeded all past records with almost $2 trillion added to the public national debt and its total approaching $3 trillion (approximately $12,500 per capita). Altogether, in the 199 fiscal years since the first budget was formulated in 1789, there has been a total of 180 fiscal years in deficit and only 19 with surpluses, most of them very small.

Economists and political leaders tend to disagree over the impact of the public debt. Most political leaders pay routine homage to the ideas of a "balanced budget," "fiscal responsibility," and "fiscal restraint," although their records in support of increased spending programs

Financial Administration

and benefits along with reduced taxes often belie that support. Economists tend to disagree over the impact of a huge public debt on the nation's economy. Some recall Alexander Hamilton's belief that, if correctly managed, a national debt can be used to control interest rates and encourage business expansion through transfer payments of interest earned on the debt. Others emphasize that the debt is an investment in the future since much of the deficit is often used to finance programs that will mature in the years ahead. Others hold that it is not a serious problem because most of the debt is "owed to ourselves," and that after adjusting figures for inflation and population growth the public debt is much smaller than it would appear to be. Economists concerned with the size of the debt, however, emphasize that the public and private debt adds up to over $8 trillion and that this huge sum has tended to weaken the use of monetary and fiscal policy to cope with economic exigencies. For them, "stagflation" (the simultaneous existence of an economic recession and serious inflation) may return as a product of continuing annual deficits. The state and local governmental portion of the debt also reflects national problems and crises, but additional problems resulting from such factors as population growth and the growing problems of health, welfare, and transportation have added to the public debt burden. Regardless of the pros and cons concerning the public debt, all indications are that it will continue to grow on all levels of government in the United States.

Regulatory Tax (286)

A tax levied by government that is aimed primarily at curtailing some unwanted kind of action and only incidentally at raising revenue. A regulatory tax can be levied (1) to reduce or eliminate some socially undesirable activity, such as the heavy taxes levied on liquor, cigarettes, and gambling; (2) to protect a product or a commodity from competition, as in the use of tariffs and discriminatory taxes, such as the tax formerly levied on oleomargarine to protect the income of dairy farmers; (3) to expand the powers of government so that certain objectives can be achieved through regulatory taxation when no constitutional authority to regulate exists; and (4) to provide help by one level of government to another in enforcing its laws, as, for example, in the case of the federal gambling tax which is aimed at helping states enforce antigambling laws.

Significance A regulatory tax offers government the flexibility needed to cope with the diverse problems of modern life. Many taxes that are levied for basically revenue purposes can and often are used for regulatory purposes as well. Estate and gift taxes, for example, are aimed at controlling concentrations of wealth in the nation. The federal income tax, definitely a tax adopted for revenue purposes, has been used to gain convictions of members of organized crime syndicates who often may have committed crimes that have gone unpunished because of the difficulty in obtaining convictions in state courts. Some regulatory taxes are a form of *sumptuary* law in the sense that they attempt to use the police power of the state to regulate personal habits that offend the moral or religious beliefs of the community. Regulatory taxes have added to the great variety and heavy tax load carried by the average citizen in U.S. society today.

Revenue Sharing (287)
A distribution of federal tax revenues to state and local governments according to the proportion of federal personal income tax funds provided by the state and local governments. Revenue sharing was provided by the State and Local Fiscal Assistance Act of 1972. The legislation imposed an allocation formula on the basis of state population, urbanized population, population weighted inversely for per capita income, state individual income tax collection, and general tax effort. Approximately one-third of the revenue-sharing funds were distributed among the states, and about two-thirds were allocated to local governments. "Local governments" included county commissions, city halls, and Indian tribal councils. There are few strings attached to revenue-sharing funds. They are general purpose monies with only three major prohibited uses. Monies cannot be used (1) for local operating expenditures for education; (2) as public welfare spending in the form of cash payments; or (3) as the local share of matching funds for other federal programs. State and local governments may use revenue-sharing dollars for capital expenditures, maintenance, and operating costs in public safety, environmental protection, transportation, health, recreation, libraries, social services for the old and the poor, and financial administration. *See also* BLOCK GRANT, 259; FEDERALISM, 47; FEDERALISM, FISCAL, 49.

Significance Revenue sharing was universally applauded in the early 1970s as the cutting edge of the new federalism. A Gallup Poll conducted in 1971 reported that 77 percent of the public endorsed revenue sharing, and that this support transcended party lines. By 1975, however, the public was not so sure. The Advisory Commission on Intergovernmental Relations reported that only 55 percent of the public supported the program. The reasons for the decline in public support were brought out in congressional debates about whether revenue sharing should be extended beyond 1977. They were (1) fiscally hard-pressed governments were likely to merge revenue-sharing funds with other revenue sources, thus reducing the political visibility of federal fiscal assistance; (2) traditional patterns of political power were retained in most cities despite revenue sharing, and, if anything, the clout of entrenched special interests increased; and (3) contrary to widespread speculation, revenue sharing had not forced changes in the structure of state and local governments. It seemed to reinforce inefficient structures where they already existed. Nevertheless, the lobby to maintain the program prevailed. It consisted of a coalition of the National Governors Association, the National Conference of State Legislators, the National League of Cities, the United States Conference of Mayors, and the National Association of Counties. Ongoing analyses of revenue sharing by the Brookings Institution conclude that, although small cities and towns have used about three-quarters of their revenue-sharing funds for new spending programs, mostly for capital improvements, bigger urgan areas with 100,000 people or more have used at least half their revenue-sharing money to keep taxes down or to avoid borrowing. The tendency of both state and local governments to use shared revenues to keep a muzzle on the tax bite rather than to initiate new spending programs appears to be increasing over time. One reason for this trend is that inflation has cut the real purchasing power of revenue-sharing dollars; thus, state and local governments must use the money mainly to keep their fiscal heads above water by maintaining existing services without raising taxes.

Schick, Allen (1934–) (288)

An American public finance specialist noted for his insightful analyses of federal budgetary processes and environments. Allen Schick has served as Senior Specialist in American Government and Public Administration with the Congressional Research Services (CRS), where he has worked with congressional budgetary committees. Schick's most frequently cited writing on public administration is "The Road to PPB: The Stages of Budget Reform," described by experts as the most complete presentation of the history of budgetary reform available. Schick explains that there are three distinct functions in any budgetary system: (1) *strategic planning*, which involves establishing goals and objectives as well as performance assessments; (2) *management control*, which focuses on the organizational requirements most effective and efficient for accomplishing a specific task; and (3) *operational control*, which is concerned with accountability policy enforcement, and limitations on spending. All of these functions play an important role in creating a stable government, as well as serving as fiscal instruments for affecting the economy. Schick is careful to observe that planning, management, and control are rarely given equal attention in any budgetary system. They tend to be competitive processes. Each succeeding period of budgetary reform alters what Schick calls the planning-management-control balance, sometimes intentionally, sometimes not. The history of reform, according to Schick, falls into three stages. The first was from 1920 through 1935, when control was the most predominant orientation, characterized by a system of expenditure accounts. The second stage, beginning with the New Deal and continuing until 1950, was characterized by performance budgeting with a focus on scientific management techniques, work units, and efficiency. The third stage had a planning emphasis and began with the introduction of planning, programming, budgeting (PPB) techniques in 1960. The evolution from a management to a planning orientation was influenced by the development of macro- and micro-economic analysis, new information and decisional technologies, systems analysis, and the convergence of planning and budgetary processes. Schick believes the advent of zero-base budgeting (ZBB) puts the budgetary system back into a control-oriented period, while also reviving performance budgeting with a management emphasis on reducing the control of Congress and executive budget offices. Schick says the desire to achieve ZBB has been thematic throughout the history of budgetary processes. *See also* BUDGET, 261; BUDGET CYCLE, 263; CONGRESSIONAL BUDGET AND IMPOUNDMENT CONTROL ACT OF 1974, 266.

Significance Allen Schick is not only a scholar of budgeting processes, he is a practitioner of some influence. He was a Congressional Research Service assistant to key congressional committees during the development and implementation of the Congressional Budget and Reform Act of 1974, which has been called the most important legislation in the field since the Budget and Accounting Act of 1921. Schick has been given both the Mosher and Brownlow awards by the American Society for Public Administration (ASPA) and frequently contributes to its journal, *The Public Administration Review*. Schick has also written an important historical and futurist study focusing on regulatory commissions entitled, "Toward the Cybernetic State."

Subsidy (289)

The granting by a government of direct or indirect financial or other forms of aid to private individuals, groups, companies, or organizations, or to another government. Subsidies are granted to serve a

Financial Administration

public purpose, such as improving the economic well-being of a group, encouraging some kind of activity, or ensuring that a service will be provided. Direct subsidies involve cost sharing or grants of money to pay for programs in which the members of a subsidized group receive payments from a government agency. When subsidies are direct, administrators frequently determine who will receive them, and how much will be granted. Indirect subsidies often involve government policies that help one group by penalizing its competitors, as in the use of tariffs to protect domestic producers from foreign competition. Some government agencies indirectly subsidize special groups or industries by limiting access to them through licensing, or by exempting them from regulations that are applied to their competitors. Subsidies also involve payments made by one government to another, as in the federal grant-in-aid and revenue-sharing programs.

Significance Alexander Hamilton, the first secretary of the treasury, incorporated a proposal for federal subsidies to private business in his famous Financial Plan and Report on Manufactures. For Hamilton, subsidies served a public purpose because they would help the nation industrialize. During the two centuries of U.S. history, billions of dollars have been paid out in direct subsidies to business, labor, and agriculture. In addition, most groups or industries have at one time or another been the recipients of indirect subsidies in the form of special tax or regulatory treatment. The determination of which groups receive favorable treatment is made through a process known as "client politics." This typically involves favorable promotional or regulatory activity by an agency toward a small group or a particular industry, with the cost spread over a large group, which often consists of all taxpayers. Some laws provide subsidies for diverse groups, such as the Internal Revenue Code which contains a host of provisions granting favorable tax treatment to various groups of taxpayers. Practically no individual or group has been overlooked in the granting of subsidies by the national, state, and local governments, although some benefit far more than others. Examples of important subsidies to private businesses today include direct grants to U.S. shipbuilders and operators. Without such grants, the United States Merchant Marine might disappear because of its inability to compete with foreign companies. One of labor's key subsidies involves payments by the federal government to workers who have become unemployed as a result of foreign competition. For agriculture, the parity price support program that involves the purchase of surpluses by the federal government to maintain price levels for certain crops has been a critical subsidy program for over fifty years. Other major beneficiaries include veterans, defense contractors, minority groups, airlines, home builders, banks, railroads, disaster victims, and the trucking industry.

Wildavsky, Aaron (1930–) (290)
U.S. professor of public administration and author who explained the political nature of budgetary processes and challenged the assumptions of planning, programming, budgeting systems (PPBS) and other attempts to introduce rationalism into the decision-making process of U.S. government. Wildavsky was dean of the Graduate School of Public Policy at the University of California, Berkeley, when he published *The Politics of the Budgetary Process* (1964), a seminal work in which he boldly described the unwritten rules and strategies of budgetary politics. He wrote that budgets of individual agencies are never critically examined as whole entities, nor are they evaluated in terms of viable, competitive, or more cost-effective alternatives. Instead, budgetary bases are assumed and repetitively approved. While program considerations are important, getting a fair share of the revenues, responding to interest and clientele groups, and developing budgets that are padded sufficiently to endure possible cuts are equally important in the budgetary process. Wildavsky believed that padding is not always undesirable and might be understood as a device for establishing high and low priorities. Various budgetary actors play predictable roles he said: the officials of an agency ask for increased funding; budget examiners advocate the agency's prioritized goals; and legislative committees fluctuate among various roles—acting as protectors of the public purse, as advocates of congressional interests, and as judges in an imaginary court of last appeal for the aggrieved. The criteria for making budget cuts are often as irrational as the criteria used in planning the budget. Simplified procedures for making cuts are often established, such as "10 percent across the board" cuts. The politics of the budgetary process do not include being the keeper of one's brother. His view of decision-making processes led Wildavsky to be an advocate of incrementalism, a critic of PPBS, and a leading theorist of policy analysis. *See also* DECISION MAKING: INCREMENTALISM, 93.

Significance   Aaron Wildavsky wrote one of the most frequently cited books in U.S. public administration—*The Politics of the Budgetary Process*—whose title has also become a descriptive phrase in the public administration vocabulary. Wildavsky not only represented the budgetary process as it exists, but defended its political nature as appropriate for the U.S. system of government because it assures the

Financial Administration

influence of clientele and interest groups. Wildavsky's criticism of PPBS and his prediction that it would fail caused him to be called by one author the *enfant terrible* of public administration reformers. Wildavsky is one of the foremost proponents of incrementatalism in the continuing debate over appropriate models for administrative decision making.

Zero-base Budgeting (ZBB) (291)
A system of budgeting that requires all spending for a program or an agency to be justified anew each year. ZBB was developed at the Texas Instruments Company in 1969 and was first adopted in government by Governor Jimmy Carter in preparation of the fiscal 1973 budget of Georgia. It challenges the principle of incrementalism in budgeting, which assumes that next year's budget will begin at or near the funding level of the current year's budget. ZBB questions the *need* for a program at *any* funding level. Its three basic operational elements are (1) identifying *decision units;* (2) analyzing *decision packages,* each reflecting a different level of effort for carrying out the work in the decision unit; and (3) *ranking* of decision packages, in descending order of importance. *See also* BUDGET, 261.

Significance Zero-base budgeting provides a means for eliminating or reducing low-priority programs. The ZBB may be used to shift resources within an agency to high-impact programs that might not otherwise receive funding increases, or it may be applied in seeking to achieve a balanced budget. The national government first became involved with the ZBB approach in 1977 when, in a letter to department and agency heads, President Jimmy Carter ordered the adoption of zero-base budgeting throughout the executive branch. The estimates for fiscal 1979 incorporated ZBB into the budget preparation process. The Government Economy and Spending Reform Act of 1976 requires a congressional zero-base review and evaluation of government authorization for programs and activities every five years. Both executive and congressional reviews address two questions: (1) Are the current activities efficient and effective? (2) Should current activities be eliminated or reduced to fund new, higher priority programs or to reduce the current budget?

7. Public Law and Regulation

Administrative Adjudication (292)
A quasi-judicial process conducted by an administrative agency to ensure that substantive and procedural rights are protected in conflicts between citizens and agencies that arise over the latter's actions in discharging their legislatively mandated or delegated powers. Administrative adjudication was developed in response to constitutional requirements that no person be deprived of "life, liberty, or property without due process of law" as articulated in the Fifth and Fourteenth Amendments to the Constitution. The spirit of this constitutional guarantee found statutory expression in the Administrative Procedure Act of 1946, where procedures for adjudicating administrative remedies are set forth. The rationale of the act is that safeguards must be available to protect individuals from "arbitrary and capricious" action by a government agency. When a "person," a term which includes corporations, is charged by an agency with wrongful conduct and is subject to sanctions, the person must have an opportunity for a hearing before that body. Procedures for the conduct of such a hearing are detailed in the Administrative Procedure Act or specified in the authorizing legislation of the agency. The proceedings are formal and are similar to nonjury, trial-type, civil court actions. The defendant in an administrative action has the right to timely notice of the date, time, and place of the hearing, as well as a reasonably definite statement of the charges. While not as exact as that required in a judicial proceeding, the administrative notice must contain statements of fact regarding the charges, legal authority of the agency, and reference to the statutes or rules alleged to have been violated. The proceeding itself permits the defendant the right to present written or oral arguments, cross-examine witnesses, and

present rebuttal evidence. The right to retain counsel is also permitted. Implicit in these proceedings is the right of the defendant to a fair and impartial hearing. The decision of the hearing officer or agency tribunal is carefully documented and included in the record of the proceedings along with notices, pleadings, rulings, objections, evidence, and the findings. Collectively these items constitute the record of the case and provide the basis for subsequent judicial review if the case is appealed. See also ADMINISTRATIVE DUE PROCESS, 293; ADMINISTRATIVE PROCEDURE ACT OF 1946, 298; DUE PROCESS OF LAW, 306.

Significance Administrative adjudication protects the individual against abuses of power by ensuring that administrative procedures meet the test of due process. Administrative adjudication, while triallike, is usually not as complex or as time-consuming as judicial proceedings and permits a more complete expression of legislative policy than could be accomplished in the courts. Burdens on the courts are decreased, and speedier consideration of individual cases is encouraged. On the other hand, adjudication has become so legalistic that, in most cases, it is necessary to retain counsel to guide one through the complex procedural maze, and, even though an individual has the right to a fair and impartial hearing, the hearing officer is employed by the agency. Administrative adjudication does provide a procedure which recognizes that abuses may occur, however, and it affords a means to check them.

Administrative Due Process (293)
The fundamentals of fair and equitable administrative procedure as defined by law, implemented by administrative agencies, and enforced by the courts. Administrative due process as a concern under statutory law began in 1939 with passage of the Walter-Logan Act. President Franklin D. Roosevelt vetoed the act on grounds it would put the federal government in the untenable position of having to defend every administrative decision before the courts. In 1941, the attorney general issued a report on administrative procedures which prompted Congress eventually to enact another law on administrative due proces. That law, the Administrative Procedure Act of 1946, provides (1) that administrative rules and orders be published; (2) that certain specified procedures be followed in formulating administrative rules and in accomplishing administrative adjudication; (3) that there be established rules concerning hearing judges; and (4) that guidelines be issued regarding hearings, evidence, and decisions. Beyond the provisions of the Administrative

Procedure Act of 1946, the principles of administrative due process relating to the protection of individual rights in cases of suspension or dismissal include (1) adequate notice of intent; (2) disclosure of reasons; (3) the right to a hearing; (4) the right of an individual to appear in his or her own behalf; (5) the right to be represented by an attorney; (6) the requirement that administrative agencies state their reasons in making determinations; (7) the requirement that an administrative official may be disqualified in favor of fairness in the law; (8) the safeguard that questions of law may be referred to the courts; (9) the right of appeal; and (10) establishment of the fact that an administrative agency making a decision must have jurisdiction over the question at issue. See also ADMINISTRATIVE DISCRETION, 86; ADMINISTRATIVE LAW, 294; ADMINISTRATIVE PROCEDURE ACT OF 1946, 298.

Significance Administrative due process affirms that administrative agencies are required to adhere to those rights which all citizens have under the Constitution of the United States. Specifically, this means that the due process clauses of the Fifth and Fourteenth Amendments are to be honored by public administrators in carrying out their duties. Administrative due process is a form of democratic control. In assuring that the individual's constitutional rights are not violated by administrative agencies, the courts are less concerned with *what* the agencies are doing in terms of policy, even personnel policy, and are more interested in *how* they are doing it. Administrative due process is institutionalized assurance that administrative agencies will carry out their duties according to standards of reasonableness and equity.

Administrative Law (294)

Rules and regulations made and applied by governmental regulatory agencies. Administrative law also includes the legal provisions used to establish administrative agencies, empower them, determine their methods of procedure, and provide for judicial review of agency activities. Their operational authority typically is delegated to the agencies by the legislative body—Congress, the state legislature, or the city council or commission. The rules and regulations promulgated by administrative agencies are directed at controlling the functions and activities of private persons and companies operating within the jurisdiction assigned to each agency. Violations of administrative law are dealt with by the agency or by an independent hearing officer. Regulatory agencies can issue "cease and desist" orders to affected companies. If compliance is not forthcoming, enforcement action can be undertaken through the regular courts. Companies may also take appeals to the regular courts if they believe they have been denied due process of law. Administrative law once dealt mainly with rate-setting, with permitting or prohibiting certain products from being placed on the market, with providing for competition when needed for effective market operations, and with requiring certain kinds of services to be offered to the public. Recently it has become increasingly involved in questions directly affecting individuals in areas such as welfare, education, disability benefits, and tort liability. *See also* ADMINISTRATIVE LAW JUDGE, 295; ADMINISTRATIVE ORDER, 297; CEASE AND DESIST ORDER, 300.

Significance Administrative law has become the most common type of law affecting people in modern life. On the local level, for example, traffic laws are often made by a traffic commission composed of appointed administrators. On the state level, hunting and fishing regulations are typically made by a commission empowered by the legislature to make binding law. On the national level, most major foreign and interstate businesses—transportation, communications, food and drugs, for example—are extensively regulated by independent regulatory commissions. In each case, the elected representatives of the people have delegated their powers to appointed administrators because they lack the time and the expertise to deal with the vast array of complex problems growing out of government's regulatory role. The main checks on those who make and enforce administrative law are found in the courts, through the process of judicial review, and in the legislative bodies that have the power to oversee all administrative operations and to change or nullify decision-making authority delegated to administrative agencies.

Administrative Law Judge (295)

A government official who renders decisions or makes recommendations to regulatory agencies concerning the issuance of administrative orders. Administrative law judges operate within a specialized field of jurisdiction—for example, in the field of labor-management relations—and are found in both state and national jurisdictions. Decisions made by the judges, or by regulatory agencies on the basis of recommendations by judges, are subject to review by the courts, which may overturn them. In the national government, administrative law judges were formerly known as hearing examiners. Under the Administrative Procedure Act of 1946, judges hear evidence submitted by competing groups and render "decisions" which take the form of recommendations to the heads of agencies. *See also* ADMINISTRATIVE PROCEDURE ACT OF 1946, 298; QUASI-JUDICIAL, 325.

Significance Administrative law judges are a product of the growing complexity of modern life and the variety of specialized issues it tends to produce. Prior to 1946, federal regulatory agencies, such as the National Labor Relations Board (NLRB) and the Federal Trade Commission (FTC), performed the three functions of making rules and regulations, enforcing them, and deciding controversies that arose. Opposition based on the belief that the prosecuting and judging functions should not be carried out by the same persons led to appointment of administrative law judges, with civil service protection against arbitrary dismissal or reductions in salary. Although part of the agency, they operate with a degree of independence. Decisions rendered by the judges are subject to appeals to their agency heads by private parties adversely affected, but if no appeal is made, the decision is final. If appeals are made and are overruled by the agency, the losing party may then appeal to a regular court.

Administrative Office of the United States Courts (296)

The agency that carries out administrative duties concerned with the operation of all federal courts except the United States Supreme Court. The director of the administrative office is appointed by the Supreme Court, and the office functions under the supervision and direction of the judicial conference of the United States. The latter body, chaired by the Chief Justice of the United States, includes representatives of all major federal courts, and it functions as the governing body for the administration of the federal judicial system. Tasks assigned to the administrative office include (1) supervising all administrative matters pertaining to the operation of federal courts; (2) examining the state of the dockets and providing statistical data concerning the operations of the courts; (3) submitting reports on the operations of federal courts to the judicial conference, to Congress, and to the attorney general; (4) determining the annual budget for all courts except the Supreme Court; and (5) carrying out various housekeeping duties concerned with the day-by-day operations of the courts. In 1967, a federal judicial center was established by Congress to carry on research and study aimed at achieving the goal of improved judicial administration. The center reports to the judicial conference, which in turn transmits useful data to the administrative office. *See also* JUDICIAL ADMINISTRATION, 312.

Significance The Administrative Office of the United States Courts provides a centralized administrative framework to facilitate the smooth operation of all federal courts below the Supreme Court. Since its creation in 1939, the administrative office has had to grow tremendously to keep abreast of the expanding judicial case load. Prior to 1939, no central administrative body existed. Since its creation in that year, the administrative office has placed its major emphasis on improving the functions of the courts by centralizing and streamlining their administrative operations. The Supreme Court, however, remains aloof from the central administration and continues to insist on handling its own administrative responsibilities. This has been done since 1972 through an administrative aide who is appointed and supervised by the Chief Justice. Most states have also recognized the importance of judicial administration by appointing judicial councils composed of judges, lawyers, and laypersons who try to apply sound administrative principles and practices to the operation of their state court systems. With crowded court dockets and a shortage of judges, judicial administration is increasingly a matter of concern for public administrators as well as criminal and civil justice experts.

Administrative Order (297)
A directive having the force of law, issued by an administrative agency to an individual or to a private company or organization. An administrative order is the means by which an agency enforces its rules and regulations as they relate to a particular party that has allegedly violated them. If infractions of a rule or regulation occur, the agency holds a hearing in which the parties have an opportunity to present their cases. After determining the facts and the law that apply, the agency typically concludes the hearing by issuing an administrative order requiring one of the parties to do or not do something. The affected party can appeal the order by bringing a case to a regular court of law that has jurisdiction. Under the Administrative Procedure Act of 1946, all administrative orders must be published in the *Federal Register*. *See also* ADMINISTRATIVE LAW, 294; CEASE AND DESIST ORDER, 300; *FEDERAL REGISTER*, 308.

Significance Administrative orders have increasingly become a part of American life as the national and state governments have sought to cope with the complexities of modern life through the promulgation of administrative law. If one company charges another with unfair competition in violation of the rules and regulations set forth by the Federal Trade Commission, for example, the FTC will then hold a hearing and may issue an administrative order requiring one of the parties to cease engaging in the unfair or illegal actions.

Public Law and Regulation

Because of the specialized nature of administrative law and the expertise required in administering it, Congress and the state legislatures have assigned responsibility for making and enforcing such laws to administrative agencies. The issuance of administrative orders as an enforcement tool has greatly increased in recent years.

Administrative Procedure Act of 1946 (298)

A major law that governs the operations of federal agencies in making and implementing administrative regulations and decisions. The Administrative Procedure Act requires (1) notice, including place and date of hearing and the substance of the proposed change, before promulgating a new rule; (2) publication of all notices and new or changed administrative orders and rules and regulations in the *Federal Register;* (3) procedures that advance the underlying principles of due process in the conduct of all hearings; and (4) the right of judicial review for any person wronged by the actions or inactions of an agency. In appeals, the courts may nullify agency actions deemed to be unfair, arbitrary, violations of constitutional rights, unsupported by the facts, beyond the powers delegated to the agency by Congress, or in violation of required procedures. Individuals affected by rule changes have a right to testify at hearings, to be represented by counsel, and to cross-examine witnesses. *See also* FEDERAL REGISTER, 308; HEARING, 310.

Significance The main purpose of the Administrative Procedure Act of 1946 is to ensure that the actions of regulatory agencies are controlled and to provide procedural justice to affected persons and private companies. Because many such agencies exercise all three functions of government—quasi-legislative, quasi-executive, and quasi-judicial—they lack regular oversight and control. As a result, the potential for arbitrary actions in their procedures and in their decisions is great. This act was aimed at reducing this potential by prescribing some, and circumscribing other, procedures and activities carried on by all regulatory agencies. By vastly increasing the scope of judicial review of administrative procedures and decisions, for example, the act greatly limited the independence of the agencies, but their regulatory effectiveness was not substantially altered.

Caveat Emptor versus *Caveat Venditor* (299)

Two different approaches to achieve protection for consumers in their purchases of goods and services. *Caveat emptor* (let the buyer beware) reflects the freedom from governmental regulations that characterizes the laissez-faire system of capitalism. It typified the nineteenth and early twentieth century periods of free-wheeling business practices that put the burden of avoiding the purchase of fraudulent, dangerous, or misrepresented products directly on consumers. *Caveat venditor* (let the seller beware) conversely places the responsibility of policing businesses on the government. Under *caveat venditor,* if a business person sells a fraudulent, dangerous, or misrepresented product to an unsuspecting consumer, it may constitute a violation of criminal or civil laws, or of administrative rules and regulations promulgated by a regulatory agency.

Significance Although both *caveat emptor* and *caveat venditor* are still invoked, the doctrine of *caveat venditor* has become more generally applicable in today's consumer-oriented world. Since the 1930s, government's lack of concern has progressively been replaced by national, state, and local regulatory laws and enforcement agencies whose main function is to protect consumers. Sellers who violate laws that prohibit the sale of impure foods or drugs, give short measure to buyers, use false advertising, sell dangerous products, or otherwise violate the rights of consumers are likely to receive disciplinary action by government. Major federal regulatory agencies that act directly or indirectly to protect consumers include the Consumer Product Safety Commission, the Federal Trade Commission (FTC), the Consumer Advisory Council, the Food and Drug Administration of the Department of Health and Human Services, and the Office of Neighborhoods, Voluntary Associations, and Consumer Protection in the Department of Housing and Urban Development. More and more, private organizations, such as those supported by Ralph Nader and his "Nader's Raiders" group of young lawyers and students, use legal, political, and lobbying approaches to safeguard consumers' rights. Although *caveat venditor* has clearly become the main approach to consumer protection, *caveat emptor* remains in force since government cannot offer complete protection for unwary buyers. Purchases and investments still need careful scrutiny and healthy skepticism on the part of individual consumers if they are to avoid being bilked by unscrupulous businesspersons who often are able to avoid legal entanglements.

Cease and Desist Order (300)

An administrative order issued by an agency to individuals or to private organizations calling on them to refrain from further violations of laws, rules, and regulations which the agency has authority to enforce. A cease and desist order is issued following a hearing by the agency, and appeals of such orders may be taken to the regular courts. Violations of an order can result in prosecution in the regular courts or in the denial of certain benefits provided by the agency. See also ADMINISTRATIVE ORDER, 297.

Significance The cease and desist order is the primary means by which administrative law is enforced by regulatory agencies. An example of such an order is the action of the Federal Trade Commission (FTC) in calling on a private corporation to stop engaging in fraudulent or misleading advertising, or to stop selling certain harmful or dangerous products. The authority to issue cease and desist orders was first assigned to the Interstate Commerce Commission (ICC) in 1887. Today, many national and state regulatory agencies have the power to issue them. This power is opposed by some of the affected businesses and by those who charge that it is an antidemocratic action involving "government by administrators through administration," with little or no accountability to the people through the electoral process.

Certificate of Public Convenience, Interest, and Necessity (301)

A document issued by a governmental regulatory agency that grants permission to an individual or a company to conduct a particular type of business, or to conduct a specific business. The criterion used by agency decision makers in granting such certificates—that it meet the requirements of public convenience, interest, and necessity—has been provided by Congress and by state legislatures to guide agencies in issuing licenses and other permits to carry on privately owned operations for profit. Typically, the issuance of certificates granting permission to engage in certain kinds of activity is determined at a hearing when the action may be controversial or when private firms compete for a certificate. See also LICENSING, 317.

Significance The issuance of certificates of public convenience, interest, and necessity is a useful governmental function for several reasons. Competition can be avoided whenever it might result in uneconomic duplication of services, such as competition in services that offer natural gas pipelines to homes, or telephone service. Regulators refer to situations that do not require competition as conditions of "natural monopoly." Certificates can also ensure that the certified companies will continue to provide services in the public interest, else the certificates might be withdrawn. When dangerous materials are involved in a business activity, certification of all engaged in the hazardous operation is necessary to protect the public. When a certificate is granted to carry on a certain type of activity, approval by a government agency may cost the company or individual a small fee, or it may be free. Yet, in some cases, the government action may be worth millions of dollars, as in the case of granting television broadcasting licenses. Because of the value involved in the granting of many kinds of certificates, constant oversight of agency operations by the legislative body and by the general public is needed.

Certiorari (302)
A writ (order) from a higher court to a lower court requiring that the record of a case decided in the lower court be submitted to the higher court for review of questions of law. A writ of certiorari (Latin for "made certain" or "certified") is the means by which most cases are appealed to the United States Supreme Court from lower federal courts and from the state courts of highest jurisdiction. Up to 90 percent of all such petitions are denied review by the Supreme Court, even though only four of the nine members of the Court need agree to review each case. The writ of certiorari is also used in the states where judges of the higher courts order cases in the lower trial or appellate courts to be reviewed. Certiorari can be used on both state and national levels to appeal decisions made by administrative agencies.

Significance The highest courts in the states and the United States Supreme Court use the writ of certiorari to select a few critical cases from among the thousands appealed to them. Of the more than 10 million civil and criminal cases decided each year in the United States, the Supreme Court reviews only about 4,000. Many of these cases involve administrative law, since it has become the most common type of law. Most cases reach the Court by writ of certiorari, but the Court hears oral arguments on only about 200 of these during each of its annual terms. Most of the petitions for certiorari from lower courts are rejected, which means the lower courts' decisions are final. The most important decisions reviewed on certiorari are those which are overturned by the higher courts and establish new precedents. Administrative rulings are increasingly taken into courts by private parties adversely affected by them, adding to the caseload burden of state and federal appellate tribunals.

Civil Law (303)

Restrictions and limitations placed by government on the freedom of action of individuals and corporations. Civil law may also limit governments through actions taken by individuals in civil cases, and governments may invoke court actions based on civil law against private parties or other governments. Civil law can be distinguished from criminal law. The latter involves violations of community norms of conduct which can be punished by fines, imprisonment, or execution. In criminal cases, the government always functions as the prosecutor. In civil cases based on civil law, no punishment can be inflicted, although the losing party in a civil case can be required by the court to pay a compensatory judgment to the winning party or undertake to meet other conditions laid down by the court in its decision. Through civil law, disputes that arise in such areas as contracts, personal injury, banking, patents, copyrights, domestic relations, automobile accidents, and business relations can be resolved through the courts. In the contemporary world, administrators increasingly are called on to make civil law of rules, regulations, and administrative orders in order to cope with the difficult and conflicting nature of modern life. More civil law is made today by administrators than by the collective efforts of the national, state, and local legislative bodies. *See also* CLASS ACTION, 304.

Significance   Civil law in the United States is largely a product of the transfer of English customary law as modified by the Constitution, the actions of Congress, the state legislatures, and local policy-making bodies and administrators in the three levels of government. The development of American civil law also reflects historic roots found in the Roman *corpus juris civilis* and the continental civil law as codified in the French Civil Code or *Code Napoleon*. Civil law encourages stable relations in a society by providing peaceful means for settling disputes. Government can also seek to implement policies by providing for civil penalties through the court system. For example, in enacting the Sherman Antitrust Act of 1890 Congress provided for criminal prosecutions and also authorized civil suit actions with triple damages to injured parties resulting from the operations of any "combination . . . or conspiracy in the restraint of trade or commerce." Although the courts cannot guarantee that judgments reached in civil cases will be complied with by the losing party, they can offer legal means, such as garnishment of the individual's wages, which help the winner collect. If the defendant has no income or assets, the civil law in most controversies cannot provide a meaningful remedy for the plaintiff who brings the case.

Class Action (304)
A civil lawsuit undertaken by one or more persons representing a large group or class of persons who have suffered similar injury or damage. In a class action case, the plaintiffs typically are supported by members of the group they represent, thus making their action financially feasible. Awards by the court may include the responsibility of the defendant to meet the claims of all who have suffered injury or damage, not just for the plaintiff in the courtroom. In making an award to a class of persons, the court will ordinarily award lawyers' fees to be taken out of the judgment on behalf of the class. The traditional rule of the courts that a plaintiff bringing a case must be able to show that he or she has been singled out and has suffered special losses in order to have standing in the court was overturned when the courts began to accept class action suits. Such cases have become commonplace, as individuals have sought to protect their own interests as well as others in a similar predicament by undertaking legal action to benefit all. *See also* CIVIL LAW, 303; LEGAL ANALYSIS, 316.

Significance Although class action suits of limited impact have been decided for some time by courts of equity, class action lawsuits with far-reaching implications have become popular only during the past quarter-century. Areas in which class action suits have been especially prominent include cases dealing with legislative apportionment, environmental and energy problems, pricing, civil rights, and the sale to consumers of faulty or dangerous goods. Although the number of such cases increased greatly during the 1960s and the first half of the 1970s, Supreme Court decisions have served to limit their use since then. In *Zahn v. International Paper Co.* (414 U.S. 291: 1973), a case involving pollution damage to a large group of persons, the Court ruled that the plaintiffs could not qualify under the diversity of citizenship jurisdiction clause unless *each* member of the class or group affected by pollution damage to their property had a separate claim of $10,000. In previous cases involving citizens of different states, the Court had applied the $10,000 minimum damage figure collectively to an entire group. In another case, the Court unanimously held that plaintiffs, in bringing an action against a stock brokerage firm on behalf of several million allegedly overcharged customers, must notify each of the persons in the class before the issue is justiciable, even if the cost of such notice is prohibitively high (*Eisen v. Carlisle and Jacquelin*, 417 U.S. 156: 1974). In *Oppenheimer Fund, Inc. v. Sanders* (437 U.S. 340: 1978), the Court further limited class action jurisdiction by requiring the plaintiffs (121,000 members of an investment fund) to be identified. The rulings by the Supreme Court have limited class action suits by some plaintiffs, but well-organized clubs and interest groups can still meet the stringent requirements needed to gain standing in the courts. In addition, in 1976, Congress granted permission for class action antitrust suits by state attorney generals on behalf of the citizens of their respective states, and recently the Supreme Court excused civil rights cases from an adherence to more stringent rules placed on other class action suits.

Dillon's Rule (305)
A rule of law enunciated in a famous case which holds that municipal corporations (cities and other local units of self-government) are legally under the control of state government and can exercise only those powers expressly permitted by the state. Dillon's rule was set forth by Judge John F. Dillon in an Iowa court decision in the nineteenth century (*City of Clinton v. Cedar Rapids and Missouri River Railroad Co.*, 24 Iowa 455, 475: 1868). In his dictum, Judge Dillon held that municipal corporations could exercise only (1) those powers expressly granted to the local unit by state constitution or statute; (2) those powers that can be reasonably implied from those granted; and (3) those powers essential for the corporation's operations. In his decision, Judge Dillon emphasized the dependent and subsidiary nature of the local units' relationship to state government: "Municipal corporations owe their origin to, and derive their powers and rights wholly from, the legislature. It breathes into them the breath of life, without which they cannot exist. As it creates, so it may destroy. If it may destroy, it may abridge and control. . . . "

Significance Dillon's rule rejects the idea that state-local relations are the same as national-state relations. The latter embrace the principle of federalism, whereas the former constitute a unitary arrangement. The dependent character of local government was first enunciated by the United States Supreme Court in the famous *Dartmouth College* case in which the Court held that cities were mere creatures of the state with charters that could be amended or withdrawn at any time (*Dartmouth College v. Woodward*, 4 Wheaton 518: 1819). Dillon's rule was merely a restatement of that basic rule of law. In the contemporary world, however, Dillon's rule has been mitigated by the home-rule movement and the efforts of local units to gain a measure of autonomy from state control through constitutional provisions. Although weakened by home-rule provisions, the basic rule set forth by Judge Dillon remains generally applicable to state-local affairs.

Due Process of Law (306)
A constitutionally mandated guarantee that government in the United States must, in all of its actions, act with fairness, justice, equity, and reasonableness. The due process of law clause of the Fifth Amendment forbids the national government to deprive any person of "life, liberty, or property without due process of law." The Fourteenth Amendment extended this guarantee against arbitrary action to limit state and local units of government. Through a process of selective incorporation by the United States Supreme Court, most of the rights of the Bill of Rights have been read into the meaning of the Due Process Clause of the Fourteenth Amendment. By this means, the rights of all persons have, in effect, been "nationalized" and are protected against deprivation by *any* government in the United States. Governments can, however, deprive any person of life, liberty, or property so long as the guarantee of due process of law is not violated. Although no precise definition of due process exists, when cases arise involving charges of denial of due process, judges examine the precedents and determine what is reasonable action under the circumstances. If the governmental action has been unreasonable, unfair, or unjust in either its substance or in the procedures used by government officials, the courts will likely determine that it has failed to meet the requirements of due process of law. Public administrators are more often charged with violating *procedural* due process than *substantive* due process since they are more deeply involved in implementing than in making public policy. *See also* ADMINISTRATIVE PROCEDURE ACT OF 1946, 298.

Significance Although the Bill of Rights is usually regarded as the cornerstone of the American system of individual liberty, the Due Process Clause of the Fourteenth Amendment has actually proved to be more important in protecting rights. Because the Bill of Rights limits only the national government, whereas most of the cases involving alleged deprivations of rights have come from state and local governments, the Fourteenth Amendment's Due Process Clause has proved to be the key constitutional provision. Every action by every government agency and official at all levels of government is subject to scrutiny and potential charges that a denial of due process has occurred. The individual, organization, or company that believes it has been treated in an arbitrary or unreasonable manner must take the initiative of challenging the governmental action in a court of law. Although state and municipal courts hear and decide cases involving claims of denial of due process, the federal courts have served as the more rigorous defenders of due process rights. The idea of due process of law was inherited from the British legal system, but the

Public Law and Regulation

American system has applied it more widely and systematically to both civil and criminal cases than any other legal system in the world. In public administration, no action can be undertaken by an agency or an official without giving some consideration to the requirements of due process of law. Even if the merits of such actions are beyond challenge, the action may be overturned by the courts if the procedure used is arbitrary or unreasonable.

Equity (307)
The application of a judge's conception of what is fair and just to settle a legal controversy or protect against irreparable harm or damage. Like the common law, equity is judge-made law, but it is applied when the common law and statutory law do not provide remedies or would be too inflexible or unjust if applied. Equity law is a body of legal rules and principles developed out of precedents established by judges sitting in courts of equity. Equity courts in the United States are usually known as "chancery" courts because equity in the English system was originally dispensed by the Lord High Chancellor. Some states have separate chancery courts, whereas others convert regular courts into equity courts on petition of the parties to the case, or because of the nature of the case. *See also* CIVIL LAW, 303; NEW PUBLIC ADMINISTRATION, 18.

Significance Administrators utilize equity in performance of their duties by requesting courts to order that something be done (specific performance) or not done (injunction). Private individuals may also use equity courts to limit the powers of administrators. A common use of equity jurisdiction is to forbid strikers to engage in violence, to block entrance into a plant or office, or to engage in destruction of property. Violations of a writ of injunction issued by an equity court can be dealt with summarily by the judge. Equity gives courts a wide degree of flexibility in dealing with potential or actual controversies that come before them. Juries are not ordinarily used in equity cases, and the court's operations are generally more informal.

Federal Register (308)
A publication of the United States government that contains a verbatim record of all executive orders, presidential proclamations, and reorganization plans. Established by the Federal Register Act of 1935, the *Federal Register* is published five times each week. In addition to publishing orders, proclamations, and plans, the *Federal Register* is required by the Administrative Procedure Act of 1946 to

publish a description of each federal agency, including its organization, authority, operations, and a statement of its general policies. Each agency must also give notice of proposed rules and regulations and of administrative orders that are the result of the agency's adjudicatory function. Affected parties can thus be made aware of forthcoming changes in regulatory law and can seek to have an influence on the agency in its final deliberations. The new rules and regulations are codified in the *Code of Federal Regulations* (CFR). Many states publish similar records of administrative laws, both proposed and promulgated. See also ADMINISTRATIVE LAW, 294.

Significance Private businesses subject to federal regulatory agency jurisdiction welcomed the congressional decision in 1935 to have the executive branch publish the *Federal Register*. The *Register* has made it possible for them to learn which administrative law requirements apply to their business operations. However, because of the increasing use of executive orders and administrative rules and regulations in the United States, the *Federal Register* has become bulky and complex, making it once again difficult for business to keep up with the latest developments in federal law. Recent presidents have requested that the *Register* be published in brief and simple language, but not all agencies have complied with these requests. Most of the rules and regulations published in the *Register* are posted by independent regulatory commissions, such as the Interstate Commerce Commission (ICC) and the Federal Communications Commission (FCC). Most relate to the kinds of service required, rights and duties of the private companies, rate schedules, licensing procedures, and general operating activities.

Grand and Petit Juries **(309)**
Two types of juries used in the U.S. system of criminal justice. A grand jury ordinarily consists of a body of twelve to twenty-three persons, selected according to law, who hear evidence against someone accused of committing a serious crime and who determine whether that evidence is sufficient to warrant bringing the accused to trial. If the grand ("large") jury indicts the individual by returning a "true bill" that officially levies charges, the accused will then be brought to trial, typically before a petit ("small" or "trial") jury of twelve persons. In the states, a grand jury may vary in size from one member to twenty-three. A one-person grand jury consisting of a circuit court judge is used in a few states so that the judge can utilize the traditional investigative powers of a grand jury and yet avoid the expense and inefficiency of using twenty-three persons to investigate

and bring charges. One-person grand juries are used especially in circumstances where the prosecuting attorney's office may be unable or unwilling to prosecute the case, or malfeasance by government officials is suspected. Whereas grand juries indict by majority vote, federal petit juries are always of twelve persons and verdicts of guilty or innocent can only be rendered by a unanimous vote. State trial juries, however, vary from five to twelve persons, and although less than unanimous decisions can be made in some states for certain types of civil and criminal cases, convictions for serious crimes require a unanimous verdict in most states. The Fifth Amendment specifies that no individual can be brought to trial for a capital or infamous crime except through indictment by a grand jury. The courts have interpreted this to mean that any crime for which the law provides punishment by death or imprisonment requires indictment by a grand jury. Members of grand and petit juries are usually selected at random from voter registration lists, but the increasing numbers of retired persons and other group members found on juries in some jurisdictions has led observers to believe that jurors are not always selected randomly. In many states, indictment by a grand jury is not required, or is limited to capital cases. When not used, indictment is secured by the prosecuting attorney who must convince the judge through an "information affidavit" that enough evidence exists to warrant putting the accused on trial. Although grand juries exercise vast powers under the common law to examine records and to summon witnesses and compel them to testify under oath, trial juries make the final decisions concerning the guilt or innocence of accused persons indicted as a result of such investigations. *See also* DUE PROCESS OF LAW, 306; JUDICIAL ADMINISTRATION, 312.

Significance The two-step process of indictment by a grand jury followed by trial before a petit jury is part of the legal process by which the truth is sought, and innocent persons are protected. Although both juries are involved in the "sifting and winnowing" process to discover the facts of the case, their approaches and procedures differ. Because the grand jury's role is expensive and time-consuming, the English who created it have abolished it, and many U.S. states have abolished or modified it. In the federal courts, however, it can neither be eliminated nor modified, except by a constitutional amendment which alters the Fifth Amendment—an unlikely action. In interpreting the Fourteenth Amendment, the Supreme Court held that its Due Process Clause does not require an indictment by a grand jury, and that the substitution in the states of indictment by information affidavit meets the requirements of fair procedure. In the case of petit juries, the Supreme Court has held that the Fourteenth Amendment's Due Process Clause requires a trial by jury for "serious crimes" (*Duncan v. Louisiana*, 391 U.S. 145: 1968), defines a serious crime as any that may involve more than six months imprisonment (*Baldwin v. New York*, 399 U.S. 66: 1970), permits states to use juries of less than twelve persons for such trials (*Williams v. Florida*, 399 U.S. 78: 1970), and authorizes a decision by less than unanimous vote (*Johnson v. Louisiana*, 406 U.S. 356: 1972). The modifications in the use of both juries in the U.S. legal process pit the strong tendency to retain the traditional forms against the need for change to cope with a dramatically changing social environment.

Hearing (310)

Fact finding undertaken by a duly authorized body to determine a course of action. In rule making, a hearing is held prior to the promulgation of a rule so that private parties affected by it will have an opportunity to present their views. In adjudication, a quasi-judicial hearing is conducted by an administrative or regulatory agency concerning alleged violations of its rules and regulations. Action by the agency, such as the issuance of a "cease and desist" order, may follow if warranted by the facts presented at the hearing. *See also* ADMINISTRATIVE LAW JUDGE, 295; ADMINISTRATIVE PROCEDURE ACT OF 1946, 298; QUASI-JUDICIAL, 325.

Significance Hearings are a required part of the procedures used in the making, promulgating, and enforcing of rules and regulations by administrative agencies. A hearing may be initiated either by an agency or by an interested private party who will be affected by the application of rules and regulations. In the national government, hearings are conducted under provisions of the Administrative Procedure Act of 1946, which spells out the requirements of the hearing process in specific detail. Agencies holding hearings concerning alleged infractions of their rules operate in a manner similar to, but somewhat less formal than, that of a court. Hearings that deal with prices charged or services rendered by private companies typically attract large numbers of participants from the consumer public. Orders issued as a result of a hearing concerning possible violations of rules and regulations have the force of law, but appeals may be taken to the courts. Judges and courts generally accept the expertise of the agency personnel and limit their reviews to questions concerning the fairness of the hearing and whether the facts revealed in the hearing justify the decisions made by the agency.

Public Law and Regulation

Injunction (311)
A writ (order) issued by a court to restrain the performance of an action that might violate the personal or property rights of others. A writ of injunction is issued by a court in an *equity* preceeding to avoid future harm or damage of an irreparable nature, not to provide compensation or justice for an act already committed, for which a court of law would have jurisdiction. Although injunctions are usually applied to stop or prevent an action, a *mandatory* injunction requires a positive response by the subjects indicated in the writ. A violation of a writ of injunction constitutes contempt of court, which can be dealt with summarily by the judge through a fine or imprisonment. Temporary injunctions have often been issued by courts on the basis of *ex parte* (by or for one party, without contest by the other party) affidavits alone, without a hearing. See also EQUITY, 307.

Significance Injunctions are often sought by private parties to secure a judicial review of an administrative action by a public official or agency. Judges have frequently used the injunctive procedure to apply their own social and economic perspectives to a current problem. U.S. labor history, for example, is filled with examples of courts issuing literally thousands of injunctions that ended strikes or seriously reduced the strikers' effectiveness. Over the years, Congress and the state legislatures as well as court precedents have moved in the direction of limiting the use of injunctions, especially in labor-management disputes. Yet it remains a powerful judicial weapon that fills a need for legal action prior to the commission of illegal or harmful acts as a means of preventing them.

Judicial Administration (312)
The general management of the court system, including planning to meet the court's case volume, overseeing clerical and other support personnel, data processing, financial management, management of calendars, jury and witness coordination, space and equipment management, and media relations. Judicial administration can also include analysis and oversight of court structure, judicial selection and discipline, and judicial training programs. Felix A. Nigro and Lloyd G. Nigro, in devoting a full chapter to judicial administration in the sixth edition of *Modern Public Administration* (1980) describe the position of judicial administrator, or court manager, as a promising new career for students of public administration. They say much of the interest in judicial administration arises from widespread dissatisfaction with the malfunctioning of both criminal and civil courts. The judge is in charge of courtroom proceedings, but he or she does

not hire or fire others who work in the courtroom. Other actors in the judicial process are assigned by independent authorities, such as the state's attorney, the public defender, or the clerk of the court. Even the bailiff is assigned by the sheriff. Judicial administration is designed to coordinate and manage this organizational support system, to free judges to focus on difficult litigation. Chief Justice Warren E. Burger described the problem judicial administration seeks to alleviate as courts being asked to interpret hundreds of new, loosely drawn statutes that "create important claims and rights, and often present grave problems affecting the functioning of state and federal governments." *See also* ADMINISTRATIVE OFFICE OF THE UNITED STATES COURTS, 296; JUDICIAL ADMINISTRATION: THE CALIFORNIA PLAN, 313; JUDICIAL ADMINISTRATION: THE MISSOURI PLAN, 314.

Significance Judicial administration is an emerging subfield of public administration. It had its beginnings in the 1930s, when the American Bar Association developed proposed standards for improved court organization and procedures. In 1939, Congress established the Administrative Office of the Courts, responsible for the administrative functions of the federal courts. An Institute of Judicial Administration was established at the New York University School of Law in 1952, and since then four separate judicial training and research centers have been established: the National Judicial College (1963); the Federal Judicial Center (1967); the Institute for Court Management (1970); and the National Center for State Courts (1971). The rapid development of judicial administration is illustrated by the fact that in 1958 only twelve states had operating offices of court administration. By 1977, all fifty states had such offices, with court managers also being found in almost every major city. By the 1980s, academic programs in judicial administration existed in over thirty universities.

Judicial Administration: The California Plan (313)
A plan for dealing with the discipline of judges without resorting to impeachment or recall. The California plan involves the organization of a commission to receive, investigate, and screen complaints against any judge in the state court system. In California, this body is called the California Commission on Judicial Qualifications. If the Commission finds a complaint to be justified, it may recommend to the state supreme court that a judge be retired for any disability that seriously interferes with his or her performance and that is, or is likely to become, permanent. This Commission may recommend that the state supreme court censure or remove a judge for willful misconduct in

office, willful and persistent failure to perform his or her duties, and habitual intemperance or conduct that may be prejudicial to the administration of justice. The judge is relieved of duties without loss of salary while the Commission's recommendation is pending. The judge may be removed from office with loss of salary if he or she pleads guilty to, or is convicted of, any felony or any crime involving moral turpitude. A judge removed by the state supreme court is ineligible for judicial office and ineligible to practice law. A judge *retired* by the supreme court is considered to have retired voluntarily. Under the California plan the Commission consists of two appeals court judges, two superior court judges, and one municipal judge, all of whom are appointed to the Commission by the state supreme court, plus two members of the state bar who have practiced law in the state for at least ten years. In addition, there are two lay members of the Commission, appointed by the governor and approved by the state senate. All Commission members serve a four-year term, without compensation, and are assisted by a full-time staff. Types of disciplinary action available for use against judges other than the California plan include (1) constitutional provisions permitting the judiciary itself to discipline or remove a judge under the state supreme court's supervisory powers to control judicial behavior; and (2) convening a court on the judiciary on an *ad hoc* basis to try specific complaints involving judges of the court of appeals and the court of general jurisdiction. Neither of the alternative methods is widely used. *See also* JUDICIAL ADMINISTRATION, 312; JUDICIAL ADMINISTRATION: THE MISSOURI PLAN, 314.

Significance The California plan was first instituted in that state in 1960 as the result of a constitutional amendment. By 1973, twenty-nine other states, plus the District of Columbia and Puerto Rico, had established commissions similar to California's Commission on Judicial Qualifications. The strength of the plan is in the existence of a permanent organization, acting on a confidential basis, to receive and investigate complaints, and take action when it is justified. Confidentiality is maintained until a recommendation for removal is made to the supreme court. Since four of the nine Commission members are not judges, the problem of a judge's reluctance to initiate action against another judge is alleviated. The greatest asset of the California plan is its preventive power. The plan recognizes that impeachment is cumbersome and time-consuming. A few states allow for removal by the state legislature by joint resolution or removal by the governor on request of the legislature. A few other states allow for recall by popular election, but each of these means of discipline is politically expensive and sometimes results in extensive campaigns.

The California plan involves the public, the bar, and the judiciary itself in a measured and flexible approach to dealing with errant judicial behavior.

Judicial Administration: The Missouri Plan (314)

A method of selecting state judges based on their merit qualifications for judicial office. The Missouri plan seeks out the best judicial candidates available through the participation of the bench, bar associations, and the lay public. Representatives from these groups are organized into a seven-member nonpartisan judicial nominating commission for the sole purpose of nominating a slate, usually three, of qualified candidates eligible to fill each vacancy. The governor of the state is obligated to select one person from the list. The nominating commission is composed of the senior judge of the highest court, other than the Chief Justice, who serves as the commission's presiding officer, three public members, and three attorneys appointed by the governor. When the governor makes his or her selection, the appointed judge runs in the next general election, without opposition, on a "retention" (yes or no) ballot. If the judge receives a majority, he or she continues in office for a full term. If the vote is negative, the judge loses office and the governor makes another appointment in the same manner. A judge serving a full term can run for reelection simply by indicating his or her wish to do so, "running on the record" rather than against an opponent. Among other common procedures for selecting state judges are (1) election on a partisan or nonpartisan ballot, and (2) appointment by the governor, with the approval of the senate, or of both houses, or appointment by the legislature. President Jimmy Carter implemented elements of the Missouri plan in the federal judicial selection system by executive order in 1977. He created thirteen merit selection panels resembling the nominating screening commissions used by Missouri plan states. *See also* JUDICIAL ADMINISTRATION, 312; JUDICIAL ADMINISTRATION: THE CALIFORNIA PLAN, 313.

Significance The Missouri plan was developed by the American Bar Association and the American Judicature Society and was first adopted by the state of Missouri in 1940. The American Judicature Society described the plan dramatically as "the gratest single event in this century in the field of judicial administration." The merit selection plan was adopted largely as a result of dissatisfaction with popular election of judges. Except for Switzerland, the United States is the only democracy in the world where the practice of selecting judges by popular vote survives. The essential elements of merit selection are training, character, and judicial temperament. But the most difficult problem in merit selection is the development of standards by which to measure these factors. The undoubted success of the Missouri plan has depended largely on the wisdom and intelligence of the members of the nominating commissions. Opponents of the plan maintain that commission membership is manipulated, panels are stacked, and the governor operates politically throughout the process. Advocates of the plan say it takes judges out of politics and secures an independent judiciary. The truth probably lies somewhere in between.

Judicial Review (315)

The power of courts to examine the actions and decisions of all three coordinate branches of government to determine if they are in accord with the federal or applicable state constitution. The power of judicial review is exercised by both federal and state courts, with the United States Supreme Court being the final judge of what is constitutional in the federal system. Although the Constitution of the United States is silent on the subject, in 1803 the Supreme Court established the precedent of judicial review by declaring a law of Congress unconstitutional for the first time in the case of *Marbury v. Madison* (1 Cranch 137). Judicial power to make authoritative, constitutional interpretations and apply them to all governmental actions has long been accepted by the American people as an integral part of the American system of government. In the field of public administration the term *judicial review* is also used to describe the process by which individual public servants can appeal to the regular courts decisions and administrative orders issued by agency officials or administrative law judges. *See also* JUDICIAL ADMINISTRATION, 312.

Significance The power of U.S. courts to exercise judicial review makes them the guardians of the constitutional system. Most democracies do not grant such sweeping power to a nonelected group. In Great Britain, for example, Parliament makes the final determination about what is consonant with the British Constitution. The exercise of such power, as the Supreme Court argued in the *Marbury* decision, is in keeping with the social contract theory that regards the Constitution as the fundamental legal agreement between the American people and their government. To be valid a contract must have an enforcement agent, and this is the role assumed by the courts. Social contract theory has often been challenged in U.S. history, but the challenges have never been successful. The role of the courts in hearing appeals from administrative bodies is also an accepted practice, although judges usually exercise a good deal of restraint in such matters because of the complexity of the economic and social problems involved.

Legal Analysis (316)
An approach to the study of public administration that emphasizes the language of constitutions and charters, legislative enactments, judicial decisions, and administrative adjudication in the definition and implementation of public values. Legal analysis stresses the written record in resolving administrative conflict. It is concerned with the legal imperatives, both positive and negative, which shape administrative decisions and actions. The concept of limited government gives rise to the legal approach, for the central question in systems of limited government is the legitimacy of the decisions and actions of public officials. The issue of legitimacy must often be resolved by reference to constitutional articles and clauses, statutory enactments, executive orders, administrative agency rules and regulations, and judicial decisions. Legal analysis believes the past often provides guidelines to the legitimacy or illegitimacy of public decisions and actions. The admonition of the United States Constitution's second article that the president "shall take care that the laws be faithfully executed" is paralleled by similar provisions in state constitutions and local charters which apply to governors and mayors. The link between law and execution is direct and explicit at all levels in the U.S. system. General public acceptance of this linkage means legal analysis is central to much of the study of public administration and dates from the earliest exercises of administrative authority. When legislative intent is not clear in providing a legal source for executive policy making and action, researchers utilize congressional committee hearing transcripts and reports, debates recorded in the *Congressional Record,* and other extrinsic data sources to establish legal parameters for executive legitimacy. Legal analysis studies judicial decisions as well. For many years, in fact, the study of "public law" comprised the main approach to the study of public administration. Analysis of judicial decisions frequently provides final resolution of ambiguous constitutional or legislative phraseology when other means have proved futile. Legal analysis looks on judicial decisions as "buoys" marking the safe channels through which public agencies may pass in controversies over agency mission, power, and services. *See also* ADMINISTRATIVE LAW JUDGE, 295; POLICY ANALYSIS, 68; QUASI-JUDICIAL, 325.

Public Law and Regulation

Significance Legal analysis recognizes that the administrative process is permeated with legal issues, guidelines, and procedures that are critical in determining values in the public sector. The historical utility of legal analysis is based on its compatibility with democratic theory; that is, the coercive aspects of government are limited by a complex system of legal restraints. Democratic safeguards provide accessible data not just to administrators, but to citizens, lawyers, students, corporate executives, and anyone else interested in what can be *expected* of government in terms of a positive conferral of power or a negative denial of power. Predictability is possible because of the permanence and stability of the legal system. The longevity of the United States Constitution and many state constitutions, most of which were adopted prior to the twentieth century, provide continuity of legal principles and processes. Judicial emphasis upon *stare decisis* (let the previous decision stand) and the judicial presumption of the constitutionality of legislative and executive acts further contribute to the stability of legal institutions. Legal analysis allows the student of administrative process to follow the "unfolding" of the law and relate this to the evolution of administrative practice. The primary weakness of the legal analysis approach is a sometimes excessively narrow view of administrative processes. Critics also say that legal guidelines may be deceptive. They offer much less precision than is claimed for them— indeed constitutional and legislative language is sometimes purposely vague—and the resulting ambiguity leads to conflicts of interpretation. The frequent five-four Supreme Court decisions on public issues of great moment reveal an unsatisfactory state of the law, according to this view. Finally, critics say that legal analysis ignores the inherent dynamics of the administrative process. Concentration on legal principle and authority overemphasizes formal structure and lacks an appreciation for human dynamics in the administered organization. Despite its shortcomings, however, legal analysis asks at least five fundamental questions about public administration: (1) What legitimate means are available in executing the law? (2) Under what conditions may an administrator exercise discretion in interpreting statutes? (3) What is the intent of the law? (4) What is the nature of administrative justice? (5) What are the sources of administrative authority?

Licensing (317)
The process by which government grants permission to an individual or a group to perform certain acts or carry on specified activities. All

levels of government—national, state, and local—exercise licensing powers. For example, the federal government, functioning through the Federal Communications Commission (FCC), grants licenses to companies that wish to operate radio or television stations. State governments, acting through special commissions, grant licenses that permit entry into such fields as medicine, law, pharmacy, teaching, barbering, and plumbing, based on qualifications and examinations. Other state licenses apply to the general public, such as those needed for hunting, fishing, driving, and marriage. Licensing is used by local governments to restrict entry into and continuing operations of certain businesses, such as bars, hotels, movie theaters, private police forces, detective agencies, and other kinds of activities that can have a substantial social impact. *See also* CERTIFICATE OF PUBLIC CONVENIENCE, INTEREST, AND NECESSITY, 301.

Significance Licensing is a powerful governmental regulatory tool implemented by public administrators. The granting of licenses to certain vocational groups and to businesses affected with a public interest means that officials can influence their operations in many ways by using the threat of withholding, revoking, or refusing to renew licenses. However, due-process guarantees require that governmental controls and requirements meet the test of reasonableness. If licenses are arbitrarily withheld or withdrawn, the courts can order officials to issue licenses to aggrieved parties. Yet, much discretion is left by legislative bodies in the hands of the administering officials, who often must choose among a number of applicants, all of whom are essentially qualified. When administrators make such choices, political and legal problems inevitably arise. Licensing is often strongly supported by clientele groups that seek to maintain professional standards or, in some cases, to limit competition.

Malfeasance **(318)**
Illegal or immoral actions undertaken by public officials. Malfeasance is performing deeds an individual or an agency is forbidden to perform by constitutional or statutory law, or by commonly accepted moral standards. According to J. D. Williams in *Public Administration: The People's Business* (1980), persons accused of malfeasance attempt to justify their actions by (1) hero worship of a leader who orders malfeasance, as in the FBI's blind obedience to its Director, J. Edgar Hoover; (2) the Adolf Eichmann syndrome, wherein an act of malfeasance ordered from above settles any doubt about its propriety; (3) fear of what may happen to one who disobeys, such as the transfer of a Central Intelligence Agency (CIA) operative to an undesirable

location; (4) fear of exposure of one's indiscretions, illustrated by generations of congressmen keeping quiet about FBI excesses; and (5) the Machiavellian ethic, that the end justifies the means. According to this ethic, Williams states, malfeasance is sanctioned because the FBI's targets include Communists, the Ku Klux Klan, assassins, and spies. Although the FBI's tactics were admittedly illegal, according to an internal memorandum of FBI Assistant Director William Sullivan in 1966, "they represent an invaluable technique in combatting subversive activities . . . aimed directly at undermining and destroying our nation." Elsewhere Sullivan defined malfeasance as a form of pragmatism. What is called burglary in the Criminal Code is a "black bag job" when carried out by the FBI. "Never once did I hear anybody," said Sullivan in testimony before the United States Senate Select Committee on Intelligence Activities, "including myself, raise the question is this course of action which we have agreed upon lawful, is it legal, is it ethical or moral? . . . we were just naturally pragmatists. The one thing we were concerned about was will this course of action work, will it get us what we want . . . ? because . . . in government we are amoral." Malfeasance deals precisely with the questions Sullivan said the FBI ignored in the 1960s: Is it lawful? Is it legal? Is it ethical or moral? *See also* ETHIC OF MEANS AND ENDS, 97; MISFEASANCE, 319; NONFEASANCE, 320.

Significance   Malfeasance is widely practiced in U.S. public administration. Williams uses the following examples from recent history as illustrations of official misconduct. (1) The Central Intelligence Agency's MK-Ultra project of the 1960s involved drug experimentation on unsuspecting human beings resulting in at least one suicide. (2) President Richard M. Nixon's obstruction of justice included withholding information from investigatory bodies, having the CIA throw an FBI investigation of the Watergate incident off course, approving the bribery of burglars to obtain their silence, and interfering with the trial of Daniel Ellsberg by offering the sitting judge an important post in the Nixon administration. The Articles of Impeachment of Richard Nixon, reported by the House Judiciary Committee in its final report to the House of Representatives in 1974, constitute a litany of presidential malfeasance. (3) The FBI engaged in breaking and entering without search warrants over two hundred times between 1948 and 1973, and FBI agents sent a note to Dr. Martin Luther King, Jr., suggesting he commit suicide in the face of evidence the FBI could reveal on his extramarital encounters. (4) The FBI wiretapped communications between a defendant and her lawyer (*Coplon v. United States*, 191 F.2d 749 [D.C. Cir., 1951]). (5) The FBI provided J. Edgar Hoover with an array of personal services at FBI expense, such as carpentry and interior design work at his private residence. These and many other examples of FBI and CIA malfeasance are discussed in *Intelligence Activities and the Rights of Americans,* a 1976 report of the United States Senate Select Committee on Intelligence Activities. The report closes with these words: "We have seen segments of our government, in their attitudes and action, adopt tactics unworthy of a democracy, and occasionally reminiscent of the tactics of totalitarian regimes. We have seen a consistent pattern in which programs initiated with limited goals, such as preventing criminal violence or identifying foreign spies, were expanded to what witnesses characterized as 'vacuum cleaners,' sweeping in information about lawful activities of American citizens." Plato warned Glaucon in *The Republic* that the guardians must be fierce toward the enemy but gentle toward the citizens. If not, said Plato, the guardians will destroy the city from within. Malfeasance on the part of public officials constitutes the kind of threat to the stability of the political system to which Plato alluded.

Misfeasance (319)
The improper performance of lawful duties. Misfeasance involves administrative activity that is within the lawful mission of an agency, but that violates constitutional standards or the public interest. Surveillance and apprehension of those committing federal crimes are the lawful mission of the Federal Bureau of Investigation (FBI), for example. But disclosing its unproved findings to congressional committees or news media representatives, rather than grand juries, is not. J. D. Williams points out in *Public Administration: The People's Business* (1980) that misfeasance is most commonly in violation of the constitutional standard of due process, as when a prosecutor used a pair of bloody men's shorts to convict a rape suspect, knowing all the time the stains were paint, not blood (*Miller v. Pate,* 386 U.S. 1: 1967). Misfeasance may also consist of a violation of the public interest by public officials, as in some of the activities of the independent regulatory commissions. The responsibility of commission members is to regulate designated industries in the public interest, not to be co-opted by them. *See also* ETHIC OF MEANS AND ENDS, 97; MALFEASANCE, 318; NONFEASANCE, 320.

Significance Misfeasance is an all-too-common occurrence in U.S. public administration. It is responsible for much reorganizational effort and congressional hearing activity. Williams points out that, in 1976, for example, the Moss subcommittee of the House Interstate and Foreign Commerce Commission found that substantial misrepresentation of the public interest had taken place in the independent regulatory commissions. The subcommittee report stated: "Our studies confirm earlier observations that the actions of regulatory agencies reflect more than anything else their primary attention to the special interests of the regulated industry and lack of sufficient concern for underrepresented interests." Misfeasance was most obvious in the Federal Power Commission (FPC), which "displayed a conscious indifference to the public" in overt disregard of its congressional mandate. Misfeasance thus was one of the reasons why Congress dismantled the FPC and replaced it with the Federal Energy Regulatory Commission (FERC) in 1977. The Moss subcommittee said the measuring rods for appraising independent regulatory commissions are (1) fidelity to the public protection mandate defined by Congress; (2) quantity and quality of agency activity; (3) effectiveness of agency enforcement programs; and (4) quality of public participation. Misfeasance charges in a court of law, however, would involve actions by public officials that are clearly improper or negligent and result in injury to others. Actions that are impolitic, unethical, or in bad taste do not constitute misfeasance.

Nonfeasance (320)
The failure of a public official to perform required duties. Nonfeasance means standing pat when a situation calls for action. According to J. D. Williams in *Public Administration: The People's Business* (1980), nonfeasance was exhibited by the Illinois Department of Mines and Minerals when it yielded to economic pressure by ignoring a report of its mine inspector at the Centralia mine. The inspector said the mine was dangerous and might blow up at any moment, which it did on March 25, 1947, killing 111 men. Nonfeasance is Governor John Patterson of Alabama failing to provide protection for Freedom Riders in 1961 as they attempted to travel on interstate buses to challenge segregated facilities. Alabama mobs then firebombed the buses and attacked the church where the Freedom Riders and their supporters had gathered, resulting in a racial conflagration. Nonfeasance is the police chief of Birmingham, Alabama, promising the Ku Klux Klan fifteen minutes without police interference during which the Klan could attack Freedom Riders. Nonfeasance is the Justice Department suspending prosecution of the International Telephone and Telegraph Company under pressure from President Richard M. Nixon shortly after ITT had offered the Republican Party $400,000 for its 1972 nominating convention. Nonfeasance is frequently a product of (1) indifference to reports or events (the Centralia mine); (2) cooptation by social and cultural surroundings (Governor

Patterson and the Birmingham police chief); (3) bribery (Nixon and the ITT); and (4) cowardice (perhaps all of the above). See also ETHIC OF MEANS AND ENDS, 97; MALFEASANCE, 318; MISFEASANCE, 319.

Significance Nonfeasance as a means of avoiding responsibility is at the heart of an observation President George Washington made in his first inaugural address. He said there is an "indissoluble union between virtue and happiness and between duty and advantage." If one does not do one's duty, he or she can neither be happy nor hold any advantage among citizens or in the office. Williams has noted that deterioration takes place in an office where nonfeasance is practiced. Where it is tolerated, it is transmitted to newcomers as acceptable behavior. Documented cases of nonfeasance, however, may be actionable in a court of law, particularly in civil suits. Usually, however, nonfeasance will be punished, if at all, by public displeasure, by budget cuts, by legislative action, or by other means that may be aimed at goading the official into performing proper duties.

Occupational Safety and Health Administration (321) (OSHA)

A regulatory agency, located in the Department of Labor, that enforces a comprehensive industrial safety program developed for private companies engaged in interstate commerce. OSHA was created under provisions of the Occupational Safety and Health Act of 1970, which authorized it to require employers to furnish a work place for employees free from hazards to life or health. Under provisions of the 1970 act, OSHA (1) develops and publishes safety and health standards; (2) issues regulations to implement its standards; (3) conducts investigations and inspections to determine whether its standards and regulations are complied with; and (4) issues citations and recommends penalties for noncompliance. An independent agency, the Occupational Safety and Health Review Commission, was established by the act to adjudicate cases involving alleged violations of OSHA regulations. The Review Commission consists of three members appointed for six-year terms by the president, with Senate consent, with one commissioner serving as chairperson. Employers have the right to adjudication of any OSHA charges of a safety or health violation discovered during an inspection, the penalties proposed, and the time permitted to correct a hazardous situation. See also CAVEAT EMPTOR VERSUS CAVEAT VENDITOR, 299.

Significance The Occupational Safety and Health Act of 1970, as currently enforced by OSHA, covers virtually every employer in the

United States. The act, with the creation of OSHA and the Review Commission, was the turning point of a long campaign by organized labor to establish government standards and regulations to govern private employers. In a typical year prior to the passage of the act, thousands of workers were killed in industrial accidents, and several million suffered disabling injuries while on the job. OSHA has helped to decrease the incidence of serious accidents, but in applying its regulations it has been attacked by critics who regard its efforts as an attack on the rights of business and regard it as a contributor to inflation because of increased production costs. The control of environmental hazards, included in the scope of OSHA's regulatory powers, has been a particularly contentious area of its operations. In 1977, the Supreme Court upheld the regulatory power of OSHA and the authority of the Review Commission to adjudicate enforcement actions in *Atlas Roofing, Inc. v. Occupational Safety and Health Review Commission* (430 U.S. 442).

Opp Cotton Mills v. Administrator of Wage and Hour Division, 312 U.S. 126 (1941)   (322)
A Supreme Court decision which held that the exercise of power by Congress to authorize an administrative determination of minimum wage levels in a particular industry is within constitutional limits. The *Opp Cotton Mills* case upheld the right of Congress to delegate legislative decision-making power to an administrative agency, and the authority of administrators to make important policy decisions even though they are not directly responsible to the electorate. *See also* ADMINISTRATIVE DUE PROCESS, 293.

Significance   The *Opp Cotton Mills* case was a recognition of the broad decision authority that must be vested in administrators to cope with the power of huge aggregations of economic power. The Court majority determined that life had become too complex and technical for Congress to legislate all governmental policy decisions. In the case, the Court accepted the idea that Congress must legislate general policies, but administrative agencies could be charged with responsibility for filling in the details and applying the general policy to specific situations. The case was a clear recognition by the Court that administrators not only "administer" but must engage in policy-making functions as well. Administrators cannot be given a free rein, however, and Congress must establish the standards that guide and govern administrative agencies in implementing statutes. Such functions as rate-making, the determination of minimum wages, and public service requirements for particular industries are logically left to skilled administrators to determine on a continuing basis. Congress has neither the time nor the expertise needed to do those kinds of tasks. With the *Opp Cotton Mills* decision in 1941, the Court reversed its tendency to interpret narrowly the constitutional authority of Congress to delegate power to administrative agencies. This tendency contributed to the dramatic confrontations between the judiciary and the supporters of the New Deal in the 1930s. Examples of this confrontation over delegated powers can be found in the famous "sick chicken" (*Schecter v. United States,* 295 U.S. 495: 1935) and "hot oil" (*Panama Refining Co. v. Ryan,* 293 U.S. 388: 1935) cases.

Proprietary Function (323)
Government's role in carrying on a business-type activity ordinarily found in the private sector. Proprietary functions carried on by government include such activities as transportation, garbage collection, selling liquor, operating recreational facilities and restaurants, and providing utility service. Although in 1819 the Supreme Court established the rule of intergovernmental tax immunity in the historic case, *McCulloch v. Maryland* (4 Wheaton 316), it later moderated the application of that rule by providing that proprietary functions carried on by a state, such as selling liquor, could be taxed by the federal government because they are businesslike in nature and are not strictly governmental (*South Carolina v. United States,* 199 U.S. 437: 1905). The precedent established in the *South Carolina* case continues to be applicable, and substantial tax income is derived from taxing proprietary functions carried on by all levels of government today.

Significance The proprietary functions carried on by many governments in the United States are viewed with mixed emotions by the public. Persons in business often complain about the unfair competition they face because the government's proprietary functions are supported by a public treasury. Supporters point out that, in most cases, the entry of government into a business-type operation is caused by the failure of private entrepreneurs to provide a service, or to provide it at a reasonable cost. Business-type functions can range from the operation of a campus bookstore, to the Tennessee Valley Authority (TVA), which is a multipurpose federal enterprise that provides water-, oil-, coal-, and nuclear-generated energy to the residents of seven southern states. Governments engage in proprietary functions for many reasons, including (1) efforts to supplement tax monies with profits earned; (2) the desire to establish a model type of operation that can be used as a "yardstick" to measure the efficiency and pricing of private companies; and (3) the ordering of a

Public Law and Regulation

service or a product not otherwise available to the public. Although the *South Carolina* precedent remains applicable, the courts have often found it difficult to distinguish between a purely governmental function and those of a proprietary nature. For example, when a city sells water to its citizens through an underground pipe system, the courts have declared that activity to be immune from taxation, whereas the sale of bottled water by a city is taxed as a proprietary function.

Quasi-executive (324)
Administrative powers exercised by agency personnel who are not directly responsible to the chief executive. Quasi-executive functions are performed by independent agencies in the national government, particularly by independent regulatory commissions. *Quasi-* (Latin for "as if it were" or "that which resembles") executive powers are exercised by such agencies in implementing and enforcing the basic congressional statutes governing agency jurisdiction, and the rules and regulations that are made by the agency within the scope of powers delegated by Congress. See also INDEPENDENT REGULATORY COMMISSION, 152; QUASI-JUDICIAL, 325; QUASI-LEGISLATIVE, 326.

Significance Quasi-executive powers are exercised by those agencies that do not logically fall into any of the three regular branches of government. In such agencies, rules and regulations are made and promulgated (quasi-legislative function), are implemented on a day-to-day basis through administrative actions (quasi-executive function), and, when violations occur, administrative law judges hear and decide the issues (quasi-judicial function). Thus the same agency performs all three of the basic functions of government in an apparent violation of the constitutional principle of separation of powers. Such agencies are often referred to as "the fourth branch of government" because their operations resemble those of the three branches, but they do not logically fall into a single branch. Although quasi-executive administration of pertinent law is generally effective, in critical situations it lacks the authority possessed by those administrators who act in the name of and under the authority of the chief executive.

Quasi-judicial (325)
Functions performed by administrative agencies that are judicial in nature. *Quasi-* (Latin for "as if it were" or "that which resembles") judicial powers are similar to those exercised by courts and judges.

Administrative law judges that are part of regulatory agencies carry out quasi-judicial functions in interpreting and applying the rules and regulations issued by the agency to situations involving private companies that fall under its regulatory powers. If the administrative law determines that a violation is occurring, the judge may issue a cease and desist order to the company. *See also* ADMINISTRATIVE LAW JUDGE, 295; HEARING, 310.

Significance In the national government, quasi-judicial powers are exercised by the independent regulatory commissions and by other administrative agencies that have been empowered by Congress to carry out similar functions, such as the Social Security Administration (SSA). The term *quasi* is attached as a prefix to such activities because, under the constitutional separation of powers doctrine, judicial powers are assigned to the judicial branch. The exercise of quasi-judicial powers, along with the exercise of quasi-executive and quasi-legislative powers by administrative bodies, helps to explain why these agencies are referred to as "independent" and why they are sometimes called the "fourth branch of government." In an attempt to maintain the constitutional separation of powers system, Congress enacted the Administrative Procedure Act of 1946. This law provides that special administrative law judges be appointed to each agency to perform the quasi-judicial functions, that they operate according to specified judicial procedures, and that their decisions be subject to review by the regular federal courts.

Quasi-legislative (326)

The role of an administrative agency in making and promulgating rules and regulations that have the force of law. Numerous agencies in the national, state, and local governments have been empowered to perform quasi-legislative functions. On the national level, for example, independent regulatory commissions are charged with responsibility to issue rules and regulations that govern the operations of private companies engaged in interstate or foreign commerce. On the state level, public service commissions make rules and regulations that apply to utilities that operate within the state. On the local level, an example of the quasi-legislative function is the action of a traffic commission, authorized by the city council to make traffic rules that have the force of law. In each case, legislative supervision and control are maintained by the legislative body that has created and empowered the administrative agency: the Congress, the state legislature, and the city council. The administrative units thus exercise only *quasi*- (Latin for "as if it were" or "that which resembles") legislative powers, and the primary authority remains with the legislative body. *See also* ADMINISTRATIVE ORDER, 297; INDEPENDENT REGULATORY COMMISSION, 152; QUASI-JUDICIAL, 325.

Significance Quasi-legislative powers exercised by administrative agencies are a product of the increasingly complex, technical nature of modern life and the attempts by government to correct abuses that grow out of the operations of giant corporations. Legislative bodies, such as Congress and the state legislatures, recognize that they possess neither the time nor the expertise to legislate in these diverse problem areas. They therefore lay down general guidelines and empower the relevant agency to fill in the details through the issuance of rules and regulations. As a result, more law today is made by administrators than by legislators. To safeguard the rights of those subject to administrative rules, Congress enacted the Administrative Procedure Act of 1946. This law requires agencies to (1) give notice of a proposed new rule; (2) hold a hearing so that the views of those affected by the proposed rule can be presented; (3) publish all new rules in the *Federal Register;* and (4) provide for appeal to the regular courts to determine such issues as interpretations and applications of the rule and its constitutionality. Critics charge that too much law is being made by appointed boards, commissions, and administrators who are not democratically accountable to the voters. Supporters point out that it would be impossible for legislative bodies alone to meet the need for government regulation, and that the powers of administrative agencies are supervised and controlled by the legislative body that created them, and through review of their operations by the courts.

Railroad Commission of Texas v. Rowan and (327) *Nichols Oil Company,* 311 U.S. 570 (1941)

Upheld an administrative decision of the Texas Railroad Commission that served as an enforcement measure restricting the amount of oil that could be taken from state wells. In its decision, the Supreme Court opined that technical issues of this kind are too complex for judicial determination. Therefore, in the absence of any evidence that the Commission's decision was procedurally incorrect or was based on insufficient facts, the Court determined that the agency's administrative order should stand. *See also* ADMINISTRATIVE ORDER, 297; ADMINISTRATIVE PROCEDURE ACT OF 1946, 298.

Significance The *Railroad Commission* case is important because it emphasizes that, in the highly complex world of administrative decision making, judges are reluctant to substitute their judgment or the judgment of jurors for that of the specialists who are charged with regulatory duties. Yet they retain the right to examine administrative rulings, upon petition of a party adversely affected by an administrative order, to ensure that proper procedures were used, that relevant laws were followed, and that the decision was based on "substantial evidence." Despite this landmark ruling by the Supreme Court, parties adversely affected by an administrative ruling continue to seek redress in the courts on the bases that it did not conform to existing law, that the agency's procedures or the complainant's procedural rights were violated, or that the evidence was insufficient to lead the administrators to their conclusions. Congress followed the lead of the court by incorporating the requirements for administrative decision making set forth in this case into the Administrative Procedure Act of 1946.

Rate-setting (328)

The process by which governmental regulatory agencies determine and prescribe the charges that privately owned public utilities and other companies affected with a public interest may demand for their product or service. Rate-setting may involve prescribing specific rates, maximum rates, or maximum and minimum rates. Rate-setting becomes a necessary function of government whenever the government limits or eliminates competition for a company by granting it a license or franchise, making it the sole company providing a product or service. Under conditions of oligopoly (where the market is controlled by a few companies and only limited competition exists), government regulation of rates may also apply, especially if the product or service is essential. While government rate-setters do not find it difficult to determine a percentage *rate* that meets the requirement of a "fair return," they have often experienced difficulty in deciding what *base* should be used to apply that rate. Theories for determining the rate base include (1) *original cost,* which includes the cost of all assets acquired when the company started its operations along with the cost of subsequent capital additions, less depreciation; (2) *prudent investment,* which starts with original costs but deducts depreciation and all investments over the years that have proved to be imprudent or wasteful; and (3) *reproduction cost,* which is based on the cost of replacing all company assets at current prices. Although the courts for many years tended to insist that rate-setters apply the prudent investment formula in determining rate structures, with the advent of double-digit inflation during the 1970s and 1980s there has been a tendency for the courts to permit a shift toward the reproduction cost theory. *See also* ADMINISTRATIVE DUE PROCESS, 293; DUE PROCESS OF LAW, 306.

Significance Rate-setting has become a common function of many regulatory agencies on all three levels of government. The national government regulates the rates of many companies engaged in interstate and foreign commerce, particularly through the actions of the independent regulatory commissions, such as the Interstate Commerce Commission (ICC), the Federal Communications Commission (FCC), the Federal Trade Commission (FTC), and the Securities and Exchange Commission (SEC). The states tend to regulate many of the intrastate operations of the same companies regulated by the national agencies. On the local level, rate-making focuses mainly on the operations of public utilities that supply needed products or services to residents and are not regulated by the state. In all cases, rate-setters must try to strike a balance between protecting consumer interests and permitting rates that are high enough to enable the regulated company to earn a fair return. Rate-setters also typically permit rates high enough so that expansions and modernization of plant and equipment can be financed out of income from consumers rather than by floating a new stock issue. The latter approach would tend to proliferate ownership in the company and perhaps have an adverse effect on stock prices. Regulated companies also benefit from having many of the rate-setters recruited from the very businesses they regulate; these rate-setters are therefore usually sympathetic concerning rate-increase requests. Also, if rates are not set high enough, the companies can appeal to the courts on the grounds that their right to a fair return has been violated, or they can appeal on some technical or procedural ground. In the 1980s, many federal regulatory agencies have been moving, along with the Congress that grants them their powers, toward a greatly reduced level of control over rates and services, with mixed results. Deregulation of the airlines, for example, resulted in competitive rates that produced many bargains for passengers in the period following deregulation, but in time most rates were increased substantially over their regulated levels.

Rule of Law (329)

A basic principle of democratic government that proclaims the supremacy of law. The rule of law is embodied in the United States Constitution where it buttresses the doctrine of limited government. Public officials are restricted in their conduct toward individuals because the rule of law safeguards the people's rights from arbitrary interference. Administrators at all levels of government are guided in a general sense and governed in a specific way by the concept of rule of law. If they attempt to substitute their own judgments for the law, the courts will overturn their actions. The rule of law, as interpreted by the courts, requires that each individual in his or her dealings with government be accorded due process of law, be treated equally, receive a fair trial if charged with violations of law, and receive the punishments or awards that are prescribed by law. In the judicial system, the term *rule of law* is also used to describe the key legal source or reasoning that is used to decide a case and establish a precedent for future decisions. *See also* DUE PROCESS OF LAW, 306.

Significance The rule of law provides the foundation for the U.S. constitutional system and for the day-by-day operations of government. All levels—national, state, and local—are guided and governed by this principle. Although the United States Supreme Court has never decided a case solely on the basis of the rule of law, the basic reasoning that upholds the principle is often invoked in deciding cases. Historically, the doctrine goes back to the Magna Charta, the Great Charter that King John of England was forced to accept at Runnymede in 1215, which ordered that the King, in all of his actions, must be governed by "the law of the land." This idea has been nurtured over a period of almost eight centuries and today constitutes the basic Anglo-American doctrine governing the operations of the two democratic systems.

Whistleblower (330)

A person working in an agency who publicly criticizes that agency's administrative practices by disclosing pertinent information to the public. The whistleblower is described by Charles Peters and Taylor Branch in *Blowing the Whistle: Dissent in the Public Interest* (1972) as a "muckraker from within who exposes what he considers the unconscionable practices of his own organization." Peters and Branch say there are actually two kinds of whistleblowers: the first type attacks the organization while he or she remains a part of it; the second is an *alumnus* whistleblower who has resigned or been dismissed. Peters and Branch say either kind must manage strong feelings about whistleblowing activity: "He must . . . cope with the stinging demands of loyalty, with the don't-make-a-big-deal-out-of-it feeling, and with the fear of retaliation." Public administrationist Phillip E. Present notes in *People and Public Administration* (1979) that Congress has created a "Catch 22" situation for whistleblowers in that the federal Code of Ethics for Government Service passed by Congress states it is a federal employee's duty to "expose corruption wherever discovered," yet the same code also says that government workers must not evade agency regulations that forbid their disclosing data from official files. Thus, an administrator who gives information to the press or even to Congress can be fired, even though the original charges may later be proved. The Committee on Governmental Affairs of the United States Senate issued a report in February 1978, entitled "The Whistleblowers," in which the committee documented the case of two employees who were fired for trying to expose corruption in the General Services Administration (GSA). One of the employees, Robert F. Sullivan, was unsuccessful in using the Code of Ethics in his defense. The Federal Employee Appeals Authority (FEAA) said in its decision on the Sullivan case: "While we do not in any way diminish the importance of the code . . . , we feel obligated to point out (1) that it is not law, and (2) that the second paragraph includes a recognition by the Congress that employees should uphold . . . agency regulations and never be parties to their evasion." *See also* ETHICS, 13; ETHICS IN GOVERNMENT ACT OF 1978, 212.

Significance The whistleblower may be a disgruntled person who has been demoted or fired for legitimate reasons, or he or she may be a truly dedicated, public-spirited citizen in the finest traditon of the public service. In either case the price of blowing the whistle is extremely high. In "The Price of Blowing the Whistle" (1977) freelance writer Helen Dudar chronicled cases of retaliation. They often included the whistleblower not being able to get another job in either the private or the public sector. Dudar described a 1977 conference of whistleblowers in Washington, DC, organized by the Institute for Policy Studies, attended by two hundred people. Some of the conferees merely bore personal grudges against agency supervisors, but many of them had, to use the words of whistleblower A. Ernest Fitzgerald, "committed truth" and had suffered for it. According to several accounts, the sessions took place "in an atmosphere of such raging anger and bitterness they could have been recorded as peaks and valleys on a seismograph." In 1969, Fitzgerald had gone before a congressional committee in his capacity as a Defense Department cost analyst and testified that a Lockheed cargoplane was costing $2 billion more than the contracted price. He is currently a one-man advisory committee to federal employees who consider doing what he did in the interest of exposing waste and corruption. "People go to him for guidance all the time," Dudar wrote. "I never advise them," Fitzgerald says, "I just tell them the probable consequences of going public. Most of them never do."

BIBLIOGRAPHY

Abraham, Henry J. *The Judiciary: The Supreme Court in the Governmental Process*, 6th ed. Boston: Allyn and Bacon, 1983.
Appleby, Paul. *Big Democracy*. New York: Alfred A. Knopf, 1945.
Appleby, Paul. *Morality and Administration in Democratic Government*. Baton Rouge, La.: Louisiana State University Press, 1952.
Appleby, Paul. *Policy and Administration*. University, Ala.: University of Alabama Press, 1949.
Barnard, Chester I. *The Functions of the Executive*. Cambridge, Mass.: Harvard University Press, 1960.
Barton, Rayburn, and Chappell, William L., Jr. *Public Administration: The Work of Government*. Glenview, Ill.: Scott, Foresman, 1985.
Bentley, Arthur F., *The Process of Government*. Cambridge, Mass.: Belknap Press, 1902.
Berkley, George E. *The Craft of Public Administration*, 4th ed. Boston: Allyn and Bacon, 1984.
Berne, Eric. *Games People Play*. New York: Grove Press, 1964.
Bernstein, Samuel J., and O'Hara, Patrick. *Public Administration: Organizations, People, and Public Policy*. New York: Harper and Row, 1979.
Bozeman, Barry. *All Organizations Are Public: Bridging Public and Private Organizational Theories*. San Francisco: Jossey-Bass, 1987.
Bozeman, Barry. *Public Management and Policy Analysis*. New York: St. Martin's Press, 1979.
Brown, Brack E. S., and Stillman, Richard J., eds. *A Search for Public Administration: The Ideas and Career of Dwight Waldo*. College Station, Tex.: Texas A & M, 1986.
Caputo, David A. *Politics and Public Policy in America: An Introduction*. Philadelphia: J. B. Lippincott, 1974.
Cayer, N. Joseph. *Public Personnel Administration in the United States*, 2d ed. New York: St. Martin's Press, 1986.

Bibliography

Chandler, Ralph Clark, ed. *A Centennial History of the American Administrative State.* New York: Free Press, 1987.
Crozier, Michel. *The Bureaucratic Phenomenon.* Chicago: University of Chicago Press, 1964.
Dahl, Robert A. *Dilemmas of Pluralist Democracy: Autonomy Versus Control.* New Haven, Conn.: Yale University Press, 1982.
Dahl, Robert A. *Pluralist Democracy in the United States.* Chicago: Rand McNally, 1967.
Dahl, Robert A. *Politics, Economics, and Welfare.* Chicago: University of Chicago Press, 1976.
Dimock, Marshall Edward, and Dimock, Gladys Ogden. *Law and Dynamic Administration.* New York: Praeger, 1980.
Dimock, Marshall Edward, and Dimock, Gladys Ogden. *Public Administration,* 4th ed. New York: Holt, Rinehart and Winston, 1969.
Downs, George W., and Larkey, Patrick D. *The Search for Government Efficiency: From Hubris to Helplessness.* Philadelphia: Temple University Press, 1986.
Dudar, Helen. "The Price of Blowing the Whistle," *New York Times Magazine,* 30 October 1977.
Fesler, James W. *American Public Administration: Patterns of the Past.* Washington, D.C.: American Society for Public Administration, 1982.
Fesler, James W. *Public Administration: Theory and Practice.* Englewood Cliffs, N.J.: Prentice-Hall, 1980.
Festinger, Leon. *A Theory of Cognitive Dissonance.* New York: Row, Peterson, 1957.
Follett, Mary Parker. *Creative Experience.* New York: Longmans, Green and Company, 1924.
Follett, Mary Parker. *Dynamic Administration: The Collected Papers of Mary Parker Follett,* edited by Elliot M. Fox and L. Urwick. New York: Hippocrene Books, 1940.
Follett, Mary Parker. *The New State.* Cambridge, Mass.: Belknap Press, 1902.
Freeman, J. Leiper. *The Political Process: Executive Bureau-Legislative Committee Relations.* New York: Random House, 1965.
Friedman, Milton. *Capitalism and Freedom.* Chicago: University of Chicago Press, 1962.
Fulmer, William E.; Strickland, A. T., III; and Thompson, Arthur A., Jr., eds. *Readings in Strategic Management.* Plano, Tex.: Business Publications, 1984.
Gawthrop, Louis C. *Public Sector Management: Systems and Ethics.* Bloomington, Ind.: Indiana University Press, 1984.
Golembiewski, Robert T., and Gibson, Frank K. *Public Administration:*

Bibliography

Readings in Institutions, Processes, Behavior, Policy, 4th ed. Boston: Houghton Mifflin, 1983.
Golembiewski, Robert T., and Wildavsky, Aaron. *The Costs of Federalism: In Honor of James W. Fesler.* New Brunswick, N.J.: Transaction Books, 1986.
Goodsell, Charles T. *The Case of Bureaucracy,* 2d ed. Chatham, N.J.: Chatham House Publishers, 1985.
Gordon, George J. *Public Administration in America,* 3d ed. New York: St. Martin's Press, 1986.
Gortner, Harold F. *Administration in the Public Sector,* 2d ed. New York: John Wiley Sons, 1981.
Gulick, Luther, and Urwick, L. *Papers on the Science of Administration.* New York: Augustus M. Kelley Publishers, 1937.
Gunn, Elizabeth. *Ethics and the Public Sector: An Annotated Bibliography and Overview Essay.* Norman, Okla.: Bureau of Government Research, University of Oklahoma, 1986.
Harmon, Michael M. *Action Theory for Public Administration.* New York: Longman, 1981.
Harmon, Michael M., and Mayer, Richard T. *Organization Theory for Public Administration.* Boston: Little, Brown and Company, 1986.
Harris, Tom. *I'm O.K.—You're O.K.* New York: Avon, 1973.
Hays, Steven W., and Reeves, T. Zane. *Personnel Management in the Public Sector.* Boston: Allyn and Bacon, 1984.
Henderson, Keith M. *Public Administration: The Last Twenty-five Years.* Monticello, Ill.: Vance, 1984.
Henry, Nicholas. *Doing Public Administration: Exercises, Essays, and Cases,* 2d ed. Boston: Allyn and Bacon, 1982.
Henry, Nicholas. *Public Administration and Public Affairs,* 2d ed. Englewood Cliffs, N.J.: Prentice-Hall, 1980.
Hill, Larry B., and Herbert, F. Ted. *Essentials of Public Administration.* North Scituate, Mass.: Duxbury Press, 1979.
Hogwood, Brian W., and Peters, B. Guy. *Policy Dynamics.* New York: St. Martin's Press, 1983.
Hopkins, Anne H. *Work and Job Satisfaction in the Public Sector.* Totowa, N.J.: Rowman Allanheld, 1983.
Hummel, Ralph P. *The Bureaucratic Experience,* 3d ed. New York: St. Martin's Press, 1987.
Jacob, Herbert. *Justice in America: Courts, Lawyers, and the Judicial Process,* 4th ed. Boston: Little, Brown, 1984.
Janis, Irving L. *Victims of Groupthink.* Boston: Houghton Mifflin, 1972.
Jun, Jong S. *Public Administration: Design and Problem Solving.* New York: Macmillan, 1986.
Kast, Fremont E., and Rosenzweig, James E. *Organization and*

Bibliography

Management: A Systems and Contingency Approach, 4th ed. New York: McGraw-Hill, 1985.

Klingner, Donald E., and Nalbandian, John. *Public Personnel Management: Contexts and Strategies*, 2d ed. Cambridge, Mass.: Winthrop Publishers, 1981.

Kramer, Fred A. *Dynamics of Public Bureaucracy: An Introduction to Public Management*, 2d ed. Cambridge, Mass.: Winthrop Publishers, 1981.

Kramer, Fred A. *Perspectives on Public Bureaucracy*, 3d ed. Cambridge, Mass.: Winthrop Publishers, 1981.

Lasswell, Harold. *Psychopathology and Politics*. Chicago: University of Chicago Press, 1930.

Lindblom, Charles E. *Intelligence of Democracy: Decision Making Through Mutual Adjustment*. New York: Free Press, 1965.

Lindblom, Charles E. "The Science of Muddling Through." *Public Administration Review* 19 (Spring 1959): 79–88.

Lutrin, Carl E., and Settle, Allen K. *American Public Administration: Concepts and Cases*, 3d ed. Englewood Cliffs, N.J.: Prentice-Hall, 1985.

McCurdy, Howard E. *Public Administration: A Bibliographic Guide to the Literature*. New York: Marcel Dekker, 1986.

McCurdy, Howard E. *Public Administration: A Synthesis*. Menlo Park, Calif.: Benjamin/Cummings, 1977.

McGregor, Douglas M. *The Human Side of Enterprise*. New York: McGraw-Hill, 1960.

McKenna, Christopher K. *Quantitative Methods for Public Decision-Making*. New York: McGraw-Hill, 1980.

McKinney, Jerome B. *Effective Financial Management in Public and Non-Profit Agencies: A Practical and Integrative Approach*. New York: Quorum Books, 1986.

McKinney, Jerome B., and Howard, Lawrence C. *Public Administration: Balancing Power and Accountability*. Oak Park, Ill.: Moore, 1979.

Magat, Wesley A.; Krupnick, Alan J.; and Harrington, Winston. *Rules in the Making: A Statistical Analysis of Regulatory Agency Behavior*. Washington, D.C.: Resources for the Future, 1986.

March, James G., and Simon, Herbert A. *Organizations*. New York: John Wiley Sons, 1958.

Martin, Shan. *Managing without Managers: Alternative Work Arrangements in Public Organizations*. Beverly Hills: Sage Publications, 1983.

Meier, Kenneth J. *Politics and the Bureaucracy: Policymaking in the Fourth Branch of Government*, 2d ed. Monterey, Calif.: Brooks/Cole, 1987.

Bibliography

Meier, Kenneth J. *Regulations: Politics, Bureaucracy, and Economics.* New York: St. Martin's Press, 1985.

Merritt, Richard L., and Merritt, Anna J., eds. *Innovation in the Public Sector.* Beverly Hills: Sage Publications, 1985.

Meyers, Marshall W.; Stevenson, William; and Webster, Stephen. *Limits to Bureaucratic Growth.* New York: W. de Gruyter, 1985.

Mills, C. Wright. *The Power Elite.* New York: Oxford University Press, 1956.

Morgan, Gareth. *Images of Organization.* Beverly Hills: Sage Publications, 1986.

Morrow, William L. *Public Administration: Politics, Policy, and the Political System,* 2d ed. New York: Random House, 1980.

Morstein-Marx, Fritz. *Elements of Public Administration.* Englewood Cliffs: N.J.: Prentice-Hall, 1946.

Nachmias, David, and Rosenbloom, David H. *Bureaucratic Government, USA.* New York: St. Martin's Press, 1980.

Nigro, Felix A., and Nigro, Lloyd G. *Modern Public Administration,* 6th ed. New York: Harper and Row, 1984.

Nigro, Felix A., and Nigro, Lloyd G. *The New Public Personnel Administration,* 3d ed. Itasca, Ill.: F. E. Peacock, 1986.

Ouchi, William G. *Theory Z.* Reading, Mass.: Addison Wesley, 1981.

Peters, B. Guy. *The Politics of Bureaucracy,* 2d ed. New York: Longman, 1984.

Peters, Charles, and Branch, Taylor. *Blowing the Whistle: Dissent in the Public Interest.* New York: Praeger, 1972.

Plano, Jack C., and Greenberg, Milton. *The American Political Dictionary,* 7th ed. New York: Holt, Rinehart and Winston, 1985.

Present, Phillip E. *People and Public Administration.* Pacific Palisades, Calif.: Palisades Publishers, 1979.

Reagan, Michael D., and Sanzone, John G. *The New Federalism.* New York: Oxford University Press, 1972.

Riggs, Fred W. *Administration in Developing Countries: The Theory of Prismatic Society.* Boston: Houghton Mifflin, 1965.

Ripley, Randall B., and Franklin, Grace A. *Policy Implementation and Bureaucracy,* 2d ed. Chicago: Dorsey Press, 1986.

Rosenbloom, David H. *Public Administration: Understanding Management, Politics, and Law in the Public Sector.* New York: Random House, 1986.

Rourke, Francis E., ed. *Bureaucratic Power in National Policy Making,* 4th ed. Boston: Little, Brown, 1986.

Schuman, David. *Bureaucracies, Organizations, and Administration.* New York: Macmillan, 1976.

Bibliography

Schwarz, John E., and Shaw, L. Earl. *The United States Congress in Comparative Perspective*. Hinsdale, Ill.: Dryden Press, 1976.
Seitz, Steven Thomas. *Bureaucracy, Policy, and the Public*. St. Louis: C. V. Mosby, 1978.
Selznick, Philip. *TVA and the Grass Roots*. New York: Harper and Row, 1949.
Shafritz, Jay M. *The Facts on File Dictionary of Public Administration*. New York: Facts on File, 1985.
Shafritz, Jay M., and Hyde, Albert C. *Classics of Public Administration*, 2d ed. Chicago: Dorsey Press, 1987.
Shafritz, Jay M.; Hyde, Albert C.; and Rosenbloom, David H. *Personnel Management in Government*, 2d ed. New York: Marcel Dekker, 1981.
Shafritz, Jay M., and Ott, Steven, eds. *Classics of Organization Theory*, 2d ed. Chicago: Dorsey Press, 1987.
Sharkansky, Ira. *Public Administration: Policy-making in Government Agencies*, 4th ed. Chicago: Rand McNally, 1978.
Simmons, Robert H., and Dvorin, Eugene P. *Public Administration: Values, Policy, and Change*. Port Washington, N.Y.: Alfred Publishing Company, 1977.
Simon, Herbert A. *Administrative Behavior*. New York: Free Press, 1947.
Simon, Herbert A. "The Proverbs of Administration." *Public Administration Review* 6 (Winter 1946): 53–67.
Stahl, O. Glenn. *Public Personnel Administration*, 8th ed. New York: Harper and Row, 1983.
Starling, Grover. *Managing the Public Sector*, 3d ed. Chicago: Dorsey Press, 1986.
Straussman, Jeffrey D. *Public Administration*. New York: Holt, Rinehart and Winston, 1985.
Sutherland, John W., ed. *Management Handbook for Public Administrators*. New York: Van Nostrand Reinhold, 1978.
Thompson, Victor A. *Modern Organization*. New York: Alfred A. Knopf, 1961.
Thompson, Victor A. *Without Sympathy or Enthusiasm: The Problem of Administrative Compassion*. University, Ala.: University of Alabama Press, 1975.
Truman, David B. *The Governmental Process*. New York: Knopf, 1951.
The United States Government Manual, 1987/88. Washington, D.C.: Office of the Federal Register, 1987.
Vocino, Thomas, and Rabin, Jack. *Contemporary Public Administration*. New York: Harcourt Brace Jovanovich, 1981.

Bibliography

Waldo, Dwight. *The Administrative State.* New York: Ronald Press, 1948.
Waldo, Dwight. *Toward a New Public Administration: The Minnowbrook Perspective,* edited by Frank Marini. Scranton, Penn.: Chandler, 1971.
White, Leonard D. *Introduction to the Study of Public Administration.* New York: Harper and Brothers, 1926.
Wholey, Joseph S., ed. *Organizational Excellence: Stimulating Quality and Communicating Value.* Lexington, Mass.: Lexington Books, 1987.
Whyte, William H. *The Organization Man.* New York: Simon and Schuster, 1956.
Wiener, Norbert. *Cybernetics.* Cambridge, Mass.: M.I.T. Press, 1948.
Wildavsky, Aaron. *The Politics of the Budgetary Process.* Boston: Little, Brown, 1964.
Williams, J. D. *Public Administration: The People's Business.* Boston: Little, Brown, 1980.
Yarwood, Dean L., ed. *Public Administration, Politics, and the People.* New York: Longman, 1987.

INDEX

In this Index, references in **bold** type indicate the entry numbers where that particular term is defined within the text. Numbers in roman type refer to entries containing additional information about a term that the reader may wish to consult for further information, e.g., Affirmative action, 23, **189,** 241, 252.

Ability to pay tax theory, 284
Abood v. Detroit Board of Education, 204
ABSCAM, 89
Accountability, **85**
Accounting, **253,** 255
Accrual accounting, 253
Action for Organization Development Program (ACORD), 171
Adjudication, 310
  administrative, **292**
Administration, **1**
  comparative public, **11**
  development, **12**
  financial, 253–291
  fundamentals, 1–29
  judicial, **312**
  personnel, 189–252
  as process, 14
  proverbs of, **112**
  public personnel, **238**
Administration-politics dichotomy, **70**
Administrative adjudication, **292,** 293
Administrative behavior, 127
Administrative Behavior (1945), 2
Administrative Behavior (1947), 88, 112, 114
Administrative bias, 107
Administrative discretion, **86,** 131
Administrative due process, **293**
Administrative law, **294,** 303
Administrative law judge, **295,** 325
Administrative man, **2,** 38

Administrative management, 238
Administrative novel, **3**
Administrative Office of the Courts, 312
Administrative Office of the United States Courts, **296**
Administrative order, 295, **297,** 298
Administrative organization, 119–188
Administrative platonism, **4**
Administrative pluralism, 8
Administrative Procedure Act of 1946, 292, 295, **298,** 325
Administrative reorganization, **119,** 143
Administrative rules, 293, 308
Administrative State, The (1948), 27
Administrative theory, **5**
Administrator of General Services, 144
Administrator plan, **160**
Adolf Eichmann syndrome, 318
Ad-valorem taxation, **254**
Advisory Commission on Intergovernmental Relations (ACIR), 47, 153, 182, 287
Advisory Council on Federal Pay, 206
Affirmative action, 23, **189,** 241, 252
AFL-CIO, 237, 240
AFSCME (American Federation of State, County, and Municipal Employees), **190,** 240
Agency
  auxiliary, **120**

415

Index

Agency (cont.)
  independent, **151**
  shop, 204
Agenda, **6**
Aggregation, 58
American Arbitration Association (AAA), 192
American Bar Association, 312
American Federation of Government Employees (AFGE), 190, 237
American Federation of Labor (AFL), 190
American Federation of State, County, and Municipal Employees (AFSCME), **190,** 240
American Judicature Society, 314
American Political Science Association (APSA), **7,** 18
American Public Administration (1980), 211
American Society for Public Administration (ASPA), **7, 20**
Analysis
  cost-benefit, **35,** 283
  force-field, **142**
  legal, **316**
  micro-macro, **59**
  policy, **68**
  systems, 62, **83,** 95
Appeals Review Board, 226
Appleby, Paul Henson, **8**
  and administrative platonism, **4**
  and ethics, **13**
  and politics-administration dichotomy, **70**
  and public choice economics, **75**
Appointment power, **191,** 242
Appropriation, **255,** 263, 275
Appropriations Committee, House, 262
Arbitration, **192,** 221, 240
Area Redevelopment Act of 1961, 225
Argyris, Chris, 114, 163
Arnett v. Kennedy (1974), **194**
Asimov, Isaac, 78
ASPA (American Society for Public Administration), **7, 20**
Assembly of Governmental Employees (AGE), 240
Assessment, 270
Assessment center, **193**
Assessor, 270
Assumptive theory, 5
Atlas Roofing, Inc. v. Occupational Safety and Health Review Commission (1977), 321
Auditing, **256,** 263, 274
Auditor, **257**

Authority, **87**
  delegation of, **96**
Authorization, 255, 257, 263
Automation, 214
Auxiliary agency, **120**
Axiomatic theory, **121**

Babbage, Charles, 63
Back, Kurt W., 171
Backdoor financing, **258**
Bailey, Stephen K., 4, 5
Bailey v. Richardson (1951), **194**
Bailiff, 312
Bakke case (1978), 189, 211, 243
Balanced budget, 260
Balance of power, 178
Baldwin v. New York (1970), 309
Balzac, Honoré de, 129
Banking regulatory system, 271
Barber, James David, 67
Bargaining, collective, **203**
Barnard, Chester I., **122**
  and neoclassical organization theory, **178**
  and proverbs of administration, **112**
  and public choice economics, **75**
Bayes's theorem, 92
Behavior modification, 38
Benefit tax theory, 284
Bentham, Jeremy, 38
Bentley, Arthur F., 66
Berne, Eric, 171
Beyond the Ruling Class (1963), 41
Beyond Words: The Story of Sensitivity Training and the Encounter Movement (1972), 171
Big Democracy (1945), 8
Bimodal convergence, 37
Blake, Robert R., 170
Blau, Peter, 89
Bloch, Arthur, 108
Block grant, **259**
Blount case (1971), **250**
Blowing the Whistle: Dissent in the Public Interest (1972), 330
Board, **123**
Board of Governors, Federal Reserve System, 271
Board of Regents v. Roth (1972), **194**
Board of review, 270
Bon plaisir, 133
Boren's testimony, **9**
Borrowing authority financing, 258
Borrowing power, **260**
Boulding, Kenneth, 91, 122
Bounded rationality, 2, **88**
Branch, Taylor, 330
Bribery, **89**

416

Index

Bridwell, L. G., 100
Brookings Institution, 259, 287
Brownlow Committee, 17, **124,** 138
Budget, **261**
  committees, 266
  cycle, **263**
  line-item, **278**
Budget and Accounting Act of 1921, 253, 256, **262,** 278
Budget and Accounting Procedures Act of 1950, 263, 274
Budget and Impoundment Control Act of 1974, **266**
Budgetary cost-benefit analysis, 35
Budget Bureau, 30, 138, 166, 261, 278
Budgeting, 180
  performance, **282**
  zero-base (ZBB), **291**
Bureau, **125**
Bureaucracy (1836), 129
Bureaucracy, **126,** 187
  and administrative organization, **119–188**
  representative, **183**
Bureaucrat, internal, **127**
Bureaucratic dysfunctions, 145
Bureaucratic expertise, **128**
Bureaucratic organization theory, 187
Bureaucratic pathology, 133
Bureaucratic Phenomenon, The (1964), 133
Bureaucratic planning, 104
Bureau of Municipal Research, New York, **228**
Bureau of the Budget (BOB), 30, 138, 166, 261, 278
Bureaupathic behavior, 101
Bureaupathological behavior, 9
Bureaupathology, **129**
Burkhead, Jesse, 266
Burnout, **195**
Business-type activity, 323

Calgin, A. D., 101
California Commission on Judicial Qualifications, 313
California initiative, 74
California plan, **313**
California v. Bakke (1978), 211
Capitalism and Freedom (1962), 281
Career service, **196,** 197, 239
Carroll, James D., 20
Case study, **10**
"Catch 22," 330
Categorical grants, 49, 259
Caveat emptor versus *caveat venditor,* **299**
CEA (Council of Economic Advisers), **267**

Cease and desist order, 293, **300,** 310
Central bank, 271, 280
Centralization, 5, 14, **130**
Central purchasing, **264**
Certificate of Public Convenience, Interest, and Necessity, **301**
Certification of eligibles, **197**
Certiorari, **302**
Chadha case (1983), 119
Chancery courts, 307
Chance v. The Board of Examiners (1976), 243
Charismatic authority, 87, 187
Charter, 148
"Chicago school," 61
Chief administrative officer (CAO), 160
Chief administrator, 136
Chief Justice of the United States, 296
Circular A-11, 279
Circular A-95, **30,** 153
Cities, classification of, **132**
Citizen participation, **131**
City-county consolidation, **155**
City manager, 157
City of Clinton v. Cedar Rapids and Missouri River Railroad Co. (1968), 305
Civil Aeronautics Board (CAB), 152
Civil case, 303, 304
Civil Code, 303
Civil law, **303**
Civil Rights Act of 1964, 189, 211, 241, 243
Civil service, **198,** 239, 252
Civil Service Act of 1883, 200, 238
Civil Service Commission, 198, 215, 226, 232
Civil Service Commission v. National Association of Letter Carriers, AFL-CIO (1973), 219
Civil service reform, 246
Civil Service Reform Act of 1883, 231, **232**
Civil Service Reform Act of 1978, **199,** 203, 226, 229, 244, 248
Civil Service Reform League, 29, **200**
Class action, **304**
Classical organization theory, 22, 63, **176,** 178
Classical public administration, 22
Classification of cities, **132**
Classified civil service, 198
Classified service, **201,** 248
Clerk of court, 312
Clientele, **31,** 289
Clientele agency, **32,** 168
"Client politics," 31, 289

417

Index

Closed model (organizations), **174**
Closed shop, 204
Closed system, 84
Coalition structure, 80
Code Napoleon, 303
Code of Ethics for Government Service, 212
Code of Federal Regulations (CFR), 308
Cognitive dissonance, **202**
COGs (councils of governments), 182
Collective bargaining, **203,** 221, 237, 248, 251
Collective bargaining agreement, **204**
Commission, 123
  form, **156**
  independent regulatory, **152**
Commission on Organization of the Executive Branch, 149
Committee on Administrative Management, 124
Committee on Political Parties of APSA, 77
Common law, 307
Community Action Agency Board, 34
Comparable worth, **205**
Comparative Administration Group (CAG), 11
Comparative public administration, **11**
Compensation, **206**
Comptroller, 257
Comptroller General, 257, **265,** 274
Compulsory arbitration, 192, 221
Computer, **33,** 40, 114
  simulation, 83
  simulation models, 283
Conciliation, 192
Confirmation of appointments, 191
Conflict resolution, 178
Congress and Money (1980), 288
Congressional Budget and Impoundment Control Act of 1974, 258, **266,** 274, 275
Congressional Budget Office (CBO), 266
Congressional oversight, 105
Congressional "veto," 168
Congress of Industrial Organizations (CIO), 190
Consolidation, functional, **143**
Consolidation, functional (local government), **159**
Constituent policy, 75, 76
Consulting, **207**
Consumer Advisory Council, 271
Consumer Price Index (CPI), 211, 276
Consumer Product Safety Commission, 152
Contempt of court, 311

Contract authority financing, 258
Contracting, 207
Contra rebels, 164
Control function (budgetary), 261
Cooperative federalism, 47, **48**
Cooptation, **34**
Coordinating, 180
Coplon v. United States (1951), 318
Coproduction, **90**
Corporation, government, **146**
Corpus juris civilis, 303
Cost accounting, 253
Cost-benefit analysis, **35,** 180, 283
"Cost-push" inflation, 277
Council-manager form, **157**
Council of Economic Advisers (CEA), 39, 138, **267,** 269
Council on Environmental Quality, 44, 138
Council on Wage and Price Stability, 138
Councils of governments (COGs), 182
Countervailing theory of pressure politics, 66
County board, 158
County equalization board, 270
County-manager plan, **158**
Court manager, 312
Courts, Administrative Office of the United States, **296**
CPI (Consumer Price Index), 276
Creative Experience (1924), 15
Creative federalism, 48
Cross-district assessment, 270
Crozier, Michel, 2, **133**
Cultural models, 2
Cutback management, **91**
Cybernetic arbitration, 37, 134
Cybernetics (1947), 134
Cybernetics, **134**

Dahl, Robert A., 106
Dartmouth College v. Woodward (1819), 305
Data processing, electronic (EDP), **40,** 58, 253, 256
Davis, Kenneth C., 86
Debt limit, 260, 285
Debt, public, **285**
Decentralization, 5, 56, **135,** 141
Decision making, **92,** 122
  incremental, **93**
  mixed scanning, **94**
  rational-comprehensive, **95**
Decision tree, **36**
Decline of American Pluralism, The (1961), 66
Deficiency appropriation, 255

Index

Deficit financing, 260
Deficit spending, 272, 285
Delegation
  of authority, **96**
  of power, 322
Delphi technique, **37**
"Demand-pull" inflation, 277
Democracy, participatory, **64**
Department, **136**
Deregulation, 152
Descriptive theory, 5
Development administration, **12**
Dewey, John, 15
Dillon's rule, 148, **305**
"Direct democracy," 64
"Direct federalism," 47, 48
Directing, 180
Direct subsidies, 289
Discipline, progressive, **236**
Discounting budget analysis, 35
Discount rate (monetary policy), 280
Discretion, administrative, **86**
Discretionary Justice: A Preliminary Inquiry (1969), 86
Discrimination, **208**
  reverse, **243**
Dismissal, 245
Dispute settlement, 192
Distributive policy, 76
Division of work, 24
Doig, Jameson W., 239
Domestic Policy Staff, 138
Double dipping, **209**
Double seniority list, 251
Downs, Anthony, 108
Dror, Yehezkel, 94, 106
Drucker, Peter, 279
Dual federalism, 47, 153
Dubin, Robert, 101
Dudar, Helen, 330
Due process
  administrative, **293**
  of law, 248, 293, **306**, 316
Duncan v. Louisiana (1968), 309
Dunnette, Marvin D., 177
Dynamics of Public Bureaucracy (1977), 189

Earmarked revenues, **268**
Earned income credit, 281
Economic Advisers, Council of (CEA), **267**
Economic indicators, **269**
Economic man, 2, 95
Economic man theory, **38**
Economic Opportunity Act of 1964, 64
Economic planning, **39**
Economic recession, 267

Economic report, 267
Economics, public choice, **75**
EDP (electronic data processing), **40**
Egger, Rowland, 3
Ego, 127
Ego state, 172
Eisen v. Carlisle and Jacquelin (1974), 304
Electronic data processing (EDP), **40**
Elements of Public Administration (1946), 27
Eligibles, certification of, **197**
Elite, **41**
Elite theory, 104
Elrod v. Burns (1976), 246
Emery, F. E., 45
Eminent domain, **42**
Empirical theory of ethics, 13
Employee Retirement Income Security Act of 1974 (ERISA), **210**
Employment Act of 1946, 39, 225, 267, 272
Enabling legislation, 257, 258
Encounter group, 171
Encounter Groups and Psychiatry (1970), 171
Encumbrance accounting, 253
English customary law, 303
Enterprise zone, **43**
Enthoven, Alain C., 83
Entropy, 134, **137**
Environmental impact statement, **44**
Environmental Protection Agency (EPA), 44
Environmental turbulence, **45**
EOP (Executive Office of the President), 124, **138,** 166, 267
Equal employment opportunity, 205, **211**
Equal Employment Opportunity Act of 1972, 189, 211, 241
Equal Employment Opportunity Commission (EEOC), 189, 227
Equalization, **270**
Equal pay, 205
Equal Pay Act of 1963, 46
Equilibrium, 66, 137
Equity, **307,** 311
  social, **23**
ERISA (Employee Retirement Income Security Act of 1974), **210**
Essentials of Public Administration (1979), 20
"Establishment," 41
Estate and gift taxes, 286
Ethic of means and ends, **97**
Ethics, 4, **13**
Ethics in Government Act of 1978, **212**

419

Index

Etzioni, Amitai, 2, 54, 94
Evaluation function (budgetary), 261
Evaluation, program, **72**
Execution, budget, 263
Executive budget, 255, 261, 262, 263
Executive Leadership and
　Management Program, 215
Executive Office of the President
　(EXOP or EOP), 124, **138,** 166
Executive order, **213,** 308
Executive privilege, **139**
Executive staff development programs,
　247
Ex officio, **140**
EXOP (Executive Office of the
　President), 124, **138,** 166
Ex parte, 311
Expropriation, 42

Fact finding, 221
Fair Labor Standards Act (FLSA), **46**
Fayol, Henri, **14,** 24, 26, 28, 65
Featherbedding, **214**
"Fed," 267, 271
Federal Advisory Council, 271
Federal civil service, 198, 239
Federal Communications Commission
　(FCC), 152
Federal Election Campaign Act of
　1972, 219
Federal Employee Appeals Authority
　(FEAA), 227, 330
Federal Employees Pay Council, 206
Federal Energy Regulatory
　Commission, 152
Federal Executive Institute (FEI), **215,**
　247
Federal income tax, 287
Federalism, **47**
　cooperative, **48**
　fiscal, **49**
Federalists, The (1948), 28
Federal Judicial Center, 296, 312
Federal Labor Relations Authority
　(FLRA), 203
Federal Labor Relations Council
　(FLRC), 203, 240
Federal Maritime Commission (FMC),
　152
Federal Open Market Committee
　(FOMC), 271
Federal Pay Comparability Act of
　1970, 206
Federal personnel system, 199
Federal Regional Councils, 182
Federal Register, 144, 213, 297, 298,
　308
Federal Register Act of 1935, 213, 308

Federal Reserve Board, 152, 267, 271,
　280
Federal Reserve System (FRS), **271,**
　280
Federal Salary Reform Act of 1970,
　241
Federal Trade Commission (FTC), 32,
　152
Feedback, 84, 137, 169
FEI (Federal Executive Institute), **215**
Fenno, Richard F., Jr., 266
Fesler, James W., 21, 29, 86, 177, 187
Field service, **141**
Fifth Amendment, 306, 309
Finance Committee, Senate, 258
Financial administration, **253–291**
Financial Plan and Report on
　Manufactures, 289
Financing, backdoor, **258**
First Hatch Act of 1939, 219
First Hoover Commission, **149**
Fiscal federalism, **49,** 153
Fiscal policy, 57, 260, **272**
Fiscal year, **273**
Fisher, Louis, 275
Flextime, **216**
Follett, Mary Parker, **15,** 66, 177
Food and Drug Administration (FDA),
　31
Force-field analysis, **142**
Foreign Service Examination, 249
Formalist-rationalist approach, 26
Fourteenth Amendment, 306, 309
"Fourth branch," 324, 325
Franke, R. H., 54
Frederickson, H. George, 18
Freedom of Information Act (FOIA),
　50
Freeman, J. Leiper, 179
French, Wendell, 163
French administrative system, 29
Freud, Sigmund, 127
Friedman, Milton, 61, 74, 281
Fringe benefits, 206, **217**
From Max Weber: Essays in Sociology
　(1946), 187
Fulmer, Robert M., 217
Functional consolidation, **143**
Functional consolidation (local
　government), **159**
Functional management, 22
Functions of the Executive (1938), 122,
　178

Galveston Plan, 156
Games, 172
Games People Play (1964), 172
Game theory, **51**

420

Index

GAO (General Accounting Office), 253, 256, 265, **274**
Garcia v. San Antonio Metropolitan Transit Authority (1985), 46
Gawthrop, Louis, 114
General Accounting Office (GAO), 253, 256, 265, **274**
General Schedule (GS), 206, **218,** 234
General Services Administration (GSA), **144,** 264
Gibson, F. K., 100
"Gigo," 33
Gilbreth, Frank and Lillian, **16,** 22, 238
GNP (gross national product), 272
Goal displacement, **145**
Golembiewski, Robert T., 11
Gordon, George J., 30
Gournay, Vincent de, 126
Governmental Process, The (1951), 179
Government corporation, **146**
Government Corporation Control Act of 1945, 146
Government Economy and Spending Reform Act of 1976, 291
Government Employee Training Act of 1958, 247
Government in the Sunshine Act, **52**
Grace Commission, 209
Grand and petit juries, **309**
Grant, block, **259**
Grants-in-aid, 49
Great Depression of the 1930s, 57
Grievance procedure, 167
Griggs v. Duke Power Company (1971), 189, 211
Gross national product (GNP), 269
Group theory, **53**
Groupthink, **98**
GSA (General Services Administration), **144**
Gulick, Luther, 14, **17,** 24
and Brownlow Committee, **124**
and matrix organization, **163**
and organization chart, 63
and POSDCORB, **180**
and proverbs of administration, **112**
and scientific management, **22**

Hage, Jerald, 121
Halberstam, David, 95
Hamilton, Alexander, 289
Handbook of Industrial and Organizational Psychology (1976), 177
Handbook of Leadership: A Survey of Theory and Research (1974), 177
"Hard" money policy, 271

Harmon, Michael H., 171
Hatch Acts (Political Activities Acts of 1939 and 1940), **219**
Hawthorne effect, 54, 178
Hawthorne studies, **54**
Follett, Mary Parker, **15**
and need theory of human motivation, **100**
Taylor, Frederick W., **24**
Waldo, C. Dwight, **27**
Hay System, **220**
Health Maintenance Organization (HMO), **55**
Hearing, **310**
Hearing examiners, 294, 295
Hearing officer, 293, 295
Henry, Nicholas, 238, 239, 262
Herzberg, Frederick, 99, 206, 224
Hiatt v. City of Berkeley (1978), 243
Hierarchical organization, 87
Hierarchy, 104, 118, **147,** 176
Homeostasis, 137
Home rule, **148**
Home rule movement, 132, 305
Hoover, J. Edgar, 318
Hoover Commission
first, **149**
second, **150**
Horizontal job enrichment, 224
"Hot oil" case, 322
House Appropriations Committee, 258, 261, 262
House Ways and Means Committee, 258
Housing and Community Development Act of 1974, 259
Humanism (organization theory), **177**
Human motivation
motivation-hygiene theory, **99**
need theory, **100**
theories, 224
theory X, **101**
theory Y, **102**
theory Z, **103**
Human Side of Enterprise, The (1960), 101
Humphrey's Executor [Rathbun] v. United States (1935), 152, 242

Id, 127
IGR (intergovernmental relations), **153**
Immigration and Naturalization Service v. Chadha (1983), 119
I'm O.K.—You're O.K. (1969), 172
Impasse resolution, **221**
Impoundment, **275**
Impoundment Control Act of 1974, **266**

421

Index

Incidence, tax, 284
Income tax, negative, **281**
Incremental decision making, **93**, 113
Incrementalism, in budgeting, 261, 291
Independent agency, **151**
Independent regulatory commission, **152**, 308, 324, 325, 328
Indexation, **276,** 277
Indictment, 309
Indirect subsidies, 289
Individual motivation, 102
Industrial management, 54
Inflation, 57, 272, 276, **277**
Information affidavit, 309
Information system, management (MIS), **58**
"In-house" structural analyses, 107
Initiative, California, 74
Injunction, 250, 307, **311**
Input, 84
  economic, 12
Input/output ratio, 233
Inputs, 45, 137
Institute for Court Management, 312
Institute of Judicial Administration, 312
Instrumental theory, 5
Intelligence Activities and the Rights of Americans (1976), 318
Intelligence of Democracy: Decision Making through Mutual Adjustment (1965), 106
Interest group liberalism, **56**
Interest groups, 290
Intergovernmental cooperation, 48
Intergovernmental Cooperation Act of 1968, 30
Intergovernmental Personnel Act (IPA) of 1970, 189, 241
Intergovernmental relations (IGR), **153**
Intergovernmental tax immunity, 323
Internal bureaucrat, **127**
Internship, **222**
Interstate Commerce Commission (ICC), 152
Interstate compacts, 182
Interstate regionalism, 182
Introduction to the Study of Public Administration (1926), 28
Intuitive theory of ethics, 13
Iran-*contra* affair, 164
Iron law of oligarchy, **104**
Iteration, 60

Jacksonian Democracy, 246
Jacksonians, The (1954), 28

Janis, Irving L., 98
Jargon, 128
Jarvis-Gann amendment, 74
Jeffersonians, The (1951), 28
Job description, **223**
Job enrichment, **224**
Job insecurity, 214
Job performance, 217, 218
Job satisfaction, 99
Johnson v. Louisiana (1972), 309
Joint Financial Management Improvement Program (JFMIP), 235, 274
Journal of Comparative Administration, 11
Judge, administrative law, **295**
Judge-made law, 307
Judgment, civil case, 303
Judicial administration, 296, **312**
  the California plan, **313**
  the Missouri plan, **314**
Judicial Conference of the United States, 296
Judicial review, 298, 312, **315**
Juries, grand and petit, **309**

Kariel, Henry, 66
Kaufman, Herbert, 67, 119, 181
Kaul, J. D., 54
Keller, Suzanne, 41
Keynesianism, 39, **57**, 267, 272, 285
Kleppe v. Sierra Club (1976), 44
Klipstein, D. L., 108
Kramer, Fred A., 20, 189

Labor-management agreement, 204
Labor-Management Relations Act of 1947, 204
"Ladder of needs," 100
Laffer, Arthur, 74
Laissez-faire, 39
Lakewood plan, 75
"Language of management," 26
Lasswell, Harold, 41, 70, 127
Lateral entry, 232
Law
  administrative, **294**
  civil, **303**
  due process of, **306**
  public, **292–330**
  rule of, **329**
"Layer-cake federalism," 47
Leadership and Productivity (1965), 101
Leadership style, 170
Legal analysis, **316**
Legal-rational approach, 15
Legal-rational authority, 187
Legislation, sunset, **81**
Legislative oversight, **105**

422

Index

Legislative Reorganization Act of 1970, 274
Legislative veto, 119
Legitimacy, 187
Lewin, Kurt, 15, 142
Liberalism, interest group, 56
Licensing, 301, **317**
Lindblom, Charles E., 93, 95, **106**
Line and staff, **154**
Line-item budget, 261, 262, **278**, 282
Line-item veto, 275
Lloyd-LaFollette Act of 1912, 240
Local government
  city-county consolidation, **155**
  commission form, **156**
  council-manager form, **157**
  county-manager plan, **158**
  functional consolidation, **159**
  mayor-administrator plan, **160**
  special district, **185**
  strong mayor–council form, **161**
  weak mayor–council form, **162**
Locke, Edwin A., 177
Locke, John, 75
Long ballot, 158
Long-range planning, 65
"Loose" money policy, 271
Low, George, 163
Lowi, Theodore, 56
Lutrin, Carl E., 211

McCulloch v. Maryland (1819), 323
McCurdy, Howard E., 75, 106, 145
McGregor, Douglas, 99, 101, 102
Machiavelli, Niccolo, 91, 318
"Machine model," 26
Macroeconomics, 59
Macro-micro analysis, **59**
Magna Charta, 329
"Malek Manual," 244
Malfeasance, **318**
Management
  cutback, **91**
  function (budgetary), 261
  functional, 22
  information system (MIS), **58**
  participative, **110**
  program, 163
  project, 163
  public, **85–118**
  science, 22, 134
  scientific, **22**
  stress, **117**
  systems, 163
Management by objectives (MBO), 65, **279**
Management Intern Program, 222
Management theory, 110

Manager form, **157, 158**
Managerial grid, **170**
Manager plan, 157, 158
Mandatory Entitlement financing, 258
Mandatory injunction, 311
Mann, Dean E., 239
Manpower, **225**
Manpower Development Act of 1962, 225
"Marble cake" federalism, 47, 153
Marbury v. Madison (1803), 315
March, James G., 26, 113
Marx, Karl, 38
"Masculine ethic," 26
Maslow, Abraham, 99, 100, 110, 177
Matrix organization, **163**
Mayo, Elton, 15, 54, 173, 178
Mayor-administrator plan, **160**
Mayor-council form, strong, **161**
Mayor-council form, weak, **162**
MBO (management by objectives), **279**
Means and ends ethic, **97**
Measuring Municipal Activities (1938), 114
Medalia, N. Z., 101
Mediation, 192, 221
Merger, city-county, 155
Merit system, 197, **226**, 252
Merit Systems Protection Board (MSPB), 198, **227**, 232, 238, 245
Merriam, Charles, 124
Merton, Robert K., 145, 173
Metropolitan area, 143
Metropolitan consolidation, 143, 155
Michels, Robert, 104
Microeconomics, 38, 59
Micro-macro analysis, **59**
Middle management staff development, 247
Miles's Law, **107**
Military-industrial complex, 80
Mill, John Stuart, 38
Millage, 254, 270
Miller v. Pate (1967), 319
Mills, C. Wright, 41, 66
Minnowbrook perspective, 18
Misfeasance, **319**
Missouri plan, **314**
Mixed scanning, 92
  decision making, **94**
Model, 79
  administrative man, 2
Model Cities Act of 1966, 30
Modeling, **60**, 62
Modern Organization (1961), 101
Modern Public Administration (1980), 312
Monetarism, 57, **61**

Index

Monetarists, 271
Monetary policy, 271, 272, **280**
"Moral administrator," 4
Morality, administrative, 13
Morality and Administration in Democratic Government (1952), 4, 8
Morrow, William L., 5, 20, 34, 67
Morstein-Marx, Fritz, 27
Mosher, Frederick, 35, 239
Motivation-hygiene theory, **99**
Mouton, Jane F., 170
MSPB (Merit Systems Protection Board), 198, **227**, 232, 238, 245
Multiplier effect, 272
Municipal corporation, 305
Murphy's Law, **108**
Myers v. United States (1926), 242

NAACP v. Allen (1974), 243
"Nader's raiders," 299
National Association of Counties, 287
National Association of Government Employees (NAGE), 240
National Association of Retired Federal Employees (NARFE), 240
National Association of Schools of Public Affairs and Administration (NASPAA), 20
National Center for State Courts, 312
National Conference of State Legislators, 287
National debt, 285
National economic planning, 39
National Education Association (NEA), 237
National Environmental Policy Act of 1969, 44
National Federation of Federal Employees (NFFE), 240
National Governors Association, 287
Nationalization, 42
National Judicial College (1963), 312
National Labor Relations Act of 1935, 204, 250
National Labor Relations Board (NLRB), 152
National League of Cities, 287
National Resources Planning Board, 39
National Security Council (NSC), **164**
National Urban Coalition, 266
Natural monopoly, 301
Need theory of human motivation, **100**
Negative income tax, **281**
Nelson, Dorothy, 312
Neoclassical organization theory, **178**
Neo-Keynesian policies, 57
Neo-Weberism, **165**

New federalism, 47, 48, 287
New Federalism, The (1972), 48
New public administration, **18**
  and neo-Weberism, **165**
  and social equity, **23**
  and Waldo, C. Dwight, **27**
New Public Administration: The Minnowbrook Perspective (1971), 18
New Science of Management (1960), 92
New State, The (1920), 178
New York Bureau of Municipal Research, 29, **228**
New York Civil Service Reform Association, 200
Nigro, Felix A., 312
Nigro, Lloyd G., 312
Nixon case (1974), 139
"Noetic authority," 20
Nomination of appointments, 191
Nonfeasance, **320**
Normative theory, 5, 18
Northrop, F. S. C., 27
Novel, administrative, **3**
Nuclear Regulatory Commission (NRC), 152
Nuremberg Principle, 165

Objectivity in testing, 249
Occupational Safety and Health Act of 1970, 321
Occupational Safety and Health Administration (OSHA), **321**
OD (organization development), **169**
Office of Administration, 138
Office of Intergovernmental Relations, 153
Office of Management and Budget (OMB), 30, 72, 138, **166**, 261, 263, 278
Office of Personnel Management (OPM), **229**, 232, 238, 245
Office of Revenue Sharing, 287
Office of Science and Technology Policy, 138
Office of Special Council, 199
Office of the Special Representative for Trade Negotiations, 138
Officers for Justice v. Civil Service Commission (1973), 243
Oklahoma v. United States Civil Service Commission (1947), 219
Oligarchy, iron law of, **104**
OMB (Office of Management and Budget), **166**
Ombudsman, **167**
One-person grand jury, 309
On-the-job training, **230**
Onward Industry (1931), 26

Index

OPEC, 277
Open Market Committee, 271
Open-market operations, 280
"Open meeting" laws, 52
Open model (organizations), **175**
"Open" personnel system, 232
Open shop, 204, 237
Open system, 84, 137
Operations research, 60, **62**
OPM (Office of Personnel Management), **229**
Opp Cotton Mills v. Administrator of Wage and Hour Division (1941), **322**
Oppenheimer Fund, Inc. v. Sanders (1978), 304
Opportunity cost, 35
Optional charter plan, 148
Order
  administrative, **297,** 300
  cease and desist, **300**
Organization, **168**
  administrative, **119–188**
  matrix, **163**
Organizational humanism, 15
Organizational system, 147
Organizational theory, 54
Organization chart, **63**
Organization development (OD), **169**
  managerial grid, **170**
  sensitivity training, **171**
  transactional analysis, **172**
Organization man, **173**
Organization Man, The (1956), 173
Organizations (1958), 113
Organizations
  closed model, **174**
  open model, **175**
Organization theory, 134, 137, 169
  classical, **176**
  humanism, **177**
  neoclassical, **178**
  pluralism, **179**
Organizing, 180
Original cost rate-setting theory, 328
OSHA (Occupational Safety and Health Administration), **321**
Output, 84
  economic, 12
Output/input ratio, 235
Outputs, 45, 137
Oversight, legislative, **105**
Owen, Robert, 233

Page, William J., Jr., 279
Panama Refining Co. v. Ryan (1935), 322
Papers on the Science of Administration (1937), 14, 17, 26, 112, 124, 180

Parkinson's Law, **109**
Parsons, Talcott, 84
Participant-observer, 13
Participative management, 102, **110**
Participatory democracy, **64,** 131
Party Politics in America (1972), 77
Party system, 77
Patronage, **231,** 239
Pendleton Act of 1883, 231, **232,** 238
Pension Reform Act of 1974, 210
Pentagon Papers, 4
People and Public Administration (1979), 330
Performance
  appraisal, **233**
  budgeting, 149, 261, **282**
  evaluation, 226
Permanent appropriations financing, 258
Permissive federalism, 48
Personnel
  administration, **189–252**
  administration, public, **238**
  evaluation, 233
  systems, public, **239**
PERT (program evaluation and review technique), **73**
Peter Principle, **111**
Peters, Charles, 330
Petit and grand juries, **309**
"Picket-fence" federalism, 153
Pigeonhole (a bill), 6
Planning, **65,** 105, 180
  economic, **39**
  function (budgetary), 261
  strategic, **116**
Planning, organizing, staffing, directing, coordinating, reporting, and budgeting (POSDCORB), 17, 112, **180**
Planning, programming, budgeting systems (PPBS), 35, 65, 261, **283,** 290
Platonism, administrative, **4**
Pluralism, **66**
Pluralism (organization theory), **179**
Pluralization, **67**
Policy, public, **30–84,** 76
Policy-administration dichotomy, 12
Policy analysis, **68**
Policy and Administration (1949), 8, 70
Policy making, 1
Political Activities Acts of 1939 and 1940, **219**
Political economy, **69**
Political elite, 41
Political executives, 239
Political model, 2

425

Index

Political neutrality, 152
Political Process: Executive Bureau-Legislative Committee Relations (1965), 179
Politics, Economics, and Welfare (1953), 106
Politics-administration dichotomy, 27, **70,** 86, 200
Politics of the Budgetary Process, The (1964), 290
Population lag, 259
POSDCORB (planning, organizing, staffing, directing, coordinating, reporting, and budgeting), 17, 112, **180**
Position classification, 218, 223, **234**
Postal Reorganization Act, 203
Postappropriation control, 274, 275
Postaudit, 256, 257, 265, 274
Potential problem analysis, 108
Power, 41
  appointment, **191**
  elite, 41, 104
  in organizations, 178
  of the purse, 255
Power Elite, The (1959), 66
PPB (planning, programming, budgeting), 283
PPBS (planning, programming, budgeting systems), 35, 65, 261, **283,** 290
Practice of Management, The (1954), 279
Preaudit, 256, 257, 262, 265, 274
Prediction, **19**
Prescriptive theory, 5
Present, Philip E., 330
President, Executive Office of the (EXOP or EOP), 124, **138,** 166
Presidential Management Intern Program, 222
President's Committee on Administrative Management, 17
Presupervisory staff development programs, 247
Prince, The (1513), 97
Principles of Scientific Management (1911), 22
Prismatic Society Revisited (1973), 11
Prisoners' dilemma, 51
Privatization, 39, **71**
Probabilistic information processing (PIP), 92
Probability index, 36
Procedural due process, 306
Productivity, **235**
Professionalism, **20**
"Profit-pull" inflation, 277
Program budgeting, 149, 261, 282

Program evaluation, **72**
Program evaluation and review technique (PERT), 65, **73**
Program management, 163
Progressive discipline, **236**
Progressive/regressive tax, **284**
Project management, 163
Property tax, 254, 270
Proposition 13, **74,** 91, 254
Proprietary function, **323**
Proverbs of administration, **112**
Prudent investment rate-setting theory, 328
Prussian administrative system, 29
Psychological man, 2
Psychopathology and Politics (1930), 70, 127
Psychotechnology, 24
Public administration, 1, **21**
  classical, 22
  comparative, **11**
  fundamentals of, **1–29**
  new, **18**
Public Administration, American Society for, **7**
Public Administration and Public Affairs (1980), 239
Public Administration: A Synthesis (1977), 75
Public Administration in America (1978), 30
Public Administration—Politics, Policy, and the Political System (1980), 67
Public Administration Review (PAR), 7
Public Administration, Theory and Practice (1980), 21, 29, 86
Public Administration, The People's Business (1980), 100, 318, 319, 320
Public Administration Times, 7
Public assistance, 281
Public budget, 261
Public choice economics, **75**
Public debt, **285**
Public defender, 312
Public employee unions, **237**
Public law and regulation, **292–330**
Public management, **85–118**
Public personnel administration, **238**
Public personnel systems, **239**
Public policy, **30–84,** 76
Public regulation, **292–330**
Public unionism, **240**
Purchasing, central, **264**
Pye, Lucian, 12
Pyramid organization, 63

Quasi-executive, 152, 298, **324,** 325
Quasi-judicial, 152, 292, 298, 310, **325**

426

Index

Quasi-legislative, 152, 298, 324, **326**
Quota systems, 251

Racial discrimination, 251
Racial quota system, 243
Railroad Commission of Texas v. Rowan and Nichols Oil Company (1941), **327**
Raison d'état, 97
Rand Corporation, 37
Rate-setting, **328**
Rathbun [Humphrey's Executor] v. United States (1935), 152, 242
"Rational behavior," 51
Rational-comprehensive decision making, **95**
Rational-legal authority, 87
Rational theory of ethics, 13
Reagan, Michael, 47, 48
Recession, 285
Recruitment, 227, **241**
Rediscount rate, 271
Redistributive policy, 76
Red tape, **181**
Reform League, Civil Service, **200**
Reform movement, 28
Regents of the University of California v. Bakke (1978), 189, 211, 243
Regional commissions, 182
Regionalism, **182**
Regressive/progressive tax, **284**
Regulation, public, **292–330**
Regulatory commissions, 151, 152
Regulatory policy, 76
Regulatory tax, **286**
Reliability in testing, 249
Removal power, 191, **242**
Reorganization Act of 1939, 124
Reorganization, administrative, **119**
Reorganization, Hoover Commission, 149, 150
Reorganization plan, 124
Reorganization Plan of 1978, 227, 229
Reorganization plans, presidential, 119
Reporting, 180
Representative bureaucracy, 4, **183**
Reproduction cost rate-setting theory, 328
Republican Era, The (1958), 28
Research, operations, 10, **62**
Reserve ratio, 271
Reserve requirements, 271, 280
Resignation, 245
Responsibility, 14
Responsible party system, **77**
Retirement, 245
Retirement Income Security Act, Employee, **210**

Retrenchment management, 91
Revelation theory of ethics, 13
Revenues, earmarked, **268**
Revenue sharing, 49, **287**
Reverse discrimination, **243**
Ridley, Clarence, 114
Rifkind, Simon H., 312
Riggs, Fred W., 11
Right to strike, 250
Right to work, 204
Robotics, **78**
Roethlisberger, F. J., 15, 54, 122, 178
Role playing, 53
Roosevelt, Franklin D., 97
Roth case (1972), 194
Rourke, Francis, 128
Rule making, 310
Rule of law, 165, **329**
Rule of three, 197

Salary Reform Act of 1962, 206
Satisficing, **113**
Sayre, Wallace, 21
Scalar principle, 14
Schattschneider, E. E., 67
Schechter v. United States (1935), 322
Schick, Allen, 35, 166, 261, **288**
Scientific management, **22**
  and Gilbreth, Frank and Lillian, **16**
  and human motivation theory X, **101**
  and line-item budget, **278**
  and public personnel administration, **238**
  and Taylorism, **25**
Second Hatch Act of 1940, 219
Second Hoover Commission, **150,** 244
Secretary, **184**
Securities and Exchange Commission (SEC), 152
Selective incorporation, 306
Selectmen, 162
Self-actualization, 100
Self-directing bureaucracies, 67
Selznick, Philip, 34
Senate Finance Committee, 258
Senatorial courtesy, 231
Senior Executive Service (SES), 199, 215, **244**
Seniority, 251
Sensitivity training, **171**
Separation from service, **245,** 248
Separation of powers, 66, 119, 152
SES (Senior Executive Service), 199, 215, **244**
Settle, Allen K., 211
Sherwood, Frank P., 279
Shibutani, Tamotsu, 53

427

Index

Short ballot campaign, 157
Short-range planning, 65
"Sick chicken" case, 322
Simon, Herbert A., 26, **114**
   and administrative man, **2**
   and authority, **87**
   and bounded rationality, **88**
   and decision making, **92**
   and economic man theory, **38**
   and neoclassical organization theory, **178**
   and proverbs of administration, **112**
   and satisficing, **113**
Simulation, 79
Skinner, B. F., 38
Smith, Adam, 82
Smithburg, Donald, 112
Social engineering, 62
Social equity, **23**
Social ethic, 172
"Soft" money policy, 271
Sorauf, Frank J., 77
South Carolina v. United States (1905), 323
Span of control, 14, 63, **115**
Special counsel, 227
Special district, 159, **185**
Specialization, 114
Specific performance, 307
Spoils system, 29, 231, **246**
Staff agencies, 120
Staff and line, 26, **154**, 180
Staff development, **247**
Staffing, 180
"Stagflation," 39, 57, 272, 285
Stahl, O. Glenn, 206, 225
Stare decisis, 316
State and Local Fiscal Assistance Acts of 1972 and 1976, 49, 287
State borrowing, 260
State equalization board, 270
State's attorney, 312
Statutes at Large, 144
Steelworkers case (1979), **251**
Stogdill, Ralph M., 177
Strategic elite, 41
Strategic planning, **116**
Strategy, 51
Stress management, **117**
Strike, 203, 250
Strike injunction, 311
Strokes, 172
Strong mayor–council form, **161**
Structural-functional analysis, 121
Structuralists, 114
Subordinates, 147
Subsidy, **289**

Substantive due process, 306
Substate regionalism, 182
Subsystem, **80**
Sumptuary tax, 286
Sundquist, James, 30
Sunset legislation, **81,** 105
Superego, 127
Superordinates, 147
Supplemental appropriation, 255
Supply side economics, **82**
Supreme Court decisions, 316
Survey Research Center, University of Michigan, 110
System functioning, 45
Systems analysis, 62, **83,** 95
Systems management, 163
Systems theory, 83, **84**

Taft Commission on Economy and Efficiency, 262
Taft-Hartley Act of 1947, 204, 214
Tax, regulatory, **286**
Taxation, ad-valorem, **254**
Tax base, 284
"Taxpayer revolt," 74
Tax rates, 284
Taylor, Frederick W., 16, **24,** 26
   and economic man theory, **38**
   and human motivation theory X, **101**
   and public personnel administration, **238**
   and scientific management, **22**
Taylorism, **25**
   and Gilbreth, Frank and Lillian, **16**
   and human motivation: need theory, **100**
   and scientific management, **22**
Teasley, C. E., 100
Tennessee Valley Authority (TVA), 323
Tenure, **248**
Tenure of Office Act of 1876, 242
Termination of employment, 245
Testing, **249**
T-groups, 171
Theory
   administrative, **5**
   classical organization, 22
   of economic man, **38**
   of groups, **53**
Theory of Social and Economic Organization (1947), 187
Theory X, human motivation, **101**
Theory Y, human motivation, **102**
Theory Z, human motivation, **103**
"Therbligs," 16

Index

Thompson, James D., 112
Thompson, Victor A., 101, 112, 165, 169
Throughputs, 84, 137
"Tight" money policy, 267, 271
Traditional authority, 87, 187
Transactional analysis (TA), **172**
Trial jury, 309
Truman, David B., 179
Turbulence, environmental, **45**
TVA, 323
TVA and the Grass Roots (1949), 34
Two-factor theory, 99

Unimodal convergence, 37
Unionism, public, 204, **240**
Unions, public employee, **237**
Union shop, 204
United Federation of Postal Clerks v. Blount (1971), **250**
United Public Workers v. Mitchell (1947), 219
United States Civil Service Commission, 229
United States Conference of Mayors, 287
United States Government Manual, **186**
United States Government Printing Office, 186
United States v. Nixon (1974), 139
United Steelworkers of America v. Weber (1979), 211, 243, **251**
Unity of command, 14, 114, **118**
Urban Council, 281
Urwick, Lyndall F., 14, 17, 22, **26**
  and organization chart, **63**
  and POSDCORB, **180**
  and proverbs of administration, **112**
User fees, 74

Validity in testing, 249
Value-free administration, 165
Vertical job enrichment, 224
Veterans' preference, **252**
Victims of Groupthink (1972), 98
Voting behavior, 59
Voucher system, 75

Wagner Act of 1935, 204, 250
Wahba, M. A., 100
Waldo, C. Dwight, 26, **27**
  and American Society for Public Administration (ASPA), **7**
  and Murphy's Law, **108**

and new public administration, **18**
"War games" simulation, 79
Washington v. Davis (1976), 211
Watergate, 52, 105, 212
Ways and Means Committee, House, 258
Weak mayor–council form, 161, **162**
Wealth of Nations, 82
Webb, James E., 163
Weber, Max, **187**
  and administrative man, **2**
  and authority, **87**
  and bureaucracy, **126**
  and classical organization theory, **176**
  and neo-Weberism, **165**
  and politics-administration dichotomy, **70**
Weber case (1979), 211, 243, **251**
Weberism, neo-, **165**
Welfare program, 281
Whistleblower, 274, **330**
White, Leonard D., **28**, 238
  and comparative public administration, **11**
  and scientific management, **22**
White House Office, **188**
Whyte, Martin King, 187
Whyte, William H., 173
Wildavsky, Aaron, 35, 266, **290**
Williams, J. D.
  and equal employment opportunity, **211**
  and group theory, **53**
  and Hoover Commission, First, **149**
  and Hoover Commission, Second, **150**
  and human motivation: need theory, **100**
  and malfeasance, **318**
  and misfeasance, **319**
  and nonfeasance, **320**
Williams v. Florida (1970), 309
Wilson, Woodrow, **29**
  and Civil Service Reform League, **200**
  and politics-administration dichotomy, **70**
  and professionalism, **20**
Wilsonian paradigm, 29
Without Sympathy or Enthusiasm: The Problem of Administrative Compassion (1975), 165
Women's rights, 189, 205, 243

Index

Work schedule, 216
Writ of certiorari, 302
Writ of injunction, 307, **311**

"Yardstick" function, 146, 323

Zahn v. International Paper Co. (1973), 304
ZBB (zero-base budgeting), 261, 288, **291**
Zero-base budgeting (ZBB), 261, 288, **291**

Edited by Cecelia A. Albert
Composed in 10/12 Baskerville
Typeset, printed, and bound by Braun-Brumfield,
Ann Arbor, Michigan